Foreword

PART A—THE REAL ESTATE PROCESS

This book presumes—as did its earlier editions over the last several decades—to introduce the subject of property management as a specialized activity of rendering service to property owners. In outline, the present edition has been divided into three parts each consisting of related chapters. This arrangement is to bring into focus the relationship between property management and real estate itself (Part A), the fact that the property manager's principal business is marketing (Part B), and the idea that the success of any business rests heavily on the strength of administrative controls (Part C).

The first chapters of this book all seek to expound those aspects of real estate that are fundamental to the development by the property manager of winning business strategies. Thus, after presenting a general overview of the field of real estate management (in chapter 1), we shall discuss various criteria by which the situation in real estate can be understood at any moment, and through which the emergent situations also can be better understood and to some extent forecast.

What will be said, in effect, is that the manager who follows the status and trend of the real estate market is thereby better prepared for his renting-leasing marketing function. It will be said further that it is through a study of monetary influences on real estate that the market conditions become comprehensible, for example with respect to the fluctuations and cyclic behavior displayed.

A core section of this first part on the Real Estate Process is devoted to the history of the rise of governmental involvement in real estate, and especially in the housing sub-fields. And, as a consequence of this evolution, and of the associated socio-economic pressures, the last chapter of Part A identifies the trend in changing forms of real estate ownership, a corollary of which is that changing forms of property management also are occurring.

PART B—THE MARKETING PROCESS

In the first chapters of this book we lay a foundation of sorts for the general subject of real estate. We speak of market conditions, monetary influences, the rising governmental involvements, the idea of real estate cycles and the changing forms of ownership.

The intent is to provide for the student a reference frame of real estate theory against which the function of the property manager can be related. We conclude that, to succeed, the property manager must understand real estate, just as those in real estate directly must understand the influences of monetary, governmental, and social pressures on their activity. It was from this point of view that we set forth at the very outset a discussion of what is involved in the field of real estate management.

Now, in this second section, we move into a consideration of the central activity of property management, namely the marketing process. And from what is presented in these chapters, it will be clear that the property manager achieves business only if he is skillful in selling, merchandising, and marketing.

The property manager's product is units of space, for example, for residential, commercial, institutional and/or industrial use, for which willing and able-to-pay customers are wanted so that high levels of occupancy will be maintained. In other words, there will always be a recurring need for marketing—as leases expire, as old units are subdivided, as new units are created, and as those economic shifts occur that affect occupancy.

The student, however, must be alerted to read between the lines in the following chapters. This is because a remark made about the merchandising of a furnished building in general will have a broad application even if the cited example relates to something specific such as a residential building. In other words, for brevity, the same point will not be repeated in each instance of its application, and the student is left to make the obvious extensions.

PART C—THE ADMINISTRATIVE PROCESS

In the last chapters of this book we will be talking about those activities and functions of the property manager that belong to the administrative process of his business. Of course, the central part of what a property manager does involves marketing, and that is why so many of the preceding chapters have been devoted to it. After all, unless there is, there will be no cash flow to justify the business, hence no business to administrate.

The administrative process provides a framework by which business can be done efficiently and on a large scale. The office arrangements, personnel selection, tenant and public relations, recordkeeping, and the like, if attended to, become the vehicle by which the business functions—ideally and automatically like a well-oiled machine.

Obviously, the larger the activity, the more crucial to success the administrative process becomes. The property manager will always know who some of his customers are, but he can't personally know all of them when there are hundreds, perhaps thousands. He can't personally make an inspection to locate all of the leaky faucets. He can't depend upon memory for the payment of monthly bills. He can't expect every tenant to meet the rental obligations on

PRINCIPLES OF
REAL ESTATE MANAGEMENT

Principles of

REAL ESTATE

MANAGEMENT

By

James C. Downs, Jr., C.S.D., C.P.M.

INSTITUTE OF REAL ESTATE MANAGEMENT

430 NORTH MICHIGAN AVENUE · CHICAGO, ILLINOIS 60611

Standard Book Number 0–912104–18–X
PRINTED IN THE UNITED STATES OF AMERICA

time—especially if it becomes known that the property manager is several months behind in the bookkeeping. And so forth.

The theory and practice of the administrative processes is an established part of the business and commerce subject area. Most students of property management will already have been exposed to ideas about administration, just as they will have had a prior exposure to ideas about marketing. In what follows, therefore, it will be understood that we wish to develop mainly those specialized topics that refer to the operation of a property manager's office.

Table of Contents

PART A—THE REAL ESTATE PROCESS

1. THE FIELD OF REAL ESTATE MANAGEMENT . . . . .

The Institute of Real Estate Management. The scope and nature of real estate management. Classification of property. Commercial properties. Industrial buildings. Residences. Management functions including analysis. The manager's role as a consultant. The Accredited Management Organization.

2. THE REAL ESTATE MARKET . . . .

The nature of real estate markets. The real estate money supply and the value of money. Occupancy as a factor. Rental price level. Local eviction suits. Employment level. Foreclosures. Mortgage volume. Building activity. Real estate sales and securities.

3. REAL ESTATE AND MONEY . . . .

Monetary influences on real estate. The history and function of money. World War II and the dollar. The postwar period. The new economy. The real estate money supply. Measuring monetary trends.

4. THE RISING ROLE OF GOVERNMENT IN REAL ESTATE .

Demography of the trend towards urbanization. Antecedents of governmental involvements. The major housing acts. The evolution of urban renewal. The significance of zoning. Slum clearance and urban renewal. Neighborhood conservation. New factors such as energy and environment. The future of the Federal Housing Authority and urban renewal.

5. CYCLIC ASPECTS OF REAL ESTATE . . . .

Characteristics of cycles. Definition of cycle as an economic term. Change in real estate trends. Lessor movements of the cycle. The end of the downswing. The dynamic cycle. The "cyclet." The cycle in a managed economy.

PART B—THE MARKETING PROCESS

Illustrations and Tables

DESIGN AND PHOTOGRAPHY CREDITS

Bob Rogers, designer
First Impression, cover jacket
   7—John Hancock Mutual Life Insurance Company
  22—Robert M. Lightfoot III
 151—Bill Hedrich, Hedrich-Blessing
 222—Chicago Architectural Photographing Company
 244—Alexandre Georges
 250—Wyatt Communications
 264—George Allen Aerial Photos Ltd.
 281—Kaufman & Fabry Company
 315—Stroback Reiss & Company
 321—Langdon Studio

Author's Preface

The significant social and economic changes which have taken place in the 27 years since the first edition of this text was published, have been mirrored in the life style and living standards of the American people. In turn they have been reflected in the design and form of the structures in which these people are accommodated.

In the affluent society of the day, large numbers of people not only have a "primary" home (most likely in a multifamily building) in the town in which they live, but they also have a "second home"—either in anticipation of their retirement, or in a resort or recreation area in which they spend their increased leisure time. The same high standards apply to nonresidential accommodations. Shopping centers are more numerous, larger and more elegant; office buildings are more extravagant, have more space per employee and are on larger sites; hotels and motels are bigger and have more elaborate amenities.

Lower birth rates and more closely controlled population have reduced the average family size, have resulted in a higher percentage of childless couples, and have created whole urban areas populated exclusively by adults who live in multifamily buildings in almost complete isolation from children. Here young unmarried people and childless couples are joined by aging citizens, whose children are grown, in centers of urban "action"—where entertainment, culture, sports, and recreation are concentrated.

All of these economic and social changes have combined to create a bigger demand for the trained property manager capable of administering larger and more complex structures, replete with the amenities demanded by the type of society that is emerging.

Little wonder that the Institute of Real Estate Management has grown at an accelerated pace—from 693 members in the decade ending in 1954 to over 2,500 members in the ten years ending in 1974. There is no doubt that this growth will continue to accelerate as our society more fully reflects these trends.

The Institute wishes to recognize its indebtedness to Walter Rose, editorial coordinator of the eleventh edition and, of course, to Robert Goldstaff, CPM, Chicago, and Edward Metzner, CPM, Louisville, Kentucky for their invaluable assistance in reviewing and critiquing the new edition's revisions. Our most sincere appreciation is also extended to Harold Brin, President of Diversified Financial Consultants, for his contribution to chapter 27, Insurance.

INTRODUCTION

In order to understand his profession, the student should have at least a basic knowledge of the history of its development.

Prior to 1890, expert management of income properties was largely restricted to two general classes of land improvement; the commercial hotel and the downtown business property. At that time residential property was mostly single-family residences and owner-occupied two- three- or occasional six-family-flat buildings. Large, multi-family dwellings were a rarity; neighborhood business properties were mainly owner-tenanted and unimportant as sources of management income.

Shortly after 1890 several major trends affecting urban real estate began to develop. First, and most important to property management, was the gradual shift of residential property from the single-family, two- and three-family building to the larger, multiple-type apartment building which reached a peak in the mid-twenties. Second was the advance in structural engineering which brought into being the steel frame building and afforded almost unlimited possibilities for vertical expansion. Parallel with this structural improvement was the perfection of elevators which provided the vertical transportation essential to the use of high buildings. Third was the beginning of the decentralization of retail business activity from the traditional downtown shopping center to busy, important outlying subcenters.

When these trends were first manifest in the building activities of most American cities, the need for property management on a broad scale was evident. However, in almost all cases the buildings which were built in these early years were sold to men retiring from other lines of business—men who found in these buildings an attractive medium of investment for their savings—men who saw in their management an interesting means of providing a post-retirement occupation. During this period (except for a brief time during World War I) residential occupancy was high, rental demand was strong, and the problem of building management had not taken on many of today's complexities.

The primary cause of the breakdown of owner management was the great rental boom of the 1920–1922 period. Many retired businessmen who had bought buildings on the theory that their investments would provide a modest living, suddenly found that their incomes had skyrocketed to unheard-of levels; that they were rich beyond any expectation. On the basis of their new incomes, new vistas were opened, old yearnings became new possibilities. The most important of these was the lure of travel and extended absences from the cities in which their buildings were located.

Faced with the problem of what to do with their buildings while spending winters at far-off resorts, owners in many cases went the to best-reputed real estate men in their locality, asked whether the real estate office could collect the rentals of the building during the owner's absence, and whether they would also pay the janitor, order the required fuel, pay the utilities bills, and forward the net proceeds to them. In these arrangements no other expenditures were made without the owner's specific instruction, and in most cases the owner planned to be in the city during leasing activity.

In almost all cases the local real estate man entered into this new relationship, purely as an accommodation to a potential sales customer. A clerk in his office was assigned to the task of rent collection, and the bookkeeper was instructed to send the owner a simple statement of receipts and disbursements at the end of each month. However in a few instances, in neighborhoods and areas where rents were highest and multifamily buildings most common, the local real estate man found himself enjoying a reasonable volume of such business—a volume sufficient to become important—notwithstanding the comparative ease of earning a handsome living from brokerage and personal speculation. Modern property management was born when the real estate man recognized that here was a real field for the future; that the greatest volume of such business would accrue to the firm or individual who paid closest attention to the properties of his clients, who tried to do a better than average job.

Before 1929 the nation's buildings were largely owned by individuals— rugged, opinionated individuals who had made their money in their own specialized fields, who carried over their individual ideas and business methods into their real estate ventures. Property managers and property management firms had operated the buildings, but they were restricted in the use of their meager and newly acquired knowledge because individual owners insisted that their buildings be operated according to their dictates. Except in a few isolated instances, the managers and management companies were "agents" in the true sense of the word. They were a brand of corporate office boys who had as many policies as they had clients; who operated their properties intelligently for intelligent owners, stupidly for stupid owners. Groping for an answer to the problem of efficiency, these "agents" either did not have sufficient freedom of action to conduct experiments on a broad scale, or they were so afraid of losing the newly found business that they lacked the courage to defy their clients' orders, even when they knew the orders were mistaken or unsatisfactory.

The great depression of the thirties (which for income real estate actually began in 1928) brought about a wholesale liquidation of the individual owner and saw the control of the bulk of the country's income real estate (especially multifamily and commercial buildings built from 1920–1929) fall into the hands of banks, insurance companies, savings societies, trust companies, and investment protective committees. It was in this fiasco that today's property management had its genesis, since, for the first time, a large volume of properties was gathered together under one ownership, one policy, and on common perspective.

In the early stages of the depression the insurance companies, trust companies, investment protective committees, and banks (after a study of the property management organizations available in the field) frequently concluded that their interests would best be served by the creation of their own property management departments. Not being familiar with the broad scope of building management problems, they accepted the common misconception that the operation of properties was centered around the collection of rentals and the maintenance of physical structure. As a result many of the men inducted into such newly formed management departments were builders, ex-architects, contractors whose work was supplemented by routine collectors and, perhaps, a law graduate. Merchandising, analysis, and real estate economics were frequently overlooked; not only because they were unknown to most of the executives given the responsibility for property management, but principally because property management in the past had not been important enough or advanced enough to warrant the training of such men.

In the years which followed the first blush of the depression—years of trial and error as their experience broadened—other points of view crept into the thinking of executives responsible for the operation of these great groups of buildings. The need for adequate analysis, market research, and scientific administration was widely recognized. In the ranks of many an organization, men were getting the training to fill that need.

The great concentrations of property ownership brought about by wholesale foreclosures during the great depression of 1929–33 were largely dissipated during the recovery years. Once again investors saw opportunity for profit and satisfactory return in real estate ownership. Individuals and partnerships of individuals—sometimes called "syndicates"—purchased properties from banks, insurance companies, and reorganization committees who were anxious to reduce their portfolios of real estate and return to their normal function as financial institutions. In many instances, property managers were retained to devote their skills to producing the highest and best use of these buildings.

The recovery of 1934–39 brought about a spirited revival of occupancy, rental rates, and property values. After war broke out in Europe in 1939 and the United States entered World War II in late 1941, all urban property was caught up in a boom which saw the demand for professional property management wane considerably. Between Pearl Harbor and the end of 1957, rental market conditions were such that it was difficult to demonstrate the need for management skills. In the first place, there was no problem getting tenants in any kind of building, because space was extremely scarce and there were more consumers than accommodations. During the war years residential property was under federal rent control and no increases in rentals could be made. Moreover, tenants were so happy to have a possession of scarce space that it was possible for landlords to eliminate interior maintenance almost completely, to lower services, and to ignore the whole process of merchandising their wares.

The wartime backlog of unfilled space demand was exhausted in the early months of 1957 as the result of high volume of new construction which was carried on throughout the contry in the years 1946–1956. During these years the gross volume of new space additions to the total inventory was greater than the growth of space demand. In early 1957 vacancies began to appear and by the end of 1963 local markets assumed what might be called "normal" characteristics. With the end of space "scarcity," rental rates were stabilized and owners of property were once again faced with the need for the skills of professionals in the administration of their properties.

In the years 1964–1970 the shift away from the single-family house as the basic housing accommodation of the American family, which began in 1958, continued. A higher and higher percentage of new housing was to be found in multifamily structures. So-called "high-rise" structures were more numerous, and the economies of scale produced larger and larger individual projects in virtually all categories of property. Thus, the field for professional management was dramatically broadened.

It was also in the years 1964–1970 that there were two developments significant to the burgeoning field of property management. The first of these was condominium ownership. This new form was widely employed in the ownership of multi-occupancy properties mostly for primary homes, but also for second homes in resort and recreation areas and, to a more limited degree, for commercial properties. Because all of these properties were multi-ownership it was highly desirable that they be managed by professionals, thus relieving the owning groups from the necessity of forming volunteer management committees for which they were not qualified. Condominiums became increasingly popular with the spread of inflation as people sought ownership of their dwellings and businesses as a protection against rent increases. This trend was a real boon to property management professionals and management firms.

Another development which resulted in a substantial number of large properties of the type generally operated by professionals was the sharp increase in the mortgage money supply. This came about as the result of a rapid expansion of real estate investment trusts of both the equity and mortgage variety. These trusts have experienced considerable financial trouble in 1974, but the buildings which they financed have been erected and serve to increase the total inventory of manageable properties. The availability of mortgage money in this boom period was also due to the corporate vogue of entering the real estate markets as well as to the very liberal financing of properties by various government agencies, notably the Federal Housing Administration. Millions of dollars were invested in limited partnerships by wealthy people interested in the tax shelter which such investments in residential property provided.

As has been true in the development of all professions, the requirements for entrance into the field of real estate management have steadily grown. An important factor in implementing that knowledge is a personality which can serve as a vehicle to convey direction, information, and inspiration at all times.

Specifically, a property manager must have a variety of skills. He must be a diplomat, because he must deal with people in their homes, must negotiate the many delicate matters which come up in what should be the closest business relationship—landlord and tenant. He must also be an advertising man and business promotion expert, since the average building he manages is not large enough to employ the specialized services of an advertising agency, yet its space must be sold to prospects promoted by its manager. He must also be an economist, a statistician, and an appraiser, because in addition to the operation of physical property he must plan the economic future of his buildings and must be in a position to set the level of rents, not only for the present, but for future periods for which he negotiates leases.

At the outset it is obvious that the student of property management cannot spend a score of lifetimes preparing himself as a qualified expert in each of the many professions mentioned above, even though, as a property management executive, he may be called upon to make decisions on matters in every one of those fields. The difficulty of obtaining the required "know-how" and the complete absence of any single source of such knowledge often causes those outside the field to believe that property management is simple, that they could easily qualify as building managers. Nothing is further from the truth.

CHAPTER 1

The Field of Real Estate Management

INTRODUCTION

The nature of society in the United States and other developed countries is such that owners of income properties, to an ever-increasing extent, entrust the management responsibilities for their holdings to professionally qualified individuals and firms. These are the real estate managers and management establishments.

The profession of real estate management is an evolving one. Its subject matter, quite naturally, flows from the underlying ideas about real estate theory and practice and from the basic concepts of management. This book deals with that subject matter by stating the *principles* as presently known and understood.

As will be seen, the field of real estate management is not now—and probably never will be—advanced completely to the point where mastery of the principles alone will guarantee the success of the practitioners. This is because the requirements and opportunities for management remain in a state of gradual and perpetual change. Permanence no longer is a central characteristic of the contemporary life styles. Populations grow and shift. And as living standards for the citizenry as a whole improve, and as the transformation continues in how and where people work, shop and play, unforetold ways emerge by which the new requirements of society are accommodated.

The field of real estate management thus is but one of many that—like the people it involves—tries to keep pace with the modern innovations.

Another aspect to be mentioned, however, has to do with the idea that real estate management, by its very nature, is something of an *art form* that relies heavily on the psychology of human relations. The successful manager in most cases is more than just a person schooled in business theory. In addition, he should be one adept in communicating at the interpersonal level, for example with owners, tenants, employees, as well as with the host of other affiliated service people.

It follows, of course, that on occasion some real estate managers will come to excel in the practice of their profession without the benefit of a preliminary formal study of the underlying principles. Such a study, however, always can be recommended as a good way for a young person to get started in his chosen profession.

1

After all, most students here and abroad are prompted to specialize in a particular area of knowledge because of the implied promise of some sort of a reward for later life. Many direct themselves to the security provided by wealth and high station in life, while others also aspire to career opportunities where service to others can be practiced. The point of this book is to show—at least between the lines—that the field of activity known as *real estate management* is one of those that offers the prospect of many rewards to its practitioners.

Real estate management, as already has been implied, may be regarded properly as a *growth* profession. Although people have been engaged in the administration of real property over most of man's recorded history, the earliest managers were ones chiefly concerned with agriculture and the problem of raising the productivity of the land from that point of view. Early on, however, men turned to the creation of shelter for dwelling and for the housing of an ever-widening range of human activities.

Real estate at any given moment in time primarily is a reflection of the functional demands of an ever-changing society, which demands of course must lie within the bounds of what is possible and profitable. Thus the growth and distribution of population, its structure and life styles, its economic, cultural and social evolution, and its technological capability have continuously altered the form and functions of real estate. The almost uninterrupted growth and progress in these elements have produced a concomitant demand for the knowledge and skills which are dealt with as the subject of this text.

In other words, as society continues to expand and change, so too does the management of its increasingly diverse and complex real properties. Accordingly, the management process today is requiring the services of more and more professionals. While such professionals may be owners of property, or direct employees of the owners, the trend is for them to be self-employed or employees of management firms.

THE SCOPE OF REAL ESTATE MANAGEMENT

Technically the term, real estate, may be defined as embracing land and the improvements (if any) thereon. A farm, a mine (with its buried mineral content), a golf course, a forest, even a desert, all of these correctly may be referred to as real estate. From the standpoint of this text, however, we need to recast the classic definition and limit it to mean the "nonagricultural property used as a location for the housing of individuals, families, commerce, industry, the professions, institutions and government—each in its broadest sense." Practically speaking, we shall be referring particularly to urban (as opposed to rural) land uses, with major emphasis on the structures thereon.

Even so defined, however, there are further arbitrary but convenient exclusions to make. For example, we do not pretend to include the highly specialized categories of hotel management and marketing, club and recreational property management, or the detailed operation of those categories of real estate which are, in themselves, separate and distinct business enterprises. Each of the latter is the subject of a body of its own literature and each boasts its own educational curriculum. While in some instances these subjects are discussed in the context of their being real estate according to our definition, we regard them as separate businesses requiring distinctly different professional expertises.

Whatever the definition, a major point to be made is that the field of real estate management has broadened even as it has grown. Historically its practitioners were concerned almost exclusively with the operation of residential, commercial, and industrial properties on behalf of individual owners who sought to be relieved of the responsibility of personally attending to the details of renting, rent collecting, property maintaining, and record keeping.

To a large extent the phenomenon, seen in the United States before World War I, of most of the real estate in the private sector being owned by individuals—and managed by them too—is a thing of the past. Of course, there still remain many individual owners who either manage for themselves or who retain others for that purpose; still, the modern trend is in quite another direction. Groups of individuals owning cooperatives or condominium dwellings; business corporations with multiple holdings; financial institutions (such as banks, insurance companies, and real estate investment trusts, etc.); educational institutions; and the various agencies of state, local, and federal governments—all have now become the principal sources of management demand.

The role of the real estate manager traditionally was associated with the maximization of income for owners and investors whose basic objective was to increase the property's return on investment and, hence, to raise the level of its value. While this is still a goal, the great growth of business corporations and institutions and the trend for increasing government involvement in the operation of property have introduced new and superficially different criteria for the measurement of managerial effectiveness and efficiency.

Being referred to here is the way modern real estate managers—as well as the owners they serve—show increasing appreciation of the various ecological-environmental impacts that attend real estate activities. And they, along with the population as a whole, now find that they must contend with the threat of future energy shortages. All in all, a mood of social obligation and concern should color every decision made by real estate managers.

Even so, owners by and large always have (indeed always will) want some sort of a profit earned by their holdings. And it is also natural for managers to want an additional profit to be earned by the rendering of services. The profit of an enterprise, however, only loosely is measured by the net average recurring income. Profit in the final analysis has to do with what people *want*, whether this be money, like values in goods or promised services, or whether this be a more subjective entity like personal satisfaction.

The successful manager or management firm, accordingly, is the one skillful in developing insight into the *values* held by the owner(s) upon which the idea of profit logically is to be based. Perhaps in a given case, ownership has a tax situation which persuades the owner to limit profits or seek a political advantage. Similarly, the owner may have a commitment to a social issue like public housing or urban renewal, or may be involved in a philanthropy, or may favor long-term advantages over short-term gains. And so forth. In short, it is the manager's role to optimize with respect to the kind of profit and advantage that is wanted.

In any case, it will be clear that, regardless of the objectives, there always will be a great similarity in the basic techniques employed by the manager —especially with respect to the nonmarketing aspects of the manager's operations. It follows that the well-rounded professional should be prepared to deal with nonprofit as well as profit-oriented assignments.

CLASSIFICATION OF PROPERTY

Here we shall use the word *property* to mean those kinds of developed real estate, the improvements on which are available for rental, leasing, and presumably also for sale (viz., whenever a willing buyer meets a willing seller). Or, if a circular definition will be allowed, we mean by the term, property, whatever it is that property managers manage, including the fixed improvements (like the buildings themselves) as well as the less permanent embellishments (e.g., the furnishings, etc.).

With the definitional reference frame just mentioned in mind, it follows that many categories of properties can be enumerated, including those which to one degree or another overlap. In what follows here, however, we shall be talking about commercial properties, versus industrial buildings, versus residences. Other categories (e.g., institutional, governmental, military properties), for example, will not be explicitly referred to as they lie somewhat beyond the scope of this introductory treatment.

Commercial Properties

Broadly defined, a commercial property is one that houses enterprises such as offices, retail establishments, entertainment and recreational facilities, and other so-called special purpose enterprises which are highly individualistic in design and not subject to categorical use.

The proliferation of commercial structures has been a characteristic of the growth of cities. In spite of the obvious geographical constraints, the trend now well established is for cities to expand in what might be termed concentric circles radiating from the earlier (traditional) downtown centers. Industrial, institutional, cultural, and governmental activities quite naturally have grown along with the satellite communities to which they were associated.

OFFICE BUILDING

Great Western Savings Center is a dramatic headquarters structure located in Beverly Hills, California. This ten-story glass tower of elliptical shape rises 175 feet from the center of a park-like setting of patterned tile walkways, cascading pools, and sweeping expanses of flowers and trees.

Indeed, as the technology of transit evolved (say, from bicycles and horse-drawn cars, to cable cars, to electric street railways, subways and commuter railroads, and finally to the ubiquitous automobile) the downtown areas were, quite naturally, the first terminus of local transportation facilities. In other words, downtowns were the major objective of population circulation. In this way, the advantages to commerce of central location to other businesses, recreation facilities, and population pools in time gave rise to vertical as well as horizontal expansions. And out of this historical circumstance, the modern high-rise office building has come into being.

Even today, in a typical city a substantial portion of the community's total real estate value is centered in the comparatively small area variously known as "downtown" or "uptown." True, there has been an accelerated decentralization implemented by the private automobile—especially in the period since World War II—which has resulted in a much wider deployment of population and office-space demands (for example, in the nature of suburban relocations). It remains still, however, that the viable central commercial centers still thrive as important focal points, especially in the larger metropolitan cities.

In recent years, however, the continuing dispersal of population has been the cause for the development of both large, multistory office buildings and smaller office structures on the periphery of ever-expanding urban areas. And most recently, office buildings have been erected in clusters in the central sections of suburban communities, at major regional shopping centers, at local airports, and at interstate highway junctions.

A number of significant trends are increasing the total demand for office space, the size of major office structures, their location, and the economics of their creation and operation. In the first place, a steadily increasing percentage of employed persons in the labor force find themselves housed in office spaces as the locus of their work. This is to be contrasted with the earlier condition where the great majority of workers in developing and developed countries had found employment on the farm or in the factory. But as productivity has increased everywhere in both agriculture and industry, and as growth and automation have occurred in fields of commerce, finance, the professions, personal services, and government, more and more workers have needed to be accommodated in offices.

There is also a second reason for the increased demand for office space, and this can be related to the rising standards of occupancy. These standards not only are reflected by the modern luxury of executive suites, but by the extension of amenities and the larger allocation of space and comforts to the routine office workers (white- and blue-collar alike). Thus, the office building has become the beneficiary not only of a greater total demand on the economy for square feet of space per employee, but also of a more extravagant use of such space in terms of internal corporate and institutional standards.

The rapid expansion of both the quantitative and qualitative demand

COMBINATION STRUCTURE

The 100-story combination commercial space, office, and apartment structure known as the John Hancock Center in Chicago is an example of the new economics of scale as well as the multiple space use which is characteristic of larger and larger land development schemes.

for office space, in addition, produced an unprecedented volume of new office construction which accelerated steadily throughout the decade of the 1960s. That this was continuing to mount in the early 1970s is a matter of record. Indeed, the new construction boom has been an across-the-board eventuality in terms of its extension over the mosaic of metropolitan areas. Never before have the downtown areas of major American core cities displayed anything like the construction volume carried out in the period described.

A study of available statistical data will show both that the total number of square feet of new space, and that the cost thereof, was in excess of any previous downtown building boom in the United States. Nor were the new records established in the downtown areas alone. The construction of office space in the outer reaches of most metropolises was even more impressive, and especially so in the suburban areas. And even the disturbing effects of inflation and high interest rates that occur cyclically (and that, indeed, are most pronounced at the time the eleventh edition of this book is being composed—summer 1974) hardly seem to indicate anything except that there will be occasional lulls in the otherwise expanding real estate markets.

Particularly pertinent to the field of real estate management are the trends manifested in the *size* of the new office buildings—both in the central downtown areas and the outlying ones as well. Elsewhere in this book we shall explore the changes in local emphasis and economic circumstances which have been noted in the construction of new office buildings. The accompanying sketch, that illustrates city-planning ideas for Chicago, presents a picture representative of other cities as well of contemporary development trends (See chapter 4). And elsewhere in this book we shall be discussing ideas about the creation and marketing of the futuristic office spaces. Suffice it to say here that economic, financial, and institutional trends have already dictated that much larger structures surely are to be constructed and created, both as to height and as to total floor-area space.

Hotels and Motels

Hotel management is the oldest (and probably the best-developed) type of property management. The "inn" was a well-known institution long before the appearance of office and apartment buildings of the modern sort. Hotel men long ago have been recognized as specialists familiar with the basic facts of physical operation and maintenance of buildings and skilled in the arts of housekeeping, food preparation, and beverage dispensing.

The hotels of the United States employ more people in their management and operation than all other forms of commercial building management combined. The science of hotel management is by far the most advanced of any division of the entire field of property management. Hotel schools in American and foreign universities were the first to offer a college major in any phase of building management. And the accounting firms which specialize in the

CHICAGO CITY PLANNING

Recommended changes in the Chicago Lakefront include the development of IC Air Rights South (predominantly residential), conversion of Northerly Island from Meigs Field to an open space and recreation area, development of Soldier Field into a community sports complex, creation of bicycle paths, expansion of park beaches, and open space with improved public areas.

auditing of hotel accounts have gathered the finest bank of operating data available for any form of building.

While hotel management primarily is concerned with the administration of city transient hostelries, the broader field embraces many subsidiary types of improved property. The operation of resort hotels today is a major world industry, giving employment to thousands of professional managers.

A number of discernible trends recently have been visible in the hotel field. Practically speaking, hotels are more and more a separate industry rather than a real estate investment opportunity. The locally owned, locally run, personal, host-oriented, proprietary establishment has all but passed from the scene. In its place is the national (owner-operator-franchiser and/or manager) hotel that offers chain reservations, chain identity, chain purchasing and marketing, and chain credit. Such operations are corporate giants and to an extent may be regarded as publicly owned by minor as well as major stock holders.

CONTEMPORARY HOTEL DESIGN

That hotels are becoming more luxurious is evidenced by such hotels as the Regency Hyatt House Hotel in Atlanta, Georgia. Note the 20-story addition—a striking tower of reflective glass. The bronze-tinted environmental control glass reflects neighboring buildings and the sky. As practical as it is luxurious, the glass includes a light and heat reflecting coating that reduces air-conditioning loads for lower operating costs and controls brightness.

While the management of hotels today is a specialty not embraced by the field of real estate management as conventionally practiced (that is, as more or less described in this book), some of the topics presented on the pages that follow have a general relevance and application to hotel-motel situations.

The word "motel" is a comparatively recent addition to the language. Its coinage correctly implies that the only technical difference between a hotel and a motel at the present time is that the cost and provision of a parking space for the guest are included in the room rate in the latter case. Otherwise there is virtually no distinction, either from the point of view of structure, accommodations, facilities, or location. The fact that originally there were great differences between hotels and motels is now only of historical interest.

Of course, the adoption of the private automobile as the major means of transportation by the American people (and indeed as an important means of transportation by other peoples of the developed world) has been a gradual process. At the present time, however, more than four-fifths of *all* inter-city travel in the United States is accomplished by this means. More than that, many businessmen who commute by air between cities will hire rental cars for their intra-city travel and thus become drawn into the prevailing transportation patterns.

Under the above circumstances, it is obvious that a steadily increasing percentage of all transient room business in the United States is automobile-related. For this reason, a large number of so-called motels traditionally have been located to capitalize on the highway patronage. This dominance of highway-oriented locations, however, has continued to diminish as it was seen that airports, satellite communities, and central areas not only could be easily reached by city beltways and expressways, but additionally afforded ready access to commercial, residential, and industrial adjacent neighborhoods.

Just as the economies of scale have dictated the construction of larger and more luxurious office spaces and hotels, so too have motels responded to the rapid rise in transient living standards. Whereas the original motels were largely proprietor-owned, with up to 30-room structures operated on a "Mom and Pop" basis—that is, with Mom being the housekeeper and maid, and Pop the manager-janitor—the modern motel establishment is a major investment property. More often than not it is hooked into a national reservation system and perhaps even has a structural connection to a major hotel-motel chain. Indeed, the ownership and management of these growing structures have moved in time from the category where yield from the property was partly capital and partly wage opportunity, to the franchise—and, more lately, to the major chain—ownerships. In fact, being followed here is the trend (pioneered by franchisers such as Holiday Inn, McDonald's and Kentucky Fried Chicken) to buy up the more successful of the units originally franchised.

In any case, it is clear that today very little distinction exists between hotels and motels, at least insofar as ownership, investment, and management are

concerned. Whereas motels were originally considered a combination investment real estate and occupational-opportunity project, they now fall into the
same category—in respect to management—as hotels.

Retail Accommodations

In perhaps no other category of commercial property has there been as
revolutionary a change in recent years as in the location, design, size, physical
structure, management, and operations pertaining to retail merchandising.
These changes have been a dramatic proof of the fact that real property
constantly and inevitably reflects the changes in the mores, life styles, preferences, and tastes of the society in which it is situated. It will be to the point
to present certain observations that describe the opportunities and challenges
which rental properties present to the property manager.

The major elements in what we choose to call the "retail revolution" in the
United States are the following:

1. A phenomenal proliferation of goods and services with which rising
   living standards have been implemented. These developments have been
   supported by the innovative genius of marketing experts, as based on
   the new technology, distribution methods and facilities, mass-media
   promotion, and consumer mobility.
2. A sharply rising consumer capability in terms of net spendable income
   available for "want-satisfaction" in the area of goods and services.
3. A marked change in the time available for, and in the attitude toward,
   the shopping sortie for the purpose of the selection and consumption
   of goods and services. For most Americans, the process of deciding what
   to buy and where, why, and when, and how to pay for it all consumes
   a substantial amount of leisure time. In fact, it may be said that shopping
   is one of the major forms of recreation in our materialistic society.
   Purveyors of goods and services have come to know that their establishments will experience the greatest sales volumes at times when the bulk
   of the population is at leisure from other pursuits. Examples: the 24-hour
   shopping centers, Sunday-openings, and the like.

Industrial Buildings

Industrial real estate can be defined as property that primarily is used for
the fabrication and distribution of manufactured goods, and for the related
ancillary activities.

By and large (but not exclusively, however) industrial plants and buildings
are owned, operated, and managed by their occupants. As such they ordinarily
are not considered as real estate investment prospects but as a part of the plant
and equipment capital required for the conduct of the business of the industrial
enterprise.

As in the case of residential and commercial properties, industrial property can be classified, for example, as heavy manufacturing, light manufacturing, and research and development. These are the kinds of activities engaged in by industrial corporations—sometimes in separated, sometimes in unified facilities. And virtually without exception, the major heavy industrial plants (e.g., steel mills, refineries, automobile plants, utilities, foundaries, appliance factories and the like) are owner managed; moreover they are essentially manufacturing facilities.

On the other hand the light manufacturing category of real estate usually means smaller buildings erected for use by manufacturers whose space requirements do not dictate any specific-use design. Such space generally is interchangeable as the varying uses may require, and is widely reserved for the servicing and distribution of manufactured products as well as for the initial fabrications.

Industrial use of real estate in most urban areas of the United States is limited to those locations where the land involved has been granted an appropriate zoning by the local authorities. In a subsequent chapter of this text, in which zoning is more fully discussed, we have included the various relevant classifications of industrial zoning which are common.

The wide use of the automobile for private transportation, the truck for goods-distribution, and the adoption of the one-story structure for manufacturing, servicing, and warehousing of goods, has almost completely changed the land requirements, location, design, and marketing of industrial property. Given the trend towards abandonment of multistory industrial buildings because of line-production methods and the fork (pallet) truck for goods handling, larger land areas became a necessity. Not only was more space needed for the flat buildings, but also for employee parking, which in recent years has become a critical factor. To obtain such expanses of land, and also to realize better access to the decentralized distribution destinations (as well as to the interstate highway facilities), industries were forced to relocate in outlying urban areas.

Light manufacturers bought, developed, and improved their own plant sites in many cases. The demand for smaller industrial facilities, however, also presented a new opportunity for land developers. Out of all of this came the concept and the establishment of what now are called industrial parks. Here alert entrepreneurs bought large parcels of raw land, and planned what in effect were industrial subdivisions. Zoning would be secured, utilities installed and streets built, along with railroad sidings where necessary. And then vacant land or buildings could be offered to prospective industrial tenants and buyers.

In a completely different category—almost anachronistic—are certain industrial properties still found in the core areas of major metropolitan centers. These are the many multistory, tenanted office buildings used for the manufacturing, servicing, distribution and office functions of companies that need the central location, but do not require an "atmosphere" environment. These buildings are often called lofts. They are to be seen, for example, in the so-called Garment District of Manhattan and in other major cities. While such lofts are obsolete economically (as indicated by the fact that they no longer are being built at the present time), they are continuing to enjoy a functional value as old buildings in locations that still have an importance. In terms of gross space volume, it is clear that lofts represent a substantial amount of potential business for the professional manager.

Other industrial property is held by many major industrial corporations such as the petroleum, lumber, paper, utility, automobile, and transportation (railroad and airline) companies. In recent years many of these companies have formed real estate divisions for the purpose of managing and developing their own holdings. This trend has represented a substantial market for the services of trained property managers.

In these connections it may be mentioned that industrial property is for the most part controlled by managers affiliated with the Society of Industrial Realtors (SIR). Although members of this organization primarily are concerned with the development and sale of industrial property, they also sometimes serve as managers. On the other hand the Institute of Real Estate Management (IREM), which like SIR also is a division of the National Association of Realtors, has a membership that for the most part is solely dedicated to the profession of property management (meaning industrial as well as commercial and residential). More will be said about the professionalism and ethics that characterize the work of IREM's *Certified Property Managers* (for individuals) and *Accredited Management Organizations* (for firms) later in this chapter.

Residences

In quantitative terms, the management of residential properties is the largest single segment of demand for the services of professional real estate managers. Not only involved is property management in the private sector, but also institutional and governmental housing as well. In the year 1970, for example, the census count indicated there were some 68 million year-'round housing units in the United States.

In the light of our theorem already suggested, that all real estate development occurs as a manifestation of the mores of the society in which it is located, it is easy to conclude that dwelling units are a sensitive factor in providing a physical expression of current life styles and attitudes. Country estates reflect the tastes of the affluent occupants; suburbias more often than not are a caricature of middle-class life; young couples blend nicely against the background of their town house apartments; and prestige condominium dwellers are never mistaken for residents of public housing. Of course, in the final analysis residences are the creation of their builders—so that present occupants either must be satisfied with the original intention, or they must provide for the desired modifications that lie within their means. As an extreme case in point, we mention that much of public housing has an appearance that reflects the ideas and judgments of the planners rather than the eventual occupants. Indeed, the latter live in such places on a "take it or leave it" basis, since they have little in the way of resources to effect changes on their own.

If dwelling units reflect the times, there is some distortion of the image also involved. For example, since the Second World War there has continued to be a substantial lag in the capability of the economy to bring the housing stock of the nation into line with the ever-changing pattern of current public demand. People move about, family units are smaller, young people insist on separate quarters, and so forth. These are some of the reasons which, in addition to the population growth, continue to put pressure on the real estate market.

One recent governmental target has been the annual construction of 2.6 million housing units. Even if this were attained, however, and maintained, it would take more than a quarter century merely to replace the present housing inventory. Thus it is apparent that a major challenge to the field of real estate management is the problem of maintaining the successful marketing of a constantly aging housing stock, the attractions of which are steadily being eroded by physical, economic, and social obsolescence.

The point already has been made that the rate of change in virtually all aspects of life has increased in an unprecedented way in recent years. Moreover, as will be noted from references throughout this text, significant further changes that are almost certain to take place in the next decade already are presently identifiable. Nowhere are these apt to be more pervasive for real estate people than in the field of residential properties. This contention is supported by remarks in the following paragraphs that deal with the various types of housing.

Private Housing (the Single-Family Dwelling)

The predominant American housing accommodation continues to be the single-family house. In 1970, for example, it accounted for almost 70 percent of the nation's housing units. Although the overwhelming majority of these are free-standing (that is, detached individual houses), the rising price of development land in urban areas has caused the home builders increasingly to turn to attached and semi-detached row houses—sometimes called "town houses." In these latter dwellings, consumers may enjoy many of the advantages of the conventional single-family house (e.g., private entrance, multistory separation of living and work spaces, backyard patio, etc.). On the other hand, the higher-density land use means a lessened land-investment cost, and this is an offsetting factor of importance to some purchasers and renters.

Normally, single-family houses are developed at a density of from three to eight houses per acre, while row houses require less than half that amount of land. In any case, the single-family residence is the prime example of real estate purchases for *use* rather than investment. Of all the occupied housing units in the United States in the reference year 1970, 37.1 percent were owned by their occupants (and collaterally, of course, by the mortgage holders). Since the statistics show that most of these owners were accommodated by single-family houses, it can be seen that a very high percentage, indeed, of single-family houses were being directly used by their occupants. In other words, it is patently clear that in such instances no professional management would be involved.

A combination of forces, however, has acted to reduce the ratio of new single-family housing units to the total of all housing construction. While the need to lower land usage per dwelling unit has been the most significant element in this decline, consumers (purchasers/rentors) sometimes have found it more desirable to rid themselves of such chores as lawn care, snow clearance, landscaping, and exterior maintenance. And once these common services were assumed on behalf of individual home owners, there was a new need for the introduction of management. This is especially true where such row and town houses are sold to condominium owners, and where all exterior maintenance becomes the responsibility of whatever agency administers the common property. This trend, it may be added, is responsible for a substantially increased demand for professional management.

Mobile Homes

The term "mobile home" more and more has become a misnomer. Of the 600,000 units of this type delivered to dealers in the United States in 1972, almost all ultimately were located on a fixed lot or pad, and hooked up to local utilities as a permanent installation on their designated location. The real difference between this type of housing unit and that which is classified as a single-family dwelling is that the former was *factory-manufactured* and delivered as an assembled product, while the latter—even if of the so-called prefabricated variety—was site-assembled and finished.

Of course, another difference is that mobile homes and the sites on which they are situated typically have different owners, while houses with a fixed location rarely do. In any case, it is remarkable that so many new mobile-home units are appearing each year.

For example, in the year 1973, these so-called mobile homes accounted for something more than one out of four housing units created in the United States. Or, to put it another way, about one percent of the total existing housing units in the USA are appearing each year in trailer-park locations. Just as the compact automobile essentially is a compromise in the field of transportation, created to accommodate those consumers who are unable to

TOWNHOUSE

This three-bedroom, two-story townhouse is located in Park Forest South, a totally planned community being developed approximately 40 miles south of the Chicago Loop. Note how the attached houses have common party walls—hence, no space between them.

MOBILE HOME PARK

Consumer use of mobile homes has indeed mounted over the years. Once regarded as a form of "shanty-towns," mobile home parks have undoubtedly taken their place in our permanent residential complex.

support the purchase, maintenance, and operation of the "standard" car, the mobile home likewise is a compromise in the field of housing for those who cannot afford to occupy a conventional housing unit.

Although the industry involved in the manufacture and distribution of mobile homes is well established and is continuing to expand in total production, there has been no comparable crystallization in the business of providing end-locations and servicing of owners of such units. A fledgling industry, accordingly, can be seen to be emerging as the result of increased discriminatory demand amongst the purchases of these units. Involved here is the business of developing mobile-home parks, the sale and leasing of improved mobile-home pads, the provision of mobile-home community facilities, and the management of completed projects. Technically speaking, this emerging industry is a property management enterprise of a specialized sort, whose practitioners must gain and possess a special expertise that relates to the attending unique requirements.

Private Housing (the Multiple Dwelling)

Of all residential units in the United States in the year 1970, almost 30 percent were designed for multiple-family dwelling. Again, referring to the total of all housing units in the USA (indicated above to number almost 70 million), 8 percent were two-family dwellings, more than 5 percent were either three- or four-family units, and almost 15 percent were in structures containing five or more dwelling units.

Prior to the post-World War II popularization of the condominium concept of ownership, however, all multiple-dwelling units by and large had been contained in residential property constructed primarily for investment. This was true in a limited sense for projects under five units (in which one usually would be owner-occupied), and in the larger sense for projects containing more than five units. In other words, the general motivation reflected the desire of owners to enjoy profits associated with land conversion and new construction. Also involved was the search for financial yield on ongoing operations supplemented by the possibility of capitalizing on the rights of future benefit in the form of value increments.

The early investors being referred to, by and large, were inexperienced in the field of real estate management. Moreover, many did not wish to assume the burdens associated with the operation of their own property; hence they were quick to seek out qualified professional real estate management services.

The last four decades have seen a phenomenal change in the location, size, design, equipment, amenities, and gross volume of apartment buildings. Ideas about the related points will appear in many of the chapters that follow. Suffice it to say as an introduction that the growth in this category constitutes a major (perhaps the biggest) factor in the anticipated increased demand for real estate management professionals.

MULTIPLE DWELLING

An example of a multiple-family dwelling situated in the center of a development renewal area is the Towers in Minneapolis. This 500-family apartment complex surrounds its own park, including recreational areas, tennis courts, and swimming pools.

Institutional and ad hoc *(Nonprofit) Housing*

We now address ourselves to the field of real estate management that basically is not related to the production of investment yield, incremental yield, or to the traditional (owner-serving) objectives of real estate in the private sector. Rather we shall be concerned with housing that is created either to serve the collateral interests of institutions, as well as those of *ad hoc* sponsors of housing groups whose goals are the provision of facilities without reference to the maximization of dollar income.

Examples of the former are colleges and universities that erect housing as a means of attracting and accommodating both students and faculty; military service installations that provide housing as a means of recruiting and retaining personnel; corporations that operate in remote (field) locations where the entrepreneurially motivated builders cannot identify economically feasible construction, and the like. The fact is well known that there are many instances where the need for accommodations is such as to warrant its creation without any promise of direct pecuniary profit. Obviously, when such projects are completed and put on an operational basis, it becomes all the more reasonable to see that they are efficiently managed in order to minimize the subsidy otherwise involved.

The second category of not-for-profit property which continues to exert an influence on the field of real estate management is what we choose here to call *ad hoc*—that is, socially motivated housing accommodation. Involved is the design that produces the best possible housing units at the lowest occupancy cost, either to benefit some specific group or to furnish the sponsors with some substantial gratification. The existing mechanisms of preferential financing for nonprofit corporations and associations have greatly stimulated the construction of this type of property. In the end, a means has been found whereby religious-related organizations, labor unions, and other charity-minded associations can implement programs of housing betterment. Housing for the aged is a case in point.

In fact, the whole area of health care provides a further example of *ad hoc* housing intended for the temporary sheltering of a broad spectrum of afflicted persons. Nursing homes, extended-care facilities, and convalescent homes likewise earn broad public interest and support (as well as government financial aid). Whereas these kinds of properties represent a highly specialized form of real estate management, they nonetheless can be the beneficiaries of many of the principles enunciated in this text.

All in all, these institutional and not-for-profit properties represent a dramatically expanding opportunity in the broad field of real estate management.

Public Housing

The ascending role of the government—federal, state, and local—is treated in chapter 4 of this text. At this point, we only wish to point to the total impact of these segments of government in supporting activities that create opportunities for the professional real estate manager and management firm.

In the 1970s the record shows some 3,500 housing authorities existing within the United States. These local agencies owned and operated just under 1.8 million low-rent public housing units. While this represents only approximately 2.5 percent of the housing units in the nation, the various authorities collectively are the largest landlord in America. Their tenants are unified by economic status and often by ethnic background. And all of the authorities, either directly or indirectly, are subject to the influence and pressure emanating from the central policy-establishing agencies in Washington.

The total property management personnel (including project managers) employed by the housing authorities, is indeed extensive. In addition to these federally supported housing accommodations, many of the 50 states of the Union (and in some cases municipalities themselves) are active in the construction, operation, and management of locally supported housing program which have been created by a wide variety of legislative and financial mechanisms. These latter groups, in turn, offer additional employment opportunities to a substantial cadre of professional managers.

In this book the position will be taken that the existence of this formidable stock of government housing is a major challenge to the creative capabilities of all citizens—and to the real estate managers in particular. Erected idealistically as a means of providing "decent, safe, and sanitary" housing for low-income citizens, the nation's public housing program has been a source of bitter disappointment to even its early most enthusiastic protagonists. While it is true that the experiences of local housing authorities have not been universally adverse to the interests of the communities in which they were located, the plight of public housing in city after city has been such as to condemn the original concept and the workings of the attending programs. It is to be hoped, of course, that a solution to the current dilemma may emerge. The role that professional real estate managers potentially can play in this evolution will be discussed further in chapter 4.

MANAGEMENT, CONSULTATION, ANALYSIS

When the real estate business was comprised solely of individuals and firms whose prime objective was the earning of commissions on the sale and leasing of real property, the public felt free to bring its problems to them for gratis advice. Recently, however, the trend among real estate people has been toward professionalism. While most of those in the field are still employed in brokerage, many of the more sophisticated, more experienced, and more respected leaders have come to view the rendering of counsel and advice as a valuable service for which the payment of a fee is justified.

INSTITUTIONAL HOUSING

Housing that serves the collateral interests of institutions is seen in the above picture of Northwestern University's Foster-Walker Undergraduate Housing Complex. Completed in 1972, the project accommodates 585 students.

The American Society of Real Estate Counselors was established in November 1953 and became affiliated with the National Association of Realtors in 1954. Its members, according to their literature, are compensated solely by fees.

As the professional status of the Certified Property Manager has been more thoroughly established, owners of income property, investors, financial institutions, and others have come to recognize the value of his counsel and analytical skill. In many instances, these owners and others turn over the complete management of their property over to a management firm, yet they feel the need of professional advice in the solution of their problems. Still others among them are considering investment in one or more properties and wish to have a professional opinion as to the desirability of doing so.

For many years, property managers (many of whom were also real estate brokers) felt that such counseling contacts gave them an opportunity to establish a relationship which might someday result in either a full management contract or a chance to earn a sales commission. Consequently, they would furnish valuable information on a gratuitous basis. Frequently, management firms would make detailed proposals containing full-scale management programs merely in the hope of obtaining future business—brokerage and otherwise.

There is no more reason why a property owner should expect to get gratis advice from a property manager than he would to obtain free medical or legal advice. One doesn't expect a visit a doctor, a lawyer, or an accountant without expecting to pay a fee for counsel received. This attitude was not self-generated by the client, but was imposed by the professional who was sufficiently confident of the value of his services to demand compensation. Generally speaking, the public is willing to accept anything that it can get free. Advice is usually worth what it costs. While this is not always true, people have a great deal more respect for counsel when they pay for it.

Because the public is not always fully aware of the obligation which is involved in seeking the counsel of the professional property manager, it is desirable for the consultant to reach such an understanding at the outset. Thus, when a client comes to your office and asks a question drawing upon your professional knowledge and skill, you simply need to ask him the question: "Are you seeking professional counsel, Mr. So-and-So?" No really worthwhile opportunity has ever been lost by seeking such an understanding.

We would point out the difference between selling services and offering counsel. The former is a matter of inspiring confidence, reciting experience, enumerating results, and introducing references or testimonials. On the other hand, the latter involves offering valuable, substantive information which, once proffered gratuitously, cannot be retrieved. The property manager who is seeking to sell his services or those of his firm should concentrate on the reasons *why* the prospective client should award him the business. Detailed information as to *how* he would produce beneficial results is the manager's stock and trade and should not be given away.

BUSINESS AND INSTITUTIONAL PROPERTY MANAGEMENT

A growing field for the professional real estate manager is to be found in the administration of property belonging to commercial and industrial business enterprises and to the nation's major institutions.

The evolution of business has resulted in the creation of vast property holdings on the part of corporations. These include office structures, shopping centers, individual retail stores, research centers, manufacturing plants, recreational facilities, inns and hotels, and parcels of land held for use, investment or speculation. In addition, hundreds of institutions (notably educational) own and operate a wide variety of property requiring skilled management.

It is not unusual for such enterprises and institutions to embrace a real estate division in their administrative or operating structures. Usually a part of the financial organization, these departments handle property acquisitions (including location analysis), new construction, maintenance and operation, financing and disposition. In most cases these real estate divisions augment their staffs with consultants in various specialties. Thus, they afford an opportunity for both fully employed personnel and for management firms. In many instances the location specialists are likewise market analysts, especially in the retail and service fields.

THE INSTITUTE OF REAL ESTATE MANAGEMENT

The first attempt at the professionalization of those who devote their lives to the operation of the nations' buildings was made in 1933, when a group of men gathered together for the purpose of forming an organization which would enable the public to identify responsible real estate managers. This meeting grew out of the fact that the first few years of the great depression of the early thirties were marked by a series of failures and defalcations on the part of real estate men who had acted as "agents" for property owners in the collection and disbursement of funds. As a result of this conference a group of about one hundred property management firms formed the Institute of Real Estate Management. In order to be a member, each firm was required to certify that it would follow certain definite practices, chief among which were:

1. That the firm would set up separate bank accounts for its own funds and for the funds of its clients; that these funds would under no circumstances be commingled.
2. That the firm would carry a satisfactory fidelity bond on all of its employees whose duties involved the handling of funds.
3. That the firm would refrain from taking discounts, commissions or other emoluments arising out of purchases, contracts or other expenditures of clients' funds, unless such income was fully disclosed to the property owner and taken with his knowledge and permission.

Although the original organization of the Institute of Real Estate Management was merely an adoption of certain ethical standards of trade practice by a group of private firms, it was significant in that it was the first step ever taken by property managers in the United States to lay down fixed principles of qualification.

In the year 1938, a few of the men who originally had established the Institute of Real Estate Management recognized that it was failing to provide a background of professionalism. It was generally agreed that the prime qualities of management could be possessed only by man as an individual; that firms and corporations, as such, could not be qualified as having "ability." A firm—John Jones & Company, for example—might be qualified to manage property so long as John Jones was its administrative head. But when John Jones retired or died or sold the firm, the character of its management might change completely. It was obvious that it was only the "*man*" *in management who could be certified to be a qualified property manager.*

Having agreed upon this fundamental thesis, the members of the Institute of Real Estate Management undertook to reorganize into a truly professional society. The firm was abandoned as a basis for membership and the organization was restricted to individuals. The bylaws of the Institute state that "*The Governing Council may elect to membership any individual who:*

A. Has been accepted as a Candidate for membership in the Institute;
B. Has paid all application and service fees as prescribed in these Bylaws;
C. Files official forms as required by the Institute, giving the detailed information requested there in full, and signs an irrevocable waiver of claim against this Institute, any of its members, employees or agents for any act in connection with the business of this Institute, and particularly as to its or their acts in electing or failing to elect, or disciplining him as a member;
D. Has been recommended for active membership by the Admissions Committee as to having met all necessary qualifications for the CPM designation as provided in the Regulations;
E. Has for not less than three years immediately preceding been actively engaged as a property manager in real estate management. The term "property manager" as used herein shall mean any person who, as an owner, employee or independent contractor, directs, controls or advises in respect to rental properties in such manner and with such degree of skill, executive ability, judgment and integrity as to demonstrate to the satisfaction of the Governing Council knowledge of and proficiency in real estate management. "Real estate management" shall mean the art or science of operating, dealing with, or otherwise handling real estate or the improvements thereon which is held for rent or for the production of income, herein referred to as "rental properties," in a manner or fashion as to produce for the owners thereof, within the limitations of applicable law and responsibility to the community, a maximum of economic return over the period of management.
F. Holds some form of membership in a member board of, or an individual membership in, the National Association of Realtors;
G. Satisfactorily passed examinations given or approved by the Institute as prescribed in the Regulations;
H. Subscribes to the Bylaws, Regulations, Code of Ethics and the Institute."

As of this writing, 4,358 have been certified by the Institute of Real Management and more than 2,700 individuals are now in active practice as Certified Property Managers.

This group of professional property managers today manage in excess of 68 billion dollars worth of the nation's assets. Although they spend approximately 61 percent of their professional time in property management, they are also involved in brokerage, syndication, counseling and appraising. The need for professional training in property management today is apparent since CPMs are called upon to manage a wide gamut of income-producing properties, including office buildings, shopping centers, mobile home parks, apartments, and condominiums.

Education as a valid criteria for professionalism in property management has of necessity risen to the fore over the past years. Generally, only the educated property manager can be expected to cope with the specialized problems presented by a culture composed of such variegated housing communities. The professional property manager today must be in a position to anticipate and deal effectively with economic, social, and political change. He can attain flexibility and foresight only through education. IREM currently offers eight courses on different aspects of property management.

Even government itself has of necessity become a giant consumer of property management services, and the Institute's 1973 course addition, "The Management of Low and Moderate Income Housing," deals specifically with the problems of managing federally assisted housing.

The dissemination of information in the real estate industry is another big problem that the Institute is tackling at present. Obviously, as housing problems tend to become specialized, channels to get timely information out efficiently and concisely must be established. That is why the Institute has a constantly expanding publications program, intended to provide professionals with the "benefit of experience and expertise" of others in the same field with the same concerns.

There is no doubt that property management is "big business" today, but it still remains essentially a service profession, answerable to both property owners and the general public. The property manager who is successful today must be fully conscious of his responsibilities for continuing self-improvement and adherence to a strict code of ethics if he is to be considered a professional.

THE ACCREDITED MANAGEMENT ORGANIZATION

The advantages of association by men in what we have come to call an "organization" have been recognized in nearly every field of human activity. The modern need for specialization has resulted in groups of technicians who have gathered together to render broader service of greater benefit to clients. Law firms have united the specialists in tax law, corporate law, and probate law. Medical men have formed clinics. And property managers have founded firms. The objectives of such alliances are sound and, therefore, worthy of professional recognition.

The Institute of Real Estate Management, although a society of individual professional property managers, is aware of the advantages to be gained by organization management. It fully realizes that the building-owning public stands to benefit from a single agency which can make available specialized

THE TITLE OF

Accredited Management Organization

being the designation awarded to Property Management Organizations meeting the high standards of Ability and Integrity established by the INSTITUTE OF REAL ESTATE MANAGEMENT of the NATIONAL ASSOCIATION OF REALTORS® in the interests of Owners of Income Property is hereby conferred upon

THIS TITLE is conferred by virtue of the authority vested in the Governing Council and upon the recommendation of the A.M.O. Committee of the Institute of Real Estate Management;
IN WITNESS WHEREOF:The Institute has caused these presents to be signed in its behalf and to have its Corporate Seal to be hereunto affixed on this day of

Executive Vice President   *President*

Certificate: This Certificate is the property of the Institute of Real Estate Management and must be returned to the Executive Vice President upon termination of Accredited status.

ACCREDITED MANAGEMENT ORGANIZATION CERTIFICATE

Management firms which have been "accredited" by the Institute of Real Estate Management are entitled to display the above certificate on the walls of their offices and to use the designation "Accredited Management Organization" in their advertising and printed matter.

services in each category of the overall field of real estate management. As a professional society which certifies the character and ability of its members, it realizes its responsibility to the public in identifying those management firms which it is willing to certify as qualified to manage property, in contrast with those firms about which it knows nothing.

It was in recognition of this need for the qualification of management firms that the Institute determined to set up standards of firm operation under which certain organizations could be "accredited." There was ample professional precedent for such action. For example, in the field of hospital management it has long been the practice of the American College of Surgeons to "accredit" hospitals. Such hospitals are examined regularly by representatives of the College of Surgeons who investigate the standards of operation, maintenance, and equipment. If the administration and facilities of the hospital are thought to be satisfactory, the institution is given "accredited" standing.

Another precedent for this type of professional rating was set by the various educational associations which rate the standing of schools and universities throughout the United States.

In the light of its desire to serve the public, the Institute of Real Estate Management in 1945 amended its bylaws to include a section relative to Accredited Management Organizations:

The Institute of Real Estate Management, after proper qualification of the applicant, may designate as an "Accredited Management Organization" (also referred to as an AMO) for the calendar year any organization which:

A. Files an application for accrediting on official forms furnished by the Institute giving the detailed information requested therein in full and signs an irrevocable waiver of claim against this Institute or any of its Members, employees or agents for any acts in connection with the business of this Institute and relating to acts in accrediting, failing to accredit, or revoking such accrediting recognition;

B. Has among its officers or as one of its management executives an individual holding membership in this Institute.

In the event of the death or the separation of the only CPM in an AMO office the firm shall be allowed ninety days after the death or separation of its CPM in which to file evidence with the Institute:

1. of the employment of a CPM as an officer or managerial executive, or;
2. of the filing of an application in proper form to qualify another member of the firm or its management executive for the CPM designation.

C. Is actively and reputably engaged in the business of real estate management in the sense it is offering service to the general investing public;

D. Conforms to the minimum standards established by this Institute for an "Accredited Management Organization";

E. Is deemed worthy by the Governing Council of the designation "Accredited Management Organization."

An organization which has been accredited shall be reaccredited upon application from year to year if it continues to meet the requirements of Section I, Article VII.

The designation "Accredited Management Organization" shall be nontransferable and may be revoked by the Governing Council in the event of any material change in the ownership or personnel of the organization or for violation of the regulations of the Institute, or for other cause.

Each organization designated as an "Accredited Management Organization" shall be entitled to the use of the designation or its initials or the official emblem on its stationary, advertising, or elsewhere in connection with its name, in any dignified and reputable manner but not in such a manner as shall have been forbidden by the Institute.

In the event of revocation or termination of the "Accredited Management Organization" designation, the organization shall immediately return its current certificate and shall cease to display anything that would lead anyone to the assumption that the organization is still accredited. The President or Governing Council may cause notice of the revocation or expiration to be publicized.

The Governing Council of this Institute may delegate its authority in relation to investigation of applicants for accrediting or reaccrediting and for all matters in connection with "Accredited Management Organization" except its authority to grant the original designation.

A CPM who offers his services through a firm or corporation shall not offer the firm or corporation as certified or accredited by the Institute of Real Estate Management, unless the firm or corporation has been designated an "Accredited Management Organization."

The foregoing description of the field of real estate management should indicate to the student that there is presently great opportunity in the management of the nation's real property. Moreover, the profession is growing steadily as the result of the operations of three trends. First, the simultaneous growth of the population and its space standards is greatly increasing the total inventory in all classifications of buildings which have been discussed here. Second, a higher percentage of all real estate can be classified as investment property.

Buildings are larger and demand professional management. Lastly, there is broader recognition of the fact that property management is a special skill, requiring the kind of training and education which justifies professional status.

REVIEW QUESTIONS

1. In this book we shall be talking variously about real estate management and property management. In what sense are these terms equivalent?
2. What is the Institute of Real Estate Management? When did it start and why?
3. When and how was property management first professionalized?
4. Can a firm become a member of the Institute of Real Estate Management? Give membership prerequisites.
5. What are the three major classifications of *commercial building* management? Describe each briefly in relation to population and economic trends.
6. What is the oldest phase of property management? Name another well-established phase of property management. Where are the opportunities in each?
7. What are *industrial properties* and what specialized techniques are essential for property management?
8. Outline the scope of *real estate management,* describing briefly the various classifications of property management?
9. List the forms of *residential building management.* Describe each briefly.
10. What does "Accredited Management Organization" mean? How is that designation secured?
11. What is the justification for excluding in this text consideration of the management of hotel properties?

SELECTED REFERENCES

Friedman, Edith J., ed. *Real Estate Encyclopedia.* Englewood Cliffs, N. J., Prentice-Hall, 1960. 1458p.
    See Part VI.

Hanford, Lloyd D., Sr. *Analysis and Management of Investment Property.* 3d ed. Chicago, Ill., Institute of Real Estate Management, 1970. 178p.

Hanford, Lloyd D., Sr. "The Value of Management." *Journal of Property Management,* Nov.–Dec. 1965, pp. 313–317.

Haught, Wilford R. "Significance of the Insignificant." *Journal of Property Management,* July–Aug. 1973, pp. 180–182.

Institute of Real Estate Management. *The Property Manager's Guide to Forms and Letters.* Chicago, Ill., 1971. 245p.

Institute of Real Estate Management. *The Real Estate Management Department: How to Establish and Operate It.* 2nd ed. Chicago, Ill., 1967. 148p.

Walters, David W. "Just How Important Is Property Management?" *Journal of Property Management,* July–Aug. 1973, pp. 164–168.

CHAPTER 2

The Real Estate Market

INTRODUCTION

The property manager who does not understand and keep abreast of the real estate market is like the politician who doesn't read the newspapers. Both try to serve a public without really knowing what that public wants.

A market has been aptly described as "a meeting of people for the purpose of trade by private purchase and sale." And the classical definition of the "fair market price" is what a willing buyer will offer sufficient to meet the expectations of a willing seller. In some markets there will be only one commodity, in others many will be bartered, bought, and sold.

It is fair to characterize the functioning of real estate markets as complicated mechanisms. This is because they may be variously concerned with land, farms, houses, apartments, office buildings, stores, city lots, hotel rooms, factories or industrial space, and the like. Moreover the real estate markets will refer—depending upon the point of view—to conditions which are found in local areas (e.g., small neighborhoods), in large metropolitan areas, in regions, or in the country as a whole.

As is well known, there are certain umbrella terms by which the broad swings in any market, including the real estate market, can be portrayed. In the sense that the country's economy can be said to be reflected by the fluctuations in the stock market, so also the underlying trend of real estate investments tends to establish an overall pattern. At different times, the stock market can be said to be good or bad or bullish or bearish. Even so, when certain stocks are climbing, others may be falling; and in the same way a real estate analyst may be reporting, for example, that the residential market is flourishing, whereas the office space market is down.

This chapter is written on the premise that there is a direct relationship between what we know as the *real estate market* and the operation of income property. It follows that no property manager can afford to be so preoccupied as to rationalize his lack of familiarity with the real estate market on the misleading idea that property managers should not be involved in the sale of property.

On the contrary! Buildings are real estate just as land and its natural assets (e.g., contained mineral resources) are. Renting is selling just as land brokerage is selling. Moreover, because the property manager's selling (renting, leasing)

30

does not in general involve any transfer of title to a new owner, and also because he must constantly resell (i.e., renew) space as it becomes vacated in the course of time, it may be argued that the property manager's proper interest in the general real estate market is actually greater than that of the real estate broker. After all, once a broker has made his sale, he is finished with that specific product, and is left free to follow the market wherever it leads—whether up or down, or near or far.

Although buyers purchase real estate both for use and for investment, the ultimate occupants and tenants of all property can be thought of as primarily users of the associated space. From an economic point of view, we must classify real estate analytically as consumer goods rather than as capital goods. Thus, it may be said that the economic well-being of real estate fluctuates to a greater extent in line with consumer conditions than with capital markets.

It is true, of course, that in recent years there has been a trend toward more widespread owner-occupancy of real estate. A very substantial percentage of property users, nevertheless, remain tenants rather than owners. In such cases, the resultant arrangement between owners and tenants is not a "purchase or sale" but instead a "leasing" of the real estate involved. This is not to deny that professional property managers increasingly are engaged in the management of many wholly (or primarily) owner-occupied spaces (notably condominiums).

The fact remains that the greatest percentage of the business of property managers still is centered around servicing the needs of tenant (nonowner) occupants. This circumstance will be of special interest from the theoretical standpoint, because it means that when a unit of space is "sold" there will be in fact no transfer of title to a new owner. Thus, the property manager is left in most cases with the requirement periodically to resell again and again previously sold but now vacated units of space. In a later chapter the special implications of this marketing process will be dealt with in detail.

In spite of the mulitiplicity of markets within the scope of real estate activities, simple measures can be used to determine whether at any given moment the markets are strengthening or weakening. For example, there are the official governmental data sources, the numerous publications of the real estate professional groups, and the current reports of various business publications.

In a subsequent chapter dealing with renting and rental markets, we shall find that all of the many individual and isolated markets are definitely linked to the general real estate conditions. The strength or weakness of these general conditions may operate horizontally over entire metropolitan areas, and may influence local conditions materially. It is for this reason that the property manager should follow the real estate market in order to understand the forces underlying current movements and pointing to future trends.

In recent decades, real estate has to a greater and greater degree become subject to national and international political, economic and social forces.

These, as is well known, have been playing a major role in all sectors of human activity. One specific factor is the increased commuting mobility of the population, which has extended the practical size of the metropolitan areas. On the other hand, in spite of these influences, the analysis of individual parcels of property essentially is a local problem. This is because real estate, in particularized form, is an immobile asset of a long-term nature, used by an increasingly mobile, impermanent set of consumers. Buildings stay put, but people come and go.

People make real estate values because it is people for whom buildings are built. Purchasing power, total numbers, and social status of people make for differences in the quality, value, and type of improvement of real estate. A highly desirable, multistory building would have no value in the center of the Sahara; it would have negligible value in a small town in Iowa; it would have a reasonable value in a small city; but it would be worth a fortune on Lake Shore Drive in Chicago or Park Avenue in New York. The same building would have these widely different values, not because of the land under the building, but because of the effect of people on the earning power of the land.

Confirmation of the fact that there is a distinct relationship between consumers and land values has been furnished by the studies that show the total value of real estate in major American cities often is directly proportional to the density per square mile of local population.

Specifically applied to the property manager's search for data on local real estate conditions, the relationship just mentioned between real estate value and people density can be analyzed in a number of practical ways. The studies that are called for, of course, are no more than lip service unless there is a sincere desire to obtain information and a willingness to consider the major details. The property manager who conscientiously desires to keep himself and his office fully informed must develop a research point of view—must have the patience to repeat the required fact gathering month after month, year after year.

What is being implied here is that the property manager owes his clients a brand of attention to detail equal to that which would be appropriate for an owner-resident of the property involved. This is true with respect to all of the management functions described in this text—including accounting for funds, accommodating individual requirements, providing maintenance, choosing tenants, and—as we are now discussing—the making of market analyses.

To set the tone of the remarks that follow, we shall assert that there are two practical methods by which local real estate trends and conditions can be measured accurately. The first is by a direct approach, refering to the factors that influence real estate values; and the second is by checking the human factors by which people are motivated and the means by which they express their preferences. The proposition that the first method can be a check on the indications of the second, and vice versa, emphasizes further the consumer goods (rather than capital) nature of real estate.

In describing the first method of analysis just mentioned, it will be advantageous to begin with an assertion so self-evident that it might be overlooked, namely the fact that real estate conditions would not periodically be growing better and worse unless there were discernible causes. In other words, we are not dealing with random events when we observe real estate cycles, and this fact will be made evident in the discussion that appears in chapter 5 to follow.

In the present chapter we shall first identify eleven factors that together embrace all of the forces to which the all-important local real estate markets are subject. Of these eleven, six may be identified as factors of *cause,* and the other five as factors of *effect.* As will be seen, the first six may be regarded as of the greater importance, in the sense that they are the ones causing the major movements in real estate economic conditions. And if the last five factors are of lessor importance, still they may be regarded as valuable indicators of the same economic conditions.

THE FACTORS OF CAUSE

The six factors of cause and their significance are as follows:

The Real Estate Money Supply and the Value of Money

The purchasing power of the commodity dollar obviously is a factor of cause in determining the condition of the real estate market. What is being referred to, of course, are the well-known monetary influences upon real estate price movements.

The overwhelming influences of cost, availability and value of money are viewed here as sufficiently important to the price, value and earning power of real estate holdings, to cause us to devote an entire chapter (chapter 3) to the subject of money, and to an identification of the effects that are produced by its recurring changes in status.

There will be no disagreement that a separate and special treatment of money and real estate is warranted both by the inherent importance of this subject, and also by the fact that the value of money at any particular time follows a trend that is outside (i.e., only partially influenced by) real estate itself. The fact is that the value of money, and therefore its availability for real estate transactions, is of paramount importance in fixing the tone of the property markets at any particular time.

Occupancy

The fundamental law of supply and demand operates unerringly in real estate as in any other commodity market. Supply in this instance means the total number of property units available for occupancy. Demand means the number of renters/lessors who are able to pay for the right to occupy these units. The overall occupancy of the property units in a particular city therefore reflects the relationship between the supply and demand for such units *at the current level of rent price.*

We say "at the current level of rent price" because any change in the rentals, up or down, affects demand. Higher rentals tend to narrow the market (and thus make the privilege of occupancy an exclusive thing); while lower rentals widen (and cheapen) the market.

Now there are a number of popularly held impressions with respect to the occupancy of real estate which, in passing, we may examine for fallacy. One of these ideas is that with each property type a "normal" vacancy expectation can be associated. Historically, the across-the-board generalization was that, on the average, properties would be unoccupied ten percent of the time. More recently, however, it is common to find it assumed that normal vacancy is at the five percent level.

The idea that the degree of occupancy averages out at some particular number is simply specious. On the contrary, the facts show that vacancy is constantly in a state of flux—either down until 100 percent occupancy is attained, or up to economically intolerable low levels of sustained occupancy. The proof of this proposition is shown in the accompanying chart depicting levels of residential occupancy in the United States between 1914 and 1970. Here no recurring pattern can be seen from one decade to the next in an interval of more than 50 years. In other words, there is no central tendency shown by the data; therefore to talk about a normal vacancy is to talk about nonsense.

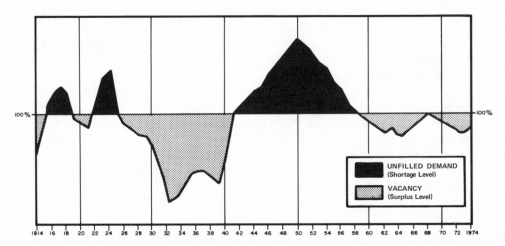

CHART SHOWING OCCUPANCY: 1914–1974

A related idea commonly believed by unschooled observers is that occupancy at over 100 percent levels is an impossibility. Whereas it is obviously true that a unit of space cannot be more than fully occupied, there have been a number of times in the history of real estate in the United States when there were more potential occupants than could be accommodated conveniently by the then extant structures. When property is thus fully occupied, however, there can be a backlog of unfilled demand which somehow is temporarily accommodated, but which continues to "overhang" the market in which the condition exists. For example, this has been historically the situation during major war and postwar periods, as the accompanying figure illustrates.

Another fallacious idea, commonly held by Realtors and managers alike, is that somehow there is a relatively fixed relationship between what people will pay for residential shelter costs and the level of their current income. The rule of thumb often quoted is that the average family can spend a fourth of its income for rent (just as presumably it can spend two and one-half times its annual income for purchased housing).* Here again, the weakness of such guidelines lies in the fact that rents and prices depend wholly on prevailing conditions of an essentially fluctuating market. In other words, only if there were a continuing correlation betwen family income and the state of the real estate market would the idea of a fixed relationship between what people pay for shelter and what they earn make sense.

In the case of commercial properties, of course, the entrepreneur will have some yardstick that will be used to limit rentals (hopefully) in the direction of maximizing profits. Clearly, however, the prevailing conditions for one enterprise most likely will not apply to any other (and perhaps not even apply to the same business at different times).

With respect to residential housing, however, it is clear that there will generally be a point beyond which the family budget cannot safely be strained. And this is the point at which the family will either accept a lower standard of housing or withdraw from the house consumer group. In the latter case the family may "double up" (married children living with parents, couples joining with others to form communes, etc.), or it may break up completely. In any case, it is in these ways that a *de facto* "greater than 100 percent occupancy" condition is possible.

In other words, for the very reason that there is no such thing as a "normal" vacancy, the occupancy ratio of individual buildings and of community shopping areas (centers) fluctuates constantly. Periods of oversupply are followed by periods of shortage. But while it is clear that ups will follow the downs, and vice versa, it is only the trend of things, rather than the rate of change

---

* These figures (if they apply at all) refer to attitudes and life styles in the USA. In France, for example, it is sometimes suggested that three-fourths of the family budget is earmarked for the kitchen and wine cellar.

or the duration of any particular trend that can, in general, be forecast.

In considering the law of supply and demand as specifically related to residential property, we must recognize the fact that there are at least two distinct types of oversupply which may result in an increase in vacancy. These we shall identify as *technical* oversupply and *economic* oversupply. (It will be evident that these types also characterize other markets including office space, hotel/motel rooms and industrial property, as well as residential property).

In the context of residential properties, technical oversupply is a theoretical condition that arises when there are more housing units than families in a given community. Strangely enough, there has never been a time in the history of the United States where the number of housing units in major cities has exceeded the number of families logically (as opposed to economically) available to be consumers of such units. Thus, technical oversupply has tended to exist only in isolated "ghost" communities, where for some reason or another the declining population has given rise to the condition.

Economic oversupply, on the other hand, is caused entirely by lack of customer purchasing power of the family units. In other words, it is the result of widespread inability through society as a whole to pay for housing at the then-current rates. A splendid example of the working of this principle was seen in the great increase in residential vacancy which started in 1929 and steadily mounted to a peak in early 1933. During this depression period, the country still continued to grow in population, while building remained almost at a standstill; * a large portion of the potential housing customers simply found themselves without adequate purchasing power. Loss of employment, failure of banks and bankruptcy of businesses in general (including those of the farmers) caused untold numbers of families to "double-up" with others, or otherwise to make shift, disbanding established family units. John Steinbeck's *Grapes of Wrath* refers to these days and these situations.

Corresponding to an economic oversupply condition, we may differentiate between two associated categories of shortages, one of which, it will be seen, includes the other. Thus we may say that a technical shortage condition exists whenever there are fewer housing units than families in a community. And, as noted above, all major cities in the United States have been continuously in a state of technical shortage, at least throughout the twentieth century. On the other hand, it is terminologically useful to define as an *actual* shortage the condition in which there are more *able-to-buy* consumers than housing units. Naturally, the existence of an actual shortage (as defined here) is predicated on the existence of a technical shortage since without more families than housing units the actual shortage could not exist.

* It was residential building that was stopped, of course, but not that of the government in the form of federal offices.

In the preceding paragraph the word *shortage* has been used as the antithesis of supply. It remains, of course, misleading to try to influence the minds of the tenant class by claiming the existence of a local shortage just because the local occupancy is high (e.g. 90 percent or greater). In other words, the distinction has always to be made as to whether the alleged shortage is due to the real scarcity of housing units, or only to the high price of these as compared to what the potential customers actually are in a position to pay.

The Question of Occupancy

Much of what can be said about the experience of real estate markets from the 1920s to the 1970s is historical prologue to contemporary conditions and bears repeating. This is to say that a recounting of the antecedents cannot help but illuminate the sense of present circumstances, even if this recounting by itself is not enough upon which adequately to base predictions of the future.

To begin, we may point to the fact that in the twentieth century there have been only three periods which might accurately be described as real estate "booms," namely the periods between 1922 and 1929, between 1946 and 1957, and between 1964 and 1969. The first two were postwar periods and the last was due to the economic impact of the American involvement in the Indo-Chinese (Viet Nam) war.

The record shows that in the present century only in major war periods has there been the necessary combination of circumstances to create a real estate boom. Indeed, these booms are seen to have been prolonged by their own momentum into the following postwar periods, except as other politico-economic factors have intervened.

With respect to the American presence in southeast Asia during the latter part of the 1960s and the early part of the 1970s, however, conditions were substantially different from those which had prevailed during the two great world wars of the present century. In the earlier cases, the war involvement had brought the productive capacity of the nation into full use. In fact, with the increased demand for production, an immediate and substantial expansion of facilities was stimulated, with a parallel upswing in employment. And as the urbanization of populations was speeded up, the demand for new housing rose sharply. In contrast, during the Viet Nam war, urbanization in the United States already was a largely accomplished fact, as was the industrialization upon which a wartime economy could be based.

There were political factors, and some with a sociological base, however, which lessened the impact on the economy of our recent involvement in Indo-China as compared with that of the earlier wars. For one thing, Viet Nam remained an undeclared war, and one that did not have the full support of the American people. And towards the end of the involvement the sharp divisions that had developed on all sides between "doves" and "hawks," etc.) had society so polarized that with the onset of the Watergate Affair, there was very little chance for a normal postwar boom to develop.

In any case, it is clear that during wartime it eventually becomes necessary to restrict construction and to limit production processes to those goods vital to the prosecution of the war effort. Even though some war housing may be undertaken in areas of extreme need, the demand for housing of all kinds and in all places will be expanding much more rapidly than can be accommodated by the economy. The typical results of such a set of circumstances are: (a) simple overcrowding in existing units; and (b) the creation of temporary quarters in trailers and rooming houses, and by the subdivision of larger into several smaller units. And, in most of these cases, the substandard housing is accepted by workers anxious to earn the high wages that prevail in the vicinity.

When, in wartime, the government is called upon drastically to increase its expenditures while at the same time curtailing the output of civilian goods, the pressures brought about by sharply increased purchasing power (against scarce products) inevitably result in the higher prices symptomatic of inflation. Since housing is basic, these conditions force sharply higher rents and values. And even though in WWII the federal government imposed rent control, these pressures forced up the *actual* cost of shelter for a very high percentage of housing consumers.

A further aspect of wartime conditions which greatly stimulates economic activity is the shortage of civilian personnel.

Historically, the wartime periods themselves are only a prelude for the boom periods that usually follow. Initially the total capacity of the country's productive effort is channeled to satisfy the high-priority needs, and shortages in consumer goods and housing are left unmet. Later, with demobilization and the return of many people to the civilian sector, pent-up demands produce an explosive surge of consumer pressure. In the case of the Viet Nam war, the government's policy for a managed economy involved promoting consumer prosperity while at the same time undertaking heavy expenditures for the conduct of the so-called "limited" war. This combination, in turn, produced an inflationary condition under which the aforementioned 1964–69 real estate boom occured.

The two great wars of the twentieth century in which the United States was involved, as well as the lesser (Asian) conflicts, have been unique in that none of the military action nor the associated destruction took place within the nation's continental boundaries. Thus the stateside American community was completely free to enjoy the special type of prosperity which war creates. Since, in contrast to this, it may be assumed that any future major war will involve a certain degree of destruction of American urban centers, the traditional pattern of a war-created boom likely will never be repeated.

Furthermore, with regard to forecasting, it seems doubtful that those conditions responsible for real estate booms in the past will ever again reappear in peacetime. This view is based on the judgment that in the future recurring periods of intensive spending are not to be anticipated, and on the idea that new construction of housing will surely continue to keep pace with normal demand. And it is only the opposite of these two conditions which can produce the situation of acute shortage in which a backlog of unfilled housing demand will mount steadily beyond the capacity of the nation's housing facilities.

Returning now to the actual history of occupancy since the outbreak of World War I, we find that from that event until the end of 1925, the nation's urban areas were in a continuous period of housing shortage. The United States was the great arsenal of production which supplied the Allied armies, and its industrial plant was sharply enlarged. Urbanization of the population was unprecedented both before and during the war. The demobilization of troops in 1917–18 (most of whom were young people in the marriageable ages) produced a sharp increase in the demand on the already overloaded housing market. Even though new housing construction was begun in earnest, after the initial period of postwar adjustment, in 1921, it was not until 1926 that a sufficient number of units had been built to cause a slight housing surplus, which showed up in the form of residential vacancy. Between 1926 and 1930, construction continued at record levels, even though the housing shortage was factually over. As a result, residential vacancy increased steadily and reached noticeable proportions by the end of 1929.

The real estate depression of 1929–34 was *not* caused by this space surplus. Instead, it was caused by the ravages of the Great Depression itself. At that time there were no cushions against unemployment. If a man lost his job, he was *completely* without cash resources. There was no such thing as unemployment compensation, relief payment, social security, and all of the other palliatives introduced after the depression was over. Thus when people lost their jobs in the depression, they were immediately forced to give up their housing accommodations and to go back to their parents or to move in with relatives or otherwise "double up." In this way, millions of housing units in the United States were vacated. When they were added to the housing surplus already existing at the end of 1929, a level of vacancy resulted that was so great as to cause an almost complete collapse of the rental and value structure.

When Mr. Roosevelt came to office in 1933, he and the Congress instituted measures that led to the limited recovery of 1933–37. It was in this period that deficit spending was undertaken in earnest and that many socially oriented bills passed the Congress which acted to increase consumer income. We use the term "limited" recovery because the upturn which started in 1933 came to an end in mid-1937. By this time, the pendulum had begun to swing somewhat in Washington and the Congress was exceedingly apprehensive over the rate of its deficit spending, with the result that its generosity was curbed. The economy of the nation lapsed into the first of what we have come to call "recessions." This recession lasted until the outbreak of World War II in

Europe on the Labor Day weekend of 1939.

Immediately following the outbreak of war in Europe, purchasing commissions from the Allied nations descended upon the United States in force. Within a brief period, they placed orders with U. S. industry for hundreds of millions of dollars worth of material. Almost overnight, employment increased sharply. Urban residential accommodations were snapped up by in-migrant workers, and the surplus of housing was virtually exhausted by the end of 1941, when Pearl Harbor precipitated the entry of the United States into World War II.

From 1941 through 1946 there was an acute housing shortage in all urban areas of the nation. Before the middle of 1942, *all* surplus had been exhausted. While it may be true that residential occupancy cannot rise above 100 percent, the fact that all housing accommodations are filled does not mean that the demand for residential space stops growing. Between 1941 and 1950 this demand for housing rose at a faster rate than the supply of new residential units—even though new housing construction in large quantities began immediately after the war ended.

In 1950, for the first time in a decade, the housing industry produced more housing units than were needed to meet the expansion of *current* demand. This meant that at long last the backlog of need was reduced. It took eight years of such catch-up production, until the end of 1957, before housing supply was brought into balance with housing demand. Beginning in 1958, the annual production of new housing units *exceeded* the expansion of new demand. This excess caused the first residential vacancy in more than 15 years in the typical metropolitan area of the United States.

The years from 1957 to mid-1963 were marked by two recessions: the first in 1958 and the second from mid-1960 through mid-1963. At about the latter date the economy began to move forward under the dual influence of government consumer stimulation and the expansion of U. S. activity in Viet Nam. Employment rose rapidly and urbanization of the population was accentuated. In reflection of these trends there was a rapid expansion of all categories of space demand—residential, commercial, industrial, institutional, and governmental. By the end of 1965 most space markets were at the "point of shortage" and the stage was set for rapidly rising rents and prices.

The situation was further aggravated in 1966 by developments in money markets which are described in chapter 3 of this text. Suffice it to say here that these monetary developments caused a decline in residential development which prevented the creation of new supply to accommodate the rising demand. Hence the shortage became more intense.

Importance of Trend Rather Than Status

The condition of inventories is recognized as an indication to which a certain economic meaning can be attached. For example, it is clear that the used and new car markets are always affected by the number of cars on hand at the dealers' lots. Similarly, when security dealers have substantial amounts of unsold bonds, there is bound to result an adverse trend in the market. The government accordingly recognizes the importance of such statistics, and studies of inventories should be given substantial weight in evaluating the probable trend of the market.

It follows that a property manager's knowledge of occupancy will in the best cases be based on a study of trend rather than only on the actual occupancy status. Already we have shown that there is no such thing as a "normal" vacancy or a "normal" occupancy. While it remains possible, of course, to compute an "average" vacancy relating to a certain period in the past where records happen to be available, such an average will yield little if any information about occupancy trends. The fact is that occupancy is never stationary—it is either moving up or down. *Which way* and *how fast* are the questions that directly bear on the property manager's current planning, and on what his merchandising policies should be.

It is of course true that unsold space is excess inventory, and thus a weight upon the real estate markets involved. On the other hand, very high occupancy indicates that there may be a space shortage, and that perhaps rental increases are justified. It follows that, to the student of local markets, a meaning sometimes can be attached to the level of occupancy as observed at a given particular time. Even so, it is the time sequence of such statistical information that is to be watched. When an upward movement is seen, one can feel confidence in the strength of the market whereas a downward trend will be indicative of a market weakness.

In any case, one must be conscious of the fact that, in the final analysis, it is the *public* (and not the managers) which actually sets the tone of the market. In periods of high vacancy, the public is alerted to market weakness by such indicators as the volume of advertising, the number of "For Rent" signs, and the publicity given to the market situation in the media. Consumers show thereafter a resistance to any demand for rent increases, and perhaps they will even counter with requests for rent reduction. Eventually, the public realizes that greater demands are possible for negotiable items in rent renewals (e.g., equipment, decorating, etc.). And property managers and the owners they represent are left to cope with the adverse situations as best they can.

In periods of high occupancy, on the other hand, the reverse situation holds. Rental space becomes hard to find; the selection of accommodations is limited; there is very little advertising, and few "For Rent" signs are to be seen. During such periods managers are alerted to raise rents, tighten negotiations, and reduce optional services.

A case in point will illustrate these ideas. In the 1925–29 cycle, the falling occupancy was the result of the inability of the economy to produce new able-to-buy families at a rate as fast as the concurrent production of new housing units. Consumer purchasing power was excellent, general business was running in high gear, and the number of families unable to afford housing remained small, yet the combined effect of these factors was to start a trend towards increasing vacancy. And the response of the public, as it noticed the trend, was to take those very actions that confirmed and accentuated this adverse trend. In fact, such historical experiences seem to confirm a rule to the effect that *the velocity of rental market decline is directly proportional to the renting public's awareness of increasing vacancy.*

And as a corollary rule we may state that *in periods of rising occupancy, rent reductions due to high vacancy are stopped as soon as the public becomes conscious of a change in the trend.* This is because increased occupancy can be related to the interplay of at least two factors, namely: (a) an increase in the total number of families (say, due to population growth, or splitting of large family groupings); and (b) a restoration of purchasing power to previously unable-to-buy families (say, due to increases in local employment, or wage levels). Either of these factors is a subject sure to be publicized in the press and, therefore, the public quickly becomes aware of the condition. In consequence, new housing customers become predisposed to accept higher rentals, and old customers (tenants) become less demanding in asking for rental reductions and the like.

Sources of Data

The decennial housing census taken in the United States is a complete enumeration of all urban properties (residential and otherwise). It includes statistics that reveal the actual vacancy of residential properties at the time the census is taken. Between census periods, the student of the housing market must base his appraisal of its strength or weakness on at least some knowledge of the occupancy situation in the local residential market.

Although there is no across-the-board enumeration between census periods, the United States Department of Commerce issues what is known as its Current Housing Report (series H-11) which reports by regions housing vacancies for homes owned and for rental accommodations. The regions are northeast, north-central, south, and west. Statistics on vacancy are given for the areas inside standard metropolitan areas and for those outside standard metropolitan areas. While these figures are symptomatic and probably can be used as a general reference for the overall trend of occupancy in the region and in the country as a whole, they do *not* have specific application in any one locale.

During periods of vacancy in individual housing units, local power companies do not remove their meters, but rather show them as idle. Since there obviously cannot very well be an occupant in a residential unit without electric current, it can be assumed that this ratio of idle meters is a valuable indicator of housing vacancy. In many cities, the power companies furnish statistics on idle meters at specific intervals, often monthly. Although the figures may not be absolutely accurate as they relate to the occupancy of local housing, when reviewed in series they certainly are representative of a trend of occupancy in a given local area.

From time to time, local organizations desiring to test the strength of residential markets are able to make arrangements with the local postmaster for mail carriers to report vacancies on their routes, which can then be related to the total number of active mail recipients. In this way, occupancy figures become available to the local analysts.

Individual property managers can, of course, keep a record of the total number of units which they operate and the number of those units currently vacant. If the property manager has a large and varied residential management account, his own figures will furnish at least a clue to the status and trend of occupancy in his area. In many instances, a number of property managers band together to combine such statistics into a larger and more representative sample of the operating experience in their local area. This, of course, gives a more valid estimate of what the actual situation may be in the community as a whole.

In the fifth factor (below), we show the importance of labor force and employment data in the *anticipation* of occupancy trends. We also cite sources for such information.

Whereas in the foregoing we have discussed the question of occupancy mainly from the standpoint of residential property, its meaning actually is the same for all types of properties, whether these be residential, commercial, or industrial. In other words, high occupancy always suggests market strength, just as low occupancy suggests weakness.

Rental Price Level

If occupancy shows us "the relationship between supply and demand at the current level of rentals," rental price levels show us the *economic strength* of the current real estate situation.

It is essential that the student of fundamental real estate economics understand one peculiarity of the rental price structure, i.e., that *there is no ability to control rental price through reduced production*. If a property manager is managing 100 buildings containing 3,000 dwelling units, his daily production of dwelling units is 3,000. In periods of reduced consumer demand most producers reduce production to offset the shrinkage in demand. Automobiles are a case in point. Automobile plants are operated at a production level which is quickly adjusted to the level of demand, thus avoiding the depressing effects of serious oversupply. On the other hand, the property manager cannot reduce his production of dwelling units in order to maintain his price level on occupied units. In some cases (as we shall see in the chapters on Modernization and Rehabilitation), the property manager can maintain price by creating new and relatively higher values in his space; but, in general, his space price is *not subject to control.* It must move upward and downward in sympathy with supply and demand.

Of course, rent controls are able to "fix" certain rentals so long as there is rigid control of possession. But during the period of the Second World War, when such rent controls were in effect under a system of guaranteed possession, the "rent market" nonetheless continued to mount. "Premium" rentals sometimes were charged by landlords operating illegally, with "bonuses," fictitious furniture sales, and other devices to tap the higher *actual* prices. On the other hand, in many areas of the world where occupancy of rental space virtually is guaranteed by eviction and rent controls, tenants often demand (and get) what is called "key money" for relinquishing possession of their space. Thus, the right to confer occupancy sometimes becomes an asset of the tenant in such cases, rather than the prerogative of the landlord!

We have already found that the *trend* of occupancy is vitally important in the property manager's study of rents. We have seen that rents will drop off steadily in a period of falling occupancy, and that the rate of their fall depends upon both the duration and the severity of the vacancy condition. We have also found that a reversal in occupancy trend stops falling rents.

Rising Rental Markets

There are two types of rent raises—"nuisance" rent raises and "economic" rent raises. In order for *either* to be operative, local occupancy trends must be upward and the community residential occupancy must be above approximately 95 percent. If an upward occupancy trend starts at a level below 95 percent, rent raises should not be attempted until enough dwelling units have been absorbed to reach this level. For example: If occupancy in your community stands at 90 percent when local employment picks up and the trend reverses, it will be futile to try to raise rentals immediately. With a 10 percent vacancy, too many owners will be glad to get your tenants at current levels; they will probably go so far as to give your tenants a concession to offset moving expense. When the occupancy has reached 95 percent, however, it is time to give consideration to increasing gross revenue. Competitive owners will be more independent, and the public will be aware of a reduced selection of dwelling places from which to choose.

A "nuisance" raise is an adjustment of rent based on the property manager's appraisal of *that amount which a tenant will pay to avoid the expense, discomfort, and inconvenience of moving.* The amount of such raise is in no sense proportionate to the tenant's rent, and is not subject to the generalization of theory. It is an amount which must be estimated by the local property manager, whose familiarity with local conditions will permit him to place a dollar-and-cents valuation on the nuisance value of moving.

The use of the term "nuisance" is not intended to indicate that the motive of the building owner, or manager, in raising rentals is based upon a desire either to annoy or to take advantage of his tenants. It is to be presumed that the conditions which have caused the rising occupancy whch has made rent raising possible have also brought about increases in operating expense and taxes which require upward rental adjustment. The owner or manager in each case will need to satisfy his conscience with respect to the fairness of this action.

"Economic" rent raises are based on the existence of shortage. This type of rental adjustment requires prior discussion of two general questions, namely:

1. When does the rent market reach the "point of shortage" required for economic rent raises?
2. How is the level of rents to be related to average family income?

Again let us illustrate the points involved by citing a representative example. By definition, the "point of shortage" begins to exist when an able-to-buy family cannot find suitable accommodations. In most cities this situation would correspond to a residential occupancy factor of 98.5 percent or more. Consider a hypothetical family with a monthly income of $1,500 presently living in a property that commands a $240 monthly rental (viz., an amount equivalent to 16 percent of this family's income).

Suppose further, in the hypothetical case under consideration, that the landlord notices that the current level of occupancy for the property is 99 percent. At the earliest moment, therefore, a demand may be made to have the rent increased by 35 percent to $325 monthly (viz., almost at the level of 22 percent of the family income). Naturally, the family's first reaction may well be to tell the landlord that the proposed rent raise is not acceptable. What will then probably happen, however, is that a search by the family for an equivalent place to live will reveal that because of the nearly saturated real estate market, any move—in addition to its inconvenience—would force the family either to pay an even higher rent or to accept a lower standard of housing. The family will agree, therefore, to the increased $325 monthly rental.

The outcome just suggested, of course, is the likely one, assuming that the property manager has based his calling for a higher rental on a correct judgment about the effective state of the market. And the lesson to be learned from the above example is that there is no fixed relationship between the level of acceptable rentals and the level of family income.

Rent remains essentially an independent factor, governed by its own law of supply and demand, and moving up and down with the movement of residential occupancy without direct correlation with the levels or fluctuations of family incomes. True, there is a degree of rental increase at which families will be forced to withdraw to lower standards of occupancy. The fact remains that the whole scale of rentals may be raised—some say from 25 to 40 per cent—whenever occupancy is high.

In all cases, of course, property managers should proceed with caution. They must be sure of the strength of the market situation. They must know enough about the income level of the tenant families accurately to gauge the point of diminishing returns on any demands for rent raises. And they must satisfy their own social consciences as to the need and desirability of any drastic requests for increases.

In fact, it should be noted, the government in one way or another (e.g., especially by rent control legislation) assumes responsibility in protecting the public against rent gouging (and, indeed, against even the appearance of it). Thus, building owners and managers have an added reason to make certain that any rental adjustments they may wish to impose are in line with the movement of other cost-of-living factors.

In the above discussion we have again chosen to illustrate the points being made by citing only residential property examples. That the same (or similar) principles hold true for other categories of properties may easily be inferred. Our simple proposition is that the strength of the real estate market is essentially established by the level of occupancy, and this is the basis upon which rental price (more or less automatically) is determined.

In this connection, reference can be made to the so-called acceleration clauses in leases by which office buildings and store spaces sometimes are rented. The intention of these clauses is to guarantee automatic rent adjustments for increased operating expenses and taxes. In the final analysis, however, it is found that such provisions have only the strength of palliatives, since the *real* rents remain adjustable only on the basis of how the occupancy trend is actually influencing the market.

As an example of these points, we should note how hotel rates usually are established on the basis of their demand. Central city hotels experience high occupancy from Mondays through Thursdays and may therefore offer lessened weekend rates. Similarly, resort hotels often offer bargains during the off-season periods.

We once considered the *necessities* of life to be *food, clothing,* and *shelter.* To these basics we must now add such things as automobiles, health protection, cosmetics, home appliances, and other highly competitive expenditures. Obviously, these added purchases must be accommodated either by increases in true purchasing power or by reductions in funds allocated to the original necessities.

Shelter has been a major item available for reduction. In some cases—a substantial number, in fact—consumers deliberately lower their housing standards in favor of improving the standards of their automobiles, apparel, travel, and so forth. Mobile homes (trailers) are often substituted for standard dwelling units by persons who wish to reduce the allocation of resources devoted to housing. This is but one example of the reduction of space as a means of cutting housing expenditures.

Sources of Data

As it collects the figures on residential occupancy, the decennial Census of Housing enumerates rental rates paid by occupants for rented residential quarters. Between census periods, the Bureau of Labor Statistics samples residential rental rates in 20 metropolitan areas in its Consumer Price Index. These figures are available to individual property managers and can be used to spot overall rental trends in the United States as a whole and in cities which may be comparable to a manager's own community.

The other sources of data on residential rental trends are far from exact, but are nonetheless useful in spotting trends. The manager can make periodic studies of his own to determine the average monthly rental per room of properties under his management. As in the case of vacancy, he can combine his own statistics with those from others in the area to get a broader sample. In some cases, managers analyze rental rates given in classified advertising to get a monthly average of offerings on a per-room basis. While all of these methods leave something to be desired from the point of view of their statistical validity, the property manager *must* maintain some degree of knowledge of rental trends if he is to analyze accurately his own market situation.

Local Eviction Suits

The level of rent collections in relation to rent billings is a significant factor in the cash income of the property being managed. The matter of *tenant credit,* therefore, becomes an important factor in market analysis. In other words, it appears to be a fact that when tenants become delinquent in their rental payments, they do so somewhat in relation to the prevailing general economic conditions.

Most tenants will tend to pay their rent promptly if they are trained to do so by a well-managed collection department. But when economic conditions produce layoffs and rising prices (as for example happened in response to the Energy Crisis of early 1974), rent collections inevitably—and immediately—reflect the growing pressure on the family pocketbook.

While the property manager knows whether rent collections are easy or difficult among his own tenants, he needs a broader perspective of tenant credit if he is accurately to measure real estate conditions in his community as a whole. Such a broad perspective can be obtained by a monthly check on suits for possession filed by landlords because of nonpayment of rentals.

Ordinarily rent suits are not filed against paying tenants. In times of typical vacancy any increase in the number of such suits shows greater pressure on family budgets and weaker economic conditions in tenant groups. Inasmuch as eviction suits vary according to season, it is well for the property manager to study the monthly level of such suits for a period of years. From these figures he can set up seasonal "norms" and adjust his monthly computations for such fluctuation.

Although the level of eviction suits is normally a barometer of tenant credit, it is also a measure of shortage in time of acute scarcity of housing. A large number of eviction suits in times of high vacancy and substantial unemployment are, as noted above, an indication of the inability of tenants to pay rent. On the other hand, when there is practically no vacancy and employment is at high levels, eviction suits may increase sharply for another reason. At such times the volume of home-ownership transfer will be increased by the purchase of homes for use by those seeking housing. The lack of an alternate residence may force the present occupant's eviction by court action. Thus, the number of eviction suits filed becomes a measure of the intensity of the shortage.

Inasmuch as the conditions under which these two different situations prevail are dramatically dissimilar, there is little chance of confusing their respective meanings.

Sources of Data

Statistics on eviction suits are maintained by the local courts in which such suits are filed. It is not necessary for the property manager to know the disposition of these suits, since the number filed will provide him with the level of legal action taken by landlords against tenants whose rental delinquency has become sufficiently serious to warrant taking such action. It is desirable that the number of such cases be recorded monthly, since this is an extremely sensitive indicator of the state of local tenant credit.

Public Assistance versus Employment Level

We have remarked more than once that real estate is primarily a consumer good, and that its market fluctuations and well-being follow consumer conditions rather than other indicator elements in the economy. Thus, a prime objective of the property manager's market analysis is to follow those statistics which can give him an accurate idea of developments upon which the fortunes of consumers depend.

There are at least three prime questions about consumers that the real estate analyst should be able to answer, namely:

1. How many of them are in the able-to-buy category?
2. What is the trend of their earnings?
3. How do they feel about spending versus saving?

The importance of considering these factors is brought out in the paragraphs that follow.

As to the first question, the monthly statistics issued by the Department of Labor will be of critical importance. They show, for example, the total number of people by geographical distribution who have registered as being available for work. Also shown are the number of persons currently employed, and the ratio of the unemployed to the total labor force.

Thus, on the basis of the latest census data one may arrive at the figure measuring the number of housing units per employed person in the USA (or subdivisions thereof). By keeping track of this kind of information as it applies to one's local community, it is possible to draw accurate inferences about housing demand. Obviously, the market never fluctuates exactly in correspondence with employment data, as suggested by the example of the person who retains his housing (at least for a while) even after losing his job.

In this connection, it may be added that published information about numbers of people collecting unemployment insurance and other forms of public assistance provides additional sources of useful data. With them the analyst may hope to have a proper measure of the strength or weakness of consumers in his area of interest.

As to the second question formulated above, it would appear that a qualitative answer is all that can be had (or in fact even needed). It is seldom possible to determine precisely how much money particular consumers possess. Even so, the trend of consumer incomes is not altogether beyond the reach of the inquisitive and resourceful property manager, and from that an indication of the gross purchasing power can then be inferred. For example, statistics on average weekly earnings, gross personal income, and the relationship of these to the Consumer Price Index usually will prove to be·most revealing.

Another sensitive indicator of people's attitudes is the record of *consumer savings*. Thus, in periods of declining public confidence (as witnessed, for example, in the post-Watergate period when the credibility of the core leadership of government itself was under direct challenge) consumers tend to increase saving and to reduce spending—as a prudent hedge against the uncertain future. These actions and the attitudes they reflect quickly tend to be reflected in the rental markets as elsewhere. Naturally, commercial, industrial, and residential markets are all involved.

To the beginning student of property management, the systematic gathering and recording of statistics on both public assistance and the size and composition of the active labor force may seem an esoteric exercise. The record shows, however, that the practicing professional who actually possesses and uses such data will not only be ahead of competitors with respect to early-warning information on the markets, but he will earn a high level of respect (and be assigned a high level of credibility) for his opinions by clients and colleagues alike.

The proliferation of welfare programs in recent years has resulted in a sharp increase in many localities in both the number and percentage of families whose incomes are dependent upon federal and state aid. In checking the magnitude of this trend, the student can take account of persons and families on emergency relief, check the aid-to-dependent children rolls, and study the statistics that show how many people are receiving old age benefits or are otherwise involved in public assistance programs.

Unemployment compensation in recent years has become an increasingly important factor in measuring the trends and stability of the residential markets. As augmented by the so-called annual wage contracts of many of the major industrial unions, this stop-gap consumer income cushions the shock of layoffs and delays the impact of unemployment on the housing market.

Finally, it may be pointed out that the great increase in life expectancy, coupled with the substantial rise in economic capability (e.g., as the result of social security, pensions, savings, and medicare), has meant that more and more senior citizens continue to consume housing after retirement from the labor force. Increasingly, these people are migrating in the direction of the sun where the rigors of winter are avoided. Thus in states like Florida, California, and Arizona we find the ratio of jobs to housing units substantially lower than elsewhere.

Sources of Data

In every major metropolitan area in the United States, the Department of Labor maintains a local employment office. In each of these offices there will be a "labor analyst" who will be in a position to provide current statistics on local and regional employment, including those that refer to trends, growth, and movement. Figures having to do with public assistance programs also are freely available from municipal, county, and state welfare agencies, and from the U.S. Department of Health, Education, and Welfare.

Family Formations

The sixth factor of cause relates to the idea that an unprecedented social revolution is occuring in the United States and elsewhere. The antecedents for this are well known. Literacy and educational opportunity are on the upswing everywhere. Racial barriers are being broken down. People now are more mobile and less subject to constraints imposed by traditional institutions. And nowhere are the changes more dramatically illustrated than in the new life styles that are forming the core structure of modern society.

In former days the record of marriage licenses was an accurate indication that a new family unit of some permanence had been formed. On the average, the family unit would be predictable as to size, growth, and composition. This was only true, however, before the relaxation of divorce and abortion laws and before the advent of the "pill."

Eventually, when the complex sociological events of the present era can be seen and studied in historical perspective, definitive statements can be made that will relate the present social changes to such questions as the concurrent fluctuations of real estate markets. Now, however, we are in a position to perceive and describe only the major facets of the phenomenon.

For example, it is clear that in the middle 1970s there is a rise in one-person families, and an increase in childless couples (both married and unmarried, and including male-male and female-female as well as the conventional male-female categories). Fertility and birth rates also are sharply down. Clearly, the impact of these differences in the social structures will have an enormous importance in determining the kinds of buildings that will be designed and marketed to meet the needs of the emerging society.

Indeed, in order that future students of real estate markets may continue to be reasonably well informed, it would appear that the census people will have to devise a whole new set of questions so that the periodic enumerations will yield relevant information.

Sources of Data

In the interim, we can only recommend that those who wish to pursue available social intelligence keep track of current marriages and divorces in the locales of interest, as being at least indicative of one aspect of conventional family formation and stability. Marriages usually are licensed by the Clerk of County Courts, and divorces are recorded in the records of the County Courts.

THE FACTORS OF EFFECT

The student who has carefully examined and considered the foregoing six *factors of cause,* will realize that there are other widely accepted indices of real estate conditions. These we refer to as the five *factors of effect.* They include foreclosures, mortgage volume, building activity, real estate sales, and real estate securities.

It turns out that there are at least two schools of thought on this subject of measurement of the strength or weakness of general real estate. One school holds that the level of *activity* in real estate is the key to the understanding of the gyrations in its values; while the other school believes that activity in itself is unimportant. In other words, the real estate market may be strong as to trend even when the activity is at a low ebb, and conversely it may be weak as to trend even when activity is at prosperity levels. This latter school principally directs its interest and concern to the *condition* of real estate as revealed by a broader range of factors (and therefore does not direct too much attention to activity criteria).

Here we prefer to divide our study of the condition of real estate markets by referring to the factors of effect as well as of cause. As will be seen, the factors of effect have an importance in that they are a *reflection* of real estate conditions (but not causes as were those described in the previous section).

Foreclosure

If a banker has a customer in the grocery business whose condition is sound enough to warrant a loan, he will be happy to take the grocer's note and advance the money. The note (ordinarily) will provide for a certain interest (which explains the banker's interest in the transaction), as well as call for specific payments by which the principal of the loan is reduced (which is the way the grocer preserves his equity in ownership). If these payments are made on schedule there will be no difficulty. On the contrary, the banker regains his money and can lend it again elsewhere (and perhaps under even more favorable terms), while the grocer for his part has his credit rating enhanced by the record of prompt and full repayment of the note.

On the other hand, if the promised repayments fail to materialize, and if at the same time the banker loses confidence that the loan ever will be repaid, he will sue the grocer even to the point of forcing bankruptcy. The important point is that the banker's suit will not cause the grocer's financial weakness, but rather is the result of a pre-existing weakness.

In other words, foreclosures are not an important cause of real estate recessions, and are worthy of notice only because an increase in the number of them indicates *an inability of real estate to pay its debts.* The holders of mortgages and real estate securities (like the banker who fears the grocer will not pay) file suits against the debtors only when they suppose the collateral real estate cannot earn a sufficient amount to repay the loans.

Conversely, the absence of foreclosures in itself does not guarantee a condition of prosperity in real estate. On the contrary, a scarcity of foreclosures only shows that real estate is paying its debts, that is *if it has any debts.* For example, in the period after the 1929–33 depression, real estate debts were so largely liquidated already that foreclosures simply disappeared. No real prosperity for real estate, however, was indicated by this drop in the number of foreclosures.

Historically, the economy has experienced alternate waves of the excessive extension of credit and the liquidation of the debts incurred through foreclosures. This pattern of events has however been changed somewhat by the workings of *inflation.* In fact, there is a new tendency to reduce the value of money as a device for "bailing out" real estate debts, and this has given rise to an alteration in the traditional real estate cyclic pattern (cf. chapter 5).

As this text is being written (summer 1974), the total extant debt of real estate in the United States is at record levels; therefore it may be predicted that there is a forthcoming liquidity crisis. Whether or not the forces of inflation will be strong enough to enable an avoidance of the classic foreclosure pattern remains to be seen.

The study of foreclosures, then, may be thought of as a means of confirming trends already detected from a prior investigation of the factors of cause. In other words, when occupancy and rentals turn downward, when the purchasing power of the commodity dollar goes up, when relief is on the increase and marriages are off, and when increasing numbers of tenants are being evicted, the conclusion is clear that real estate is losing its earning power. And the loss of earning power leads first to unpaid debts, then to creditors taking action. This action is called foreclosure.

As a historical note, it may be added that once the financial debris of the Great Depression (1929–33) had been cleared away, foreclosures continued to be uncommon well into the mid-1950s. The fact was that during the period from 1934 through 1957, real estate could easily support its debt, and did. Both values and rental were increasing steadily so that, generally speaking, real estate was able to carry an even larger and larger debt. Beginning in 1958, however, when the first postwar surplus space began to appear, rentals tended to stabilize. Then, the earnings of real estate—in some cases, at least—turned downward. And at the same time, it must be added, money conditions began to promote a sharp increase in real estate's debt.

In view of the trends just mentioned we can see why real estate began to experience greater difficulty in supporting its debt structure, and why the number of foreclosure suits (as well as the dollar amount of default) began a gradual but steady increase throughout the United States. In fact, foreclosures had risen to such a level by the end of 1966 that notice had to be taken of them. As the money shortage of that year eased, however, foreclosures declined again, only to increase when the pressure of the 1970 recession caused further defaults on mortgage payments.

In this introductory textbook it is not our aim, of course, to give a complete historical account of what has happened, any more than we can report on what is likely to be happening in the future. It is enough to notice from the few examples given that phenomena such as trends in foreclosures follow the cyclic movements in the real estate market.

Sources of Data

Statistics on the number and dollar volume of foreclosures are not universally available for all local areas. In many localities, however, either the courts or some local agency (for example, a title company) will maintain some records. In other instances, foreclosure suits are reported in the legal journals, from which property managers can extract information about numbers and associated dollar value.

Mortgage Volume

In the final analysis, most loans reflect the lender's confidence in the borrower and/or in the security that is offered as collateral. Loans made on real estate are no exception to this rule unless there is some compensating third-party guarantee (as in the case of Veterans Administration loans, etc.). In other words, lenders must in general feel that the real estate is sound, that it will retain or increase its value, and that it can earn sufficient sums to provide for the repayment of the loan.

Increased volume of mortgage lending *reflects* a revival of confidence in the safety and desirability of real estate, but it does not *cause* the improved real estate conditions. This is the point of importance. And, conversely, when real estate's trend is downward, and when the factors of cause are showing unfavorable movement, then it follows that mortgage volume will drop off. This will happen because fewer people will have sufficient confidence to make the needed loans.

In this connection a most important consideration is the way the rate of interest (plus other associated mortgage charges) influences the mortgage volume. In other words, when the money lending rates are high (as they have been recently in 1966, 1970, 1973–74, and thereafter), borrowers tend to put off the assumption of new debt—either until rates come down or until other factors persuade them to accept the current high rates.

That interest rates have been rising over the last three decades is well known—and to some extent astonishing. In the USA in the 1940s, they were in the 4 percent range; in the 1950s they were in the 5 to 6 percent range; in the 1960s they were in the 7 to 8½ percent range; while in the 1970s they have risen to more than 10 percent (in 1974) and are still rising. The rates quoted are for "prime" single-family home loans. Those for apartments and other income property in general are substantially higher.

The influence of money rates upon real estate activity is more fully discussed in chapter 3.

Sources of Data

In most counties throughout the United States, it is the so-called county recorders who compile statistics on the number and dollar volume of the monthly trust deed entries. And in those cases where the data are not released by the public authorities, they will be privately gathered and released by savings and loan associations and by the mortgage bankers.

Building Activity

In spite of the great stress placed upon building as a factor in real estate prosperity, it essentially cannot be considered as one of the causes. Rather, building activity is simply a reflection of the *practical* value of land, and is nothing more or less than an indicator by which one can evaluate the financial potential of vacant land.

As a matter of fact, building in substantial amounts tends to depress real estate by introducing new supply and cutting the scarcity factor in both commercial and residential space. Thus, a high volume of building, in many instances, has been a warning of lean periods to follow, and this is to be seen in periods (for example, in 1928) when the factors of cause were already pointing to the oncoming storm.

It is true, of course, that a large volume of building is often seen as stimulating the national prosperity, but it must be understood that unless such volume is paralleled by a corresponding increase in the volume of consumer demand, real estate will probably be in for a downward trend.

From one point of view it may be said that the construction business in the United States is the largest of all enterprises. That is why housing starts in the country are taken as one of the most important indices of the national economic well-being. For example, in some sections of the country it turns out that more than 15 percent of the total employed labor force will be engaged from time to time in new construction. Thus, it would miss the point to discount entirely the influence of high building volume on the local economic strength.

When surplus space grows to such proportions that private construction is seriously curtailed, the resulting cutbacks tend to aggravate the situation by further reducing the number of consumers for such space. In other words, if 1,000 carpenters are laid off because of a reduction in local construction, it is at least possible that a substantial number of them will move on to other areas (or be otherwise forced to diminish their own spending as housing consumers). It is for that reason that we have concluded that unless a volume of construction is paralleled by a corresponding increase in the volume of consumer demand, real estate is in for a downward trend.

Sources of Data

Virtually all communities—especially those in metropolitan areas—issue statistics on the current volume of new construction. Some of these releases merely cover the number of building permits and the total dollar volume of construction undertaken. More and more, however, these statistics are being reorganized to indicate classifications of construction (commercial versus residential, etc.), types of residential structures, and other valuable break-downs.

The data referred to above are usually available through the building departments of cities, suburbs, and counties.

Real Estate Sales

Throughout the history of real estate operations in the United States, the question: "How's business?" has almost always elicited a reply based on the point of view of the salesman, the subdivider, or the developer. If real estate was enjoying a volume turnover of ownership, if sales were frequent and at higher prices, then the answer to the question was that the real estate business was good. The broad inference of the answer was that *conditions* in real estate were good.

From the point of view of the analyst of real estate, however, a brisk market in real estate sales is significant only because it indicates the possibility of successful liquidation, of a relatively high liquidity in real estate at a given time. Such a condition *reflects* the public need for and confidence in real estate, but it does not in any sense *cause* better real estate conditions.

Speaking of liquidity, it should be pointed out that most people erroneously believe that real estate tends to be a *frozen* asset, that it should not be classified as *liquid.* This is not necessarily true. The prime reason that real estate has been thought of as nonliquid is that in a declining market its owners tend to cling to their former ideas of value, hence are unwilling to price their property realistically at the level where buyers are operating. In appraisal parlance, value is sometimes defined as "that price at which an informed buyer will buy and an informed seller will sell a given piece of property." This definition assumes that buyer and seller will be *equally well informed* as to value. Especially in a declining market, it is likely that the buyer who has been exposed to various properties in the market and who must justify the prudence of his purchase is better informed than the seller. This is also usually the case in a rising market where the buyer is generally better informed, hence willing to pay for a property more than is required for the seller to acquiesce in a sale.

It is significant to point out that there is no *precise* method of reporting real estate prices similar to the systematic and specific quotation of stock prices. Most real estate owners—when asked the value of their property—are inclined to respond by quoting a value which is a combination of incomplete information and wishful thinking. The stock owner is under no such illusion. When asked what his stocks are worth, he consults the market quotations, which are a matter of daily record.

The emerging importance of *condominium* ownership already has had a marked impact upon the volume of real estate sales since World War II. Both the construction of new residential units and the conversion of existing rental space to this relatively new form of ownership, have greatly expanded the opportunities for brokers and salesmen. More than that, the trend towards this type of ownership is to be seen in commercial properties as well. Although it is observed that the money-lending rate increases of 1973–74 momentarily arrested the trend towards condominium arrangements, it must be noted that so long as inflation continues the advantages of condominium ownership will be appreciated by the public at large.

Source of Data

Recorders of deeds in virtually all areas issue statistics on real estate transfers. Obviously, however, not all transfers can be counted as sales (as in the case of inheritances from deceased previous owners, divorce settlements, and the like).

Real Estate Securities

In the last ten years especially (1965–75), there has been a dramatic growth in the volume of real estate securities in the hands of the public. Billions of dollars have been invested in real property, for example: (a) by the purchase of stocks and certificates of beneficial interest in real estate investment trusts;

(b) by the purchase of limited partnerships and shares in syndications; and (c) by other purchase modes wherein investors buy *paper* to indicate their implicit participation in real estate ownership and/or in its financing.

While the securities that are issued to the public in these processes (e.g., as shares of stock, trust certificates, etc.) tend to fluctuate in general sympathy with the stock markets themselves, the degree of nonconformance exhibited in particular instances indicates the effect of an independent judgment about the desirability of real estate as compared to other categories of investment.

In the recent past, for example, real estate securities have climbed faster than corporate securities, just as real estate itself exhibited an increased value trend in the same period (1965–70, for example). More recently, however, as the 1974 congressional elections were being approached under the cloud of the Watergate scandal, real estate securities have been dropping farther and faster than corporate stocks, even though the price of real estate has remained fairly stable.

The property manager who seeks to keep informed as to price-value trends in the real estate marketplace must therefore keep an eye on the security market fluctuations. This is because the security markets are a much more sensitive indicator of current investor response than are the real estate markets themselves.

From a historical point of view, it will be of interest to recall that originally real estate securities consisted largely of individual mortgages. And transactions in them were for the most part between individuals and their bankers, with information about these transactions outside the domain of public information. In periods of real estate prosperity, sound mortgages frequently would sell at a premium. In periods of depression, they might in fact be discounted by owners desiring to liquidate.

In the depression of the 1930s, the failure of earnings of buildings securing real estate bond issues caused a wholesale reorganization of the financial structure of such buildings. First mortgage bonds in most cases were converted into stock, or into certificates of beneficial interest in liquidating trusts. Inasmuch as many of the bond issues floated in the 1920s were for large sums of money (and moreover were sold in small denominations to a widely scattered group of investors), those owners of stock who needed to liquidate their newly aquired shares were forced to find a market for such sales.

It was in these ways that organizations were eventually set up in the major cities to handle a volume of over-the-counter sale of real estate securities. These organizations would post list prices for the securities and then record actual prices of the various transactions. In this way there came into being a market for real estate securities, and a method for recording the present liquidation value of the various real estate stocks. The widespread involvement of the public as investors in the real estate trusts quite naturally followed. Also, in the course of time a number of national corporations dealing with rental and ownership of real estate have gained listings on the major security exchanges (meaning that public price quotations are available daily to the property managers).

Since the price of securities reflects the actual desirability of the property behind the investment, the fluctuation of such security prices gives a broad indication of public interest in real estate. This is why we have included in our study of real estate conditions the recommendation that the analyst be familiar with the real estate security trends. That these trends are not to be taken as a factor of cause follows from the fact that high security prices do not alone make for optimum real estate conditions (but rather the reverse).

Source of Data

Stocks of corporations specializing in real estate and collateral activities are now listed on the major exchanges of the country. In fact, there are several averages of real estate security prices (like Dow-Jones averages) that are available to property managers as indicators.

CONCLUSION

The full knowledge of the six factors of cause and the five factors of effect described in this chapter is obviously integral to any appraisal of actual real estate conditions and the trends to which at each moment in time they may give rise. That the information is to be gathered frequently, on a regular basis in the light of associated economic, political, and sociological considerations which influence life in general (including the fluctuations of the real estate market) will be self-evident to the experienced property manager.

REVIEW QUESTIONS

1. Name the factors which are important in reflecting real estate conditions, and explain each briefly.
2. What are the primary factors of *cause?* Give the significance of each in influencing local real estate.
3. How can local trends influencing real estate be measured?
4. Who sets real estate values?
5. Name several factors which influence improvement of real estate.
6. Explain *technical* oversupply and *economic* oversupply.
7. To what degree does a *downward* occupancy trend affect the real estate market, and how can it be caused?
8. Under what conditions can rents be increased? Describe types of raises, and give examples.
9. What is meant by the *point of shortage?*
10. What is meant by *tenant credit,* and what barometer can a property manager use in measuring *tenant credit?*

11. Why is the family on relief a problem to the property manager? What must he know about this family?
12. How did the market for real estate securities and liquidation values come about?
13. How does U. S. involvement in a major war affect our housing market?
14. In what respects do real estate markets correspond to the operation of a super-market, and in what other respects do they correspond more to a wheat market?
15. In most instances the purchase of real estate for commercial/industrial uses would be identified as a capital investment. How is it then that real estate can be described as consumer goods?
16. Montaigne said: "No man profiteth by the loss of others." To what extent does this idea apply to real estate markets?

SELECTED REFERENCES

Pearson, Karl G. *Real Estate: Principles & Practices.* Columbus, Ohio, Grid, Inc., 1973. 456p.
See chapter 1: *The Scope and Significance of Real Estate.*

Ratcliff, Richard U. *Real Estate Analysis.* New York City, McGraw-Hill Book Co., 1961. 342p.

Ratcliff, Richard U. *Urban Land Economics.* New York City, McGraw-Hill Book Co., 1949. 533p.

Ring, Alfred A. *Real Estate Principles and Practices.* 7th ed. Englewood Cliffs, N. J., Prentice-Hall, 1972. 631p.
See chapter 3: *The Real Estate Market.*

Smith, Halbert C. and others. *Real Estate and Urban Development.* Homewood, Ill., Richard D. Irwin, 1973. 481p.
see chapter 11: *Analyzing Real Estate Markets.*

Weimer, Arthur M. and others. *Real Estate.* 6th ed. New York, N. Y., Ronald Press, 1972. 831p.
See chapter 9: *Real Estate Market Analysis,* and chapter 5: *Economic Characteristics of Real Estate.*

CHAPTER 3

Real Estate and Money

INTRODUCTION

It is a common belief, even among less-travelled businessmen, that money has a fixed value. Up until the substantial revaluations that occurred during the worldwide monetary crises of the early 1970s, it was common to hear it suggested that *a dollar is a dollar* under any and all conditions in the economy. This naive view is as perverse as it is pervasive. So strong is the myth that many years ago IBM decided to make its now-famous computer card identical in size to the pre-depression-era dollar bill. That the dollar has shrunk (in more ways than one) since then, and that it no longer carries the reassuring statement that the "bearer on demand" can have a fixed amount of silver in exchange, are circumstances that insular Americans prefer to overlook.

Simplistic people are prone to attribute the fluctuations in prices of goods and services to the changing values of the commodities involved. With Locke (who said: "Commodities are movables, valuable by money, the common measure."), they ignore the fact that money itself changes in value—from day to day and from year to year. They find no merit in the argument that $100 would buy a much greater quantity of pork chops, shoes, and rent a hundred years ago than now. Too bad!

In a way, of course, the hundred-dollar example just cited begs the question as much as it answers it. The public does not like to think that the butcher controls his scales with a magnet, or that the surveyor employs a rubber yardstick. "Is a pork chop a better standard than a 100 dollar bill?" is one way to phrase the troubling question. The fact that a dog would have a definite answer, but an economics student not, underscores the prevailing confusions currently existing.

Against this background we now set out to understand the influences of money on real estate markets. And our proposition is that *money is more important to the level of real estate activity, and to its well-being, than is real estate itself.* By this we mean simply that the availability, cost, and inherent value of money tends to be more important for determining the activity level in the trading of land and buildings, and for fixing the prices offered and accepted in the exchanges, than any of the other factors of cause and effect that were discussed in the previous chapter.

An example or two will bring the ideas into focus. Consider the case of a home being offered for sale at a cost of $30,000 for land and all improvements. If a mortgage for 90 percent of the purchase price can be arranged at a 6 percent interest rate, the monthly (uncompounded) cost of borrowing $27,000 for a year will be $135. On the other hand, suppose that an 8 percent interest rate is to be charged, then the borrowing cost on the same principal, and for the same period, will be $180 monthly.

Now, for the additional occupancy cost involved ($180 − $135 = $45 monthly), the buyer gets no more land, no more brick and mortar, and no better location. Since his earning power remains the same, it is possible that, depending upon the interest rate offered by the lender, the $30,000 home either can be bought, or it cannot.

In another example, suppose one is the owner of an apartment building that throws off an annual return of $50,000. Let us say that the money markets are such as to make a 7 percent earning a competitive rate of return suitable for real estate investments. Then the capitalization of that stream of income would be some $714,500 (= $50,000/0.07). But, suppose that the money markets are such that one may expect a 10 percent return on investments. In this latter case the value of the same building will have dropped to $500,000 (= $50,000/0.10).

It is obvious in either of the above two cases that a change in the money rate alone results in a completely altered financial impact upon the value of the real estate—including categories for residential use, or for investment.

This controlling influence of money over real estate has been proved time and again in the actual market place. For example, in 1966, and again in 1970, and especially in 1973, the record shows that the level of real estate activity and its earning power were dramatically altered by momentarily rising money lending rates (that eventually exceeded—for the first time—10 percent). The consequence was that real estate sales declined, mortgage lending dropped, and new construction was reduced. And all of these outcomes occurred in periods when the demand for space remained high in the years mentioned.

To one degree or another, almost everyone is in the money business. People who labor in any of the vineyards of the economy have essentially similar ultimate goals. The forefathers of the American Dream spoke of our right to life, liberty, and the pursuit of happiness. Translated into simple English, this means that all but the most altruistic aspire to a reasonably good living standard, seek to provide educational opportunities for their children, and hope to provide old age security while at the same time establishing an estate. The common denominator to which all of these goals ultimately can be reduced, however, has the sense of being money dependent.

Property managers professionally are in the money-making game, the rules of which are similar to those that are involved in real estate brokerage itself.

If money is of such common and basic interest, all the more wonder that most should be so ignorant about what money is, how it should be valued, and what it can do. In the present context, this means that the property manager should develop more than just a casual understanding of how the fluctuations in real estate money supply and value govern leasing and rental operations.

MONETARY INFLUENCES ON REAL ESTATE

There is a historical relationship between the price of real estate and the purchasing power of the dollar. Real estate prices invariably climb when the purchasing power of the dollar declines. Conversely, real estate prices always decrease when the purchasing power of the monetary unit rises.

Obviously, the working of a fundamental law of economics is involved since inflationary periods are always ones where goods and services (as well as other entities, like real estate) cost more, just as deflationary periods are ones where things cost less.

Of recent years there has been a tendency to relate the purchasing power of dollars to the Consumer Price Index issued regularly by the Bureau of Labor Statistics. Once known as the Cost-of-Living Index, this measurement of purchasing power is widely used by labor unions as a means of adjusting wage rates to the fluctuations of dollar value. This Index is based upon analysis of price movements in several categories of consumer expense, such as food, housing, apparel, transportation, medical care, personal care, reading and recreation, and "other goods and services."

When we analyze the components of this Consumer Price Index we find that it contains what can be called "monopoly" factors. For example: under *housing,* the consumer pays for his utilities (gas, electricity, etc.). The rates of these utilities are not subject to wide fluctuations. In almost all instances, they are governed by local utility commissions. In the case of *transportation* a similar situation prevails. Thus as we study the fluctuations of the Consumer Price Index we find a tendency for them to lag behind price movements in, for instance, spot commodities.

For many years, our studies of the relationship between real estate price movements and the value of the dollar were based upon changes in the monetary unit as reflected by the series known as the "Irving Fisher Purchasing Power of the Commodity Dollar" which was computed monthly for the Federal Reserve Bank System. This series began in January 1926, on which date the purchasing power of the United States dollar was arbitrarily determined as $1.00. The purpose of this statistical series was to measure the fluctuation in the amount of commodities which could be purchased by the dollar in any given month subsequent to January 1926.

A study of this index shows that the dollar remained fairly constant in purchasing power until the year 1929, but that beginning in 1930 deflation in the general economy produced a trend which in the early part of the year 1933 brought the value of the dollar to a peak purchasing power of $1.81. By the year 1948, under the inflationary influence brought about by World War II, the purchasing power of this index dollar had dropped to $0.586.

Especially in the period following our entrance into the Korean War, we noted that real estate prices moved up much more rapidly than did the Consumer Price Index. When the hysteria of the post-Korean inflationary scare subsided, we found that real estate prices tended to decline whereas the Consumer Price Index continued its climb.

At about this same time the computation of the Irving Fisher Commodity Price Index for the Federal Reserve Bank System was discontinued, forcing us to accept another index of dollar value which would be representative of real estate price fluctuations. Real Estate Research Corporation of Chicago developed a new series known as the "Purchasing Power of the Real Estate Dollar" based upon a number of factors, including construction costs and spot commodity prices.

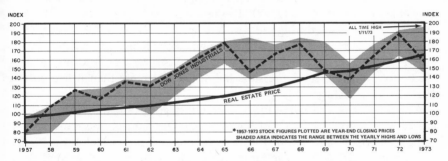

THE RERCO INDEX OF REAL ESTATE PRICE AND INDEX OF DOW-JONES INDUSTRIAL AVERAGES

The reason we feel that real estate prices fluctuate with greater similarity to commodity price movements than to consumer price movements is because all real estate transactions are "spot" sales. For example, the employee of Sears Roebuck in Waterloo, Iowa, who is transferred to Newark, New Jersey, must, under all ordinary circumstances, place his home in Waterloo, Iowa, on the market for sale. If he is not an unusual man in terms of his financial status, he will need to sell the Waterloo house before he will be in funds sufficient to purchase a house in Newark. This means that his house in Waterloo must go on the market for immediate sale to a buyer willing and able to make the purchase. Thus it will be found that real estate prices can vary widely within a comparatively short range of time, whereas fluctuations in the Consumer Price Index are relatively slow. Thus a purchasing power index based upon commodity prices is much more apt to parallel real estate price movements than is one based on the BLS index.

As an example of the effect of dollar values on real estate prices, we cite the imaginary case of a six-room house built in a stable residential area of any typical city during the year 1926. Let us suppose that this house as of that date cost $10,000. Let us suppose, further, that upon its completion it was purchased by an architect and that it was subject to a $6,500 mortgage which had been placed by the builder with an insurance company.

Along came the depression which began in 1929 and the architect-occupant became unemployed. By 1932 he had exhausted his savings and his ability to meet payments under the mortgage. Since it was impossible at that time to liquidate his house at an amount even equal to the balance of the mortgage, foreclosure proceedings were instituted, and in the latter part of 1933 the insurance company came into possession of the house. Being unwilling to continue in ownership of real estate, the insurance company, let us suppose, placed this house on the market in 1934 for $6,000. It was purchased by an owner-occupant, who kept it until 1937, at which time it was sold for $7,000. This buyer, in turn, resided in the house until 1944, at which time he sold the same house for $8,750. The 1944 buyer kept the house until June 1946, when he yielded to an offer of $12,500. The buyer of the house in June 1946, had an opportunity to sell during the post-Korean inflationary bulge of early 1951 at a price of $13,000. The peak of the value of the house was reached in the year 1957 when it might have been valued at $14,500, over twice its value at the bottom of the great depression and 45 percent more than it had cost in 1926, 31 years before.

As noted above, the end of the housing shortage in 1957 in the *typical* local market saw a gradual easing of house prices. Our subject house dropped in value to, perhaps, $13,000 in 1961. In the prosperous years of 1961–1966 it rose again to $14,000 in the latter year, principally because of land price increases.

Although this is a theoretical house, the circumstances of its erection, sale, and resale are typical of the price fluctuations which applied to thousands of urban houses in the period covered. As we analyze these changes in the price of a soundly built home in a stable residential neighborhood, it is obvious that the *intrinsic* value of the property could not have changed during the period in a manner indicated by the price movements. Certainly there is no reason why the house should have lost 40 percent of its value in the first eight years of its life. Moreover, there is no real reason why the house should be worth an amount exceeding its cost more than 30 years after it was built, namely at a time when, according to bookkeeping schedules of depreciation, it should have depreciated by approximately 60 percent.

The reason for these sharp price changes must be in the fluctuation of the dollars in which values were stated. If this is so, it is axiomatic that the student of real estate management should acquaint himself with the fluctuations of money value and the methods of measuring such changes.

THE HISTORY AND FUNCTION OF MONEY

Courses in money and banking are offered to most students of economics, and we shall not attempt here thoroughly to explore the subject. However, since the monetary influences on real estate markets are so significant, we shall attempt to give the student a few basic ideas on the history and function of money. Whereas money was widely used in early Phoenician and Egyptian times and in the Golden Age of the Mediterranean, the lapse into the so-called Dark Ages produced a society and economy in which its use was extremely limited. In medieval times the immobility of people and the limited nature of goods for trading enabled the simple processes of barter to accommodate the needs of men.

With the advent of the merchant and craft guilds, under which people in certain areas specialized in and developed the manufacture of particular types of goods, there again arose a need for some commodity which would have universal value, and which could serve as a medium of exchange. Any universally valued commodity which is suitable for use as a medium of exchange can be described as *money.* In order to be suitable for wide use as money, the commodity should have the qualities of portability, durability, and scarcity. A number of commodities met this requirement, but none was so admirably suited as the precious metal, gold.

The coming of the Industrial Revolution, with its greater mobility and its broader supply of goods, brought a greatly increased demand for a universal money. Those who accumulated gold and traded in metal found it extremely difficult actually to transport the physical metal from one place to another in every case. Problems of storage, likewise, became troublesome for those who accumulated wealth in the form of money.

To accommodate the requirements of those owning and spending the precious metal, numbers of goldsmiths entered the business of providing storage for this metallic wealth. In order to serve the convenience of their customers, they would issue receipts for gold when it was stored with them. These receipts, or "chits," when issued by well-known firms of goldsmiths, would be accepted as good tender in lieu of the actual delivery of the required weight of the metal.

As trade and travel broadened and grew more complex, the difficulties involved in the transfer of money increased. There arose out of these problems the need for the issuance of money by a central agency whose "chits," or notes, would be universally recognizable and would enjoy a validity based upon widespread confidence and careful control. The logical agency to undertake such a distribution was the local government.

Inasmuch as trade was carried on widely between the nations of the world and individuals therein, it became necessary to establish a single worldwide unit of value against which individual currencies could be measured and stabilized. Thus it was that England in 1816 established what was henceforth known as *the gold standard.* This gold standard simply meant that the British Government guaranteed to its nationals and to the rest of the world that for each currency unit issued, a certain weight of actual gold had been stored in its vaults, so that on demand the holder of this currency could claim redemption of his paper money in gold.

Subsequent to the adoption of the gold standard by England, this same standard was embraced by most of the nations of the western world, with the individual national currencies valued in relation to one another by their guaranteed gold content. This criterion of money remained in effect, with the exception of a brief period during World War I, until 1931, when England under the strain of the depression was forced to abandon her guarantee as to the level of the gold backing of her currency.

In a few instances during this period, individual nations (notably Russia, Germany, and France) temporarily abandoned the validity of the relationship between the amount of their currency in circulation and the amount of their gold stocks. In each case a disastrous inflation resulted from a complete breakdown in their publics' confidence in money, caused by the issuance of untold volumes of unbacked currency by hard-pressed governments.

As the depression of 1929–1933 broadened and seriously involved the United States, the strains on our currency increased to the point where the United States in early 1933 itself abandoned the gold standard. Whereas for purposes of international trade the United States dollar retained its fixed weight of gold, it was no longer permissible for the citizen to own gold coin; debts were no longer required to be paid in gold; gold notes were withdrawn from circulation by the treasury and our currency became irredeemable in the precious metal. The value of money was henceforth to be self-evidently determined only by the relationship between the amount of money in the economy and the amount of goods available for purchase therewith.

Almost immediately after the United States went off the gold standard, commodity prices rose sharply. The purchasing power of the dollar dropped from $1.81 in February 1933, to $1.395 at the end of 1933. Generally speaking, the typical citizen of the United States did not attribute this rise in prices to our abandonment of the gold standard, or to any change in the value of the dollar in his pocket or in his bank account. He merely thought recovery was under way with prices moving up in reflection of better times.

One of the reasons the Government determined to abandon the gold standard was that it desired to engage in a spending program by which it hoped to stop the disastrous deflation of 1929–33.

There lived in England in this period a man named Lord Keynes, an economic philosopher, who had evolved a theory that governments could reverse the adverse trends of business by undertaking programs of wholesale spending which would set the wheels of commerce and industry into motion, reviving general prosperity and relieving unemployment. Keynes' followers believed that when this reversal of trend had been accomplished, and when commercial and industrial activity reached sufficient velocity, then the government could recapture its original investment in "pump priming" by taxes against the accelerated volume of income and trade. This philosophy was embraced by the Roosevelt administration and became known as *deficit spending.*

Although the people of the United States were not much impressed by these financial manipulations, the purchasing power of money was gradually driven down by these inflationary measures until in February 1937, the purchasing power of the dollar reached a low of $1.102. This decline in the value of the United States currency had been accomplished through substantial *deficit spending,* under which the relationship between dollars and goods had changed sufficiently to produce a relatively higher availability of goods. The productive genius of the country, however, once reanimated by this deficit spending, began to produce goods at a rate faster than the increased amount of money in the economy, and deflationary forces again operated.

The so-called recession of 1938–1939 set in, and we witnessed a gradual increase in the purchasing power of the dollar from $1.102 in February 1937, to $1.279 at the end of August 1939.

WORLD WAR II AND THE DOLLAR

The virtue of a stable currency lies in the confidence with which people regard its future purchasing power. Inflations have sometimes been called periods of *distrust spending.* At such times people fear that the money in their pockets or in their banks will be worth less in the future, and hence they are anxious to spend it today in order to obtain the best possible trade for whatever goods they may desire.

The war in Europe broke out on the Labor Day weekend of 1939. On the following Tuesday morning in hundreds of stores over the whole United States, scores of women snatched up every available pound of sugar. They were acting on their memory that during World War I sugar had been in acute shortage. Although they probably did not realize it, their mental process went something like this: "I had better rush out and buy sugar, because I am afraid that there will be no sugar to buy tomorrow." This was the beginning of a period of *distrust spending* which accelerated gradually during the period prior to Pearl Harbor and broke out in inflationary flame immediately after that fateful day in December 1941.

More decisively, the outbreak of World War II in Europe caused the immediate liberation of foreign funds for expenditure in the United States. Foreign purchasing commissions arrived by the score, placing orders for millions of dollars of goods. This, in turn, caused a sharp increase in employment, a rapid rise in industrial production, and a resultant increase of money in our economy. This increase in the amount of dollars in the economy was quickly matched by a concomitant increase in the amount of consumer goods available. As a result, there was no great immediate change in the purchasing power of money.

In early 1941, however, it became apparent that the funds in the hands of European countries were not sufficient to meet their demands for materiel. It also became increasingly clear that the United States might shortly be embroiled in the war and, hence, steps should be taken to increase our own military preparedness. These facts served as the background for the enactment of the Lend-Lease Act, under which additional millions were liberated for the purchase of United States goods and for arms. At the same time the Selective Service Act was passed, promising the withdrawal of thousands of men from the labor force, and consequently threatening a shortage of labor.

These measures resulted almost immediately in a sharp drop in the purchasing power of the United States dollar from $1.17 in February of 1941 to $0.996 at the end of the year. During the year 1941 a gradual awareness of impending war came over people of the United States, and they subconsciously engaged in a *distrust spending* spree which pushed industrial production of consumer goods to the highest point since 1929.

Shortly after the Japanese attacked Pearl Harbor in December 1941, it became obvious that the economy would shortly need to be converted to all-out war production, and that consumer goods in many categories would have to be shut off completely in favor of military materiel. This meant that our people would be fully employed, that wages would increase, and that there would be a shortage of goods for the people to purchase with their new, higher earnings. Unless some measures were taken to assure an equitable distribution of the dwindling supply of consumer goods and to prevent outrageous price increases which would tend to vitiate the nation, we would find ourselves in an uncontrollable inflation. To forestall such an eventuality, the Congress passed price control regulations, under which essential goods were rationed, rents were controlled, and prices and wages were generally frozen.

In spite of the fact that it was impossible to hold an inflexible line against the forces of inflation, the price control efforts of the government during the period of World War II were generally successful. The purchasing power of the dollar—which stood at $0.996 in the month of Pearl Harbor—dropped only to $0.866 during the month of victory over Japan. Whereas this purchasing power figure represents the price movements of principal commodities, certain other elements in the economy experienced a sharper price rise. Among these other elements were wages and real estate.

During the period from January 1, 1939, until VJ Day, the federal debt was increased from 41.9 billion dollars to 267.5 billion dollars. Federal spending during that portion of this period in which the nation was at war reached fantastic levels. In one six-month period the increase in the government debt—

principally spent for war purposes—amounted to more than 60 billion dollars. This was indeed a period of sharp inflation from a monetary point of view, but the *effects* of that inflation in terms of price rises were held in check through the observance of price control regulations by the majority of the people. Although there was some hoarding and some black-market trading, most of the people were brought close enough to the actual war that they observed the rules of fair play as laid down by the government.

THE POSTWAR PERIOD

As soon as victory over Japan was achieved, the typical citizen of the United States felt that this type of *fair play* was no longer a responsibility. More and more goods were channeled through black markets, and fewer and fewer price regulations were effective. The fact was that the *actual inflation* had taken place during the war, but that its effects had been *delayed* by control measures. Once the war was over, the dikes which held back the great accumulations of cash in the hands of consumers were broken and a flood of purchasing power (greatly in excess of the then current production) spread out into the economy. The tremendous hunger for consumer goods, which had characterized the long war period and which represented a giant backlog of demand for virtually every type of product, was manifest in the spending behavior of the consumers.

Since it was impossible for the economy to convert to peacetime production in time to take the impact of this flood of purchasing power, the competitive bidding of consumers for limited available merchandise resulted in a sharp increase in the general price level. The purchasing power of the dollar dropped from $0.86 in the month of VJ Day to $0.568 by July 1948. The most drastic drop was experienced in the first full year of the postwar period, 1946, when the value of the dollar dropped from $0.855 to $0.663.

Because the demand for goods of all types spread over the entire economy, virtually all prices responded to the buyers' push. This was especially true in real estate since the long wartime ban on building had produced a serious shortage in all types of structures—residential, commercial, and industrial. Because of the fact that the production of additional housing facilities for families, business, and industry requires a longer period of time than most consumer goods, the bidding for existing facilities was especially spirited and the price rise was somewhat higher than that of the economy as a whole.

Theoretically, the end of the war produced the setting for a technical *deflation*. Once the victory was obtained, the government program of fantastically high spending was brought to a sudden stop. The giant facilities for production, which had been created during the war period to produce war materiel, were liberated for the production of consumeer goods. These increased production facilities were more than sufficient to produce the amount of goods required by the economy for *current* consumption. Thus, once the backlog of accumulated demand was satisfied, it was apparent that deflation would set in.

In spite of the postwar conviction that a depression was bound to ensue as the result of the fantastic increase in production facilities, no such economic cataclysm had occurred through mid-1970. Unquestionably, new forces are at work in the economy—forces which may tend to inhibit the operation of so-called natural economic laws. These new forces are referred to elsewhere in this book.

THE NEW ECONOMY

The social and political life of man, in recent years, has been changing radically in America—indeed, in most of the other developing and developed parts of the world too. Attending these changes, and stimulating them, have been substantial alterations in the nation's and the world economies. These influences are especially well seen in the monetary field.

What we refer to as the new economy has been in a state of evolution almost continuously since the marker year, 1931. Although many of the changes that have occurred and have been embraced since then have already been described above, a recapitulation now will bring to the fore the rationale of its current manifestation.

First and most significant is the idea that the new economy has the character of being responsive to whatever it is that people, in general, want. The latter, of course, is best expressed through political action, as directed towards the obtaining of the desired economic benefits. Examples follow.

Historically people always have sought and hoped for the hedges and guarantees that would guard against the "slings and arrows of outrageous fortune" to which the aged especially are subject; hence, Social Security. Likewise, in modern times people have had the audacity to appeal for relief against the threat of future unemployment; hence, unemployment insurance programs. Similarly, people have reacted negatively against the mounting costs of health care; hence such programs as Medicare and Medicaid. And more and more people are wanting to be able to buy things while still earning—but not fully possessing—the money for the purchase price; hence the emergence and continued growth of consumer credit. Similarly, people have wanted the government to insure their loans on housing to the extent that the money lenders would be satisfied with modest down payments; hence, the Federal Housing Administration. And the like.

As things have evolved, the question of whether or not the people could afford the gratification of these various desires has been of secondary importance. The majority of Americans have simply hoped that, without resort to socialism or allegiance to the idea of a welfare state, somehow, and by some miracle, they would be taken from the cradle to the grave by the capitalistic system, but without the need to pay the full price that unsubsidized free enterprise demands. This made it necessary for the system itself to be both innovative and flexible, just as the population of mid-America was asked (in fact, asked itself) to ignore the planned economy of which they were the privileged beneficiaries. In other words, the situation demanded an "open-ended" economy that was not hemmed in by fixed, too-rigid rules.

In chapter 4, the whole history of the rising governmental involvement, as affecting certain aspects of private lives, is discussed. This topic will be presented as it would be written by the student of recent history, and without any authorship bias. In other words, when talking about the new economy it is best to talk about the way things are (i.e., deal with the facts), rather than to reminisce about how they might have been in some former time.

The fact remains that the *modus operandi* that has been employed by those responsible for the emergence of the new economy is the device of a planned inflation followed by whatever planned remedial actions might thereafter be indicated. And, as will be seen, the principal difference between the new economy and the old is reflected in the fact that the currencies of nations no longer are bound by a fixed relationship to gold (pegged, as will be recalled, in former years at a stated—inflexible—level).

A milestone in the most recent history of the emergence of the new economy was the notification by President Nixon on August 15, 1971 to the peoples of the world at large that the United States would no longer freely convert dollars into gold. While citizens of our country had of course not been able to convert their currency into the precious metal (in fact, had not been allowed either to own or trade in gold) for a long time, this notice to the world that the United States henceforth and officially would forsake the gold standard as a backing for its currency came as a shock.

As noted above, inflation has been in almost continuous long-term progress over the entire history of our country—especially since 1933. In consequence, the national debt of the United States in the meantime has risen from some 16 billion dollars in 1930 to more than 470 billion dollars at the end of 1973. And the upward swing continues up to the writing of the present edition of this book.

Our main concern here, however, is to examine how the new economy differs from the old with respect to real estate. In the first place, and perhaps most significantly, the old economy (with its inflexible relationship to gold) was said to follow a "boom" and "bust" pattern. Under the optimism that would always prevail in times of prosperity, real estate owners and developers followed the pattern of borrowing heavily for funds by which they hoped to improve property. Moreover, inevitably, this would create a surplus of such property. The result would be that rents and occupancy would tend to decline under the pressure of competition.

Inasmuch as real estate debts traditionally have been incurred on the premise of an assured profitability of new properties, a wave of foreclosures would occur when properties produced insufficient cash to support the debts that had been allowed. The ultimate result would be a real estate depression.

Under the new economy that has been operating now for more than forty years, however, debts tend to be liquidated by inflation rather than by default. As an illustration, take the case of a hospital built in 1968. Suppose originally the cost of a two-bed room had been set at $44 daily, but that between 1968 and 1973 the room rate had been doubled to $88. Suppose further that the hospital in question had required a $15 million loan for its construction, and it was anticipated that the loan would be retired through income based on the $44 daily room rate. But in the inflation of the hospital bed rates from 1968 to 1973, the doubling of the room rates did not change the dollar-fixed $15 million loan. Thus, it would become relatively easy for the hospital to liquidate its debt by paying off the obligation in dollars that cost only fifty cents in relation to their 1968 value.

The illustration of a hospital has been used because in that five-year period, the price of hospital beds advanced more than any other type of rental income property due to the *selective inflation* which was experienced under the pressure of Medicare.

We have used the term "selective" advisedly, since in terms of inflation all prices do not necessarily rise uniformly. On the contrary, individual prices will increase by differing amounts depending upon the relationship of demand to supply of certain goods and services. As an example, consider how food prices rose dramatically in the summer of 1973, as the result of an emerging food shortage linked to the simultaneous prosperity in most of the free world, plus the wheat deals with Russia and China. Or as another example, consider how petroleum prices rose dramatically in the fall of that very same year, in consequence of the energy crisis brought on by the Yom Kippur War and the following Arab oil embargo. Yet, at the same time, other prices barely registered the then-rampant selective inflation. (That later, in 1974, the characteristics of a more general inflation could be seen, is another story beyond the focus of this book.)

In any case, real estate often selectively experiences an inflation in price. For example, when there is a space shortage in housing, office space, retail store space, or in buildable land, then it will be the prices in that particular category of property that tend to rise. Obviously, one of the reasons why real estate failed to register an across-the-board increase in the latest phase of inflationary pressure in the United States was the oversupply in virtually all markets. Thus, in the fall of 1973, it could not be said that any kind of space was at anywhere near "a point of shortage" (with the possible exception, however, of single-family houses). Under these circumstances, it was not possible for landlords rapidly to increase rents, or for sellers likewise to raise prices, as much as had been the case between 1946 and 1956 when all space had been in short supply.

In these connections, it will be of passing interest to observe that in 1973, inflation in the constituent elements of real estate appeared to be proceeding at a pace faster than inflation in real estate itself. Land prices had risen sharply; property improvement costs were up; labor and material costs were peaking; operating costs and real estate taxes were accelerating; and so forth. Naturally this meant, in many cases at least, that the finished product, when occupied at existing rents, was unable to produce a sufficient cash flow to support the total costs. And the difficulties then experienced, it will be recalled, were further compounded by the very high cost of financing that prevailed during the subject period.

Another difference between the new and old economy, as these terms are being employed here, can be found in the practice of borrowing all of the money needed to complete real estate developments. Thus, from 1971 to 1974 the level of money supply was so high, and the competitive pressures to lend it out so great, that the average builder-developer could raise more than 100 percent of the needed amount by approaching a combination of available money sources. This encouraged the practice of "borrowing out" which means, simply, that the developer of a project could obtain *all* of the necessary money without investing any funds of his own.

The term "equity" that, under the old economy, had meant the amount of the owner-developer's funds that were directly invested in the project, has rapidly become obsolete under the "borrowing out" conditions of the new economy.

THE REAL ESTATE MONEY SUPPLY

There is a group of economists who believe that the art of business forecasting is principally one of keeping close watch on the money supply available to the total economy. This money supply is defined as the total amount of currency outstanding plus the total demand deposits in all of the nation's banks. The theory of these economists, who are called monetarists, is that increases in the gross money supply tend to stimulate the economy, and that decreases in the money supply act to depress busines activity. The total money supply of the nation has increased dramatically over the years—sometimes at a higher rate, sometimes at a slower rate, but very seldom is it actually reduced. The control of the money supply is in the hands of the Federal Reserve Bank system and is a principal tool in the hands of the managers of the economy.

Real estate has its own special money supply. It secures the bulk of the funds which it uses from one or more of the following sources:

Savings and Loan Associations

These institutions are a prime source of real estate capital. Whereas, traditionally, their loans were virtually confined to single-family houses, they are now active in all forms of income properties. In addition, through their service corporations, they can allocate a limited portion of their capital to entreprenurial enterprises.

Relying almost solely on the savings of the American people for the source of their funds, they are sensitive to the rise and fall of individual thrift. Moreover, they are sensitive to the competitive situation in the savings money markets. When rates offered by others are higher than those legally possible for such institutions, they are subject to widespread *disintermediation.* At such times, their lending capacity is restricted by their cash inflow.

Savings and loan institutions are a significant factor in providing the money supply available to real estate borrowers. The gross savings of these institutions at the end of 1972 were approximately $227.8 billion.

Banks and Bank Holding Companies

Commerical banks traditionally have operated mortgage loan departments in conjunction with their savings departments. The object has been for the banks to be in a position to accommodate their savers when home mortgages were required. In addition, these banks have sought to make interim construction loans on nonresidential and apartment buildings on the basis of a take-out of permanent financing provided by others. Finally, these banks have the policy of frequently making mortgage loans through their commercial departments to business customers.

In the middle of the 1960s, the banks had entered into a new era with the authorization of so-called bank holding companies, under which banks could acquire businesses in a limited number of specifically nonbanking enterprises. A prime target of these acquisitions was the mortgage banking field. In the following ten years, most of the leading mortgage banking firms then extant were bought by the proliferating bank holding companies. There was an obvious advantage to these purchases. This grew out of the circumstance that bank holding companies can issue "commercial paper," and use the proceeds to finance projects in the real estate field. The additions to the real estate money supply, thus made available, totalled countless millions of dollars.

Real Estate Investment Trusts

Also in the 1960s, a substantial addition had been made to the real estate money supply by the adoption of the Real Estate Investment Trust Act. This enabled qualified trusts to operate for their beneficiaries, and still pay no federal income tax or capital gain tax on income or gains distributed to their share holders. The proviso was simply that the trusts should distribute at least

90 percent of their ordinarily taxable income to the shareholders annually.

Such trusts (called REITS) were organized by a wide variety of sponsors, including mortgage bankers, bank holding companies, realtors, life insurance companies, and other groupings with a capability in the real estate field. In effect, the development under discussion made it possible for small investors to get a "piece of the action" in the real estate field, just as the buyers of mutual fund shares gain the opportunity to acquire an interest in a broad portfolio of stocks. Generally speaking, these REITS were of two kinds, namely: (a) those owning real estate both for gain and income, and (b) those engaged in the mortgage business.

The funds that the public has invested in REITS, in most cases, have been leveraged by borrowings. The investments that have been made by shareholders are thus employed as *equity* in borrowing against mortgages. Thus, the gross assets of REITS will be substantially greater than were the initial contribution of the investors.

Up to the present writing (mid-1974), there are more than 200 such trusts in the United States with assets of over $15 billion.

Insurance Companies

For many years the insurance companies (particularly the life companies) have been a major source of real estate capital. Being capable of long-term investments, these companies can invest substantial amounts of money (usually up to some fixed proportion of their investments).

In recent years, with advancing rates of inflation, the patterns of participation by the insurance companies have changed materially. This has been because long-term mortgages (20 years, for example) are unattractive in inflationary periods. Therefore, in the mid-1960s these companies sought to protect themselves by claiming participation in the rights and future benefits of ownership. Modes adopted for this purpose have been assigned to be either a share in the ownership or a share in the profits to the lender.

The Corporate Conglomerate

To add to the flow of capital into real estate over the last 15 years, the various sources of expanding capital mentioned above have been joined by a virtual avalanche of business corporations which sought to participate in the promise of the profits offered. These groups accordingly have purchased all forms of enterprises in the field, including those of land developers, mortgage bankers, real estate consultants, home builders, mobile and modular manufacturers; any kind of company that offered access to the supposed bonanza.

The net experience of these corporate investors has been less than favorable, at least through the year 1974. In fact, the record shows that this sort of involvement has fallen off in the 1970s; still, earlier substantial funds had poured into real estate markets in the way here described.

Syndications and Partnerships

The lure of tax shelters for individuals has gained ground steadily since the advent of income taxes. Real estate ownership (especially of the residential sort) offers superior attractions in this area. Financial and real estate entrepreneurs were quick to discover that there were profits to be made by offering such opportunities for participation in real estate investments. This was because, on an after-tax basis, such measures provided much higher yields than were available to savers in any other media of investment. The funds thereby added have swelled the already massive amounts of new money supply made generally available to developers and promoters from the various sources.

In passing, the opinion may be offered that, since the quality of these investments has been quite varied, there may eventually be a resultant widespread disappointment on the part of investors. Nonetheless, syndications and partnerships have provided major sources of money supply in real estate markets.

The Government

The role of government in real estate is treated separately in the next chapter of this text (chapter 4). Suffice it to say here that both the federal and state governments have participated in a dominating way, especially with respect to stimulating the flow of capital into housing markets.

It is obvious from the foregoing remarks that an unprecedented change has been experienced over the last 15 years in the money to real estate relationship. Not only have the elements of *availability, cost,* and *value* of money each undergone radical revision, but the *speed* with which such alterations have occurred, and the *extent* to which they have taken place, have picked up remarkably. This tells the property manager that he must prepare himself to interpret monetary developments with the same level of knowledge and competence that he possesses for real estate itself.

In other words, to properly manage property, one must first understand the inner workings of the real estate market (chapter 2). This, in turn, is achieved only when the pervasive role of money in real estate (chapter 3) also is comprehended.

MEASURING MONETARY TRENDS

Historically, the economy has found itself in one of three possible monetary situations. The first of these may be described as a period in which money is extremely plentiful and is being pumped into the economy at a more rapid rate than goods are being produced. This is a period of *inflation.* The years from 1941 through 1946 were a classic example of such a period. Workers were fully employed at high wages, but they were unable to buy the products of their labor.

The second type of condition in which the economy finds itself is one in which goods are extremely plentiful and money is increasingly scarce. This type of period is known as *deflation*. It was classically illustrated in the years 1929 to 1933.

The third type of condition is one we have chosen to call *unflation;* it might also be described as *prosperity*. This is a condition in which there is an ample supply of both money and goods and a high velocity of exchange between the two *without any marked change in price levels*. This type of situation prevailed in the years 1924 to 1928, 1946 to 1948, 1955 through 1956, and again from mid-1962 through 1965.

It should be understood that the above reference is primarily to so-called *consumer prices*. Actually, as noted previously, real estate experienced a mild *deflation* in the years following 1957 and, in the money crisis of 1966, *income real estate* declined sharply, along with stocks, bonds, and other income-producing capital investments, as abnormally high interest rates forced the use of sharply higher capitalization rates in its appraisal. On the other hand, real estate for *use* (as, for example, single-family houses, farmland, and industrial plants) did not suffer in the 1966 situation and, in some cases, increased in value because of improved *current demand* for such *use*.

It would seem apparent that the United States and the rest of the free world now are on a course of what may prove to be *permanent inflation*. Whereas our economic training and the experience of history would lead us to believe that ultimately such a course will be in the direction of a complete debauchment of money, we nevertheless must deal with the subject of money values always and only as we find them. As this text is being written, the United States is suffering far less from inflation than are many other countries in the capitalistic world. Indeed, the U.S. dollar seems to be strengthening on the world's currency markets, at least for the moment. The so-called gold bugs, of course, can be expected to continue clinging to their hopes that the precious metal once again will emerge as the world's standard of monetary control, but the counterindications cannot be overlooked.

The student of real estate management, if he is to forecast economic events, must place himself in a position to anticipate the movements of the purchasing power of the dollar. To reach conclusions in this field, a wealth of data is available from government and private financial publications which provide benchmark figures on commodity prices, wages, interest rates, the money supply, construction, and other important factors. It should be a routine matter for all property managers systematically to examine these statistics each month to interpret the recorded trends.

Ours is a managed economy under which both the factors of supply and demand (which ultimately establish actual markets) are heavily influenced by political action on both the world and domestic fronts and by government administrative action. The unprecedented events of the 1970 recession are a case in point. The Energy Crisis faced in 1974 offers another example of how political failure (in part, at least) has affected the supply and demand balance in a critical area.

Generally speaking, the value of the monetary unit (in our case the dollar) is established by its relationship to goods and wages. When money in the economy is increased at a rate faster than the production of goods, prices increase and money becomes less valuable. Conversely, when the gross amount of goods and labor in the economy outweighs the amount of money, prices decline and money becomes more valuable.

In any event, real estate price is extremely sensitive to the value of the monetary unit and fluctuates in sympathy with monetary trends. These trends, as well as all of the factors in the economy, are in a constant state of flux and must be studied continuously by the manager who would conscientiously perform his responsibilities to clients.

REVIEW QUESTIONS

1. Give a definition of *money,* and what governs its selection as a basis of exchange?
2. What brought about price control regulations, and what result did these controls have on real estate?
3. When did the United States go off the gold standard? What happened to the value of money?
4. Explain what is meant by *distrust spending.*
5. What should a property manager know about the purchasing power of the dollar and why?
6. What is meant by *deficit spending,* and who originated the basic theory? Explain in detail.
7. Where can a property manager look for factual help on interpreting money trends?
8. Give an example of the value fluctuations from date of erection in 1946 to January 1969 of a five-room, stable, suburban-area house which cost the original owner $12,000 and passed into three subsequent owners' hands in the 23-year period. Justify your answer.
9. Define the following: prosperity, inflation, deflation with respect to the economy of the country.
10. How should the value of certain monies be measured? When do real estate prices usually go up? When do they go down?
11. How did the establishment of the gold standard come about? When and by whom first established?

SELECTED REFERENCES

Dahlberg, Arthur Olaus. *Money in Motion.* (New York City, J. De Graff, 1961.) 141p.

Hanford, Lloyd D., Sr. *The Real Estate Dollar.* Chicago, Ill., Institute of Real Estate Management, 1969, 120p.

Smith, Halbert C. and Carl T. Tschappat. "Monetary Policy and Real Estate Values." *Appraisal Journal,* Jan. 1966, pp. 18–26.

CHAPTER 4

The Rising Role of Government in Real Estate

INTRODUCTION

The United States has existed, in a manner of speaking, first as a concept and then as a nation, for about 200 years. The Declaration of Independence signed in 1776 asserts that governments derive "their just powers from the consent of the governed," and that they are instituted to secure for all nations "certain unalienable Rights" such as "life, liberty and the pursuit of happiness."

In this same historical period the rule of law and responsible government have emerged in one way or another, and to one degree or another, almost everywhere in the world. The trend, most would agree, has been a part of a natural evolution where widespread awareness and articulation of human aspirations have come to the fore.

In other words, the *necessity* of government seldom will be contested (anarchists excluded), especially wherever a move towards government *for* the people and away from tyranny can be noticed. How else can there be a rule of law, and how else can the principles of equity and self-determination be served? These are the basic justifications of government. This acceptance does not mean there will be no opposition (antagonistic as well as loyal), but it underlies the commonly accepted view that even a bad government is better than no government.

And so there are governments, and even the worst of them have a broad base of public support.

On the other hand, the pervasive role of government in influencing, controlling and dominating the affairs—indeed the destinies—of the citizenry even in the advanced democratic nations, comes as a surprise. There is a widespread feeling among Americans, for example that modern government represents a departure from the original plan and conception and that it has grown too big and too complicated to be responsive to the aspirations of the population at large.

Of course, the annals of human affairs confirm that it is not unusual for outcomes to bear little resemblance to the original anticipations. This is hardly to say that there is no causal relationship between the antecedents and the events that follow, but rather that the direct relationships, more often than not, are obscured by the passage of time. Moreover, the logical nexus between human intentions and human actions is made all the more ambiguous by the fact that people tend to be motivated by a self-interest not always logically consonant with the rhetoric of their idealism.

The nationalistic sensibilities of many, however, contribute to a widespread (but perhaps illusory) belief that a status quo in government can (in fact, *should*) be preserved at all costs. They view government at any particular moment, as a contemporary expression of what the founding fathers with incredible foresight originally had in mind. That this is a primitive, sometimes naive notion of shaping events to conform to hypotheses about how Jefferson and his colleagues would have regarded the matter, will be assumed here without elaboration.

Suffice it to say that the history of civilization has been a record of change, sometimes abruptly felt, but more often so gradually experienced as to be detected only by the professional observers. A growing child does not appear to change from day to day, but a comparison of annual school pictures will confirm his development. So it is with government in the United States and elsewhere. Today official Washington seems to exercise a role (sometimes referred to as a concentration of power at the federal level) far beyond the original intention.

The situation can be explained in terms of the contributing factors. One of these involves the population growth and its attending urbanization during the first half of the present century. All of a sudden there were too many people too close together, and it was natural, perhaps imperative, for centralized government to step in to maintain order and to provide for needed services. Another factor has been the encroachment of socialism and the upheavals that have followed as minority groups strive for parity in housing, education and employment opportunities. A further factor has been the dislocations caused by the great wars and threats of wars in recent times. Since people alone are powerless to cope with such factors, governments more and more have assumed the responsibility for dealing with them.

At the same time society is becoming computerized. Even the personal side of one's life is subjected to pressure for more and more regimentation. But, as the population and the size of government increase, the absolute dimensions of man remain more or less the same. Small wonder, therefore, that the individual should come to feel so insignificant and powerless. Small wonder that the big bureaucrats (by now, fully computerized) step in, ironically often with neither invitation nor opposition, to perform their largely self-appointed role. It is as though the consent of the governed is sometimes measured by the complacency of the electorate, indifferent to participation as individuals in the political process.

In this chapter we deal with the rising role of government in real estate. We have in mind, of course, the situation in the United States. We shall see that the rise has been rapid, sometimes faulty, and often misunderstood. But to suppose that government will abruptly diminish or withdraw its involvement in (and influence on) real estate is no more justified than to suppose that the Secretary of Housing and Urban Development is soon likely to be withdrawn from Cabinet rank and eliminated.

A HISTORICAL ACCOUNT

Demography of the Trend Towards Urbanization

The term *real estate* is an urban term. In agrarian societies and farm areas, one doesn't speak of "real estate;" one talks of *land*. Certainly the field of real estate management is strictly an urban opportunity. While there are many managers of farms, theirs is an entirely different profession calling for training and skills of another order. Since this is the case, the student of real estate management should be conversant with the history of our present urban society as a basis for understanding and participating in the great social challenges of our day, for example urban renewal.

The United States started out as a rural country. It is said that 97 out of every 100 of the early settlers worked on the land in order to eke out a living for themselves and for the other three (probably the minister, the storekeeper, and the public official) who worked in the settlement. As our population grew and as the techniques of farming improved, more people were liberated (or driven) from the land. Thus began a trend toward the urbanization of our population which has been continuous—save for short periods in the depths of depressions—ever since. For many years the majority of townspeople were engaged in production. But just as technological improvement reduced the number of people needed to grow the nation's food, so did it lower the proportion of the population engaged in the manufacture of goods. As a result, more people were free to earn their living from services, the professions, and in government. In the year 1957, for the first time in any society anywhere, more than half of the workers in the United States neither *grew* nor *made* anything. Obviously the most desirable setting for this concentration of service activities is logically the city.

The urbanization of our population has been an accelerating trend. For example, in the year 1850 the total civilian population of the country was 23,192,000. As of that date 3,544,000 or 15.3 percent of the people lived in cities. By the year 1900 the total population had grown to 75,995,000, and 30,160,000 or 39.7 percent were city dwellers. In the period 1950–1956 while the civilian population increased to 164,308,000 (a gain of 9.8 percent), the population of the standard metropolitan areas increased to 96,235,000. This was an increase of 14.8 percent and brought the population in the Standard Metropolitan Areas up to 58.6 percent of the total for the country. In 1960 the total United States population had moved up to 179,323,175. On this census date 112,885,178 persons lived in 212 Standard Metropolitan Areas. This was 63.0 percent of the total population as compared with 59.0 percent of the total population which lived in 168 Metropolitan Areas in the year 1950. In April 1965, by which time the total United States population had reached 192,185,000, 64.4 percent resided in Standard Metropolitan Areas and 35.6 percent lived in nonmetropolitan areas. Only 5.7 percent of the total population resided on farms. Thus, 29.9 percent of the total population in 1965 was in nonmetropolitan, nonfarm areas.

According to the 1970 census the increase in total population was 24 million. There were more than 203 million people living in the United States. Of these less than 20 percent lived in nonurban locations. The population increase was more than 13 percent over 1960. By now the central cities were growing by less than one percent, while the suburban ring was increasing in population by more than 24 percent. It should be noted that these trends can also be observed outside the United States, especially in the developed countries.

In this context, it may be noted that since the 1970 census, the population growth in the U.S. has dropped to its lowest level since the mid-1930s. For example, in January 1973 the population growth was estimated at 7.8 persons per 1,000 (the lowest since the 1937 rate of 6.7 per 1,000). And, in reflection of the same trend, 1972 saw more than one million fewer births than the peak year of 1957. In other words, whether for good or for ill, abortion laws, the accelerating and already widespread use of contraceptive methods, and changing social attitudes, point to the birth rates approaching the vanishing point in the not-so-distant future.

Government Involvements in the Past

For many years property owners in the United States suffered no interference with their ownership or in the perogatives appertaining thereto. The property owner could use his land as he saw fit. He could improve it in any way he chose, following whatever design or plan that suited his fancy. The building could have any purpose. If it was his home it was his castle. The owner could even leave the land vacant as a forest of weeds.

Local governments acting under their police powers were the first to encroach upon those real property rights that historically had been sovereign. Gradually legislation was enacted, usually in the interest of safety and health. Codes were established for the regulation of buildings, to control occupancy standards, to implement fire regulations, and to guarantee the reliability of the construction materials.

An early instance in which the common good was allowed to infringe on the rights of owners was the adoption of zoning codes by many cities as early as 1905. More and more, ordinances came to be enacted to limit the uses to which various properties could be put. In many cases, these arbitrary regulations would radically change the value of the properties involved. Still, since they were imposed as the acts of duly elected local governments, they were generally accepted by a public inclined to approve acts taken for the general welfare.

Today most cities in the United States rely on zoning ordinances to control land use within their boundaries. One notable exception is Houston, with its metropolitan population of several million steadfastly avoiding the imposition of zoning restrictions.

The federal government, for its part, entered the housing arena in 1931. At that time President Herbert Hoover convened a national conference to examine and consider the methods that might be adopted and employed to alleviate the problems precipitated during the early years of the depression. The main problem, of course, was to find ways to help the economy.

As a result of the recommendations of this conference, the federal government embarked on a series of administrative regulations and legislative actions, commencing in the first Roosevelt Administration, and continuing up to the present, whereby Uncle Sam more and more has become an active partner and participant in the field of housing.

The devices which the governmental agencies historically have employed, have been four-fold in nature. In summary form these may be identified as:

Indirect Influences

Quite early the government designed actions which would have influence on housing as the result of monetary, fiscal and credit policies aimed at maintaining prosperity by combating inflation.

Direct Financial Influences

These were steps aimed directly at increasing the total supply of housing through credit and institutional arrangements other than direct financial aid. Examples of these influences are the creation of the Federal Housing Administration to issue mortgage insurance, and the Federal National Mortgage Corporation to help establish secondary markets in mortgages.

Direct Housing Subsidies

These actions were aimed at increasing the supply of housing directly available to low-income households. Examples of this are the Section 235 and 236 programs of the Federal Housing Administration enactments.

Community-Related Programs

These were actions aimed directly at influencing the general structure of urban areas, and also of public attitudes towards the newly developing communities. Examples are the interstate housing program, urban renewal and the model cities programs.

Although housing *per se* has never been a major political issue in the minds of the majority of the people in the United States, traditionally it has been in the minds of politicians. Thus housing has been one of the planks in the platforms of major political parties in recent elections, and housing has been a part of the action programs of every president since the depression years. A culmination of sorts, of this courtship between political office seekers and that segment of the electorate interested in housing, was the establishment of a Department of Housing and Urban Development (HUD) to supervise and coordinate the activities of the Federal National Mortgage Association (FNMA), the Federal Housing Administration (FHA), the Public Housing Administration (PHA), the Voluntary Home Mortgage Credit Program, the Urban Renewal Administration, and the Community Facilities Administration. The first Secretary of HUD, Robert C. Weaver, was the first black in American history to serve in the President's cabinet.

In this connection, it is important to consider the fact that, by and large, most voting people and families in the United States have not regarded their housing as unsatisfactory. It follows then that most political issues based on the questions of housing would not particularly serve the interests of the sponsoring candidates, since the voting public would be neutral to programs that seemed only to provide what was already possessed.

On the other hand, there is little doubt that the housing legislation that eventually resulted has been directed to the fulfillment of the American promise, especially for those deprived and disadvantaged citizens who, because of poverty or race, traditionally have had little voice in the electoral process. Indeed, the record shows that, over the years, literally millions of American families have been forced to live in less than "a decent and suitable living environment"—contrary to what later was promised for every American family by Congress in the preamble of the Housing Act of 1949.

To clarify the matter—since it was those who least exercised the vote who needed the housing most (and, conversely, those who exercised it most who needed the housing least)—another force was necessary to bring about the modern revolution of government involvement in the question. And here it may be argued that the most powerful influence contributing to the early housing legislation was the building and construction industries (seeking profitable markets), the building trades groups (seeking full employment) and the mortgage bankers. Indeed, it would appear that the United States has "backed into" most of its housing legislation as the result of a desire to accommodate the self-interest of these groups, rather than to achieve the social gains that the legislation apparently provides.

The Major Housing Acts

Every President of the United States, from Hoover to Nixon, and every Congress from the 72nd to the 93rd, has had a hand in the development of the United States Housing Policy. Actually, many of the proposals have resulted from the deliberations of various commissions and conferences called by the presidents. The Congress itself very often has had special committees from which have flowed the several bills that eventually became the law of the land.

The agencies which actually supervise and administer the housing programs over the year, have been subject to a certain amount of revision and reorganization by presidential order. In the final analysis, however, the functions and responsibilities of these agencies have been fixed by a series of housing acts passed by Congress over the years. Among these, the most important are the following:

The National Housing Act

This Act, passed on June 27, 1934, created the Federal Housing Administration with authority to insure long-term mortgage loans made by private lending institutions on houses. The clear aim was to insure lenders against loss on loans for financing home alterations, repairs and other improvements.

The United States Housing Act of 1937

This Act created the United States Housing Authority. The aim was to provide loans and annual contributions to public housing agencies for low-rent housing and slum clearance projects. This law was passed in September 1937.

Housing Act of 1949

While there were many laws passed by Congress during the World War II years, the first really comprehensive housing legislation was passed by the 81st Congress on July 15, 1949. This Act established the nation's housing objectives and the policies to be followed in obtaining the desired objectives. Title I of the legislation authorized one billion dollars in loans and 500 million dollars in capital grants over a five-year period. It also provided for advances of funds to localities needing assistance in slum clearance, and community development and redevelopment programs. Title III amended the United States Housing Act of 1937, and authorized federal contributions and loans not to exceed 810,000 additional units of low-rent public housing over a six-year period. Title IV authorized research and other studies aimed at reduction of housing construction and maintenance costs being incurred in the increased housing production. Title V provided a new program of technical service loans and grants, and an expanded farm housing research program for the improvement of farm housing and other farm buildings. In addition, the Act provided for an extension through August 31, 1949 of FHA Title I, Section 608, dealing with rental housing mortgages and insurance operations. It also provided for a half-billion dollar increase in the FHA Title II mortgage insurance authorization. Finally, the Act also provided for a decennial census of housing.

Housing Act of 1954

This Act liberalized the FHA mortgage insurance programs, by providing for more effective assistance in the construction of new housing and in the repair and purchase of existing homes. Further, it liberalized the FHA cooperative housing program; authorized a new mortgage insurance program for housing for servicemen, enacted provisions to prevent abuse of the FHA loan insurance program, entered a new charter for the Federal National Mortgage Association under which FNMA was empowered to provide a secondary market for FHA and VA mortgages, and provided special assistance to special housing programs by which the portfolio of mortgages held prior to the new charter could be liquidated. But that was not all. The Housing Act of 1954 broadened commercial involvement in clearance and redevelopment programs by authorizing federal assistance for the prevention of the spread of slums and urban blight. The mode for accomplishing this was to underwrite rehabilitation and conservation of blighted and deteriorating areas. Further, the Act authorized assistance for an additional 35,000 public units. It required that a community must have a workable program for the prevention and elimination of slums and blight, as a prerequisite for federal assistance to urban renewal, to low rent public housing, and to certain FHA mortgage insurance programs. The Act also established the Urban Planning Grant program, and authorized advances for the planning of a reserve of planned public works. It extended the public facility loan program under the Reconstruction Finance Corporation Liquidation Act, and placed the loan authority in the hands of the Housing Administrator. Finally the Act of 1954 provided additional authorizations for the Farm Housing Program, under Title V of the Housing Act of 1949.

The Housing Act of 1968

Although there was a considerable amount of legislation in the intervening years (1954–68), the next really important statute was the Housing Act of 1968 which for the first time elevated the position of the Director of the Housing and Home Finance Agency to cabinet rank, thus creating the new Department of Housing and Urban Development. This legislation was created as the result of a Presidential Commission on Urban Housing headed by industrialist Edgar F. Kaiser. The commission was appointed in June of 1967 by President Lyndon Johnson. Among other things, it recommended that the Congress adopt a ten-year production goal of 26 million additional housing units, including at least six million for the lower-income population groups. Thus, for the first time, legislation provided for housing subsidies on a very broad scale. Section 235 of the Act authorized the subsidies for single-family housing, while Section 236 introduced them for multi-unit rental housing. In the twelve titles to the Act a number of important subjects were included, such as: the development of new technologies for more economical building; the establishment of a National Housing Foundation; new community planning and guarantees for urban renewal; mass transportation; secondary mortgages; housing partnerships; and public housing.

The major thrust of this last bill was negated in January 1973 when President Nixon—fresh from his remarkable re-election victory, but as yet untouched by the Watergate scandal—terminated housing subsidies. The effectiveness of the legislative efforts of the previous decades already had been threatened by the dramatic failure of the so-called operations breakthrough program which had been mounted by the home manufacturers. Finally, in 1974, federal involvement in the housing markets was further curtailed by the unprecedented rise in mortgage interest rates, and the continuing inflationary spiral in the costs of new construction. Subsidies ended in order not only to reduce federal expenditures, but also the program were not working as anticipated and there was proof of some graft and corruption.

The historical account given above, and repeated on the following pages where the specific example of urban renewal is considered, reflects a continuous rising involvement of government in the affairs of real estate. The legislative actions that have been taken are the result of a *potpourri* of factors and influences. Almost everything that has been done by the Congress can be given the interpretation that the motivating force was a concern about the interests of the people to be housed (especially the poor people). Another interpretation is that the Congress is known sometimes to act out of the desire of its members to secure their re-election. More than that, administrative actions (such as the one just mentioned in which President Nixon in 1973 chose to terminate housing subsidies) are rooted in the preferences of special interest groups—regardless of the rationales that accompany the announcements of policy changes.

In other words, it is a complicated business to discuss objectively and fully the interplay between the involvement of government in housing (or the lack of it) with the other prevailing and mediating circumstances. While a connection of some complicated sort must exist, it does not appear that past events are representative enough to permit a perfect forecasting of the future. What has been happening, as summarized in the historical accounts presented on these pages, is just an example of logically possible outcomes. Beyond taxes and death, the only thing certain about the future is that other things will be happening, some *like* past events, some *because* of past events; but many of the future events surely will be so much of their own nature as to astonish even the professional forecasters when they occur.

The Evolution of Urban Renewal

Traditionally and historically, Americans regard the ownership of private property—*especially land*—as a sacred right. Millions of immigrants came to this country drawn by the possibility of land ownership. Here the ordinary man could acquire land to use it as he wished without interference from the authorities. Aside from this thirst for land the typical immigrant to the United States had several other characteristics; he was young, he was uneducated and illiterate (in English at least), and he was poor.

In a society as dynamic as that of the United States, where population growth was unprecedented in world history, and where the rise of the individual's living standards was phenomenal, the society as a whole took on another characteristic; it disliked anything old—the old world, old goods, old houses. The standard pattern developed something like this: An immigrant arrived and took up residence in a house which belonged to a predecessor immigrant who had prospered and moved on and out to a new home he had built to suit his new living standard. At a slightly later date the original immigrant built still another house of an even more impressive size and style at a location even farther from the site of his original residence. His successor (having "done well" in the meantime) moved into the original man's second house, and a fresh new immigrant came along to occupy the original immigrant's first house. During the process, living standards in this fabulous land moved up apace, with the result that obsolescence in older houses was rapid and dramatic.

As some of the original immigrants or their children grew rich, they expressed their newly won prosperity by the erection of large mansions. Meanwhile, rapidly expanding commerce and industry needed the space at the center of the city for new facilities and plants. Thus the original immigrant housing was torn down and the residents *all* pushed on and outward toward the periphery. However, when the wave of new immigrants got out to where the original man had built his mansion, their poverty prevented their occupying the house as it was originally designed—as a *single-family* structure. However, the house was too good to demolish, so it was "converted" to multiple occupancy and the process of creating *slums* was under way. This same process was evidenced in the original multi-family structures close-in to the center of the city. Here the original buildings did not have inside plumbing or hot water, or, in many cases, tenants shared the bath facilities.

These buildings (also too valuable to destroy in view of the pressure of growing population) were also "converted" to more intensive use. The two major ingredients of *slums* (overcrowding and deterioration) were increasingly evident in the core of most of our major cities. Other ingredients of *slums* were: poor original construction, lack of facilities, inadequate city services, unplanned development and overcrowding of land.

The widespread incidence of these abject living conditions became a matter of concern among students of our social structure, progressive legislators, and many apprehensive public officials. In England, where a Labor Government was in control after World War I and where a serious housing shortage was resulting from urbanization, Parliament passed a law in 1919 providing for state assistance in the creation of new housing, which was the forerunner to our own housing legislation. Even prior to this date, the English had taken steps (on the basis of public health) to regulate the nature and operation of housing accommodations. English government involvement in housing dates back more than 100 years. Steps to do something about housing were also taken in Holland, Germany, Sweden and other European countries.

As pointed out above, the complete and unfettered right of private ownership was a part of the American creed. People were loath to sponsor or promote public action which would violate these rights. In New York a Board of Health was created in 1866 and the first Tenement House law was enacted in 1867. Further legislation was passed in the year 1901 but, because housing legislation cannot be retroactive (except in certain health and safety provisions), the continuing consumer pressure made old, obsolete, substandard and therefore cheap buildings a scarce commodity and hence preserved their earning power and their value. As in all cities, these old buildings were too valuable an "asset" to destroy. Only recently have U.S. cities tightened up their housing and building codes as well as their enforcement programs.

In the first three decades of the twentieth century many states and local governments enacted legislation to curb the rights of private ownership in real property. These steps were designed in the realm of public health and welfare. New York, where urban problems were most numerous and critical, was the first city in America to pass a zoning ordinance (1916).

The Significance of Zoning

The basic aim of zoning ordinances passed by municipalities over the country shortly after the turn of the century was to protect the locational *integrity* of individual parcels of land, to assure *sustained* desirability for local areas; to bring land developments into line with *planned objectives,* to assure *compatibility* of use of land, and to control *densities.* As has been true in so many other instances, acting under democratic principle the people banded together to use governmental powers to protect their *common* interest.

Whenever the common good is substituted for individual advantage, the action results in depriving certain individuals of rights and benefits. In this instance, prior to the creation of zoning ordinances, a man who owned a house on a corner lot in a residential neighborhood was free to convert the use of his land to a gasoline filling station regardless of the deleterious effect that such an improvement might have on other houses in his neighborhood. This disregard of the interests of others resulted in chaotic conditions.

Since their original passage, zoning regulations have been perfected and strengthened by more rigid ordinances, by increasing public recognition of the desirability of controlled land use, and by court rulings. As might be expected, the tightening of zoning controls has tended to increase the rewards for either their violation or disavowal.

Under normal circumstances, the value of urban land increases with the intensity of its use. Land which may be worth $500 per acre when zoned for agricultural purposes can frequently bring many times that price when zoned for single-family residences at a density, let us say, of three or four families per acre. If this same land can be zoned for townhouses or garden apartments at a density of 15 to 25 families per acre, it obviously will take on a still higher value. Zoning for multi-family apartment buildings with still higher densities per acre will, of course, produce even greater values. If this same land is zoned for industrial use (assuming it is suitable for such use economically) the value may go to levels in excess of $50,000 per acre. More than that, under certain circumstances of development for commercial purposes, the land may go to completely astronomical levels, where values are no longer computed on an acreage basis, but rather in terms of dollars per square foot.

In a dynamic economy like the one in which we live, it is not necessarily desirable to freeze forever the pattern of land use. It becomes prudent from time to time to amend zoning ordinances to bring them more nearly into line with current planning objectives. It also frequently is advantageous to change the individual use of a given parcel of land prior to changing the overall zoning ordinance. This practice is called "spot zoning" and is generally considered objectionable by both planners and zoning authorities. Safeguards against such practice are written into most local zoning procedures.

Because the conversion of property from a lower to a higher intensity of use or from a lower to a higher zoning category is extremely profitable, and because amendments to zoning ordinances are only granted by honest officials when persuasive factual arguments are advanced, skills of the property manager are frequently called upon in the preparation of studies to be used as the basis for expert testimony before zoning boards of appeals and the courts. The employment of these skills should be offered only when the property manager is convinced that the objective of the client is soundly conceived from the point of view of the common good.

Slum Clearance

As might have been expected in view of the *laissez faire* tradition in the United States, the entrance of local, state, and federal governments into the area of the control, financing, and creation of real property met with formidable and continuing opposition on an ideological as well as practical basis. Whereas some of these attitudes were undoubtedly influenced by self-interest, many people and organizations felt genuine and sincere concern over what they described as the "creeping socialism" of government intervention in the real estate economy.

On the basis of the facts, however, some things had become obvious to the capable analyst. One of these was that the only method of attacking areas of greatest urban blight was through wholesale clearance of slum property and the redevelopment of these areas with new structures. If sound, viable neighborhoods were to be re-established, new projects of significant size had to be developed. Such new developments could not be limited solely to residential use, but, based upon the needs of the community, might also include industrial, commercial as well as private and public institutional uses.

Because, as noted above, slum properties continued to be valuable to their owners, it proved economically unfeasible for redevelopers to acquire slum buildings (even where the right of condemnation was extended for this purpose), demolish them, and redevelop the cleared land. Some governmental assistance would be required as a means of "writing off" the residual value of the slum buildings which were a plague to urban society.

Actually the government subsidy required in the typical instance is a sound public investment. New property raises the tax base of the area, it eliminates the heavy expense of providing public services to slums, and it creates higher values in adjacent properties and stimulates other rehabilitation and redevelopment. On the basis of many dramatic demonstrations of these facts, the slum clearance program has steadily earned broader and broader public support.

One early experience of cities which chose to avail themselves of the slum clearance opportunities afforded by government help was that slum clearance activities *alone* are not a solution to the problem of providing a "decent, safe, and sanitary" housing unit for every urban American family. The wholesale clearance of slum buildings and the consequent displacement of slum families —unless paralleled by concomitant steps to safeguard the physical integrity of neighboring properties—often merely clear slums in one area and create new ones elsewhere.

Neighborhood Conservation

It became apparent that steps would have to be taken to build a backfire against the spread of blight especially when slum clearance programs were being carried forward.

It is possible to classify urban neighborhoods into five general categories, as follows:

1. The *new developing neighborhood* is an area in which extant buildings are of recent construction, where further growth is taking place, and where there is land available for still further improvement.
2. The *established sound and dynamic neighborhood* is an area in which virtually all of the land has been improved. Continuing residential desirability is causing *self-redevelopment* through conversion of land use (for

example, the demolition of single-family homes and the substitution of apartment buildings) and through rehabilitation, modernization, and upgrading of existing structures.

3. The *sound, aging conservation neighborhood* is an area in which virtually all land is improved and where the average age of structures is generally from one to ten decades old, where housing units are being used as originally designed, as opposed to being *cut up* or *converted,* and where educational, cultural, and spiritual institutions are virile and active, where family composition is normal and healthy. (See Appraising Comparative Values—chapter 7.)

4. The *changing, deteriorating and obsolescent neighborhood* is an area much like three as to age and percentage of development, but where many of the buildings have been cut up and converted, where overcrowding characterizes a substantial proportion of the dwelling units, where there is greater transiency of tenancy, where the character and vitality of local institutions has been undermined, where large amounts of property are in disrepair and some are in dilapidation.

5. *The slum neighborhood* as defined in the Illinois Blighted Areas Redevelopment Act of 1947, "means any area of not less in the aggregate than two acres located within the territorial limits of a municipality where buildings or improvements by reason of dilapidation, obsolescence, overcrowding, faulty arrangement or design, lack of ventilation, light and sanitary facilities, excessive land coverage, deleterious land use or layout or any combination of these factors, are detrimental to the public safety, health, morals or welfare." Webster's International Dictionary defines a slum as: "A highly congested, usually urban, residential area characterized by deteriorated, unsanitary buildings, poverty, and social disorganization."

Whereas vigilance must be practiced in *all* neighborhoods as a means of preventing deleterious developments and uses, the major attention of cities was first directed at those classified in paragraphs numbered three and four above. The limitations of our national resources make it unlikely that this problem of the changing, deteriorating, and obsolescent neighborhood can be cured through wholesale slum clearance at any time in the foreseeable future. Thus some mechanism would obviously be required to *prevent* the deterioration of sound neighborhoods and to *arrest* the spread of blight in those neighborhoods already infected with its virus.

The Urban Renewal Program

Almost immediately after his election to his first term in the White House, President Dwight Eisenhower appointed what was known as the President's

Advisory Committee on Government Housing Policies and Programs. This group was representative of the housing industry, labor unions, citizens' organizations, and the financial community. The federal government had been concerned with housing finance, public housing, and urban redevelopment (slum clearance) only, but the committee realized there was need for a more comprehensive approach to the creation and maintenance of healthier cities. The term "urban renewal" was actually coined by the President's Commission to describe the new, total program.

Recent Developments

The last few years have seen a continuing expansion of the various components of the housing programs in the United States. There has been increasing emphasis on providing a number of ways through which it would be possible for the individual family to obtain housing in accordance with its space needs and the capacity to pay; there has been fuller recognition of the artificial separation of the central city and the metropolitan ring; there has been better understanding of the relationships of the various housing, urban renewal, public facility and social programs to each other. With that recognition has come a broader understanding of the need for modifications in administrative structures—at the federal as well as the local level.

One perhaps gets the meaning of these programs most clearly by reading the Presidential message of Lyndon B. Johnson of January 26, 1966, transmitting recommendations for city demonstration programs, as well as that of February 26, 1968, transmitting a message on housing and cities. This holds true, as well, for the message by President Nixon on the "State of the Union" of January 22, 1970, and his message on "Population" on July 19, 1970. It is particularly significant that *every* administration in the past three decades has followed much the same theme in the development of housing and urban programs.

The major concern of the Nixon administration in its first years has been the reduction of the rate of inflation to what has been called "manageable" proportions. This, in turn, has limited the amount of money available for the vast array of programs. Notwithstanding these constraints, the Nixon administration submitted the proposed but now superseded 1970 Housing and Urban Development bill, which had for its major goals:

1. To provide dwelling units for low-, moderate- and middle-income families more efficiently by streamlining and consolidating existing HUD programs.
2. To attract substantially greater private sector investment in low-cost housing by eliminating unnecessary bureaucratic requirements and establishing uniform criteria for subsidized housing programs.
3. To make the assistance programs more responsive to the needs of local

communities by basing eligibility limits and construction requirements on income and cost factors prevalent in the community.

4. To include the optimum number of low-income families in rental and home ownership programs by deepening the maximum subsidy that is available.

The 1970 Housing Act was intended to: (a) consolidate the numerous authorities scattered throughout existing law into a number of broad, flexible programs; (b) eliminate obsolete, or duplicatory agencies; and (c) improve existing operations and subsidy programs. The most striking example of the consolidation and simplification is to be found in Title I of the new bill—the Mortgage Credit Assistance Act. Under its provisions, the number of existing FHA programs is reduced from approximately 50 to eight. In place of over 40 existing authorities dealing with home and rental housing, there would be one new program to cover all unassisted home mortgages and one new program embracing all subsidized rental projects.

The Property Manager and Urban Renewal

No professional group should be more interested in maintaining the desirability of our cities than property managers, whose very livelihood depends upon an inventory of sound income structures, especially in the residential field. The manager's first interest in urban renewal should be that of a citizen anxious to be of help in the general welfare of his community. It would seem obvious that he would be in the forefront of organizational efforts to arouse the citizens and public officials to the challenge of improving the desirability of their cities as places in which to work and live. The real demonstration of the superiority of the American way of life will face its ultimate test in the city. For it is in this complex that the bulk of our citizens will live and meet their destiny. Certainly life in these cities has not filled the promise of our country or the promise of our era. That it can and must do so is the opportunity and the mandate of urban renewal.

As a practical professional matter, the urban renewal program offers many opportunities for the employment of real estate skills. Urban renewal and redevelopment areas must be identified and delimited. In view of his capability in property and neighborhood analysis, the manager is uniquely qualified to carry on surveys and to counsel authorities. Appraisals must be made of the properties to be acquired as well as of the land to be reused. Projections must be prepared to show the type of property best suited for the reuse of the land, and these buildings must be financed, constructed, and managed upon completion.

In the important work of conservation, rehabilitation, and rejuvenation which will, in the final analysis, be the determining factor in the overall success of urban renewal, the property manager will find great opportunity for his entrepreneurial as well as professional skills. Whereas government financial and legal aid is fundamental to the initiation of action, urban renewal is really a private enterprise program. Hence, the ultimate goal is the restoration and preservation of sound, privately owned, and privately operated improvements.

SOME PREDICTIONS

The future of housing subsidies is uncertain. As things have been developing, from the 1930s and 1940s into the 1970s this is not a time for prophecy.

There is little doubt that the typical American city today contains large areas of substandard structures (most notably in the residential category) that need to be replaced by well-designed, modern structures if our cities are to retain their economic vitality and basic desirability.

It is also probably a fact that if we are ever to be free of the necessity of devoting so large a proportion of our total national income to hot and cold wars, we will need to cushion the resultant sharp drop in government expenditures by a substitute for the defense program and only urban renewal is an effective substitute. Urban renewal not only stimulates construction, but it also acts to stimulate markets by destroying structures at the same time it erects new ones. Moreover, urban renewal also acts to motivate expenditures in a wide variety of fields unrelated to new building.

So runs one way of thinking, but expectations derived from knowledge of what has happened in the past, and from understanding of future needs and possibilities still leaves us only with guesses. What follows are thoughts about the future, but not full predictions.

Under study here implicitly has been the question of whether or not the historical government involvement in assuring housing for all who need it, should take the form of subsidies (i.e., in the form of a housing allowance), instead of offering housing itself. This question is being actively dealt with presently by agencies representing the governments of several community and city locations. This is a *central* question.

The fact remains that at each moment some good and some bad can be seen in the way things have been done, and are being done. Out of this review we should only hope to find some guidance about the best way to deal with the future eventualities.

Government already has been immersed "ankle deep, and head-first" in the real estate business over the last forty years (or more). Government will not pull out abruptly from any further involvement in housing. Agencies like government always have the potential of overexpending their budgeted allotments. And there are too few counterindications for the proposition that it is the nature of the beast for bureaucracies to be self-perpetuating.

That does not tell us, however, whether the role of government in real estate will *in*crease or *de*crease. New factors are involved. Some of these have political, economic and social bases; others have a physical base such as the environmental and energy questions discussed below. What would happen if there were a disastrous war? What would happen if the oil-rich nations of the so-called Third World upset the world economy by destroying the sense of money (already so abundantly in their possession)? And what will happen if and when the have-not people and the have-not nations wrest more and more control from the traditional establishments? In the long range, only time can tell.

In the short range, however, some things can be said about the likely government response to the emerging crises in the quality of the environment and in energy supply. These physical factors will affect future land uses. And we can say something about the future of the FHA and the urban renewal programs, as to what course government will be following.

The New Factors (Environment, Energy)

The wave of expansion of land uses that occurred as a result of the private and public development in the three decades following World War II has been marked especially by the destruction of the environment. The consequences and the effects have been both emotional and physically disastrous. Nature lovers and ecological purists have responded in chorus to the clarion call of the book, *Silent Spring,* by Rachel Carson, a prophetic volume that envisoned the doom that would soon ensue from an unchecked multiplication and expansion of human activities.

The enthusiasm of the environmentalists, together with the uncontestable virtue of the majority of their proposals, have proved to be extraordinarily effective for identifying issues around which citizen groups could mount pressure for the imposition of governmental controls backed up by citizen review. The result, as the record shows, has been a wave of activity sweeping the country, and a dealing with questions centered around land use and pollution (which in turn bears on *which* land uses are possible).

As it turns out, those who have been recruited into the movement have included not only the foes of despoiling the environment, but also those with selfish interests who have wanted to impose exclusionary controls under the guise of alleged ecological benefits. High-growth areas have been most susceptible to the appeals of the self-interest groups, and this has led to one cynical definition of an ecologist as "a person who, having arrived somewhere, wishes to prevent anyone else from arriving too."

Whatever may have been the source of the movement's popularity, the result has been an unprecedented flurry of governmental activity that has had the effect (if not the intent) of harassing and thwarting the objectives of the land developers. At the level of the federal government, the Environmental Protection Agency was authorized by the Presidential Order of July 1970. And today, virtually every state in the Union as well as most large cities also have departments specializing in the regulation of air and water pollution, noise abatement and waste treatment.

Thus, various states have enacted coastal protection laws and regulations which restrict residental, commercial and industrial development within specified distances of coastal boundaries. The availability and treatment of water has come under close scrutiny, and hundreds of communities have shut off growth until a greater capacity can be provided for by utilities. In a nutshell, all newly proposed land developments and redevelopments are considered from the standpoint of their possible impact on the environment before go-ahead permits are granted.

Many of the proposals that have been put forward have proved so extreme as to be impractical to implement. Some espouse so-called no growth measures which either are impossible or undesirable to achieve. Keeping in mind the old saying that "one man's medicine may be another man's poison," it is clear that value judgments are involved in defining the actual meaning of terms such as "undesirable," "impossible" and "impractical."

In the end things are determined by what people want, and by what they are willing to pay in added costs. The hope is, of course, that politics can be kept out of the operations and rulings of the Environmental Protection Agency. Only in this way is there the chance for EPA to steer a course that fully balances man's local tendency to establish a poisoning presence in the environment, against man's global aspiration to see Nature preserved.

But environmental impact concerns affect not only proposals for new land use, but also existing use. Consider the example of an apartment building that loses comparative value because at some later time the construction and nearby location of an interstate highway presents a noise nuisance. In this case, the existing apartment building is not the problem, nor indeed would the construction of additional residental spaces in the vicinity present an adverse environmental impact *per se*. Noise pollution, which is the environmental impact that flows from the high-use thoroughfare has, however, the effect of substantially decreasing the desirability of the residential units. And this aspect is what deserves the concern of the property manager and owner alike. Perhaps the conclusion will be that while the highway brings noise it also brings the convenience of accessibility; but still the pros and cons must be evaluated in the long run. And the student can imagine other examples of the sort just presented that display the question of environmental impact as being a two-sided coin.

In the senses just being discussed, the emergence and recognition of the energy crisis in the middle 1970s also will be of interest to the property manager. This is because energy shortages affect the continued use of existing properties.

Two passing examples will suffice to make the point.

(a) Residential, commercial and industrial properties, the access to which depends upon the availability of cheap and plentiful gasoline for automobiles, may lose in value during periods of petroleum shortage.

(b) Properties in the categories just mentioned, where initial values were largely based on air-conditioning, abundant heating fuel and other energy-using utilities and facilities, likewise will lose in these values during periods of energy shortage.

And, again, students can think of other obvious examples of energy availability being directly linked to the desirability of particular properties.

But the questions of energy and environment actually and significantly are linked. With a shortage of petroleum, pressure may be brought to bear on the EPA to relax regulations on the burning of high sulfur coal even though the adverse effect on air quality is well known. And further, energy and environment problems are linked in the sense that either or both can be solved as soon as the public agrees to provide enormous research and development funds—in billions of dollars—for example, to harness less-pollutant energy sources such as the thermal energy radiated from the sun, and the geothermal energy that can be extracted by circulating water through the bowels of the earth.

Finally, it may be added that the energy question is a two-sided coin too. Not only do the present shortages affect the continuing use of existing properties, but they forebode serious limitations on future building and redevelopment. This aspect is a concern to the property manager because obviously properties are needed before they can be managed.

The Future of FHA and Urban Renewal

Up to now we have described the broad movement of the government into the real estate field. We have examined the impact which it has had on the field itself, and we have related this matter to the real estate management profession.

As noted, the two agencies whose work has most significantly affected both the real estate field itself and the opportunities of the management profession are the Federal Housing Agency (FHA) and the Urban Renewal program.

Originally started as a program to stimulate the construction of single-family houses through the insurance of mortgages, the Federal Housing Administration eventually became the major force in the entire housing market, including multi-family rental housing construction. The insurance plan by which FHA assumes the risk of mortgage guarantees is relatively simple. The proposed borrower makes application to the FHA for mortgage insurance as a part of the application, then presents his plans and an appraisal for the completed project. When the FHA has reviewed these plans and specifications and has approved the appraisal, it commits itself to the issuance of a policy of mortgage insurance. This is then issued to the private agency which makes a loan. In the event of a default in the mortgage, the private mortgagee forecloses on said mortgage and presents his claim to the Federal Housing Administration. Debentures are then issued (which are fully guaranteed as to principal by the federal government to the mortgage holder).

During the early years of its operation the Federal Housing Administration conducted an exemplary insurance program from the point of view of its observing the principles of sound business. It adopted and put into being standard housing practices which unquestionably raised the level of home building quality.

By the year 1954 the FHA momentarily freed itself of debt to the federal government. In 1954, the agency also survived the threat of a major scandal under its Section 608 program. Developers throughout the nation had in many cases been able to arrange insurance on loans which not only covered the land and buildings involved, but were for additional sums. These "windfall profits" were widespread enough to have reduced public confidence in the agency. However, Section 608 loans were discontinued and the practice brought to an end—at least for the time being. The FHA resumed its exemplary performance.

Under the housing act of 1968, the FHA was called upon to desert its sound business practices and pursue a program designed to procure social gains. In consequence its underwriting criteria were increasingly ignored. Moreover, the change in administration occasioned by the elections of 1968 caused it to lose much of its trained personnel and hence much of its administrative skills.

In 1972 a consortium of the National Association of Home Builders, the National Association of Mutual Savings Banks and the United States Savings and Loan League engaged Dr. Anthony Downs to make an appraisal of the effectiveness of housing subsidies. His report,* published in 1973, observed that many of the failures of housing subsidies were caused by poor management of the projects involved, not because the original idea of the subsidy was lacking in validity. This dramatically illustrated the lack of emphasis on experienced management and proper training of the personnel employed and pointed up the need for the recognition of properly trained managers.

As this edition of the Principles of Real Estate Management is being prepared, the fate of the FHA is somewhat uncertain. The function of mortgage insurance is increasingly being provided by strictly private companies such as the Mortgage Guarantee Insurance Corporation and others. Because of money rates, the FHA is practically being excluded from the mortgage markets and the restoration of its competitive capability is under question. Indeed, the future of mortgages themselves, is open to question.

* 1973, Lexington Books (Div D. C. Heath) *Federal Housing Subsidies: How Are They Working?*

The next most important aspect of the federal program in terms of its impact on the practices followed by local governments in their planning and operating procedures is the Urban Renewal program. This operation, originally conceived of as strictly a slum clearance program, has, like all bureaucracies, been considerably broadened over the years since it was originally conceived. One of the original statutory provisions of the Housing Act of 1949 required that "a workable program for community improvement (which shall include an official plan of action, as it exists from time to time, for effectively dealing with the problem of urban slums and blight within the community and for the establishment and preservation of a well planned community with well organized environment for adequate family life) for utilizing appropriate private and public resources to eliminate and prevent the development or spread of slums and urban blight, to encourage needed rehabilitation, to provide for redevelopment of blighted, deteriorated or slum areas, or to undertake such of the aforesaid activities or other feasible community activities as may be suitably employed to achieve the objectives of such a program."

The further provision was that this workable program on the part of local communities should be observed in order for those communities to "utilize funds for renewal and housing programs." Probably this provision did more to raise the standards of planning and code observance in the average American city than any other single thing. Since virtually all such communities desire to avail themselves of the opportunities provided by federal funds, they immediately sought to comply. The quality of local planning, code enforcement and local community services was raised in the entire country, as was the level of sophistication in such areas.

Whereas most Certified Property Managers are still to be found in the private sector of the economy, so too are the properties which have come into being as the result of expanded government influence. Most of the properties erected under all of the programs envisaged above have, in fact, been built by private developers. On the other hand, one cannot overlook the substantial increase in properties built by nonprofit corporations under the provisions of various statutes. The government itself employs thousands of persons who would be better prepared for their jobs if they were certified property managers. The whole trend of both public and private business in the U.S. points toward further professionalization in the management of real property, whether operated on a purely private basis, or managed by semi-private or nonprofit corporations, condominiums, or agencies of government.

REVIEW QUESTIONS

1. Name the principal Housing Acts starting with that of 1934, and through library research compare them with respect to intent and actual provisions.
2. Characterize the housing legislation (if any) that has been enacted since the publica-

tion of the 11th edition of this book. In any case, discuss the Nixon administration position with respect to the 1972–73 legislative proposals.

3. Compare the various zoning laws that apply to your state and municipality of residence, as affecting real estate development and property uses. Contrast these regulations with those which apply to some other state and other muncipalities. To what extent do you see the value and importance of federal zoning laws?

4. Write an essay about the pros and cons of urban renewal, slum clearance and low cost (subsidized) housing. Conclude with your own recommendations for eliminating defects and minimizing problems in the future.

5. Make a contrast in the categories of professional problems confronting property managers dealing with urban renewal properties on the one side, and luxury apartments on the other. How do you think the earning potential of property managers working in these two areas should compare.

6. Identify the ways the public's concern about environmental impacts is important to the work of the property manager. How about the public's response to the continuing prospect for a national energy shortage.

7. Give your opinion about the book discussion of the future of the Federal Housing Administration.

SELECTED REFERENCES

David, Philip. *Urban Land Development.* Homewood, Ill., Richard D. Irwin, Inc., 1970, 549p.

Downs, Anthony. *Federal Housing Subsidies: How Are They Working?* Lexington Books, 1973. 141p.

Smith, Halbert C. and others. *Real Estate and Urban Development.* Homewood, Ill., Richard D. Irwin, 1973, 481p.

Soloman, Arthur P. *Housing the Urban Poor, A Critical Evaluation of Federal Housing Policy.* Cambridge, Mass., The MIT Press, 1974, 229p.

CHAPTER 5

Cyclic Aspects of Real Estate

INTRODUCTION

In this chapter we shall be talking about real estate cycles. A common dictionary definition describes a cycle as "a period of time within which a round of regularly recurring events or phenomena is completed—as in the business cycle." The key word is *recurring,* which implies that there will a repetition of the events or phenomena in following cycles. A different concept is that of a fluctuation, which is a movement back and forth or up and down as a continual or irregular variation.

Real estate, of course, is a part of business, and if it is fair to suppose that business cycles exist then the idea of real estate cycles has a similar relevance. A cycle, if there is one, will be displayed as a graph in time of some measure of the state of business. For example, in chapter 2 we saw a graph in which the measure of occupancy of residential units (given as the percent of available units that were occupied at various points in time) was plotted against time over a 60-year interval. Interpreted in one way, it may be argued that this graph shows a cyclic phenomenon, since a recurrence is seen in the rise of occupancy during major wartime periods followed by a fall in occupancy in the later postwar periods.

In another interpretation, however, the graph just mentioned can be taken as an example of a plot of a fluctuating phenomenon. The latter, like cyclic phenomena, also is displayed by a graph in time of some measure of the state of business. Whether a particular graph pertains to fluctuations rather than cycles, depends upon the interpretation of the business analyst as to whether the phenomena therein displayed are a succession of random or of recurring events.

If the graph under discussion has recurring features that encourage the analyst to predict future states of business on the basis of the past, he can then say he is dealing with a business cycle. But if the past record does not seem to display a sufficiently regular trend upon which future events can be forecast with confidence, the analyst must conclude that he is dealing with business fluctuations rather than business cycles.

For example, in the case of the cited occupancy graph in chapter 2, even the staunchest believer in business cycle theory would be hard pressed to infer with any certainty what occupancy will be like at some future time like 1999.

Thus, while his guess about next year always will have some validity, in the instance under discussion any five-year (or longer) prognostication appears to be only a flimsy guess.

To make these reservations at the onset is not to suggest that the concept of business cycles has no merit. On the contrary, applications of the concept are made every day in real estate as well as other fields, much to the benefit and profit of the businessmen involved. The trick, of course—and every weather forecaster will be glad to confirm this—is to discriminate between those cases in which the future *is* or *isn't* adequately and discernibly correlated to the past.

In what follows we shall be dealing only with examples of situations in which measures of the strength and condition of real estate markets, when plotted against time, serve to reflect the presence of recurring cycles. Such cases may not always be so clear-cut as to motivate the analyst to risk large sums of money on long-range predictions. On the other hand, the cyclic character of the phenomenon under study should be so evident that no one will be inclined to infer that only random fluctuations are involved. This means that, at the very least, the time graph has a form which makes its cyclic outline plausible when looked at in retrospect.

It must be added that the record of a cyclic phenomenon should encompass a period of time long enough for evidence of the recurrences to be clearly seen. For example, the cyclic character of the rotation of the moon around the earth will not be apparent to the casual observer on the data provided by a happenstance glance of a few seconds. The position of the moon in the sky should be studied for at least several months. (That some people can look at the moon for a lifetime without gaining any understanding of what is happening, simply confirms that it takes intelligence and a trained eye to recognize the cyclic behavior—and not only in the heavens, but in real estate as well).

CHARACTERISTICS OF CYCLES

In the first three chapters we have studied the various factors which are responsible for the condition of real estate at any given time. The principal reason for our identification, isolation, and analysis of these factors was to be able to measure the movement of real estate conditions from weak to strong, or from strong to weak. Our findings indicated that each of these factors is in a constant state of flux, that *movement* is the essence of the problem.

Observers of real estate markets and activity over long periods of time have found that when conditions favorable to real estate cause a strengthening of one factor, the others likewise are apt to react favorably. Moreover, it has been found that the history of real estate conditions has been a series of periods in which favorable trends prevail for awhile, only to be replaced by unfavorable trends which also extend over a span of time.

Most of us are familiar with the term *cycle.* The term is used in astronomy, physics, biology, mathematics, and economics.

Virtually everyone who has had any contact with business charts has seen one or more graphs on which the movements of business over a long period of years have been drawn. These charts center about a long horizontal line, the length of which represents a certain number of years. This line is generally identified as *normal.* Deviations from this so-called *normal* are represented by dots placed above or below the line. These dots mark the year in which conditions are charted, as well as the level of those conditions. If business is above normal for the year, the dot is placed above the line. The distance above the line is determined by the percentage or rate by which conditions in that particular year are above the normal level. Conversely, if business conditions are below normal for the year, the dot is placed below the line, likewise by a distance representing the deficiency.

When the dots are joined together by lines, the lines will then form a curve. It will be found that this curve will cross the *normal* line at intervals, sometimes going *up* and sometimes going *down.* A cycle of business activity is completed each time the curve crosses the normal line *while moving in the same direction.* In other words, a full cycle represents the movement of the curve from the normal line upwards to the top level of the business activity, downwards across the normal line to the bottom of the downswing, and then back to the normal line again.

Period, Frequency and Amplitude

There are two variable factors in cycles: *frequency* and *amplitude.* The frequency of a cycle refers to the reciprocal in length of time required for the completion of the cycle. This time interval is called the *period* of the cycle. The distance between the peak of the curve and the normal or zero line is the *amplitude* of the cycle. The amplitude indicates the height of the boom, or the depth of the depression.

Most of the wall-type charts which delineate the movement of business over the years show a series of line curves which appear to have *regular* frequency and *identical* amplitude. It would appear from these charts that business is good for a certain number of years, then reverses itself and is bad for a like number of years. It would seem that each time a peak of prosperity is reached, it is just as far above normal as the previous peak; and that each time a depression comes along, it is about as far below the normal line as the previous low. Moreover, it would also appear that the normal line always represents an identical position; and that *normal* is a stationary condition.

There is some difference of opinion as to whether or not real estate operates

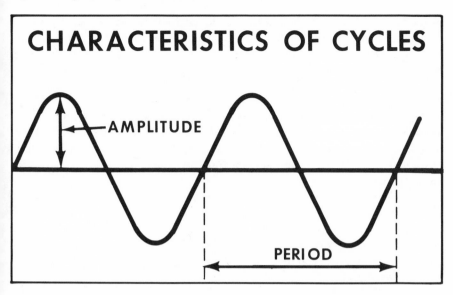

CHARACTERISTICS OF CYCLES

The above chart illustrates the meaning of period, frequency and amplitudes in cycles.

in fixed-length cycles; yet there is no doubt of the fact that, in the past, the real estate economy has experienced a series of good years followed by a series of bad years. Thus, there is wide acceptance of the cyclic theory as applied to real estate. The basic trends are always *directional*—either up or down. Once established, these trends, if upward, continue to a prosperity or activity peak; if downward, they continue to the low point of inactivity or depression. Although the strength of these trends sometimes varies during such a broad movement, the direction seldom changes.

To examine what happens in the real estate economy in the operation of a normal cycle, let us follow the course of real estate from the high point of one upswing to the high point of another. During the course of this example the student will note that certain events will be influenced by the operation of *general* business. We shall discuss later the relationship between real estate and general business.

At the top of an upswing of real estate activity, the following conditions usually prevail in the factors which we isolated and discussed in previous chapters:

Money Values

In all business and real estate upswings the value of the dollar declines. From a strictly monetary viewpoint, the peak is reached when the public recognizes that money either will be harder to get in the future or that it will be more

valuable, i.e., that prices have reached the peak. This information comes to
the public from diverse sources and produces an attitude of *distrust saving.*
Just as *distrust spending* characterizes periods of *inflation,* so *distrust saving*
is a characteristic of periods of deflation.

Residential Occupancy

The peak of a real estate upswing is always characterized by an increase
in residential vacancy. The housing shortage, which inevitably marks the span
of the upswing, stimulates residential construction to the point of creating
more new housing units than are warranted by the actual demand based on
ability to buy or rent.

Rent Price

The peak of rent price is usually reached shortly before the peak of the
general real estate upswing. It is usually reached at the time of the greatest
backlog of unfilled demand—hence, when there are the greatest number of
bidders for space.

Eviction Suits

At the high point of real estate prosperity, eviction suits resulting from
nonpayment of rent have reached a low point. Consumer condition is good,
rental demand is good, and there is no reason for default in rent payments.
Eviction suits brought about by the scarcity of housing have become less
numerous because the high level of construction has begun to ease the housing
shortage.

Relief-Employment

Employment is at a peak at the top of the real estate cycle. The number
of families on relief rolls generally has increased ever so slightly, due to the
inability of marginal people to obtain employment in the last few months of
the boom.

Family Formation

Even if love is a constant factor in society, the number of marriages is
influenced by political and economic factors. The highest marriage rates are
reached when employment is at the peak, when confidence in the future is
strongest. Over the history of marriage and real estate the peaks of the two
nearly always have coincided.

Real Estate Sales

The peak of real estate activity in terms of the number of transfers of real
estate usually is reached simultaneously with, or just after, the peak of the
upswing, depending upon the operation of the other factors listed.

New Construction

The peak of the volume of new construction in an upswing is almost always reached *after* the peak of real estate as a whole. The reason is that the momentum of the upward trend stimulates the planning of building projects at an accelerated level. Because there is a lapse of time between the planning of these projects and their actual erection and completion, the highest volume of actual building is usually experienced after the other more sensitive factors have already turned downward.

Mortgage Financing

Studies of the volume of mortgage financing seem to indicate that mortgage lending, like new construction, reaches its peak some time after the top of the general real estate upswing. One of the reasons for this lag is that mortgage lending is closely related to construction activity. Another is that the confidence of moneyed groups tends to outlast that of ordinary consumers. Moreover, in the very earliest stages of the downswing, those who have not yet been affected by the decline in income are apt to increase their savings. Lending institutions are likely to require investment outlets for funds and, as a result, continue to channel money into mortgages. Moreover, interest rates paid by real estate borrowers—tempted by what they feel are the peak earnings of the boom—are apt to be high enough to lure lenders who are not well informed as to the underlying status of the real estate market.

Foreclosures

At the peak of real estate prosperity, the number of foreclosure suits is at low ebb. An extremely sensitive factor, the foreclosure index is among the first to indicate that the *up* trend may have dissipated itself; that a downswing is in the making.

Real Estate Security Prices

We have mentioned that the moneyed groups of the nation are usually not the first to sense the end of an upswing. As we shall see subsequently, the general public has the greatest awareness of impending trend change, since in part its attitude affects the swing. Real estate security prices, like mortgage activity, seldom turn down until after other factors have begun to evidence the change.

Causes of Major Changes in Trend Direction

We have said that there is a relationship between major swings in the curve of real estate activity and the curve which delineates the trends of general business. The principal link between the two curves is the *consumer*—whose status is the all-important factor in the economy. Generally speaking, the true peak of the two curves is reached *simultaneously,* because both general business and real estate are dependent upon the financial condition and the mental attitude of the consumer.

At the peak of general business and real estate activity, the consumer is working full time. His wages are at their highest point and his purchasing power is being fully utilized—both to complete cash transactions and to anticipate future earnings through credit purchases. At such times the consumer is sanguine of the future. He has no fear of loss of employment or curtailment of earning power. He is willing to commit himself to a financial program based upon a continuation of his present earnings. It is characteristic of the public in periods of peak prosperity to feel that the economy has entered a *new era;* that man has solved the problem of sustaining business activity. What, then, causes a reversal of trend?

During every business and real estate upswing the production facilities of the economy are greatly enlarged. Perhaps this enlargement comes about because of the tremendous physical requirements of a war, or because of the existence of a large backlog of demand built up during the lean years of a previous depression. Perhaps there are other causes. In any event, once the industrial producers recognize that there is a demand for additional goods, they undertake a program of plant enlargement in order to capitalize upon the expanded markets. Population growth is a factor in this new, larger market and its impact is always felt when an upswing gets under way.

The free enterprise system is theoretically self-adjusting. When the need for increased plant facilities arises, prices are pushed up by heavy demands for finished goods. As a result, profits from the manufacture of goods can be raised by those who have the production facilities. These increased profits act as a lure to new capital because of the promise of high earnings. The new capital is used for the construction of new production facilities.

Students who have any knowledge of air movements know that wind is created by the rush of air from an area of high atmospheric pressure to one of low pressure. In some respects capital is like this air. Whenever and wherever a "low" pressure of production exists in an area of high pressure demand, capital rushes in from everywhere. In theory, the plant expansion stimulated by enlarged demand should attract only sufficient capital to construct enough extra capacity to handle the enlarged demand. Practically, however, the demand has always been blown up to an abnormal level by the fact that it not only represents the expanded *current* demand, but embraces the *backlog* of demand stored up during the lean period.

Since there is no overall control of production facilities nor any exact system of measurement of *current* demand, the history of our economy has tended to be a record of over-expansion of plant facilities during times of peak demand. Too many people, and too much capital, are attracted to the "low" pressure areas, and the momentum of the movement results in over-correction of the shortage condition.

When the backlog of demand finally is used up [1] and the need for goods settles back to the level of *current* demand (as opposed to *current* plus *backlog* demand), it is necessary to slow down the rate of production pending some further development of additional demand—as the result of further population growth, accumulation of new backlog, or some extraneous dynamic event such as war.

At the peak of an upswing, the economy is geared to the full use of the expanded production facilities. This means that plants are operated at capacity with a full complement of employees; that these fully employed people are spending freely in the economy and retail establishments are operating at high velocity; that service establishments are extremely busy; that the demand for all types of facilities has caused an expansion identical with that experienced in the field of direct production.

As soon as the production facilities of the country begin a slow-down —meaning a drop in industrial employment—there is an immediate effect in those areas of the economy which are supported by industrial workers. Of equal importance, there is a sudden awareness of the fact that the peak has been reached—at least by those who first learn of the layoff of workers. This awareness raises the specter of unemployment and of curtailment of earning power. Even those who have not yet been affected by the layoffs immediately suffer a change of attitude. Their confidence in the future is replaced by concern for the future. Therefore, their willingness to spend freely and to commit future earnings for current needs is decreased. The change in their pattern of spending produces an additional brake on general business activity.

Now during the course of the upswing one of the major sources of employment was the very creation of new plant facilities which were thought to be needed to cure the maladjustment between supply and demand. New factories, new homes, new store buildings, new service establishments—all of these were being built simultaneously in order to enable capital to take advantage of the lush market. Keep in mind now that these new facilities were not *all* needed; that the need was being measured against an *accumulated* demand. Thus, when the backlog demand was used up and only *current* production was needed, there was certainly no need for new plants. This meant that the thousands who were engaged in the expansion program automatically were laid off.

In the process of the downswing, prices are reduced in order to attract higher volumes of business. The purchasing power of money increases, with the result that debts incurred during the period of cheap money are harder

---

[1] In addition to the backlog of demand left over from a previous period of shortage, the expansion of the economy during periods of prosperity introduces new demand in the form of higher living standards. This *expansion* acts like a backlog in that it disappears once the economy settles on a plateau, however high.

to repay. Liquidation becomes necessary to raise funds to meet debt payments; there is pressure to reduce payrolls to offset declining incomes. And, as the decline goes full blast, the upswing is over and the downswing is confirmed.

THE CHANGE IN REAL ESTATE TRENDS

Real estate is a consumer product. Its value is established by the demand evidenced by consumers. Its status can be measured by consumer status. Although there is some lag between action in consumer markets and the resultant reaction in real estate, the relationship is positive and the reaction certain.

The real estate economy is separate from the general business economy, yet its broad sweeps are influenced by, and are usually parallel to those of general business. The causes of major change in trend apply to real estate as well as to the economy as a whole.

Although real estate (land and buildings) might factually be classified as *durable,* from an economic point of view, it is still a *consumer* good. We saw in chapter 2 that there was no fixed relationship between the number of logical consumers of real estate (families) and the number of housing units which will be purchased or occupied in any given period. There never have been as many housing units in the United States (or anywhere else in the world) as there have been families. Thousands and thousands of families have always shared housing with others, or have lived in makeshift quarters that could hardly be called housing.

Families can only become housing consumers when they can pay the going price (purchase or rent) of housing. In lean times, when unemployment is high and when consumer incomes are low, a substantial percentage of families is unable to afford individual housing—notwithstanding the fact that costs of housing simultaneously will be down.

When an upswing in the economy takes place, the number of employed people increases sharply and the level of income of all the people likewise rises. This means an expanded demand for housing by people who suddenly find themselves able to support individual housing unit consumption. New buildings are needed, new land is needed; not alone for houses, but for factories, stores, service buildings, amusement centers, schools—for every conceivable kind of use.

In real estate, as in general business, the heightened demand causes higher prices; acts as a lure to new capital. There is the same rush into the areas of low pressure; the same momentum and the same over-correction—all following inexorably.

There is, however, one significant difference between real estate and general business—particularly industry. When the industrial output in any type of manufactured goods is found to be in excess of supply, production schedules are curtailed and the output reduced to the level of demand. In this manner inventories of manufactured goods are kept at relatively low levels and price demoralization is avoided—or at least limited.

In real estate, however, when consumer income is reduced and thousands of families are forced to withdraw from the consumer markets, there is no possibility of reducing the inventory of space available. Since buildings are relatively permanent, all of the units of housing, all of the stores and offices and all of the service buildings which were built to accommodate peak demand remain standing and are continuously in competition with all other units. For that reason price demoralization is always greatest in the real estate field, since prices ultimately must be reduced to a level where families will find it possible again to become consumers again.

The End of the Downswing

As we pointed out, the free enterprise system is theoretically self-correcting. When demand exceeds supply, new facilities of supply are created until their production capacity exceeds demand. Then there is a period of correction, during which demand is allowed to accrue to the point that new facilities again are found to be needed.

We have seen how the forces which create an upswing are finally dissipated, and how a downswing gets under way. The cyclic theory indicates that such a downswing lasts for a certain span of time, after which the trends are reversed again and an upswing begins.

How does this change in trend come about? It is axiomatic that a depression is a *shrinkage,* rather than a complete *cessation* of business. Essential activity goes on in the economy during the period of adjustment; people continue to eat, to wear clothes, to consume goods of all kinds. The rate of consumption is lower for some things, but for others the rate of actual consumption is the same. It is largely the rate of replacement which changes. Depreciation and obsolescence take their toll and the inventory of goods in the hands of the public declines. A large part of the residual wealth of the country remains in the hands of those who own it, but it is in relative *suspension,* not employed dynamically for the benefit of the economy.

During the whole period of the downswing those consumers who have been able to maintain relatively good incomes are afraid of resuming a normal purchasing pattern, and they deliberately exhaust their inventories of goods rather than enter the markets for replacement. While the population may grow constantly during the downswing, the impact of this quantitative increase is not felt because of the decline in the gross purchases by the average individual within the population.

At some point in the process, however, it is no longer possible to postpone purchases. Consumers re-enter the markets, lured by low prices and driven by acute need. As this individual goods crisis is reached by increasing numbers of able-to-buy individuals, production facilities feel the demand for greater output. Additional employees are then needed. The growth of buying produces a market reaction and prices are firm to higher. Those who have deliberately refrained from making purchases are fearful now that they may miss the opportunity to capitalize on low prices, and they rush into the markets to build up their inventories. The momentum now increases and the upswing is on.

In real estate the first evidence of an upswing is an increase in occupancy not brought about by rate reduction in either rent or purchase price. When rising occupancy reaches a certain level, prices and rents begin to move up. When these rents and purchase prices reach the point where they will support additional construction, new buildings begin to go up and land is again in demand. As the forces of demand expand, the cycle is then completed.

Lesser Movements of the Cycle

In the above discussion of the *upswing* and *downswing* we have envisioned a cycle of some duration; one which proceeded in each direction to its ultimate limits. Whereas real estate cycles generally are of comparably long duration, business cycles sometimes are completed in a relatively short length of time.

It is not always true that production facilities are pushed to capacity in periods of upswing, or that deflationary forces are exhausted before a downswing is ended. Frequently the backlog of accumulated demand is exhausted before additional plant capacity is needed. In the period 1933–37, for example, the economy experienced an upswing partially stimulated by government activity, and partially supported by the accumulated demand built up in the years 1929–33. This upswing never did give sufficient momentum to use up the productive capacity then extant. By the end of 1937 the joint stimuli were largely exhausted and the curve of business turned downward. The dynamic factor of World War II introduced a stimulus strong enough to produce a major upswing which completed the cycle.

Real estate is slower to react to these short-term influences. As we have seen above, the permanent nature of real estate inventory causes sharp price adjustments in order to maintain relatively high occupancy. There is thus never a large "stand-by" capacity available to place on the market to absorb the impact of the upswing. For that reason, once real estate has hit the bottom of a downswing and has started up again, its course is not easily disturbed by minor, short-term adjustments in business conditions. Similarly, once real estate starts downward as a result of overbuilding, it is seldom rescued from this trend by minor spurts in the general economy.

THE CYCLE IN A MANAGED ECONOMY

In theory, the free enterprise system is self-correcting. Periods of prosperity contain the forces of self-attenuation by stimulating over expansion of production facilities. Likewise periods of depression are self-exhausting, since they build up backlogs of demand which ultimately break the bounds of consumer restraint. The whole process has been likened to the swing of a pendulum.

However, endless fluctuation of affairs from boom to bust, and from bust to boom, entails excesses in both directions which are needlessly wasteful of physical and social resources. In the evolution of democracy the public has come to believe that political power should somehow be employed for the betterment of economic status. The initial objective of the body politic in the field of economics was to reduce the *amplitude* of the business cycle—to *level out* the business curve.

The first real attempt of this kind was made in the depression of 1929–33, and has been partially described in chapter 3 when we discussed the introduction of deficit financing. It was commented upon further in that same chapter in the discussion of the future monetary influences upon the real estate market.

Whether it will be possible for governments to permanently and effectively flatten out the curve of business, by lowering the amplitude of successive moves above and below the line of normal, has yet to be proved. However, it is increasingly apparent that efforts will be devoted more and more to that vital end.

In real estate, these efforts have already assumed an important role. In housing, the government has taken a number of steps which have changed the entire course of real estate economic events. Among the moves in this direction, in the decade of the 1930's, were the formation of the Home Loan Bank System, the operation of the Home Owners Loan Corporation, the formation of the Federal Housing Administration and the Public Housing Agency. In the forties the government imposed rent control, formed the Defense Housing Administration, created the Veterans Administration, the division of Slum Clearance and Urban Redevelopment and other agencies which vitally affected the course of real estate events. Moreover, through its control of consumer and construction credit, as well as its allocation of materials in the immediate post-Korean period, the government was a major factor in determining real estate trends in the middle years of the fifties. In addition, government action in crop support, and in such consumer supports as unemployment compensation, social security, aid to dependent children, old age benefit, etc., has been of great importance in stabilizing the nation's real estate markets. There is every indication that the fiscal powers of the government will continue to be employed in the future in an effort to "level out" the excessive oscillations of the business curve.

The Dynamic Cycle

In chapter 3 it was pointed out that the history of monetary units throughout their existence has been one of a long-term trend toward lower value. Monetary unit trends have been a dynamic factor in the economic history of man; their very movement has provided a certain stimulus to the economy.

It is not only money which evidences a long-term dynamic quality in our economic history; it is also the standard of living of men as measured by the level of consumption. It is important for the student to recognize this fact in his study of the operation of the cyclic movement of business and real estate.

As we noted at the beginning of this chapter, most charts purporting to show the movement of business over a long period of years indicate movements above and below a long, horizontal line labeled "normal." On these charts this "normal" is viewed as a fixed level of activity from which business moves either up or down. Such charts present a false picture, however, when the level of normal in one period is *higher* than in the previous period.

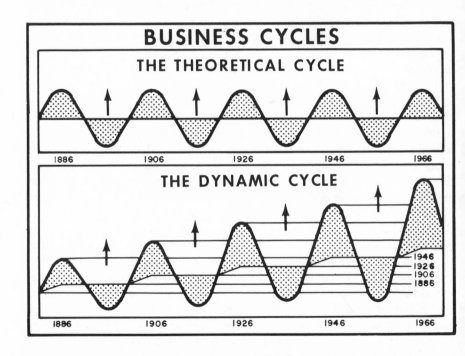

The above chart illustrates the difference between the idealized static cycle and the dynamic cycle. It will be noted that in the dynamic cycle the normal line customarily moves upward in each succeeding cycle. It will also be noted that the amplitude of each succeeding cycle on the upswing is greater than the amplitude of the previous upswing. What is termed the static cycle shows a horizontal base line (control tendency) of uniform period, frequency and amplitude.

If the business and real estate cycles operate on a pendulum it is a pendulum with a moving fulcrum. "Normal" is a line which moves upward during the course of every upswing to reflect the resulting higher standard of living. If we measure the standard of living of the typical citizen of the United States over the years of our history, we find a positive progress which is evidence of the amazing dynamics of our society. Not only have wages gone up in sympathy with the declining value of the dollar, but wages have advanced in *true income* to the worker in terms of the goods and services which he has been able to afford. The availability of energy and power per person, food per person, raw materials per person, and services per person has increased steadily throughout our economic history. This is the quality of the *dynamic* cycle under which our economy operates.

An example of the *dynamic normal* as applied to housing is furnished by the changed standards which have been experienced in the United States almost continuously since its inception. Today a standard unit in our residential market contains equipment which was unheard of a century ago. It is presumed that a dwelling unit today will contain a heating unit, one or more bathrooms, a kitchen complete with stove and refrigerator, adequate electric wiring—all installed under the advanced standards of modern building codes. It can be said that no enclosed space in the U.S. today—residential or commercial—can be rated "grade A" unless it is air-conditioned. In other words, as year follows year, our concept of a standard unit of either residential, commercial or industrial space is apt to change completely—always in the direction of a higher level of utility, physical comfort, and technological progress.

The "Cyclet"

Historically, the period of real estate cycles has varied from 18 to 25 years. On the basis of the *idealized cycle,* we should have experienced a major depression 25 years from the low point of real estate activity reached in 1933. In other words, according to a long-held theory, we should have been at the bottom of a cycle at least by the end of 1958.

However, as noted above, the prime objective of the managed economy under which we have lived since 1933 has been to *flatten out the business curve,* to put an end to the widespread misery and economic upheaval of major depressions.

In their effort to put an end to marked amplitude (height and depth) in the business cycle, the managers of the economy have been unable to produce a flat plateau of prosperity. At least up to the present time, they have been unable to produce a *stable* economy. However, they *have* been able to reduce the *length* of the *period* and the *magnitude* of the *amplitude.*

For example, in the postwar period we have seen a series of *upswings* and *recessions.* In 1946 we experienced an all-time peak of prices and prosperity. Under the influence of controls and cutbacks we lapsed into a recession in early 1947. The degree of this decline frightened the managers into an all-out stimulative effort which produced the boom of 1948, with its apprehensions over runaway inflation. Once more controls were imposed and credit tightened, with the result that we entered the recession of 1949. Then came the Korean war with its bulge of *distrust spending* which produced the crest of 1951 and, once again, the imposition of controls. By 1954 we were back in a recession, this one steep enough to cradle the all-out resuscitative drive which produced the record activity and prices of the 1955–56 boom. Once again (this time more seriously) the brakes were applied to the economy with sufficient pressure to push us down into the recession of 1958. Recovery was once more set in motion. It produced many new records in 1959, but the new prosperity was short-lived. As the first months of the so-called soaring sixties unfolded, the U.S. economy settled into its *fifth* postwar recession. It bottomed out in 1961 and was succeeded by the *boom* which began in mid 1963 and lasted until the early months of 1969. This economic surge was characterized by a rapid increase in general employment, an accentuation of urbanization and a re-sumption of accelerating price inflation. Consumer trends were so strong that even the "money crunch" of 1966 (which did, momentarily, slow down residential building) did not interrupt the increase in space occupancy and the resulting rise in prices and rents. By early 1969, however, the government's *war against inflation* produced money market conditions which ushered in the recession of 1970.

As the chart of residential occupancy given in chapter 2 shows, it is possible for housing demand to greatly *exceed* supply, even when occupancy reaches 100 percent. This unmet demand is called *backlog.* It grew steadily during the actual war years and expanded even more rapidly in the period of 1946–50, when the full impact of demobilization and renewed consumer spending further enlarged the housing demand.

Beginning in 1950, peacetime housing construction got under way in earnest. For the first time in over a decade, the U.S. housing industry that year produced more units of housing than were needed to meet the demand. In other words, beginning in 1950, new construction began to dissipate the size of the housing backlog. By January 1, 1958, this backlog was completely exhausted and the first vacancies began to appear. Between that date and early in 1965, a combination of circumstances (the very momentum of the building industry, the unique availability of mortgage money, and the vigor of the entrepreneurial system) acted to prolong a high level of residential building —beyond the amount actually needed in the private housing sector.

We have called these short-term swings in the economy "cyclets." It is interesting that they exhibit the characteristics of what we have described previously as the dynamic cycle. Each new peak is higher than its predecessor.

The whole process has been fed on inflation, which has been diagnosed by many as the major malady of the managed economy.

The term *inflation* often has been used erroneously in speaking of real estate. The long period of rising consumer prices which characterized the postwar period has not been paralleled by increases in rentals and real estate prices. In fact, there have been several short-term periods of real estate *deflation* between January 1940 and the present. This has been especially true in urban residential income property and farmland. For example, industrial wages increased an average 428.04 percent between 1940 and April 1970. On the other hand, the rent segment of the Consumer Price Index increased only 91.9 percent on the average between 1940 and January 1970. Similarly, the index of prices received by farmers (prepared by the U.S. Department of Agriculture) dropped from a peak of 313 in February 1951 to 281 in April 1970.

The fact is that *scarcity* is an essential ingredient in the impact of inflation on rentals and real estate prices. It is virtually impossible for general economic *inflation* to affect real estate markets whenever there is substantial vacancy. Moreover, periods of such vacancy do not always parallel the relationship between *money* and other consumer goods.

REVIEW QUESTIONS

1. If you wanted to know the *status of the uptrend* in real estate—whether it was at its height, or on the way up or down—what would you do? Why?
2. What is meant by *accumulated demand?* Is this a sound basis for expansion? Explain your reasoning.
3. What are the *variable factors* in a cycle? Define each.
4. The activity of real estate shows change. List the various conditions which you can expect to find and make a brief statement on each.
5. Define *cycle* in the real estate field. Draw a graph showing a full cycle in residential real estate.
6. Is the period of *normal* always the same? Justify your answer.
7. Name a difference between the real estate market and the clothing industry when the supply begins to exceed the demand.
8. In which sense, if any, can cyclic phenomena be regarded as a special case of fluctuating phenomena?
9. Summarize in approximately 200 words how cycle theory can be used to forecast real estate trends. Then in a sentence of 25 words or less, restate the same idea in capsule form.
10. Explain the meaning of the statement: "The status of real estate is measured by consumer status."
11. Give an example of how the amplitude of some business cycles can be diminished by "managing the economy." Can the period of cyclic phenomena likewise be influenced? Explain.

SELECTED REFERENCES

Alberts, William Wallace. *Business Cycles, Residential Construction Cycles, and the Mortgage Market.* University of Chicago, 1961, 105p.

Gordon, R. A. "Are Business Cycles Passé?" *The Mortgage Banker.* October 1963, pp. 27–28.

Moore, Geoffrey Hoyt. *Business Cycle Indicators.* Princeton, N. J., Princeton University Press, 1961.

Real Estate Analyst. St. Louis, all issues, 1932 to present.

CHAPTER 6

Changing Forms of Real Estate Ownership and Management

INTRODUCTION

In this last chapter of the first part of this book devoted to ideas about real estate, we not only draw attention to the new and revitalized forms of ownership that have become popular and widespread in the last several decades, but we also introduce the subject of property management as practiced for these ownership forms. Preliminary ideas about property management have already been referred to in the overview of the subject given in chapter 1. And in the chapters to follow many of the specifics about what property managers do, and about the ways in which they work, will be explained in detail.

Specifically, in what follows, we shall talk about corporate ownership of investment real estate by syndicates and real estate investment trust arrangements, and by cooperative apartment and condominium ownership modes. Finally we shall refer again to the subject introduced in chapter 4—the way government itself is involved in real estate ownership through its public housing authority programs. And throughout this section there will be discussion of the new opportunities for property managers that the emergence of the new ownership forms has brought into being. Obviously, to fully understand the impact of these developments, it will be worthwhile to reflect on what has happened in the past.

The Historical Antecedents

In the beginning, real property in the United States was almost totally owned, by individuals, either alone, or in association with other individuals as partners, joint tenants or tenants in common.

The framers of the Constitution were afraid that the ownership of land in the United States might follow the pattern of Europe, where large land holdings were both common and of a nature to thwart the ambition of ordinary people to own property. So great was the fear of people in this country that land would fall into the hands of large estates, institutions or combinations of the wealthy, that for many years it was impossible for corporations and large businesses to own property.

As the wealth of the nation grew and an affluent society emerged, it was actually the demands of the people that they be permitted to invest in real estate which resulted in most of the changed forms of ownership which have been adopted during the past three or four decades. These demands grew out of the fact that real estate itself was being packaged in larger and larger projects, including multi-family dwellings, office buildings, and motels. It was obviously impossible for all but the very rich to *own* such large properties individually. Because of the desirability of participating in such ownership, devices by which people of modest means could *share* in such ownership were developed. Another factor in the spread of real estate ownership was the tax benefits which accrued to individuals who participated in real estate ventures. As this movement continued, the desirability of participating in such investments increased and even larger numbers of people were interested in real estate investments.

In the 1920s millions of dollars worth of real estate bonds were sold to small investors who wished to participate in the higher yields which such securities offered. These securities, available as they were in denominations as low as $100, attracted a very substantial number of buyers, and each of the holdings represented a portion of the major mortgages which were placed on the larger projects of that era.

The depression of 1929–1933 was in a sense a revolution in income property ownership in the United States. The financial debacle of those years converted thousands of split mortgage (bond) holders into unwilling stockholders, and the recovery which followed produced two entirely new types of real estate owners. The first of these was the individual who for the first time was able to become a home-owner as the result of the extremely favorable mortgage terms which were created by government. The second type was what we might call the "split-equity owner" who became a member of a purchasing syndicate.

In spite of the tremendous impact of the new type home-owner on real estate markets, we are concerned here principally with the new buyers of income property, since the real estate manager's involvement is mainly with that type of property.

The thousands of bondholders whose bonds were converted into stock in the process of reorganization were—theoretically at least—*unwilling* owners of real estate. It had never been their purpose to take an equity position in real property. They did not wish to assume the risks of ownership, but were interested originally in a type of security which would pay a fixed interest rate and which would have a stable value. The courts in which these real estate bond reorganizations were accomplished were aware of this and, in most cases, the new corporations which they created to hold title to the reorganized real estate were essentially *liquidating* in character. The voting power of the newly created common stock was generally vested in three or more trustees. The trust agreement under which they operated clearly stated that it was the aim of the trust to liquidate the property. Even where the formal trust agreements failed to contain such instructions, it was understood that the purpose of these corporations was to hold title to the property until a satisfactory sale could be consummated.

In other words, in the fiasco of efforts to contend with the depression of 1929–33, there were bondholder committees set up to act on behalf of those bondholders whose projects securing the bonds had wound up in default. Under the terms of the subsequent reorganizations, it was decided that these bond holders should share in the ownership of the properties which they acquired through foreclosure. To accomplish this, the bondholders were issued stock in new owning corporations in place of their bonds. Thus, for the first time, the corporation became a widely employed form of real estate ownership, with former bondholders becoming stockholders.

In addition to the new stockholders discussed above, thousands of properties came into the hands of banks, insurance companies, trust companies, and other agencies which had originally been in the position of *lender,* rather than owner. In the case of banks, regulations in many states forbade their ownership of real estate and required liquidation of foreclosed properties within a limited period of time. In virtually all instances, the former lending agencies were under pressure to rid their portfolios of the type of asset represented by actual ownership of income real estate.

Because of these pressures a great deal of property was placed on the market. Since the economy had lately experienced a major depression, the funds of potential buyers had been subject to atrophy. Moreover, the experience of the depression had caused many conservative investors to frown on real estate as an investment medium—especially in the light of the fact that lower prices in other forms of equity made these latter investments extremely attractive.

Deflationary periods are by very nature marked by a dearth of cash. The sellers of income real estate recognized this fact and provided for the sale of large properties under terms requiring very small down payments in relation to the total purchase price. In most cases the new buyers were required to put up only 10 percent of the total cost of the building—a considerably lower percentage of the purchase price than had ever been acceptable.

Strangely enough, there were substantial numbers of people who thought that the purchase of income real estate under these circumstances represented an attractive speculative investment. These potential buyers did not propose to venture all of their capital in such investments, but were willing to take a small percentage of an ownership combination. Such combinations were called "syndicates" and were, in effect, partnerships of a limited nature formed to buy, own, and operate a specific piece or pieces of property.

Alert real estate managers in this period saw a unique opportunity. First, as brokers they could earn a commission through the sale of such income property; and they could organize a syndicate to become the buyer. Second, if they used their commissions to make up a part of the syndicate, they would become partners in the ownership of the property and unquestionably could control its management. Thus the formation of such syndicates represented a threefold advantage to the manager. It provided him income from brokerage, income from management, and potential profit from investment.

Although the uniquely favorable investment opportunities of the early recovery period gradually disappeared as the result of higher prices and greater market activity, the imposition of higher income taxes in subsequent years served to continue the interest of investors in the field of real estate. Tax advantages, which were appealing to a specific type of investor, brought some new buyers into the field. Inflationary trends which tended to give real estate an advantage as a "hedge" produced other buyers. The uniformly successful experience of syndicate members in real estate ownership made syndicate investment attractive to still other prospective buyers. A combination of these circumstances made the ownership of real estate by this type of limited partnership a large factor in the potential operations of the real estate manager.

One of the major disadvantages in the real estate management business is that under ordinary circumstances the manager is exposed to the loss of property under his management for reasons not in any way related to the character of the management service which he renders. Such loss of business frequently results from the sale of the property by the owner, the death of one or more of the owners, the dissolution of a partnership, or any one of a score of reasons. In some especially discouraging instances, the very efforts of the manager are responsible for the loss of business. If by especially creative work, he raises the level of the income of a property to a point where its value makes liquidation attractive to the owner, the manager is apt to lose the management of the building as a result of the excellence of his management job. In any event, the stabilization of management accounts is one of the problems of the property manager—one which can be solved through the participation in and formation of adequately financed and properly organized ownership syndicates.

CORPORATE REAL ESTATE OWNERSHIP

The advantages of corporate ownership of real estate are many and varied. Among them are that the stockholder in such a corporation has no individual liability; only his capital contribution is at risk. The corporation is also an entity in itself, entirely apart from the identity of its stockholders. Stock in the corporation can be sold or otherwise disposed of at will. Additional capital can be raised by the issuance of new securities or by borrowings. Owners of such stock can offer it as collateral for borrowing.

While these benefits made the corporation an ideal vehicle for the reorganization of the thousands of properties which fell into financial difficulties during the depression, there were substantial disadvantages in employing the corporation in the case of deliberately planned real estate investments. The most important of these by far concerns taxes. Property held in corporate form results in the payment of two kinds of taxes. First there is the tax levied against the corporation, and then there is the tax paid by the individual stockholder when he withdraws profits from the corporation in the form of dividends.

Although there are benefits from the use of the corporate form of ownership under certain circumstances, these are financially esoteric and applicable only under certain unique circumstances. Generally speaking, however, it is not practical for corporations to own real estate.

The practical reason for the pressure to create devices whereby a substantial portion of the public might become investors in real estate was to make tax advantages available to such investors. With income taxes at a constantly higher rate, such tax shelters are of greater and greater advantage to those whose incomes are "sheltered" by deductions for depreciation and losses allowed by the regulations.

Four forms of real estate ownership are most widely employed to provide these benefits. These are syndicates, cooperatives, condominiums, and real estate investment trusts (REITS). Because both syndicates and REITS involve the sale of securities to the public by syndicators and underwriters, they should be viewed as separate from condominiums and cooperatives.

Syndicates

Theoretically, a syndicator is a real estate promoter or developer who caters to the public's desire for investment in real estate which might otherwise be out of their financial reach. A syndicate may be created to buy real estate with the purpose of holding it for a period and selling it at a gain. On the other hand it may be formed with the idea of investing in income-producing real estate and holding it for the income and tax shelter which it will produce until it is finally resold. The syndicates themselves are usually of two types: private syndicates which range in size from four to five participants to larger groups, sometimes as many as 100 persons, each of whom figures to benefit from the tax shelter available or the public syndicate which includes an unlimited number of participants. The syndicator or promoter of the syndicate usually takes the role of a general partner and the participants take that of limited partners.

There are several roles which the property manager can fill in the total process of syndication. He can be the syndicator or general partner, and, if so, he has the first call on the management of the properties syndicated.

Unfortunately, many syndicators who operated in the period from 1965 to 1974 fell victim to the problems derived from the extravagant promises which they made to investors on the basis of the optimistic conditions at the time. In consequence, many of these syndicators were forced to the wall by subsequent events in the money market. And, as has happened many times in the past, small investors who took the securities route through partial ownership faced disasterous results, not only in syndicates but in the investment trusts as well.

Although many ownership syndicates are composed of wealthy individuals who have more or less limitless funds to place at the disposal of the syndicate-forming real estate manager, their number is decreasing and, as a class, they are not apt to be real estate investors. Thus the property manager, who seeks to stabilize his business by the promotion and formation of ownership syndicates, usually must draw his participants from among the ranks of those with moderate means who are financially sound for real estate investment purposes.

At the outset of such activity, the manager must be familiar with the laws (both federal and state) which govern investment activity and which may be applicable to the proposed operation. The manager should check his promotional scheme with his attorney, in order to make certain that the activities are in no sense illegal and that his personal liabilities in the promotion are thoroughly outlined and understood. The manager must be extremely careful to protect his reputation and to avoid any possible criticism or litigations.

The first step in the actual promotion and formation of an ownership syndicate involves the selection of a suitable property for investment. This selection should be made from a number of potential submissions, and should be based upon a series of careful analyses as recommended in other chapters in this text. Certainly the manager will wish to submit only those properties which enjoy the highest likelihood of success, even though they may be offered to prospective clients as genuinely speculative investments. Inasmuch as the property manager is urged to join in such ownership syndicates (at least to the extent of his commission), his interests in the successful operation of the syndicate will be identical with those of his partners. Because it is the manager's prime objective to create a satisfactory permanent investment, there is little use undertaking an operation which cannot be so regarded.

Once a suitable property has been found which has stood the test of careful analysis, then the manager is ready to solicit his prospective partners. It is true that a large percentage of investors base their judgments primarily upon confidence in an individual, but a prospectus should be prepared giving the basic facts of the investment. This summary should be reviewed carefully with the prospective partners in order that all will be made thoroughly familiar with the nature of the investment. Obviously such a prospectus should be an exact statement of the facts as revealed by a feasibility study, and should not contain exaggerations.

Once the ownership syndicate has been formed, the building purchased, and operations commenced, the manager should exercise all possible influence for the adoption of a conservative program of operation. If possible, the syndicate members should be persuaded to accept limited dividends on their ownership, reserving excess funds for contingencies or for application against the debt on the property. Most members of typical syndicates are persons who live primarily on *earned* income, who are investing primarily for security in subsequent years. Thus, they are not especially hungry for current income and will be willing to support any program designed to give additional security to their investment. The manager should recognize that once a syndicate has been formed and placed in operation, the only threat to his continued management of the property lies in the possibility of a default on the debt obligation. In case of such a default, the syndicate would be frozen out of ownership. The management of the property in all probability would be taken away by the lender. Either of these eventualities is a tragedy for the manager, and is to be avoided at all costs. Obviously the most certain method of escaping a possible default is the retirement of debt.

The operation of syndicates represents a special type of public relations for the manager who is either a participant in or operator of such combinations. Syndicate members assume the role of clients of the manager and their continued satisfaction with the operation of the enterprise is extremely important. Reports of operations should be sent to syndicate members on a regular basis (either annually or semi-annually) and meetings should be held periodically to advise the members of the progress of the investment. If at all possible, the manager who has formed such syndicates, as a participant or not, should develop alternative investors who can take over the position of any individual syndicate member who wishes to liquidate his share of the investment. Thus an element of liquidity can be provided, at the same time protecting the permanence of the syndicate, and assuring the permanence of the management of the property which is owned by the syndicate.

Managers must realize that conditions are not always favorable for syndicate formation. In the course of a major downswing in the real estate cycle the manager may be forced to withdraw completely from such a field of activity. Certainly in such periods it is inadvisable to purchase real estate on thin margins. If syndicates are to be promoted and formed in such periods, the ownership of the property should be *outright,* and not subject to debt which might take precedence over the investment position. The desire of the manager to enlarge his business and to establish its permanence is constantly subject to market analysis. The findings of such an analysis should be the *ruling force* in decisions relating to client investment.

The REITS

The second method of broadening the participation of the public in real estate investments which was popular in the period 1965–1972 was the real estate investment trust. This form of investment was made possible by the Real Estate Investment Trust Act of 1960. Qualified real estate investment trusts obtained special tax treatment which required no federal income nor capital gains tax providing they distributed to their investors at least 90 percent of their ordinary taxable income. People who were wealthy enough to purchase entire properties were granted tax shelter as proprietors of such holdings. It was only democratic that equal advantages be given to those who could buy only a fraction of a piece of real estate instead of the entire property. It was for such fractional owners that the Real Estate Investment Trust Act of 1960 was passed. If conservative practices had been followed, the real estate investment trust would have been a desirable investment, but, as has been the case so many times in the past, the promoters and underwriters of a large percentage of real estate investment trusts overestimated their capacity to produce returns for the investors. The average real estate investment trust's equity was heavily leveraged by mortgages on the properties which it owned, sometimes exposing its equity to a debt of as much as four times its size.

In 1974 because of high interest rates, the interest on this leverage debt proved too much for most REITS and many were forced to the wall.

There was nothing essentially wrong with the real estate investment trusts except the judgment of certain promoters. In most cases the underwriters took a much larger slice of the initial offering than would have been true in promoting a normal corporation. More than that, excessive loans were made and the managerial judgment of the trustees was frequently poor. As this text is being written, the ultimate destiny of such trusts is uncertain.

Cooperatives

Two other forms of ownership have come into wide use. The first of these is the so-called *cooperative* which was widely employed in the period from 1920 to 1950, but which has diminished in importance during recent years. Cooperative ownership was most often applied to residential development, principally apartments.

When persons buy a cooperative apartment, they do not actually own the apartment itself, but rather own shares of stock in a cooperative corporation which, in turn, owns the building of which the apartment is part. In exchange for ownership of so many shares of stock in that corporation, the buyer is given a proprietary lease on a specific unit of space within the building owned by that corporation.

Reasons for the purchase of cooperative apartments are varied. Initially, people were prompted to join in a cooperative venture when the apartment markets were such that all types of residential spaces were not being offered by conventional builders. For example, people who wished luxury units of large size often banded together to build buildings with large units simply because they were not being offered by builders. People also bought cooperative units because, by so doing, they were able to share in the advantages of home ownership. The fact that interest and taxes could be deducted brought substantial savings especially to people in higher income brackets. Another mode of cooperative apartment purchases was tenancy by mutual consent by which owners were able to set up their own criteria as to who might share in the accommodations in the building.

One of the major disadvantages of the cooperative form of ownership lies in the method of its financing. Since the building is owned by a corporation which is the borrower under the mortgage, each apartment theoretically owes a proportion of the total mortgage. Thus the occupant does not have the option as to whether or not he finances his premises. Moreover the amount of money which the individual occupant owes is not within his control but is decided upon by the board of directors of the corporation, usually at the time the building is new. The mortgage, for example, might have been for a substantial amount of its value, say 75 percent. Thus initial purchasers would be required to come up with only 25 percent as a cash payment. As the apartment grew older, however, and as the single mortgage was paid down, subsequent owners would have to come up with more cash—sometimes as much as 75 percent in the event that the total mortgage was paid down to 25 percent of value. In addition, the new buyer would have to pay for any increase in the value of the total unit. As a result of this need to pay higher cash sums, the original owner may not be able to sell his unit for anywhere near as much as originally when only a 25 percent down payment had been required. This proved to be a substantial disadvantage in many instances, but until the advent of the condominium apartment, no alternative was available.

Condominium Ownership

The most revolutionary development that has occurred in real estate ownership in the United States in the last two decades is that of the condominium. Entirely new in concept in this country, condominium ownership has been employed in Latin America and western Europe for many years. The word *condominium* means "joint ownership" and was initially used in Rome to designate countries operating under joint rule. Condominium ownership is most widely employed in areas where inflation is a continuing factor. Its spread in the United States has broadened as inflation has risen. Whereas virtually every kind of real estate involving multitenant occupancy can be owned in condominium, including single-family home developments, apartments, commercial buildings, and resort properties, the ownership concept is most frequently employed in multifamily dwellings.

This is the way it works. That portion of the real estate which is actually occupied by the individual tenant is owned by him in fee simple, whereas that portion of the development which he shares or uses in common with others is owned jointly, or in condominium. Thus, in an apartment building the condominium owner has full title to his unit, while the land, foundation, heating and plumbing systems, halls and entrance ways are owned jointly by him and the other occupants of the building. The condominium apartment may be mortgaged separately in the same manner as a single-family house and, as such, it is assessed for real estate taxes just as though it were a detached piece of property.

Condominium ownership is almost ideally suited for certain types of resort property. For example, suppose you own a condominium in Florida and wish to spend a month a year there prior to retirement. In the other eleven months of the year you would sublease the unit for possible profit or at least to recover some of your costs. In this period you would be delighted to be rid of the responsibility of maintaining the property, watching over it, and protecting it from mildew, hurricanes and vandals. The condominium plan is a unique and ideal solution to this problem. Its management will not only lease your unit but will watch over it during your absence. This relieves you of the physical problems of the property and provides tax advantages by enabling you to consider your condominium as an income property, subject to depreciation under certain circumstances.

CORPORATE MANAGEMENT

As pointed out above, a high percentage of the original corporate ownership of real estate was involuntary. However, in the comparatively brief period during which the corporate ownership of real estate has been permissible in many states, such ownership of the nation's real property on a *voluntary* basis has steadily increased. Therefore, the real estate manager must be prepared to administer the affairs of property owned by corporations—not only the management of the real property owned by the company, but of various matters of the corporation itself.

The management of corporate affairs involves responsibilities over and above those embraced by the management of real property. These extra duties of corporate management are frequently called *fiscal services.* The availability of such services under one roof with the property management organization is a definite advantage to the corporation, and for this reason is an asset to the management firm in the solicitation of building management under corporate control. In the light of the fact that the percentage of buildings owned by corporations is steadily increasing, it is expedient for the management organization to equip itself to provide these fiscal services.

Among the more important routine services which are included in the so-called *fiscal services* offered corporations by management companies are the following:

Directors' Meetings

The affairs of most buildings owned by corporations are principally administered by boards of directors. The officers of such corporations ordinarily are inactive in cases where the management of the corporation's property is in the hands of a competent agency.

Directors' meetings are held on regular dates but at varying intervals. Some boards of larger properties meet monthly, others bi-monthly, and still others quarterly or semi-annually. Where the corporate affairs are competently managed, the management firm plans the board meeting, and prepares the agenda to be considered. The agenda, together with the supporting data, frequently are mailed to members of the board in advance of the meeting in order that they may familiarize themselves with the problems on which decisions will be required.

A representative of the management firm (usually the account executive) attends such meetings and acts as operating counsel for the board. He is available to furnish technical interpretation on the various matters under consideration, and to answer questions of board members respecting current operations. In many cases, this representative of the management firm takes the minutes of the meeting and does all of the routine work normally carried on by the secretary of the corporation. These minutes are transcribed and distributed by the management office, and are recorded in the minute book after final approval by the board.

Although directors' meetings of corporations owning real estate should preferably be held on the premises owned, the management firm should be able to provide a satisfactory conference room in which such meetings can be held at the option of the directors.

Stockholder Contacts

In corporations wherein stock is widely held, stockholders frequently make written inquiries about the affairs of the corporation and often make personal visits to the corporation management on one or more matters in connection with stock ownership. All such references are ordinarily handled by the management firm which is providing the *fiscal service*. The account executive for the corporation must, therefore, be familiar with all of the corporate problems, and must be in a position to interview these stockholders or to answer any written inquiries.

Annual meetings of the corporation require the same type of planning noted above in connection with directors' meetings. The annual reports of the corporation to stockholders are prepared in rough draft by the management firm for submission to and approval by the board of directors. Corporations of all types are giving increasing attention to the preparation of annual reports, and are making a serious effort to acquaint stockholders more and more with the details of the enterprise in which they have an ownership interest. One of the objectives of these annual reports is to heighten the interest of the stockholder in the affairs of the corporation.

Bookkeeping

The fiscal agent is in complete charge of the books and records of the corporation. This represents an accounting department activity which transcends the mere maintenance of operating records on the building owned by the corporation. It involves a substantial amount of collateral detail, including the filing of capital stock tax returns, the preparation of income tax returns, and the preparation and filing of social security and other governmental forms. Summary reports of these activities are prepared for presentation to the board of directors, so that they may know the financial condition of the corporation as well as the operating statistics on the individual building.

Stock Operations

In the section above devoted to syndicate promotion and management, we discussed the participation in syndicates by the manager. Frequently managers also desire to protect the stability of their business by becoming stockholders in corporate enterprises which are under their management.

The activities of management in the purchase and sale of stock in corporations under their administration is subject to question in certain cases. It is generally felt that management is perhaps in a position to enjoy the benefits of information which are not available to stockholders as a whole, and which therefore give management a preferential status in determining whether to buy or to sell securities. In large corporations, the Securities and Exchange Commission demands that management make known its operations in the field of stock purchase and sale, and under certain circumstances it regards such operations unfavorably. Certainly in cases where the manager is in any sense in a fiduciary capacity, it is unethical for him to trade in the securities of those corporations in which such a relationship exists. It would certainly be desirable for a manager to discuss stock purchases with his attorney or financial adviser, to make absolutely certain that his position is above criticism.

In any case it would appear that the financing of equities in real estate in the future will increasingly involve participation by the saving and investing public. Within such regulations as may apply on the federal and state levels, the sponsorship of corporations in the field of real estate ownership represents an opportunity for the creation of stable and satisfactory management business. Such sponsorship should be based upon extremely careful analysis and upon the manager's conviction, beyond reasonable doubt, that the enterprise envisioned has a definite likelihood of success.

GOVERNMENT-SUBSIDIZED HOUSING

Just as corporate forms of real estate ownership are a new development in the second third of the present century, so also is the involvement of government at all levels (federal, state and municipal) in the subsidization of various public housing arrangements. Of course, government has been in the real estate business all along—in activities as diverse as the ownership of its own office buildings, warehouses, museums, veterans hospitals, research and development centers, military training and proving grounds, and the management of extensive public lands (e.g., the national and state parks).

The innovation was the establishment of public housing in the 1930s under the Works Progress Administration (WPA) to stimulate the economy by creating employment. There followed the public housing of the 1940 war years for factory workers migrating to northern industrial centers from the rural south; the public housing of the late 1940s and early 1950s to alleviate the postwar housing shortage problems; and the public housing of the 1950s to date aimed at dealing with the economic problems of low-income citizens.

In the three categories of subsidized public housing just mentioned, the intent was to engage in *temporary* measures only, until passing problems (unemployment, war-time population migrations, postwar housing shortages) were eliminated. On the other hand, public housing today, in many cases provided for minority groups (defined either ethnically or by age-category— for example, senior citizens' housing) has been undertaken with the thought that there would be a *permanence* to this sort of government involvement in real estate.

As a case in point, we may list some facts about the Chicago Housing Authority which has been in existence since 1937. Today (mid-1974) it provides more or less permanent housing for some 153,000 people (that is, to more people than are living in any Illinois city outside of Chicago). The value of its property, more than one thousand buildings, is a half billion dollars. While some rentals are collected, operating expenses are provided chiefly by subsidies received from the federal government. (Permanent financing is provided through 40-year bonds sold on the private market, but the principal and interest of these bonds is paid by the federal government—along with an operating subsidy.) The Housing Authority's policies are formulated by commissioners appointed by the Mayor of Chicago with concurrence of the State of Illinois. Programs are administered by a permanent staff headed by a director who reports to the Board of Commissioners. These now include a Family Housing Program, a Housing Program for the Elderly and a Leased Housing Program. Racial occupancy is 82 percent black, 17 percent white and one percent Spanish-American. Two-thirds are minors and one-tenth are elderly persons. More than half of the households receive public assistance.

Public Housing Programs in U.S. Ranked by Size of Program (Federally funded)

Rank	Total Units	Family	Elderly	Leased
1	New York City (80,488)	New York City (68,887)	New York City (9,015)	Los Angeles (3,052)
2	Chicago (40,040)	Chicago (29,575)	Chicago (7,727)	Boston (2,990)
3	Philadelphia (22,361)	Philadelphia (20,291)	Minneapolis (5,010)	Chicago (2,738)
4	San Juan, P.R. (15,877)	San Juan, P.R. (14,930)	Cleveland (3,660)	New York City (2,586)
5	Boston (13,377)	Baltimore (11,328)	Newark (2,770)	Portland, Ore. (1,797)
6	Newark (12,869)	Atlanta (10,526)	Seattle (2,656)	Oakland (1,600)

Sources: HUD Reports as of 6/30/72 for family and elderly units; as of 12/31/71 for leased units.

Ratio of Public Housing to Population in America's Six Largest Cities (Federally funded)

City	Total City Population	NUMBER PER 100,000 PERSONS			
		Total Units Operated	Family	Elderly	Leased
New York City	7,894,862	1,020	873	114	33
Chicago	3,366,957	1,189	878	230	81
Los Angeles	2,816,061	404	263	33	108
Philadelphia	1,948,609	1,148	1,041	55	52
Detroit	1,511,482	603	545	54	4
Houston	1,232,802	232	205	0	27

Currently the median income of new households being admitted is only $2,300. Other data are shown in the accompanying charts.

The need for housing subsidies in the United States is a reflection of three permanent and pervasive conditions:

1. There are many poor people in this country who are unable to purchase adequate housing on their own. Current figures indicate that almost 15 percent of the population are below the poverty income level.

2. The relatively high quality standards for new building make it difficult to accommodate the requirements of potential buyers with low budgets.

3. In spite of the progress towards integrated housing, middle and upper-income households still wish to relegate poor people to other neighborhoods.

Chicago Public Housing Program

Name	Year Completed	Number of Apartments	Total Population
TOTAL COMPLETED DEVELOPMENTS		41,524	153,102
TOTAL FAMILY DEVELOPMENTS		30,274	137,693
Jane Addams Houses......................	1938	988	2.760
Julia C. Lathrop Homes	1938	920	2,515
Trumbull Park Homes......................	1938	447	1,445
Ida B. Wells Homes.......................	1941	1,652	5,965
Frances Cabrini Homes....................	1943	581	2,455
Robert H. Brooks Homes	1943	833	3,260
Bridgeport Homes	1943	138	610
Lawndale Gardens.........................	1943	125	575
Altgeld Gardens...........................	1945	1,477	6,785
Wentworth Gardens........................	1947	422	1,780
Dearborn Homes	1950	799	2,875
Leclaire Courts...........................	1950	315	1,620
Harrison Courts..........................	1950	125	267
Maplewood Courts........................	1950	131	374
Ogden Courts.............................	1952	135	668
Archer Courts.............................	1952	147	325
Loomis Courts	1953	126	273
Victor A. Olander Homes..................	1953	150	530
Philip Murray Homes	1954	500	2,095
Gov. Lowden Homes.......................	1954	128	655
Leclaire Courts Extension	1954	299	1,380
Harold L. Ickes Homes....................	1955	797	3,280
Grace Abbott Homes.......................	1955	1,199	4,670
Ida B. Wells Extension	1955	641	2,465
Olander Homes Extension..................	1956	150	530
Gov. Henry Horner Homes	1957	916	4,365
Prairie Ave. Courts	1958	326	1,075
Prairie Ave. Courts Ext.	1958	202	830
Cabrini Extension.........................	1958	1,896	8,330
Stateway Gardens.........................	1958	1,633	6,790
Rockwell Gardens	1961	1,126	5,450
Brooks Homes Extension	1961	449	1,960
Horner Homes Extension	1961	736	4,065
Clarence Darrow Homes....................	1961	479	2,265
William Green Homes......................	1962	1,092	5,355
Washington Park Homes....................	1962	1,443	8,940
Robert R. Taylor Homes...................	1962	4,311	25,405
Lake Michigan Homes......................	1963	457	2,695
Hilliard Center	1966	342	1,415
	1967	300	1,800
Hyde Park................................	1967	12	52
	1968	6	41
	1969	109	520
	1969	97	580
Lincoln Park.............................	1969	18	100
Lawndale Area New	1969	186	1,130
	1970	187	1,025
	1970	151	745
Madden Park Homes.......................	1970	450	2,050

Chicago Public Housing Program (cont'd.)

Name	Year Completed	Number of Apartments	Total Population
TOTAL ELDERLY DEVELOPMENTS		8,045	9,394
Lathrop Apts.	1959	92	116
Washington Park Apts.	1961	92	115
Lake Michigan Apts.	1963	124	143
Parkview Apts	1963	181	210
Bridgeport Apts	1963	14	21
Yates Garden Apts	1963	28	33
William C. Jones Apts.	1963	116	145
Wicker Park Apts. & Annex.	1964 & 70	237	267
Shields Apts	1964	116	136
Garfield Park Apts.	1964	151	181
Judge Fisher Apts	1964	200	224
Eckhart Park Apts. & Annex.	1965 & 69	399	452
Thomas F. Flannery Apts.	1965	250	302
Midwest Terrace Apts.	1965	129	159
Armour Sq. Apts. & Annex	1965 & 70	392	481
Patrick F. Sullivan Apts	1965	482	539
Franklin Blvd. Apts.	1965	157	179
Hattie Callner Apts	1965	151	168
Britton I. Budd Apts	1965	173	188
5040 N. Kenmore Ave. Apts	1966	136	154
1039 W. Hollywood Ave. Apts.	1966	117	147
Hilliard Center	1966	363	427
4945 Sheridan Rd. Apts	1967	201	239
Judge Slater Apts. & Annex	1967 & 70	407	479
Maj. Lawrence Apts	1967	193	238
Judge Green Apts	1967	154	169
Clark & Irving Apts	1967 & 70	357	420
Hyde Park.	1967	22	28
661 E. 69th St. Apts	1968	125	151
Kenneth E. Campbell Apts.	1968	165	188
4645 Sheridan Rd. Apts	1968	235	267
4930 S. Langley Ave. Apts	1968	174	197
Lincoln & Sheffield Apts.	1968 & 70	394	430
2111 N. Halsted St. Apts	1969	138	155
2140 N. Clark St. Apts	1969	100	112
4250 S. Princeton Ave. Apts.	1970	339	373
6400 Sheridan Rd. Apts	1970	450	518
6401 S. Yale Ave. Apts.	1971	224	293
3245 S. Prairie Ave. Apts	1973	267	350
TOTAL LEASING PROGRAM		3,205	6,015
Leased by elderly individuals or couples		2,356	2,627
Leased by non-elderly families		849	3,388

UNDER CONSTRUCTION
(2 Developments—330 Dwellings)

Housing for Elderly (1 site).. 212 Apartments
Housing for Families (6 sites)..................................... 118 Apartments

IN DESIGN AND LAND-PURCHASE STAGE

Added to these conditions are the adverse effects of inflation and the high cost of borrowing money whenever (as in mid-1974) these exist. Public housing in one form or another with the attending governmental involvements, will be in view for a long time to come.

Public housing projects, by one definition, are those that provide housing for the most economically deprived people under conditions where the government pays construction costs with bond issues. The property owners have no mortgage payments to make and rents are set at about 25 percent of the tenants' adjusted income (plus government subsidies) in order to provide for an operating budget.

Other types of governmental involvement in subsidized housing include plans where rebates are returned to the promoters to make up the difference between the mortgage at one percent interest and that of the market rate; three percent interest 100 percent mortgage loans for 40 years to certain nonprofit organizations and 3½ percent interest 90 percent mortgage loans to certain limited dividend companies, and a rent supplement program where an additional subsidy is paid directly to sponsors for a limited number of tenant families unable to pay even the "basic" rent.

The sheer volume of current levels of subsidized housing programs creates a heavy demand for property managers who are skillful in balancing the interests of the various parties (owners, governmental sponsors, tenants, citizen-action groups), and in defusing situations which may become foci of social unrest. Given the fact that public housing can have various locations and involve various groups (suburban versus inter-city, garden versus high-rise versus town-house, elderly versus large family, etc.), it is clear that not all of the management problems will be encountered in every situation. Sometimes the manager will be called upon to be sensitive to the human rights of tenants regardless of their ability to purchase higher quality housing on the free market. Often they must cope with the problems of fatherless families, working mothers, or teen-age dominance. Communication must be established across ethnic, racial, economic and religious barriers. Often an enormous amount of paper work will be involved because of the imposition of bureaucratic controls.

Thus because of the emergence of subsidized housing, involving large and complicated management problems that relate to social and political as well as to physical questions, a whole new specialized field of property management has opened.

REVIEW QUESTIONS

1. What is meant by *syndicate ownership?* How does it affect real estate management operations?
2. Name the *extra* duties involved in corporate management.
3. What took place in property ownership during the depression years, 1929 to 1933, that is of significance to real estate managers?

4. Describe how you would go about forming a syndicate.
5. What is corporate management?
6. How has voluntary corporate ownership developed—is it increasing—or decreasing?
7. What is an alternative investor? Why should a property manager be interested in developing alternative investors?
8. How important are annual reports to stockholders? Why are they necessary and what are today's trends in the preparation of such reports?
9. Suppose there is a downward trend in real estate. Would you form a syndicate? Would it differ in any way from one formed in an upward real estate trend? Explain.
10. What services can be offered a corporation by real estate management in addition to the managing of property, and what is the value thereof?
11. What briefly are the essential provisions of the law and its regulations on real estate investment trusts?
12. Explain the workings of real estate investment trust arrangements.
13. Explain why property managers of public housing should have empathy for the population to be served, be good in communication skills, and themselves be free of personal problems.

SELECTED REFERENCES

"A Capsule Survey of Tax-Sheltered Investments." *Real Estate Investors Report* (Apr. 1974) pp. 7–8.

California Real Estate Association. *Apartment House Syndication for Small Private Investment Groups, A Case Study* (Los Angeles, Calif., 1973).

California Real Estate Association, *How to Syndicate an Apartment House* (Los Angeles, Calif., 1971) 127p.

"Careless Co-op Owners Can Lose Tax Deductions," *Mortgage and Real Estate Executives Report* (July 3, 1972) pp. 6–7.

Casey, William J., *Real Estate Investments and How To Make Them.* New York, Institute for Business Planning, 1972, 329p.

Crandell, Larry, *Corporate Real Estate Development and Management* (Prendents Publishing House, N. Y., 1971) 294p.

Konter, Lawrence J., "Apartment Syndication As a Form and Type of Development and Ownership," *Farm and Land Journal,* (April 1970) pp. 8–10.

Mead, Sedgwick, Jr., "Ownership of Real Estate as a Corporate Investment." *National Market Letter,* (March 1974) pp. 5–7.

Neilson, Gordon J. "Apartment Management by Syndication," *Professional Builder,* (Feb. 1972) 146p.

Practicing Law Institute, *Development and Financing of Condominiums,* Real Estate Law and Practice Course, Hardbook Series No. 86, 1973, 824p.

Ware, Ridgeley P., "The Once, Now and Future REIT," *Journal of Property Management* (March–April 1973) pp. 75–78.

"What Kinds of Real Estate are Corporations Seeking? When, Where, Why, How?" *Real Estate Forum* (Aug. 1972) pp. 33–36.

"Why Corporate Investors Need the Real Estate Specialist," *Mortgage and Real Estate Executives Report* (Aug. 2, 1971) pp. 1–2.

CHAPTER 7

Appraising Comparative Value

INTRODUCTION

Property management involves, among other things, selling space, and selling starts with setting values in accordance with the realities of market demand.

In the final analysis, it is a profit system that is operating. The major function of the manager is the conversion of space into use by persons able and willing to pay a competitive monetary consideration for the right of such use. Almost invariably property managers are paid for their services in proportion to their success in the actual production of gross revenue. They are kept employed, however, to the extent that they produce the highest possible net revenue over a period of years. This is why any analysis of the property management process leads us to consider a whole series of activities under the general topic of *producing gross income.*

The activities of appraising comparative value presented in this chapter may be divided into several major steps, each of which embraces several minor phases, as will be seen.

According to one tongue-in-cheek definition, "Mathematics is what mathematicians do, operating with symbols invented just for that purpose." Similarly, we may say that property management is what property managers do with properties made available just for that purpose. In any case, it is not the argument, "Which came first, the chicken or the egg?" Buildings exist and others come into being. From time to time, owners seek out and retain managers to operate these properties.

Property managers for their part cannot afford to accept blindly any assignment. They will want to know something about the type, condition, and associated facilities of the property under consideration. They will need to know something about the neighborhood involved. And, ultimately, they will want to undertake a full market analysis, to complete the appraisal of what is termed the *comparative value.* With the information thus obtained, the property manager can form a judgment about the likelihood, in particular instances, of earning a profit both for himself and for the owner interests.

138

PROPERTY ANALYSIS

The appraisal best starts with a personal visit to the property under consideration. If the building is occupied in part or in whole, special arrangements naturally will have to be made to guarantee adequate entry. Being accompanied by the owner(s) and/or the former manager(s) has both pluses and minuses in this kind of expedition; therefore, both kinds of visiting may be in order. It is solid information, such as the following, that will be wanted:

As to the Structure:
1. What is the size of the property (how many individual units does it contain)?
2. What is the desirability level (visual impression—age, style, landscaping, approaches, public spaces, tenancy character)?
3. What are the sizes of the units (how many rooms contained)?
4. What is the level of desirability of the units' design (room size, layout, closets, exposure, general facility)?
5. What is the level of desirability of the units' equipment (hardware, plumbing, stoves, refrigerators, electric fixtures, bathroom treatment, window treatment, etc.)?

As to its Physical Condition:
1. What is the physical condition of the building's exterior (masonry, sash and trim, roofs, porches, walks, curbs, etc.)?
2. What is the physical condition of the building's interior (entrances, lobbies, halls and corridors, lockers and laundries, public spaces)?
3. What is the condition of tenant spaces (decorations, floors, shades or blinds, general maintenance)?
4. What is the condition of the building's equipment (heating plant, machinery, elevators, furniture and furnishings, carpet, linens, vacuum sweepers, tools, etc.)?

The inspection of all of these items, and their careful recording, is the property analysis. In this examination of the property, the manager becomes thoroughly familiar with the merchandise he is charged with selling to the public, and the physical structure he is to maintain for his client. It is probable that the average manager will inquire about the present rents in the building (if it is completed and occupied when he is given its management), yet it is not necessary that he do so. In fact, it is preferable that he does not.

The technique of *appraising rental values* is the same for existing buildings as for proposed buildings. The truly expert manager does not allow himself to be influenced by the rentals which another manager has set on the building. Any judgment on rentals reached by a manager at the conclusion of this first visit is apt to be erroneous; moreover, such a judgment would be definitely synthetic since the *property analysis is only the first step in a broad program of gathering data pertinent to a sound estimate of the true rental value of the space in the property under consideration.*

Neighborhood Analysis

Having visited the property, and having recorded the data necessary for an adequate *property analysis,* the second step is the analysis of the neighborhood in which the building is located. In this connection, a word of warning: *Neighborhood analysis* is not to be confused with miscellaneous recollections of a section of town with which the property manager imagines himself familiar (or is reminded of by historical accounts.)

The *science* of property management, as practiced today, leaves nothing to so-called incidental experience, and does not permit the substitution of "memory" or "impressions" for accurate, reliable data. Therefore, unless the manager has previously, indeed recently, made an analysis of the particular neighborhood in which the building is located, he is bound by duty to himself and his client to go through the exacting processes of gathering all of the required information.

What Is a Neighborhood?

The common definition of a neighborhood is sometimes stated as "the region lying near where one is or resides, adjoining or surrounding dwellings collectively, in the vicinity." Such a definition does not fully enable a property manager to isolate an area surrounding a particular property from which he can gather data significant to his study of that property. Actually, from the manager's point of view, a neighborhood may more succinctly be defined as *an area within which there are common characteristics of population and land use*. In rural areas, a neighborhood may be made up of many square miles; but in highly concentrated city areas, a neighborhood may consist of only three or four blocks, or the vicinity of a major intersection of streets.

Since to study a neighborhood requires first the fixing of its boundaries (so that it may be isolated from the rest of the community), the manager must determine its limits. In many cases the boundaries of neighborhoods are obvious geographical or man-made barriers such as rivers, lakes, ravines, railroad tracks, parks, and boulevards. Frequently, obvious changes in the character of land use and population occur on the other side of such barriers, and the trained observer of people and buildings will have no difficulty in fixing the boundaries of the neighborhood in which he wants to gather his facts.

In many cases, however, neighborhood limits are not visually discernible even to the trained observer. In such cases the manager can obtain assistance from United States census data, newspaper research offices which study neighborhood characteristics for circulation information, city librarians, school boards, welfare agencies, statisticians, and other reliable sources. By observation or from other sources the manager will in the end be able to isolate the neighborhood in which his property is located.

In this connection, the opinion may be offered that the practical life of the average neighborhood usually is between 30 and 50 years, as measured from the time it has first reached a peak in desirability. This is a rule for the United States; still there will be important exceptions that can be found (for example,

Beacon Street in Boston, the Near North neighborhoods of Chicago, Nob Hill in San Francisco, etc.).

Perhaps the processes of deterioration here alluded to will not mark the future as much as they have the past. Much depends upon the far-sightedness of present and future urban planners, and upon the skill of architects and builders. But dynamism in America has always been a factor to keep the pot boiling and to bring about change even where just a few years before it could not be foreseen. For these reasons the property managers must keep alert to the emerging trends.

Now, after the neighborhood has been delimited, what data must the manager gather in the second step toward scientifically appraising the rental value of his property? Most important is *population,* since people make value in real estate, and since trends in population are reflected by trends in neighborhoods. Let us suppose, for the purpose of illustration, that we have found that our neighborhood is a square mile in size. These are the population facts to be uncovered:

Trend in Numbers

It has been observed frequently that "population growth is the keystone of real estate prosperity." Whereas this is a true generalization when applied to a town or city as a whole, it is not applicable always to a neighborhood. For example, a neighborhood that has been completely built up with homes may suddenly show an increase in population. This, rather than indicating an improvement in values, may reveal a change from single-family occupancy to cheaper, rooming-house tenancy. For that reason the manager must correlate his study of trend in numbers of population to the percentage of land development in the neighborhood under analysis.

If an area whose land has been completely developed shows an increase in population without simultaneous new building operations, then other factors must be analyzed. On the other hand, if a neighborhood in which, let us say, there is only a 25 percent land development shows a population increase paralleled by building activity, then the area is probably in good trend (scheduled for higher values and greater public acceptance).

Trend in the total population in any neighborhood must be interpreted by the manager in terms of land use and the economic level and character of that population. A study of total numbers of people is not in itself conclusive data, when the population is either stationary or on the increase. It is generally safe however to conclude that a neighborhood losing population is in bad trend.

Economic Level

From the point of view of appraising the economic level of population, no better method has yet been devised than the determination of average rentals or purchase price within an area. In a system in which purchasing power is the common denominator of relative social desirability, the property manager engaged in studying a neighborhood must know the level of its purchasing power before any conclusion can be reached about the rental potentials of a particular property. Generally speaking, a neighborhood in which the average rental for residential units is $200 will not support even a single property whose rentals are $800. Likewise, it may be said that the general level of comparative neighborhood rentals tends to move downward (due to age, obsolescence, and deterioration) over a period of years, and that the existence of isolated low rentals in a neighborhood tends to drag down higher rentals.

The average residential rental level in a neighborhood reveals the character of facilities (commercial and social) that the neighborhood can support; the amount it can contribute to the maintenance of its own desirability; and, from the standard point of view, the desirability of its population.

Family Size

As noted elsewhere in this text, the unit of consumption of residential real estate is not population as such, but the family. If there is a community of 1,000 people in which the average family numbers five people, then there will be an effective need for 200 units of housing. If, however, the average family numbers only four, then the same community will require 250 units of housing. For that reason, the analyst of a neighborhood must know the current average family size in his subject neighborhood, and its trend (for example, as now influenced by the "pill").

In this connection, it is pertinent to observe that already for the past half century the size of the average American family has been shrinking due to increased economic pressure, to control of family size, to increase of divorce, and to greater longevity. Today, one and two-unit families are not uncommon.

These trends are particularly effective in urban centers, and have given rise to what we may call "social obsolescence," a vitally important factor in neighborhood study. In many cities there are neighborhoods, desirable essentially from a locational point of view, that were designed to house families of five and six persons. Although these buildings may be sound of structure and reasonably modern in design, in general they are not suited for occupancy by families of two and three persons (the very rich being here excluded).

The typical remedy for such "social obsolescence" is the conversion of such buildings into rooming houses, light housekeeping suites, and other uses designed to avoid bringing on the earnings-paralysis of "blight."

The exception to this rule is neighborhoods of outstanding consumer pressure, where many older buildings frequently are converted into more profitable properties by making them available to a greater number of families, without thereby too much reducing the level of their desirability.

Facts pertaining to neighborhood size, from census studies or other sources of information mentioned previously, are extremely useful and illuminating to the property manager. Families of large size indicate the presence of children—a fact that in middle to upper-middle income areas usually indicates residential stability (while in substandard areas it can mean the opposite). On the other hand, the smaller the size of the average family, the less stable the tenancy often is in terms of length of residence. In fact, the presence of large numbers of one and two-person families once was thought to be evidence of a high degree of transiency, but today with the new life styles, this may indicate the presence of couples who either have raised their children, or never had or wanted any.

Domestic Status

Really a subheading of the "Family Size" study, the domestic status category embraces that part of the census information which reveals the number of divorced persons, the number of single and married persons of adult age, and the number of new (e.g., communal) relationships existing.

Population Composition

In a society existing under constantly changing influences, there are significant shifts in the population composition. Examples of these trends are the so-called bulge of post-war babies, the great increase in senior citizens, and the sharply reduced age of initial marriage. Each of these factors has significance in local real estate market analysis.

Population Mobility

When all of the above population data are assembled, it is wise for the manager to recheck the information from the point of view of the *actual change* taking place in the population character, if any. It is possible that a neighborhood may not have changed for, say, twenty years insofar as its total population is concerned, but the people who are resident in the area *now* may be different in economic level and different in family pattern.

Another phase of neighborhood analysis involves the manager's study of land use within the area. This study should provide him with two types of information about the neighborhood's residential buildings—their general character, age, condition, and visual desirability, and also the type of accommodations that are afforded to the renting public.

The observant property manager, after establishing the boundaries of his neighborhood, can obtain satisfactory information on the character, age, condition, and visual desirability of the area's buildings by, for example, driving through its streets and observing the structures. For the data regarding accommodations, he must make adequate inquiry concerning the size of units in the zone's buildings, examine sample units, and obtain prevailing rentals at which the various sizes and types are being offered for rental.

In this phase of his study, the property manager will begin to correlate the supply, as revealed by the units in the area, with the demand, as indicated by the population studies. He will become aware of whether the size of the units matches the size of the families and whether the rentals of the area are reflecting strength or weakness in the volume of demand. He will, in short, know if the demand pattern matches the supply status.

NEIGHBORHOOD VERSUS NEIGHBORHOOD

In the previous section, we have attempted to define a neighborhood by suggesting an analysis of its characteristics and a means for delimiting its area. Perhaps the most essential characteristic of the free enterprise society is *change.* Within the typical urban area, neighborhoods seldom are static in the characteristics we have examined. As the result of new area developments, old area redevelopments, population changes, obsolescence, and shifts in circulation patterns, some neighborhoods will be gaining in desirability and acceptance, while others will be declining.

In the years from 1941 through 1957, when virtually all space in U. S. metropolitan areas was in a state of acute shortage, property consumers found it impossible to move about as they might have liked, or to select the accommodations they preferred. A prospect for an apartment, house, store, or office was forced to accept whatever space was available. For example, if a newly arrived citizen was told that the most desirable place to live was in neighborhood A, he might have scoured neighborhood A for accommodations for himself and his family entirely without success. If further he had been given neighborhood B as a second choice, he might have experienced the same negative result. Thus, he might have been forced to accept residential space in some neighborhood C merely because that was the only area where space could be found.

With the growth of surplus space in nearly all categories of the real estate market beginning in 1958, consumers once more enjoyed the traditional right of selection based on their ideas of desirability. This freedom of expression in locational decision making served to restore local dynamism, and also to widen the margin of desirability between neighborhoods which had been missing during the prior, long period of shortage.

The boom of the late sixties, however, reintroduced a space shortage in virtually all categories of property. Rentals and prices remained strong through the early part of 1969 in all areas, and continued to rise in the most desirable areas through the early part of the 1970 recession. In marginal and submarginal areas, however, the markets exhibited some weakness.

Property-Neighborhood Relationship

The first step mentioned here in appraising rental value was the *property analysis;* the second, *neighborhood analysis.* The third step is the study of the *relationship of the particular building scheduled for management to the neighborhood in which it is located.* Already familiar with the neighborhood's buildings, their character, age, and exterior desirability, the manager can now compare his own building to those of the neighborhood and note the characteristics ranking above or below the average. He can also note the style, character, and size of the building's units and their relation to the competition and the evident demand. And, most important, he can analyze the *location* of the property, from the point of view both of its relation to competing buildings within the neighborhood and of its relation to the metropolitan area in which the neighborhood itself is located. All of these observations bring the location factor into perspective.

In this connection, it is important to direct attention to the semantics of the conceptual meaning of the usually self-evident derivatives of the Latin word, locus (place). In the real estate profession there is no word more significant than *location,* yet its exact meaning, as related to specific property, is most difficult to define. As a matter of fact, location, as applied to real estate, has many meanings—it means one thing when used in connection with industrial property, another when related to commercial property, and still another when used in describing residential property. We shall concern ourselves in this chapter only with its definition as related to *residential property.* And we shall say that location in this specific connection means the comparative advantages of dwelling on a site weighed from the point of view of the factors listed in the following table.

Table of Desirability Factors in Location Analysis

I. Transportation (public) [1]
   A. Distance to points of departure of various media
   B. Frequency of departure from those points
   C. Comforts of relative transportation facilities
   D. Type of passengers apt to be encountered on typical trip
   E. Time required to travel to main objectives
   F. Cost of travel to main objectives

II. Transportation (private) [2]
   A. Distance to main traffic arteries
   B. Ease of driving to main objectives
   C. Time required to travel to main objectives
   D. Fare of taxicabs to main objectives
   E. Environment through which one must travel
   F. Parking facilities

---

[1] Street cars, buses, service cars, elevated lines, subway, or other forms of transportation (commonly considered utilities) which operate on fixed routes, schedules, and fares.

[2] Transportation media operated by the owner, or owner's agent, over routes chosen by the owner, e.g., private automobiles and taxicabs.

III. Convenience
    A. To shopping subcenters
        1. Distance to necessity dispensaries
        2. Ability of local center to supply wants
        3. Facilities of local shops (delivery, service, prices)
    B. To recreational facilities
        1. Theaters: type of entertainment, prices of admission
        2. Sports centers
        3. Parks and public recreational facilities
    C. To educational facilities
        1. Kinds of schools (public, private, and parochial)—elementary, junior high, senior high, junior college, and four-year college or university
        2. Distance and type of transportation
        3. Hazards (or lack of them) enroute for children
    D. To churches—denominations, services, social values
IV. Social Advantages
    A. Reputation and social acceptance of neighborhood
    B. Existence of social organizations within the area, membership requirements, relative activity and availability, and cost
  V. Personal and Property Safety [3]
    A. Relative local record for crimes against persons
    B. Current statistics on crimes against property

In any analysis of location from the point of view of the tabulated factors, it must be kept in mind that our definition stated that location meant the "*comparative* advantages" of a site, as measured in terms of the above factors. There is no such thing as *absolute desirability* in location of real estate. Moreover, the relative importance of the above criteria is constantly changing in the eyes of the consumers. With the threat of an energy crisis (first noted by the public at large in the fall of 1973), proximity to places of employment took on a new priority. On the other hand, location in reference to churches no longer can be regarded as an important factor.

Market Analysis

In the scheme of things presented here, it is worthy of note that thus far the property manager who is setting out to make an *appraisal of rental value* has not as yet concerned himself with any expression of value. The processes recommended here have involved only the gathering of objective data dealing with people, buildings, and their relationships. The fourth step in the technique

---

[3] This is a comparatively new criterion of location desirability. Previously, it was not thought to be pertinent enough to include as a separate item of consideration. As of 1974, however, it is (next to schools) the single most important factor to prospective space consumers.

of *appraising rental value* (market analysis) does not yet contemplate giving attention to the rental value of the specific product actually to be sold by the property manager. Rather, it specifies his becoming familiar with the general markets for the *specific type* of merchandise.

In chapters 2 and 5 we have discussed broad general conditions which we have identified as the "real estate market," but we now turn our attention to the many smaller markets that the manager must isolate and analyze when appraising the rental value of a specific property. Any beginning student of property management probably knows that there are many individual markets within the structure of real estate—commercial space markets, store markets, apartment markets, single-family residence markets, etc. He also must know that, in order to appraise the rental value of any given unit of space, the said unit first must be classified as to its market and then be related to a measurement of that market. It is the process of measuring a specific space market for which the term "market analysis" as here used has been coined.

Individual real estate markets are difficult of measurement for three main reasons. First, there is *no exactly comparable unit of measurement* in residential space. For example, in the grain market, measurements are taken in terms of bushels of corn, each bushel being just like every other bushel. In the stock market a share of stock in a given issue is identical with every other share in the same issue. But in real estate, one apartment may differ greatly from another, and there is no exactly comparable unit of measurement (that is, from one building to the next).

The second difference in the analysis of real estate's submarkets is that there is no *central point of trading.* In the case of grains, the great trading centers are boards of trade; in the case of stocks, trades are made on central exchanges. However, rentals are not made at a central point, but are being made in buildings, real estate offices, and landlord's homes scattered over an entire neighborhood (or city).

This scattered trading results in the third major difference between real estate markets and other markets, i.e., *there is no systematic recording of sales and reporting of prices.* When a bushel of corn is sold in the Chicago Board of Trade, the sale is immediately recorded and broadcast to the world over an international wire service. Likewise, the sale of a share of stock in the United States Steel Corporation is instantly broadcast to the world through tickers. In real estate markets, however, there is no full recording of sales by an organized agency, and transactions are considered the business of the individual lessee and lessor—confidential business, at that. (Note that the recording of deeds of sale often does not require the disclosure of the exact consideration.)

Since without loss in generality we may be primarily concerned here with the problem of residential property, we shall confine our discussion of market analysis technique to that field. In so doing we must recognize that there are virtually scores of different markets within this one field. Among the major classifications of these markets we find markets for multistory apartments, markets for "walk-up" apartments, markets for unheated flats, markets for duplexes, markets for row and town houses, for single-family dwellings, and for other general classifications of residential space. These markets vary both between communities and between neighborhoods, and we shall presume that any manager, given a specific property to manage, can easily decide into which classification any property's space should be placed.

Having identified the general classification, the market analyst must further isolate his market into denominations of size and character. For example, if a specific property is an apartment building containing one-, two-, and three-bedroom apartments, the markets for units in each of these classifications must be individually analyzed. Each of these markets will have a separate supply-and-demand factor; each will have a different price range. The manager must answer the following questions with respect to each market:

1. How many apartments are available within the area?
2. What is the *average* character of the buildings in which they are located?
3. What is the *average* unit in this specific market (as to layout, equipment, etc.)?
4. Based on facts obtained through the neighborhood analysis, what is the trend of families within the area that are logical consumers of this particular sized unit—is there an increase or decrease?
5. What is the present price of this *average* unit?
6. What is the occupancy of all of the units of this type—above, below, and corresponding to the *average*?
7. What was the price and occupancy condition a year ago—what is the trend of each?
8. How do these trends compare in steepness of rise and fall with the trends as revealed in a study of the real estate market as a whole?

Armed with this and all of the foregoing information, we are ready to proceed to a conclusion in our process of appraising *rental value.*

The Rental Schedule

In all fairness it must be admitted at the outset that there is no method of placing a rental schedule on any kind of property that can be said unequivocally to be the *exact* price for rental in a free supply-and-demand market. All rental schedules are necessarily *estimates* of a true price—are, in the final analysis, opinions of the persons in control. The degree of correctness of these *estimates* is determinable only by actual results expressed by public reaction and reflected in occupancy records attained both by the property as a whole and by the individual units.

If we are to place a price upon units within a multifamily residential property, we must first determine the occupancy we desire to maintain in the building during the period in which the price is to be effective.

As we have noted above, the level of production of automobiles, televisions, or overalls may vary from day to day, from month to month, or from year to year. Moreover, the manufacturer can control his production by operating his plant at varying capacities, can shut down altogether if there is a condition of oversupply in the markets for his product. In addition, in the case of most products for sale, the chief cost is made up of the materials and labor within the product itself. Only a small percentage of cost is made up of charges for plant equipment, taxes, etc.

In the case of income property, on the contrary, production is not controllable. On the contrary, it is the same, day in and day out, year after year. A 50-apartment building produces 50 apartments every day of the year, and at least 75 percent of the cost of producing each of the 50 apartments is incurred day after day whether the building is operated at 25 or 95 percent of capacity. It is obvious, of course, that the aim of good management is to operate at the level of 100 percent occupancy (or as close to that as is possible without underpricing the units).

The larger a building is, the simpler it is to set a realistic rental price schedule, however. This idea can be illustrated by the example that, in the larger building, increasing the rental of a single unit (even to the point of not finding a customer) is a cheap way to test the market with small loss to the total income. On the other hand, the same experiment undertaken on a smaller building runs the risk of having the percentage vacancy at a high level.

Concerning the rental schedule, we shall continue with the assumption that we have been given a building containing one-, two-, and three-bedroom units. Beginning with the one-bedroom, we must first determine what is meant by a *typical* one-bedroom unit in the community in which our subject property is located. In Chicago, for example, a *typical* one-bedroom unit contains a living-dining combination room, a bedroom, bath, and kitchen. The walls are painted, the bath is tiled and contains a tub-shower, the kitchen has cabinets and stove and refrigerator. Floor covering is carpet, windows have shades and the unit is not air-conditioned. It is what we call a *base unit* in the one-bedroom market—a standard against which all one-bedroom units can be measured.

In this connection, it will be realized even by the beginning student that the history of housing and other building space (in the United States) has been one of steadily rising standards, at least up until the mid-1970s. Air-conditioning, as an illustration, sometimes is taken for granted, especially in the hot climates (Houston as opposed to Minneapolis, for example); still it remains true that the average rental unit in the USA will for a long time be priced without central air conditioning, given the problems currently being posed by the Energy Crisis.

While *typical* units may vary appreciably as between communities, each community has such base units in its various markets, and these will be easily identified by the property manager with even a modicum of experience. These base units, likewise, will have a standard price at any given moment—a price which we shall call *base price*.

Now, after the manager has identified the base unit in the one-bedroom apartment field and has discovered its current *base price* for the neighborhood in which it is located, his next step is to make a minute comparison between the value factors in his own one-bedroom apartment and those to be found in the base unit. Unless his own apartment is exactly typical and is itself a base unit, it is most likely he will find that it has deficiencies or overages in value. For example, the exterior character of his building may be better or worse than the exterior *of the typical* building; the room sizes of his apartment may be smaller or larger than average; the equipment in his unit may be more or less desirable than that of the base unit. The factors of comparison between the subject apartment and the base unit are factors of value in residential space. The accompanying table brings this idea to the fore.

Table of Factors of Comparison and of Value

I. Exterior Appearance
   A. Architectural character
   B. Maintenance of streets and walks
   C. Condition of lawns and shrubs
   D. Sightliness of signs and lawn fences
   E. Cleanliness of basement or main floor windows
   F. Taste and standardization of window treatment (shades, blinds, etc.)
   G. Condition of sash and trim
   H. Absence of clothes lines, milk bottles on sills, or other evidences of slovenliness in tenancy
   I. Cleanliness of service areaways, rear porches, courts, and stairways
   J. Indication of good tenant deportment, as in the case of the absence of children playing boisterously in areas where tenant disturbance would inevitably result
   K. Absence of bicycles, sleds, baby perambulators, etc., in places where nuisance or unsightliness would result

II. Public Spaces
   A. Appearance of entrance doors and halls—kickplates and handrails; hardware and door checks; mail boxes and information signs; cleanliness of floors or carpets; and condition of walls, hand rails, spindles, etc.
   B. Character of building as reflected by the physical atmosphere of the rental office (neatness, orderliness, and decorative taste)
   C. Appearance of lobbies and corridors

EXTERIOR APPEARANCE

The character of any building may be reflected by such factors as architectural character, maintenance of streets and walks, or condition of lawns and shrubs. The above building is situated on Nun's Island, a small, wooded land mass lying adjacent to downtown Montreal in the St. Lawrence River. (Photo by Bill Hedrich, Hedrich-Blessing)

    D. Cleanliness and pleasant atmosphere of laundries, storerooms, and basement space

III. Reaction of prospect to building personnel (exclude renting agent)
    A. Courtesy of receptionist
    B. Treatment of tenants as revealed in conversations overheard in renting office
    C. Appearance and deportment of employees contacted during the inspection
    D. System of employee control to ensure proper impression

IV. Interior
    A. Factors of plan—room size, wall space, closet facilities, convenience of layout, and circulation
    B. Factors of equipment—lighting fixtures, refrigeration, stove, plumbing fixtures, etc., and window treatment
    C. Factors of appointment—wardrobe equipment, built-in bookcases, etc.
    D. Factors of beautification—decorations and finishes, colors, design of fixtures and hardware, floor treatment, etc.
    E. Factors of exposure—light, view, prevailing winds, exterior noise

If each of the above factors of comparison is a factor of *value,* it is to be presumed that the degree by which each factor is either *less* or *more* desirable than the base unit will also be a degree by which the price of the subject unit should be lower or higher than the base price. In theory such a presumption is correct, yet two notable facts must be recognized as counterindications.

In the first place, each market has definite *economic limits* beyond which prices cannot be raised, regardless of the degree of desirability in each of the factors. For example, let us suppose that our subject one-bedroom apartment is in a neighborhood in which the base unit rents at $175. Let us further suppose that in a more desirable adjacent neighborhood this unit has a base price of $250. The chances are that if we add values to our subject unit in sufficient amount to justify a $250 rental, our prospects would prefer a base unit located in a more desirable neighborhood at the same price.

Illustrating this principle in other fields of merchandise, we know, for instance, that there are *economic limits* for automobiles in the so-called low-price field. If General Motors were to add gadgets to a Chevrolet in sufficient quantity to make its price equal to a Pontiac or Oldsmobile, most of its prospects for Chevrolet cars would move over into the Pontiac and Oldsmobile consumer groups. All values are related in terms of desirability in the mind of the general public, and neighborhoods, like specific products, have *economic limits* beyond which it usually will be fruitless to venture.

In other words, there is a point of diminishing return in the installation of added values—a point at which better equipment or accommodation fails to

INTERIOR APPEARANCE

Factors of comparison and of value must be taken into consideration both internally and externally. An example of a well-appointed apartment is illustrated above by such factors as floor treatment, wall space, room size, lighting fixtures, window treatment, light, and view.

be economic, a point at which even the installation of gold doorknobs will not bring a higher price. Thus, in the final analysis, the actual rental to be placed on the subject unit must be fixed by the *opinion* of the manager—an opinion, however, arrived at after he is fortified with the wealth of data provided by the several steps discussed above. These steps are to provide the manager with a sound knowledge of product, market, and competition. The final process of setting the rental schedule (which we call the *base unit-rate approach*) then will have a surprisingly low percentage of error, provided all of the previous steps were taken conscientiously.

It is pertinent to point out that the use of the *base unit-rate approach* leads to the establishment of rental schedules on the basis of value comparability. Constant changes in style, design, and unit composition produce concomitant alterations in the standard base unit. For example, pressures of increasing cost have virtually eliminated the traditional dining room from apartment units and small homes, and such equipment as garbage disposals, dishwashers, and laundry machines are rapidly coming into broad use. At some point in the future, it would appear, a standard four-room unit will be made up of two bedrooms, living room, and kitchen. Even now the dining room in a small apartment is a renting liability, since most young couples do not have furniture for a full-size dining room, nor do they wish to purchase it. Moreover, it is the history of appliances that they quickly pass from luxury status to common usage. At one time, electric refrigerators were considered a *plus* factor of value, justifing an extra $10 per month rental. Now they are considered a part of the standard base unit.

It is obvious that the employment of a comparative method of establishing rental values imposes the constant necessity of reviewing the bases for the comparisons of value criteria. Only by regular space-shopping sorties can the manager be certain of the validity of his conclusions.

Rent Paying Capacity

In our discussion of the rent price level in chapter 2, we pointed out that the average U. S. family has lowered its rental payments to approximately 15 percent of its income in place of the long-accepted ratio of approximately 25 percent ("one week's pay out of every four for rent"). This change has taken place over a 30-year period and has resulted from two prime factors:

1. The phenomenal rise in family incomes in the period since 1939—because of sharp increases in wages and the significant rise in secondary workers.
2. The dramatic increase in living standards. The old "food, clothing, and shelter" complex of the family budget has given way to a much more complicated and insistent set of demands including automobiles, appliances, cosmetics, beauty care, hospitalization and life insurance, as well as intensive recreation and travel. In consequence, a steadily lower percentage of average family resources has been allocated to shelter.

RENT PAYING CAPACITY

In chapter 2 we pointed out that the average tenant does not (any longer) follow a rule-of-thumb relationship between what he earns and what he is willing to pay as rent. All that really can be said is that people seek to pay the minimum for which they can obtain what they accept as satisfactory accommodations at tolerable locations.

Rentals in the U. S. tend to be lower than in most of the other areas of the free world. In Japan, for example, a two-bedroom (two-bath) unit in a high-rise apartment building may typically cost as much as the equivalent of $1,500 monthly. In Latin America, virtually all such units are owned by the occupants (or, in some cases, paid for on a daily rate); while in Europe, current rentals also are measured in terms of astronomical figures (except in those instances where rent controls apply).

This disparity between domestic and foreign levels of rent can be explained by the historical policy of the American federal government to ensure an oversupply of residential units under the prevailing circumstances. This policy has been implemented by the device of making liberal financing available for long-term loans. And, as we have discussed in some of the previous chapters, rents can be increased dramatically only when there is a condition of shortage in the market place, which condition usually has been avoided here by governmental pursuit of the policy of stimulation of financing.

In recent years, it may be added, there has been a dual market for residential space. One is to the traditional family with school-age children who might find it difficult to pay one-fourth of a $12,000 annual salary for rent. The other is the "working couple" family who with the same annual earning might be ready to pay as much as (or more than) even a third of their income as rental.

As we look to the future, however, we can anticipate that real estate markets may become tighter (meaning that rentals will rise). This prediction is based on the idea that it will become steadily more difficult to create new income property in the United States. On the one side, there are the rising financing charges, the increasing construction costs, consumerism, and all of the constraints presented by political protectionism. On the other side, there are the emerging concerns about the relationship of building to environmental impacts and to the question of future energy supply for any uncontrolled sprawl in the construction of new buildings.

REVIEW QUESTIONS

1. How would you as a property manager estimate the true value of a residential building? Describe briefly step by step.
2. Define a *neighborhood* from the point of view of a property manager.
3. How can the *economic level* of population be determined?
4. What is said to be the *keystone* of real estate prosperity? Is this true in every case?

5. Outline what data the property manager should accumulate when visiting a residential building he has just acquired.
6. When is a neighborhood usually considered to be in *bad trend?*
7. How would you go about making a *neighborhood analysis?*
8. Why is an analysis of the population in a neighborhood important?
9. Define *location* as applied to residential property. Name the factors involved, and describe each briefly.
10. How would you determine the value of residential space in various units of your residential building?
11. What is meant by *market analysis?*
12. What is the *base unit-rate approach?*
13. How can a property manager find out if the demand for property is in proportion to the supply?
14. What must the property manager know about the market for his *specific* residential building? Use a hypothetical building as an example.

SELECTED REFERENCES

American Institute of Real Estate Appraisers. *The Appraisal of Real Estate.* 6th ed. Chicago, Ill., 1973. 608p.

Hanford, Lloyd D., Sr. *Feasibility Study Guidelines.* Chicago, Ill., Institute of Real Estate Management, 1972. 131p.

Hanford, Lloyd D., Sr. *Analysis and Management of Investment Property.* 4th ed. Chicago, Ill., Institute of Real Estate Management, 1974. 178p.

Kinnard, William N., Jr. *Income Property Valuation,* Lexington, Mass., D. C. Heath & Co., 1971. 510p.

CHAPTER 8

Creating a Management Plan

INTRODUCTION

In any commercial venture it is not just a "good" result that is wanted, but rather the "best." Simplistically we may think that whenever a net profit (in money or in kind) is shown by a given transaction, the outcome can be called satisfactory; still, it will only be when the net profit has been maximized that the outcome can be classed as optimum. The creation of a management plan is aimed at uncovering that particular strategy which, upon application, produces the greatest yield as against all others.

In modern businesses, planning strategies are arrived at by applying decision-making theory. Given a background of uncertainty, *how one still arrives at a good result* is the foremost question. If the manager knew in advance all of the factors that determine the outcome of a particular decision (plan), and if he had at his finger tips all of the data necessary to take these factors fully into account, there would be no problem. In most instances, however, conditions will be less than ideal. A decision must be made on the plan to be adopted even though certain critical information will be lacking.

The basic rule upon which decision theory is developed is embodied in the idea that the so-called least-prejudiced result will be obtained when one uses all the information that is available, but not more. This idea, technically referred to as "maximizing the uncertainty," follows from the idea of David Hume who, long ago, pointed to the foolishness of basing plans on the presumption of knowledge not actually possessed. It also embodies the still older idea of the Greek philosopher Socrates, who pointed to the greater foolishness of not taking into account all of the facts that actually are known.

In this chapter we give a prescription by which the property manager can create a plan that is based on the realities of the situation. This does not mean that intuition drawn from proven experience factors is to be ignored, but rather that bias and unfounded guesses are to be avoided as much as possible.

The point is that the best management plan always has the character of being the one where risks have been minimized as much as possible simply by the adoption of strategies based on common (logical) sense. Before one can proceed, however, a set of value judgments must be identified and adopted. Otherwise the property manager will not have a clear idea of his goal. Is it a short-term gain that is wanted, or will early losses be accepted as the price to pay for a long-range profit? How much will prestige, business reputation, promises of future business, and the like be valued in comparison to dollar payments?

In other words, it is good business to do good business, but first it must be known what the business is. The property manager with ten equivalent spaces to rent may price them at the level of $500 monthly each, and find only one taker; or, he may price them at $50 monthly each, and have no vacancies. However, either procedure misses the mark if it can be shown that a $200 monthly rental will (on the average) keep half of the spaces filled. This, in a nutshell, is the sense of the problem that confronts the property manager as he seeks to create an optimum management plan.

The adoption of a rental schedule is based upon the value of space *as we found it* when we took over the management of the building. We have not given consideration to the possibility of changes in the design, equipment, or facility of the property or its spaces. Instead, we have contemplated a rental schedule intended to set a value on the units in their present form, having in mind putting them into a state of good repair and cleanliness before offering them to the public.

As we have noted above, property management is a socio-economic service designed to create the "greatest possible net return" from a given building over a "period of years" described as its "remaining economic life." The mere mention of the term "greatest possible" suggests the presence of alternates; the inclusion of a "period of years" suggests long-term planning. In this sense the property manager may be compared to a ship's pilot who sets out across the sea. He must first have an objective; he must then decide upon a course to reach his objective; and, finally, he must have a set of instruments and charts which will serve as implements to keep him on his course. To carry the comparison further, the property manager must first decide whether or not the building *in its present form* will be the vehicle to "the greatest possible return"; if not, he must then plan such changes as will put him on the course to such a return; and, finally, he must set up a projection of his earnings (a budget) by which he can hold those earnings on a true course toward that objective.

Following our example of the property manager who was given a building containing one-, two-, and three-bedroom apartments, we have thus far watched him make a property analysis in which he became thoroughly familiar with the physical structure of the building. We have seen him move through the several processes which lead to the creation of a rental schedule. His next step is the setting up of a preliminary budget. Simply expressed, a budget is nothing more or less than a statement of probable receipts (gross rental schedule less allowance for vacancies and bad debts), *less* estimated expenses for operating, taxes, and insurance. The net balance will be the return the owner may expect to receive from the building in its present form and condition.

If our property manager has found his building's apartments, as presently constituted, highly competitive in the present market, and if he has found that the pattern of demand exactly matches the pattern of the units which he has to sell, then of course the building will be merchandised "as is," and the budget outlined above will serve as his operating plan. If, on the other hand, the analyst has found that the equipment in the building is not up to the standard set by competition and that the one-, two-, and three-bedroom apartments are located in a neighborhood in which the demand is almost exclusively for studio and one-bedroom units, then the manager must investigate the cost and probable return from the installation of competitive equipment and from the remodeling of the premises into units which match the pattern of the market.

The answer to these alternatives lies *entirely* in the economics of their creation. In other words, the manager must make up alternate budgets based upon the installation of new equipment or the remodeling of the building; must analyze the rental schedule which might result from the changes in value of the space; must consider whether or not the owner is justified in making the expenditures involved in each separate program. In a new building, designed to serve a known market in a growing or crystallized community, we can presume that the owner, architect, mortgage banker, and manager have together maximized their planning skills. In older buildings, however, the need for alternate plans is constantly present (both when the manager takes over a new property, and periodically when he is rendering a conscientious service on properties being managed), and therefore deserves some study here.

Rehabilitation

It would seem proper that a text of property management should have for one of its prime objectives the clarification of terms used in the profession. Among such terms there are perhaps none so misunderstood in meaning as the words *rehabilitation, modernization,* and *alteration (remodeling).* The term *rehabilitation* has no particular connotation when used in connection with so-called alternate programs in the creation of a budget. Actually, *rehabilitation* simply means the process of *renewing* the equipment, surfaces, or materials within a building because the said equipment, surfaces, or materials are failing to serve satisfactorily the purposes for which they were intended. In other words, rehabilitation means the restoration to a satisfactory condition without a changing of plan, form, or style.

Thus, it is *rehabilitation* to install a new stove in place of one that has worn out; to repaint a wall whose surface has lost its qualities of protection, beautification, or cleanliness; to re-lay roofing on a roof which has outlived its ability to keep out water; and so forth. Rehabilitation is not a special activity to be performed at any particular time by the property manager. Rather, it is normal maintenance which has been neglected either by the manager himself or by his predecessor. Its special place in the budget comes only as a result of the fact that the property manager who takes over a new account will need to explain to his client that the heavy maintenance expenditures he is called upon to make in the first year are really the result of some previous neglect (i.e., are *rehabilitation,* not maintenance).

Modernization

The trade magazines that serve the property managers of the nation place great emphasis on *modernization.* This is because they know manufacturers of paints, stoves, refrigerators, and a host of other products spend great sums annually on advertising items used for replacement and reconstruction. As might be quickly guessed from its root, *modernization* is simply the employment of *new style* in either maintenance, rehabilitation, or alteration.

A property manager *modernizes* when, instead of replacing a faucet with a replica of the faucet which is worn out, he buys a *new, streamlined* faucet. Likewise, he *modernizes* when he replaces old hardware with hardware of new design instead of just duplicating the hinge or doorknob being replaced. *Modernization* does not describe a specific activity, it merely indicates current style conformity.

Alteration (Remodeling)

It may be said that rehabilitation and modernization, as described above, have for their primary purpose the lengthening of a building's economic life, from the standpoint of its *present design.* For example, in our case-study building of one-, two-, and three-bedroom apartments, *rehabilitation* and *modernization* would result in these apartments' enjoying the maximum functional and style appeal of which they are capable. As we have indicated above, however, it might be considered desirable to change the social function of the building so that it would serve a different type of family unit—to remodel the four-, five-, and six-room apartments into units of one, two, and three rooms. In the process it might be the property manager's intention to have the new units conform to current styles, in which case he would plan to modernize at the same time he *altered.* In still another instance the style-character of a building might conceivably have become so obsolete that it would be necessary to *alter* in order to carry out a *modernization* scheme.

As defined here, *alteration* means the *changing* of a structure. Thus, it is possible to *alter* without *modernizing* (as in the case of an apartment building which needs a change in social function, but which desires to maintain its present period styling), just as it is possible for a building to *modernize* without *altering* (as in the case of the property which streamlines its fixtures without making any structural changes).

BEFORE ALTERATION

Sorely needed alteration was required for this apartment building in order to lengthen its economic life. (See p. 163 for final result.)

The Economics of Alternates

We must take for granted the fact that the conscientious property manager, taking over a building, often will ask his owners to rehabilitate the property as soon and as completely as is economically possible. It is simply unsound to attempt to merchandise a building in which equipment or facilities are not up to the maximum public appeal. Likewise we must assume that the able property manager will *modernize* as he *rehabilitates,* since he must realize that the success of his building over a period of years will depend upon its constant ability to compare favorably in appeal with its competition.

In the average case, rehabilitation will not cost a great deal more than the maintenance that was put off; modernization will cost very little (if any) more than replacement. It is always desirable to maintain the physical welfare of a building, and always desirable (at no greater cost) to keep styling at peak-appeal levels. The question of whether or not to change the structural character of a building, however, is one that requires close analysis of the probable return on invested capital, the so-called alternates of alteration.

Before we give attention to the actual (structural) remodeling of the building whose future is being considered, we should recheck the neighborhood data to make certain that the plan for such projected work has validity in terms of the life expectancy of the remodeled building. For example, it was noted in the previous chapter that the average neighborhood in America tends to peak out in desirability and—from that point forward—proceeds to approach total deterioration asymptotically. And, when the process has reached a certain point of decay, the expectation is that the neighborhood remnants will be bulldozed out of existence for rebuilding from scratch.

Exceptions, of course, may be cited. In most of the older cities there will be neighborhoods possessed of what may be called a "destiny" that gives rise to periodic renewals and a prolonged existence. Involved here is the expression of confidence by consumers, born out of nostalgia if not out of business acumen, that persuades them to invest their money and creative skills through the purchase of deteriorating and dilapidated properties. Such areas as Georgetown in the District of Columbia, the *"Old Towns"* in various cities, and Sausalito in the Bay Area of San Francisco are examples of neighborhoods that have been reclaimed by people who saw in them the opportunities for recapturing the charm and gracious living of bygone times.

In spite of these exceptions, however, one of the most spectacular failures in the history of U.S. housing programs overall has been the fiasco of rehabilitation. Whether undertaken by public agencies, private corporations, labor unions, or not-for-profit associations, the several attempts in recent years to upgrade the physical condition of the central city ghettos have proved to be abject failures, by and large. This matter has already been referred to in chapter 4 (with respect to the governmental involvements). In all categories of cases, however, the candid explanation for the failures seems to relate to

AFTER ALTERATION

The process of modernization through alteration is illustrated above. Note, however, how the building still maintains its period styling. (See p. 161 for "before" photo.)

the fact that the residents who have occupied the rehabilitated units simply have not been capable of protecting the newly reinstated physical and environmental integrity of these properties over their required economic life expectancy.

In any case, at the outset funds invested in the alteration of any building should be considered from two separate points of view:

1. As funds added to the *current* economic value of the building, that is, as funds needed to animate the total value of the property.
2. Separate funds invested to create "added" value to a going enterprise.

As an example of the first type of alteration, let us suppose we managed a ten-apartment building of fifteen rooms each. We will imagine that the building was in an exclusive section with good consumer demand, but due to changes in the social and economic structure of the typical urban family it was impossible to obtain tenants for fifteen-room apartments at any price. Then the *current* economic value of this building would be zero, since the building would have no earnings. Thus, the funds needed to alter the property into apartments of two and three bedrooms (which program, we shall assume, has been judged the highest and best use of the land) would be considered the owner's total investment in the building when completed. In this instance, the process of determining the economics of the alteration would be identical with the process of deciding whether or not to build a new building.

The economic life of the completed project would be estimated, a budget of income and expense set up, proper amortization computed, and the probable net return to the owner established. Depending upon the earning requirements of the owner and the risks involved, it would be decided whether or not to proceed. The most important requisite of proper analysis of this type of problem is the arrival at a *realistic* conception of the building's *current* value before considering the return on the *whole investment* at the time of its completion. Most owners resist the writing down of properties to the proper point of departure, from which alteration returns can be computed.

The second type of alteration involves the expenditure of funds to increase the earnings of a building beyond the limits of its present capacity to earn—whether or not functional alteration is necessary. For example: Let us suppose that we have a building containing one-, two-, and three-room apartments in an area in which one-, two-, and three-room apartments represent the highest and best use of the land. Let us further suppose that the main floor of this property is designed to contain a very spacious Spanish-type lobby and also three stores. Let us imagine further that the apartments in the building were being offered to the public at their maximum attractiveness, and that their values had been built up to the physical limits.

In this case, it would not be possible for the management to increase rentals without losing tenants to buildings of greater general desirability. On the other hand, it might be found that by spending $10,000, management could cut down the size of the lobby, increase its visual desirability, and, at the same time, install two more stores in the space now being poorly used by the public. The procedure in this instance would contemplate the manager's preparing (or having prepared for him by competent people) complete plans and specifications for the work to be done. He would then obtain estimates for the complete cost of the necessary work, plus amounts to be spent for furnishings, decoration, etc. While this was being done he would proceed with an analysis of the income possibilities afforded by the new stores, as well as an estimate of the increased apartment rentals that could be attributable to the improved lobby. He would also determine to what extent the changed structure would affect the operating expense of the property.

When these various steps had been taken, the decision of the manager as to whether or not he should proceed would be based on one of two premises:

1. That the expense of the change could be completely amortized within a stated period; or
2. That the increased value of the property in reflection of the new money invested would make the move profitable.

In the first instance, we assume that the manager represents an owner who has no thought of selling the property. In that case the requirement of complete amortization within a stated period (during which an adequate return is produced) is sound economic judgment. In the second case, the alteration is motivated by a desire to raise the selling price of the property involved. In such a case the decision is based on the profit that will immediately accrue from the expenditure itself. Buyers of furnished apartment buildings sometimes gauge the value of a building at a certain number of times its gross revenue. If a manager is operating such a building for an owner who wishes quickly to increase its value for sales purposes—and if he finds he can spend $75 on an apartment with the result that its rental value will be increased $5 per month—the expenditure of $75 will result in an annual increase of $60 per year. Even at a three-times-rent ratio, a profit of $105 would thus accrue to the owner.

While we understand clearly that the above illustration is questionable from the point of view of sound appraisal, the facts are that buildings are bought and sold every day on yardsticks of gross revenue. In the light of such thinking on the part of buyers and sellers, property managers must recognize the possibilities of this kind of modernization and alteration.

OWNER'S CAPITAL REQUIREMENTS

Returning now from a consideration of "alternate" operating plans to the actual budgeting of income and expense, we find in many instances that when a manager takes over a property for management the owner will say: "Here is my building. Manage it as you see fit, but you *must produce* such-and-such an amount each month in order that I may pay my interest, taxes, and prepayments, and so that I may pocket a modest profit."

If the building is soundly financed and is in good condition, there will be no particular problem in such a request. However, if your estimate of obtainable income (less reasonable operating expense) clearly indicates that it will be impossible properly to maintain the building and at the same time meet the owner's capital requirements—then, by all means, remedy the situation through the arrangement of proper financing or refuse to accept the management of the property. The capital requirements of the owner in no sense should dictate the policy of the manager to his own financial disadvantage.

Good management is a constant. It cannot be adjusted to the owner's cash needs. The property manager who accepts properties under conditions that prevent him from doing what he knows should be done will soon have the reputation of being a poor manager and will eventually lose his employment. The manager's prime responsibility is to himself. He must early and clearly understand that he cannot be a financial magician—no matter how badly he may need a particular piece of business.

THE "END OF THE LINE" BUILDING

For the first time in American history there are a substantial number of properties in both small and large cities that truly can be said to have *negative* value. This situation grows out of the circumstance that eventually the accumulated tax delinquency exceeds the current resale level; hence, even the so-called tax buyers avoid bidding on such parcels. The only possibility of restoring value to this real estate is by completely razing whole contiguous areas of urban blight, re-planning them, and starting anew.

The standard situation in which "end of the line" building conditions are reached finds an owner in possession of a building (almost always in a deteriorated or deteriorating neighborhood) in which the rent-paying capacity of tenants has been declining. This is the result of units being vacated by higher-income tenants who have moved on to superior accommodations in more desirable areas. Two other factors also appear to be present in such situations. First is the case where the present owner has sought to maximize his income stream by holding expenditures to the barest possible level. Second is the case where the caliber of tenants in such marginal buildings is such as to downgrade its housekeeping—both inside and outside of the housing units themselves. As a result of this combination of circumstances, the property's deterioration is accelerated. In the process, the building runs afoul of the city's housing, health, and building officials; it is cited for code and health violations; its tenants withhold rents. In the end, vacancy rises while rents decline. Finally, the owner finds himself in a negative cash-flow position (even after default on property taxes) and under threat of prosecution by public authorities. In desperation, he abandons the property.

It is worthwhile to repeat that most efforts of private and semi-private and public agencies to engage in so-called rehabilitation projects in submarginal areas have proved to be abject failures. The simple fact is that, in a market-oriented society, subcultural poverty groups cannot sustain standard housing units. The answer to the problem must be found in an entirely new approach.

REVIEW QUESTIONS

1. Can the *money needs* of the owner dictate the policy a manager is to follow?
2. What is meant by an *alternative* operating plan?
3. Define *rehabilitation,* and give an example.
4. What basic premises should be used by a manager when proposing alterations? Give an example.
5. Name two types of alterations involving the expenditure of funds and the resulting economic value of the property.
6. What is a *budget?* What is its value?
7. What is *modernization?* Give an example.
8. What is the sense of an "end of the line" building? What can owners do with them? What role can be played by the property manager in such instances?
9. What does decision theory have to do with the creation of a plan (for example, a management plan)?

SELECTED REFERENCES

Hanford, Lloyd D., Sr. *Analysis and Management of Investment Property.* 3d ed. Chicago, Ill., Institute of Real Estate Management, 1970. 178p.

Hanford, Lloyd D., Sr. *The Property Management Process.* Chicago, Ill., Institute of Real Estate Management, 1972. 86p.

Moyer, Jack L. "Elements of Management Planning." *Journal of Property Management,* May–June 1971, pp. 140–142.

The Real Estate Management Department: How to Establish and Operate It. 2nd ed. Chicago, Ill., Institute of Real Estate Management, 1967. 148p.

CHAPTER 9

Merchandising Residential Space

INTRODUCTION

People have to live somewhere. Because of the affluence of Americans (and also because of the year-around climate conditions in the United States), the vast majority have some sort of a roof over their heads. In the urban context, the places of residence are houses (single or multifamily), rooming houses, apartment buildings, dormitories (for example, those associated with institutions), and hotels and motels.

Other categories of lesser importance also can be mentioned in passing. A jail is a dormitory residence of sorts, just as Pullman accommodations correspond to a hotel on wheels. And then there are the summer camps in the suburbs, the mobile homes and trailer parks, hospital beds, nursing homes, military barracks, and other lodging forms so specialized as to need no further mention here.

In fact, this chapter deals only with the merchandising of residential space in the sense of renting or leasing for substantial periods of time. In particular, we shall want to emphasize those aspects that will be of interest to the professional property manager (and resident manager, in some cases) who deals with the renting and leasing of homes and apartments on behalf of the owner interests. (In chapter 11 some of the special but related aspects of managing residential spaces of the condominium/cooperative types will be mentioned as a separate topic.)

Obviously, we shall not be referring to the occupancy of residential space where the occupants themselves are the owners, since in general there will be no property management function involved (except in the condominium/cooperative contexts just mentioned). True, there are some points of contact between the real estate function of selling residential space and the marketing process that holds the attention of property managers. Mention already has been made of this in the first chapters of this book; therefore, now and in the following chapters we are ready to concentrate on those functions and topics of prime and unique importance to the property management profession and to the practice of its various specialized activities.

The process of disposing of available space is most generally called *renting.* Its companion activity—the completion of arrangements to keep a tenant who is already in the space for an additional period—is usually called *renewal.* Both of these processes are frequently referred to as *selling* or *merchandising*. It has always been the opinion of the writer that *renting* and *renewal* are properly described as *merchandising* rather than *selling*.

A sale may be defined as "the transfer, from one person to another for a consideration, of the possession and right of use of some particular article of value to both parties." Such a transfer can only be accomplished if three things have happened to the buyer. First, he must have been given an *opportunity* to buy; second, he must have the *desire* to buy; and, finally, he must have the *ability* to pay for the article purchased. *All* of these three factors are requisite to a sale. Whereas both *selling* and *merchandising* are activities designed to result in the kind of transfer of articles described above, there appears to be a distinct difference in technique as between them.

For example, *selling* seems to be more properly identified with the effort to transfer articles from one to another person who was not previously known to want the article, who hadn't previously admitted a need for the article, and who may not previously have had an opportunity to purchase the article. Selling of this type is well exemplified by life insurance. Here the salesman must seek out his prospect, must create in his mind a desire for life insurance protection in general and for the salesman's offering in particular, and must determine how much life insurance can safely be bought by his prospect. Similar in technique is the sale of magazine subscriptions, encyclopedias, and services of all kinds. *Merchandising,* however, is the type of activity involved in creating *specific desirability* in a particular article which people are already known to be using almost universally—and then pointing out values in that article that will appeal to the buyer. Buyers in this classification furnish themselves with the opportunity to purchase. Whether or not they buy depends largely upon the ability of the merchandiser to present a product which meets with specifications of the buyer and to present it in such a manner as will reveal all of its values.

Excellent examples of this type of exchange are dress shops and haberdasheries. In the former case, a woman comes into a shop and asks to see a dress. The woman has thereby furnished herself the opportunity to buy, and has admitted her desire to buy. The clerk who takes care of her and the store for which the clerk works are both merchandisers. The store has sought to create an atmosphere which would be conducive to comfortable selection. It has purchased a line of dresses which it believes have wide appeal in the consumer groups it hopes to reach. The effectiveness of the clerk lies in her ability to determine the customer's tastes; her ability to produce from a large stock of dresses just the one which the customer will buy.

In the case of the man who goes into the haberdashery, steps up to the counter and announces, "I want to buy a necktie," the situation is precisely the same. The clerk's chances of making a sale are dependent upon his ability to produce from the stock a necktie which will match the taste of the buyer.

While it is true that in many instances the clerk can clinch a sale by pointing out values in the particular tie which the customer might not have seen ("it is an excellent match for that suit—it has a wrinkle-proof lining, etc."), the customer obviously was already sold on the idea of buying a tie before he ever saw the clerk.

Applying this type of analysis to the *renting* of homes and apartments, we conclude that *renting* is merchandising, rather than *selling*. It is never necessary to convince anyone that he ought to live somewhere; that he ought to occupy a room, an apartment, or a house. The reason is clear. People already do live somewhere, just as they eat and wear neckties or dresses. The property manager's problem thus centers upon getting known customers to see his particular space, to desire his particular space—and getting the type of customers who are able to pay his prices. The solution of this problem thus involves three major activities of the property manager, each of which is discussed as a subtopic in the following pages.

GETTING TENANTS TO THE PROPERTY

Since merchandisers of shoes, dresses, and neckties know that the public is buying such items of apparel every day, their first problem is to get the public to see *their particular* shoes, dresses, and neckties. The answer to that problem is found in various ways involving, for example, advertising and promotion, reputation (which is a combination of advertising and satisfied customers), and location. These merchandisers know that the greater the number of people who see their merchandise, the greater will be their volume of sales. The availability of numbers of anxious-to-buy customers (as in the case of 100 percent commercial locations) is known as *consumer pressure,* and is the condition sought by all who deal in those types of merchandise which the public is known to want to buy.

Precisely the same principles of merchandising apply to the renting of space. Following the sequence of the steps toward producing income which have been discussed thus far in this volume, we now contemplate a building upon which a rental schedule based on scientific market analysis already has been placed. We are ready to show our space to prospective customers. Our job is to *get prospects.* Our decision as to the most effective and most economical procedure will depend on several factors, chief among which are:

Building age—In the case of a new building it should be a good deal easier to attract numbers of prospects to the property than in the case of a building which has been completed for a long period. The natural curiosity of women shoppers who have watched the new building's progress over the period of construction, plus the keen desire of the renting public to live in such a building, will act to generate a good deal of renting activity. This curiosity about, and anxiety for, new space will vary with the number of competitive structures under construction, but it is safe to say that a new building has much greater self-generated prospect pulling power than an older property. This extra pulling power is needed badly in the case of a new building. The reason is simple. A new building needs to rent 100 percent of its space at one time, while the average standing structure of a residential character needs to rent less than one-third of its space in any given year.

To take full advantage of the interest and curiosity generated by the commencement of a new building's construction, developers may be inclined to construct a display model (especially when the project is noteworthy because of size and/or intended function). For example, models may be employed that are exact and full-scale replicas of the spaces eventually to be marketed, with furniture and decorations (even flowers) in place. Thus, prospective tenants can see exactly the possibilities of what they will be renting or buying, in advance of occupancy. In cases where it is not possible to create such models

BUILDING SIGN

The above sign indicates to the passerby the facilities of the property and how information is to be obtained.

in advance of the building's completion, such display model units can be set up later. In any case, there should be signs prominantly displayed that acquaint the public with the intended function(s) of the building under construction, the size of its units, how they may be inspected, and whom to contact about renting and buying.

Building size—The number of units to be rented or sold dictates the business promotion and advertising program of every merchandiser from chewing gum to automobiles. Quite naturally, the building manager will need fewer able-to-buy prospects to rent a home, than he will to rent a 2,500-unit housing project. Under a proper rental schedule and with proper promotion, there should be a definite relationship between the number of units for sale and the number of qualified prospects required.

As a rule of thumb, five *qualified prospects* per unit should be sufficient to lease out many properties. If more are required, then something is wrong with the price, the effort, or the attractiveness of the merchandise. If the property rents on the basis of a sale for each two qualified prospects, then price should be strengthened. This ratio is applicable to unfurnished buildings with units of normal size in ordinary price ranges. Furnished apartments of the one-, two-, and three-room type should rent on a one-to-three ratio; large apartments, houses, and de luxe units will require from six to nine prospects per sale. The prospects required thus vary with the size and character of the building and influence the decisions of the manager concerning his promotion program.

Building location—All of us are in the habit of associating volume of business with location when we think of retail trade in standard items. We seldom couple location with cost-of-business-production—the factor which makes certain locations most valuable.

For example, many impulse merchandisers (cigarettes, liquor, candy, etc.) will pay higher-than-normal rentals for relatively small spaces at high-traffic locations. This, of course, reflects the economics of the situation, in which the net return is greater from the payment of a premium rental than from the payment of a lesser rental plus advertising in the same total amount. Kiosks, office building cigar stands, the newsboy's square yard of space on a busy street corner advertise themselves enough by their physical presence. Likewise, for certain stores handling widely available merchandise, proprietors often will accept high rentals for premium locations simply as an expression of their promotional policy. And people have other good reasons to want to reside in high-rent districts.

On the other side, however, in recent years Americans have come to depend more and more on private automobiles for shopping. Originally the appeal of the newly formed shopping centers to store owners and renters was the lower occupancy costs associated with outlying (suburban) locations. In the meantime, of course, this advantage has more and more been lost because of the counteracting costs of providing elaborate shopping center facilities (parking areas, child nurseries, enormous modern buildings with air-conditioning, etc.). Even so, situations continue to exist where cut-rate stores will be located in low-rent (less desirable) locations, to attract those customers who (forgetting that gasoline is not free) will drive to the ends of the earth in search of a bargain. And so it is with residential space.

ADVERTISING

In the light of the fact that a building properly priced usually needs only five prospects per unit for sale, the manager who is contemplating a promotion program for a building must know the number of prospects for his particular building which will be produced by the building itself. In other words, he must accurately estimate the strength of the *consumer pressure* which the neighborhood is exerting upon the type of space he will have for sale.

If the building is located in a densely populated area in which occupancy is high, if the building's suites are of a size most in demand within the area, and if the rental schedule matches closely the consumer purchasing power within the area, then there will be no need for a sizable appropriation for prospect production. On the other hand, if the building is located in an area of comparatively sparse population (as, for example, a newly developed neighborhood), if there is very little compatibility between the size of the units being offered and the demand pattern (as in the case of a de luxe building of nine-, ten-, and eleven-room apartments on the Gold Coast of Chicago), or if the price level of the unit is far above the average purchasing power of consumers, then a carefully thought-out program of advertising and promotion is vitally necessary. Having analyzed these three factors thoroughly, the manager now knows:

1. The number of prospects he needs.
2. The number available
3. The need for an advertising and promotion program

In his previous work on neighborhood analysis, market analysis, and rental schedules, the manager obviously will have discovered the sources from which he can expect to draw his tenants. If his building needs to promote prospects, he also knows where they may be found and on what basis they must be attracted. His only problem is the selection of media to use in reaching prospects at the lowest possible cost.

Since the subject of advertising and business promotion is one of the few in the realm of property management on which there is any extensive literature, comparatively little space in this book will be devoted to this subject. However, we will mention the types of advertising that are suggested, without going into the relative merits of each or the methods of their creation. The chief types are described in the next few paragraphs.

Signs at the Building

Every residential building (whether or not it is 100 percent rented) should have at least a small and tasteful sign on it. This, quite properly, will inform interested prospects of the name of the manager (resident or otherwise), the general type of units contained within, how further information is to be obtained, and the like. Sometimes (for example, at vacation resorts) information can be given about rental prices and the present vacancy situation.

Some managers (indeed, some residents), of course, may feel that a sign on a building is degrading; but such an attitude clearly can be to the disadvantage of the owner and manager alike. A discretely placed sign tends to develop prospects—and prospects are the lifeblood of the business. An unobtrusive sign that provides the essential information in most cases may be regarded as a "must."

Signs Elsewhere

The use of signs as institutional advertising is good practice. Moreover, the use of boards and wall displays for certain types of buildings is also sometimes effective. The difficulty with this latter type of advertising is that the circulation is generally quite meager and that it can be employed successfully only on large properties.

Newspaper Advertising

In most cities where there are two or more newspapers, one tends to be the dominant force in classified advertising. Thus, one newspaper more than others becomes the place where apartments and houses are most widely advertised along with the personals, help wanted, lost and found, and other classified notices.

Classified newspaper advertising is a basic medium employed in the United States by managers and landlords. As the average size of residential projects has increased in recent years, developers have relied to an increasing extent upon so-called display advertising. For example, this is a common mode for the original marketing campaign of a new property. And, in the metropolitan areas especially, the major newspapers will periodically (e.g., weekly) publish special real estate sections with information of interest to property owners, realtors, managers, tenants—in fact, to the public at large. No other medium of advertising can reach so many people with such comprehensive coverage.

TV/Radio Advertising

The use of TV advertising usually is effective in the description and presentation of new properties that are for rent, lease, or condominium purchase. It is also costly, but less so in the smaller communities. This means, usually, that in large communities a payoff will be realized only in the advertising of large

Welcome aboard The Spirit of Ballena Village.

It doesn't float...It moves a little.

Your apartment at the "land yacht" in Alameda comes with all the things you'd expect from a luxury apartment. Wall to wall carpeting. Hotpoint kitchens. Everything.

But it also comes with a lot of things you wouldn't expect...starting with a phenominal view of San Francisco and the Bay.

Add swimming pools, a recreation club, gymnasium, saunas and a yacht basin almost at your doorstep. They're the things that make life at Ballena Village more

like a luxury cruise than life at a luxury apartment.

The price? Anything but luxurious.

Rents are from $185.00.

See for yourself. Take the Alameda Tube to Webster Street. Right on Central Avenue, 5 blocks to 1375 Ballena Boulevard. Phone: 865-2225. If you forget the directions, come to Alameda and ask for the Yacht Harbor.

Ballena Village Apts.
1375 Ballena Boulevard
Alameda, California
865-2321

Raintree South is more than a good buy.

See for yourself how the natural rustic settings of these 3 to 5 bedroom homes can provide you and your family with the best in gracious country living.

And while you're there, inspect Raintree's championship golf course featuring bent grass greens and Bermuda fairways. Both the golf course and Raintree's Country Club facilities are convenient to Raintree South.

So do yourself and your family a favor. Take a look at Raintree South this weekend. With soaring property prices in south Charlotte, it could be more than just a good buy. Drive out Providence Road past Hwy. 51 to Raintree Lane and follow the signs.

🌲 Raintree South Telephone 364-6711

Ridgegate
Town Home Village
A Wider World of Sports

It's 'round-the-clock fun to live at Ridgegate, a unique town home village complete with five separate recreation centers. Tennis courts right at hand for day and night use. Or practice your best dive into a pool that's free of wall-to-wall people. Like variety? For starters, you might try paddle tennis and shuffleboard, and then, when the sun's over the yardarm, avail yourself of one of the large sheltered patios. Have a party. Enjoy! All this without venturing outside Ridgegate's guarded gates. But perhaps golf's your bag! Choose among several Palos Verdes Peninsula courses. Hire a horse (or board your own at one of the several local stables), and explore the many nearby bridle trails. When not otherwise involved, there's the whole blue Pacific Ocean to tempt you. Surfing, sport fishing, boating for the fun of it. If it sounds great, be sure you own a luxurious Ridgegate Town Home. A beautiful, quiet place that lets you rest up for the next busy day. Come see!

2, 3, & 4 Bedrooms, 1½ and 2½ Baths
A Palos Verdes Peninsula Address

from $45,900 to $61,500
Excellent Conventional Financing

Sales Center open daily from 10 a.m. to 6 p.m.
Hawthorne Boulevard at Highridge Rd.
Palos Verdes Peninsula
Telephone: (213) 377-6777

Another quality Peninsula project of S. H. Morris Development Company

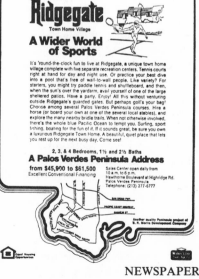

If you can't have a Mediterranean villa this year, you can have a Villa on Travis.
From $32,500.

Inspired by the noble Roman villas, The Villa on Travis is a hillside village set into the cliffs rising from Lake Travis. Each condominium captures the informal charm and sophistication of the European villa; each is carefully placed to preserve the ecological balance.

Whether you select a Villa as a year-round residence or a weekend retreat, you'll enjoy the excitement of resort living, plus the value of a fine home. And what choices there are—everything from intimate, one-story flats to two-story homes.

With spectacular fire-mile views of Lake Travis. And much more, including: 2-4 bedrooms, fireplaces, private decks, built-in kitchens, utility areas, walk-in closets, private golf carts with each residence, tennis, handball, swimming pool, exercise gym, private entertainment facilities, saunas, and private dock.

The Villa on Travis is two miles west of Mansfield Dam on RR 620. Telephone (512) 266-1361 and make an appointment to preview this exciting way of living.

The Villa on Travis
Lakefront Condominium Homes/OPEN SUNDAY

NEWSPAPER ADVERTISING

The above advertisments illustrate careful thought as to style and copy as well as reflect the character of the various properties.

(multiple-unit) properties that have selective appeal for particular classes of able-to-pay viewers.

Radio advertising also involves careful analysis of its cost-to-prospect ratio. Some, for example, hold to the idea that even radio advertising makes more sense when undertaken in the smaller communities (for example, on suburban stations).

Radio and television advertising has been a part of the American scene for the last 50 and 30 years, respectively. Even so, the potentialities have not been exhausted for any of the markets addressed. Real estate advertising in all its forms represents an occasional event in the life of the average purchaser (who at the same time may be consuming—and consumed by—two packs of cigarettes a day and 20 cokes a week, or who spends 200 hours a month in self-amusement, or who makes 2,000 telephone calls a year). Through future innovations, however, the present imbalances may be lessened. Perhaps someday TV viewers will be provided with an electronic way to choose their advertisements as well as their programs. In any case, it is up to the property manager to find the ways in which the new and emerging media modes can be utilized for his particular advertising objectives.

Direct Mail Advertising

Although we have observed that every family is a prospect for a home or apartment, we definitely do not imply that they are prospects necessarily for *your* apartment or house. To be of use to you, they must first be qualified as to family size, family ages, income, location preference, and habits of living. If families can be selected who qualify as bona fide prospects for *your* building, then direct mail advertising is a highly effective medium. The preparation of copy and the extravagance of its format, however, are secondary to the selection of those to whom the finished piece is mailed. Most purchased lists are highly inefficient and should be used sparingly. The only safe method for the manager to employ in using direct mail on the average building is the preparation of his own list on the basis of local and private information.

If direct mail advertising is selected as a medium, the copy for the piece and its format should be aimed directly at the intelligence and/or the income level of the selected recipients. Costly mailing pieces unselectively aimed at people frequently create the wrong impression and lose their effectiveness. Inferior pieces sent to the above-average groups produce a negative result such as a lack of confidence in the building or in the organization promoting the building.

THE ECONOMICS OF ADVERTISING

Here we have deliberately refrained from elaborating upon methods of preparing advertising. That subject is beyond the intended scope of this text, and there are many books on advertising theory and practice available to the interested student. There has been very little written elsewhere, however, about the economic considerations that confront the property manager when he contemplates the advantages of advertising. Accordingly, that subject will now be discussed briefly.

By the phrase economics of advertising, we mean simply *when* to advertise, *how much to spend* for advertising, and *how to judge the effectiveness* of advertising.

In the usual case, the buildings controlled by professional property managers are too small to require so-called *institutional* advertising—advertising designed to raise the prestige of the firm in the given community. Practically speaking, the only reason for advertising any building is to develop prospects in sufficient number to fill the vacancies which exist at the present or are known to be coming into existence at a future date. Thus, the answer to the question *when to advertise* is definitely related to occupancy condition. If there are no vacancies and no prospect of vacancies, no advertising is needed. In large buildings, where continuous turnover is normal, it is quite possible that continuous advertising is needed.

There is no set rule that can be applied to the amount of advertising necessary for any individual property. As we have noted earlier in this chapter, some buildings are so located and so designed that they generate sufficient *consumer pressure* to provide enough prospects to maintain satisfactory occupancy without any advertising. Other properties are so isolated from the renting public that the only practical method of obtaining prospects is through advertising. In the former type of building, the manager can decide upon his advertising program by asking himself the following question: "If I advertised in known media, could I increase the *consumer pressure* upon my units sufficiently to enable me to increase rents or occupancy; and, if so, would the amount of expenditure necessary to produce the increased volume of prospects be a profitable investment?"

This question can easily be answered by experimenting with advertising in various media. The probabilities are that if the building's units are properly priced, the experiment will prove that advertising for this purpose will not pay. However, any manager of a large property owes it to himself, and his client, to make frequent experiments of this kind as a check against his price and his market.

In the case of the smaller, isolated property which has difficulty in attracting prospects through the simple process of posting a sign indicating vacancy, the need for advertising is obvious. Here the amount that should be spent can be determined only by analysis on a cost-per-prospect basis. For example, in periods when there is a comparative shortage of dwelling units, the insertion of a small classified ad, which tells the renting public that there is a five-room apartment at such-and-such an address at a rental of $200 per month, may bring ten prospects to the building, two of whom would have rented the apartment. Suppose this ad cost $30; then the cost per prospect would have been $3.00 and there would, of course, be no question as to the advisability or effectiveness of advertising.

On the other hand, let us suppose that renting conditions were not good; that there was an abundance of vacancy in the community. Suppose further that the manager inserted an ad at a cost of $20 and got only one prospect for his $265 apartment. He would know that he needed (on the average) five prospects in order to make a lease, and would immediately conclude that his ad would have to be repeated for five days in order to get a deal. Certainly he would consider that the expenditure of $100 for a one-year lease on a $265 apartment would be good business, so he would conclude that he should continue his advertising for the five-day period.

Let us suppose, however, that it was necessary for him to advertise in a weekly publication (or that the only effective advertising day in his daily paper was Sunday), and that he would, therefore, probably have to wait five weeks to get his lease. Then, of course, he would have to compute the value of the waiting time as an added cost of making a deal, since the property manager essentially sells *time,* not *space.* Five weeks' time in itself would be worth slightly more than $265, and adding the cost of the advertising, the new tenant would cost him over $365.

Now, the solution of the property manager's dilemma in this case revolves around the question whether or not the apartment (believed to be worth a $265 rental according to the current condition of the local market) should be given to the first prospect who offers $250. This offer, of course, represents a $15 per month rent reduction that over the period of a year would amount to a $180 loss. On the other hand, the manager might have occasion to speculate that the cost of advertising to find a customer willing to pay the asking price of $265, plus the loss of waiting some weeks for a response, would overall make it sensible to accept the $250 monthly rental offer as soon as it was offered.

In other words, as in all phases of business and other activities that depend heavily upon decision making, a choice is to be made among several alternatives. More than that, there will be a background of uncertainty that makes it impossible to choose between the alternatives so that the probability of failure is reduced to zero. To complete the primitive example given above, the property manager strives to zero in on the asking price that guarantees a maximization of the net profit to the management/owner interests.

The answer to the problem being posed depends mostly upon two factors, namely, the trend of the market at the time and the number of apartments of the same type in the building in which it is located.

If the trend of the market (because of high vacancy and a lack of favorable trend in the general business picture) is downward, then the manager is well advised to make the reduction involved in the cheaper method of obtaining a new tenant. If the market trend is upward, then the manager will do well to consider a second factor, namely, "How will my reduction in this price affect the tenants in the other apartments?" If he feels that the reduction in the case of the vacancy will affect the price of his other units, then he should deliberately wait as long as is required to find a customer willing to pay the asking price.

From these examples we see that the question of when and how much to advertise is merely one of common sense applied to the problem on a simple cost basis (cost being figured, not in the amount of money spent for the advertising itself, but on *the net cost to the building after combining the cost of vacancy with the cost of advertising*). Many property managers think only in terms of the cost of the purchased advertising and are not conscious of the often greater cost of property vacancy.

Judging the effectiveness of advertising is simply a matter of keeping accurate checks on the number of prospects produced by various media and then determining the prospect-producing cost of each. The most effective medium is the one that produces the prospect at the lowest cost, time, and volume considered.

THE TECHNIQUE OF RENTING

Simply expressed, the technique of renting is the process of creating the *desire to buy* in people to whom we have given the *opportunity to buy*. This *desire to buy* in the mind of the buyer results from the creation of maximum value in the product shown to the buyer, plus the complete exposition of value by the person who exhibits the product.

It is obvious even to the beginner in property management that the condition of the space shown is a factor of great importance in success or failure in stimulating the desire of the prospect. The procedures for putting space in the condition of greatest visual desirability are maintenance procedures, discussed in chapter 28. We shall concern ourselves here only with the manager's deportment in exhibiting space. It is assumed, of course, that the space being shown has been well cleaned and given a fresh appearance.

Given a buyer who has already indicated his or her interest in the merchandise for sale, the ability of the salesman to make that buyer accept his merchandise at the price he asks depends entirely upon the salesman's pointing out sufficient value in that merchandise to warrant the buyer's parting with the amount of money required to obtain possession. In other words, the duty of the salesman is to see that the prospect gets *all* of the pertinent information which could produce a favorable decision and that the information be transmitted in a courteous, considerate, and sympathetic manner.

Prospects are never *sold* an apartment or house which they do not want. The prospect who presents herself at your building has already answered several questions in her own mind; has already taken many steps toward reaching a conclusion that your merchandise meets her qualifications. No doubt she has already concluded that the general location is suitable. She has felt reasonably confident that the price is somewhere near her budgeted allowance for rent, that the size of the units, as either advertised in the paper or stated on the sign in the front of the building, meets her needs, and that the building's exterior at least does not arouse sufficient sales resistance to warrant her passing it by.

It is improbable that any rental agent could change a prospect's mind on any of these basic requirements, regardless of the artifices he might employ. Moreover, it would be unwise for him to seek to do so. This is because the prospect should not pay more than she can afford for rent, should be sufficiently well satisfied as to location to assure her permanence of residence, and should be housed in quarters which are soundly suited to the requirements of her family.

We have spoken of the tenant who presents herself at your building. Before continuing to discuss her reception at the building, let us examine the recommended technique of the property manager when the prospect, instead of coming directly to the building, comes to the property manager's office, and asks for a list of apartments. The lazy and inefficient manager will dig into his desk, produce a list, and hand it over to the prospect. The good manager, who realizes that prospects cost money and are vital to his success in maintaining high occupancy, will first try to find out the prospect's requirements for location and range of price and size of the apartment or number of rooms in the house. If he does not happen to have a dwelling which comes within the specifications of the prospect, he will frankly tell her so. He will create goodwill for himself and his firm by thanking her courteously for having called, and will take her name for future use when he might have something that will fill her needs. The smart merchandiser realizes that his merchandise cannot possibly have universal appeal, and he saves his sales efforts for those prospects whom he has a fair chance of converting into actual tenants.

There is no substitute in renting for *accompanying* a prospect to the space which she is to see. No matter how thoroughly the manager describes the unit and points out its values before sending the prospect to see the dwelling, the average prospect's memory is short, her ability to visualize limited. The manager should either go with the prospect to the building, or buildings, or arrange to have a qualified janitor or caretaker on the premises when she arrives.

If it is impossible for him to leave his office, then it is his duty prior to her leaving to carefully point out all of the values of the apartment or house. For purposes of review, we refer the reader to the table of values contained in the portion of this text which deals with setting the rental schedule. Each of these factors can be related specifically to the building, or buildings, which the manager is recommending for the inspection of the prospect. In this connection it is important that the manager select only those which most nearly fit his prospect's requirements and submit not more than three buildings for inspection. Many prospects are lost by showing them so much merchandise that they become confused. More are lost by their being discouraged by the task of visiting too many properties.

The process of pointing out values in a product is a fascinating part of the merchandiser's work. It presents an endless opportunity for imagination, for experimenting in the intensely interesting realm of human influence. Very frequently the simple exposition of values can produce results which would ordinarily be considered impossible, in the light of common conceptions. For example, it is likely that if you were approached with a proposal to trade $2 for a twenty-five cent piece, you would scoff at the proposition as ridiculous.

However, if the person who offered to make the trade told you a story about the twenty-five cent piece, explaining that it was a special coinage in commemoration of the Columbian Exposition—that there were only five hundred like it in the world, that they were eagerly sought after by numismatists the country over—very soon you would probably be willing to trade $2 for this twenty-five cent piece. Actually, you would have been shown value which you did not know existed, thus creating in your mind a desire stronger than your desire to keep the $2. This same technique is the basis of successful renting.

Showing the Unit

If you have been the type of property manager who shows a prospect through a house or an apartment by simply opening the front door and leading her through the various rooms, then you have weakened your sales presentation. For just as there is a technique of what to say in order to sell Fuller brushes, there is a preferred technique in the presentation of a house or apartment for rent. When the prospect is first met at the building, the manager should approach her courteously and, with a smile, say: "My name is Jones, the manager (or rental agent, caretaker, janitor as the case may be) of the building." Almost invariably the woman will respond first with her own name, and will then state that she is interested in a certain type of dwelling unit.

If the building has an office the exhibitor should ask her to step in, and should proceed to determine as fully as possible her requirements as to price, space, and equipment. He should learn as much as possible about her family and their requirements. He should then ask her to accompany him to inspect an apartment which he believes will exactly suit her needs. On the way to the apartment he should begin pointing out values in the building itself: the exterior; character of tenancy; the method of maintenance employed; the neatness of entrances, halls, and corridors; the service offered and the various facilities (such as laundries, recreation rooms, etc.) which the building affords its tenants; the policies of management which ensure peace, quiet, and wholesome comfort; and the safeguards which promote and maintain safety for the residents.

When the apartment which is to be shown is reached, the exhibitor should say as he opens the door: "Here is an apartment which I think you will like." Then, in an unobtrusive way, the exhibitor should watch his prospect carefully to see what she is examining and point out the values of that particular thing which she may not be able to see. For example, if she looks out of the window, point out to her the most pleasant things about the view. If there is no view, but plenty of light, tell her the value of such optional window treatments as venetian blinds and the special price the building has procured for tenants who desire to buy them. If she looks at the stove, show her how easily it works and how clean it has been kept. On her first cursory inspection, do not force this information upon her, but simply watch the things she has selected to look for, since they are the most important in her mind. As she looks at them, give her the qualities of those particular things which would make them most attractive.

During the first look about, note the values which she is missing. If she appears to be sold and ready to take the apartment, say no more, but guide her to your office for the filing of an application. If she is apparently not sold to the point of closing immediately, then point out the values which she overlooked by saying, "Did you notice that the hardware throughout the apartment has been refinished, that the closet off this small hall is especially handy for linens, that the bedroom is away from the living room and is unusually quiet if your neighbors happen to be entertaining?" The manager should never appear anxious over a deal. He should offer these additional points of information in a manner which simply indicates his own enthusiasm for his building, as contrasted with high-pressure salesmanship.

When the apartment has been thoroughly examined, the prospect will certainly ask the manager one or more questions. These he should answer completely without going into too much detail and again without exhibiting any undue anxiety over the hoped-for decision. When the prospect is ready to leave the apartment the manager should not reveal any desire to delay her departure. He should maintain a casual, sympathetic interest, but while leaving the apartment he should tell her about the conveniences and advantages of location and the qualities of the neighborhood.

In his original interview in his office he learned something about her family and her manner of living. In his talk on the neighborhood he can draw on this knowledge to point out special values. For instance, if she has children, he can tell her about the school facilities, the distance and way to the schools which serve his building, and the comparative safety of the route which the children travel. If she has no children, he can tell her how close they are to the movies, to churches, and to activities in which he thinks she may be interested.

In the case of unfurnished apartments, most prospects do not rent on their first visit, especially if a woman is alone. She usually must come back to show the unit to her husband or roommate. Notwithstanding this fact, the manager should give her an opportunity to announce her decision at once, and should make one leading statement to that end. We use the term *announce* her decision advisedly since, in most cases, the woman shopper will have made up her mind on the basis of the values which she has seen, but will hesitate to *announce* that decision until she has had another person's confirmation of her judgment.

From her attitude the manager can generally tell whether or not she has been favorably impressed, as she will usually say that she will be back at a specific time, or she will make some statement of specific nature. If and when she has made such a statement, then the manager can adroitly press for a specific appointment, his concern being expressed on her account, and still not indicating anything but a genuine interest in having his building enjoy her tenancy.

It is obvious that a woman prospect will not bring her husband or room-mate to see an apartment on a return visit, unless she has seen values in that apartment which have caused her to make a favorable decision.

On the second (accompanied) visit, the woman takes the role of the sales-man. Knowing her companion, she is much more likely to dwell upon those values that will prove effective. It is safe, therefore, for the manager to adopt the attitude that there is no real need for him to supplement her descriptions and arguments.

In this connection, it is worth noting that the changes in life styles that have marked the last two decades (and that promise to be even more important in the future) have introduced a number of tenant types who do not conform to the conventional family patterns. In some cases these groups (for example, so-called swingers) in fact become a market target; but in other cases they may be made unwelcome. The old adage to the effect that "birds of a feather flock together" applies to the compatibility of people living together in the same residence, as it does to other aspects of social life.

It is significant to note that almost anyone can be taught to do a reasonably good job of space merchandising. While there is no substitute for a pleasant personality, the process of showing an apartment successfully does not demand the same caliber of salesmanship that is needed in the type of selling which creates the whole desire for the thing to be sold. We again note that the apartment prospect already wants an apartment, and the job of the manager is to make the desire apply specifically to his apartment.

We have pointed out that the probabilities of actual rentals are greatly increased when the prospect is accompanied by a person trained in the values which the unit affords. We also are cognizant of the fact that many buildings do not warrant resident rental agents and that many management offices cannot afford to send a man or woman along with each prospect who comes to the office to inquire for a dwelling place. However, in most buildings of between six and fifty units (it is recommended that all buildings of over fifty units employ a resident space exhibitor), there is a resident janitor or caretaker who can be trained to show apartments. This training is more fully discussed in a separate chapter of this book, but we simply point out here the fact that a management organization or a property manager will be more successful if an exhibitor accompanies each prospect, provided that exhibitor has been trained in the technique of renting.

THE TECHNIQUE OF RENEWALS

From almost every point of view, it is more important to renew a lease than to make a new lease. In the first place, there is no danger of the loss through vacancy which inevitably occurs in a normal market when one tenant moves out and another must be found to take his place. In the second place, it is always cheaper to satisfy an existing tenant than to condition an apartment or house for a new tenant. Finally, a building enjoys greater stability of character if it is made up of long-term tenants.

The technique of renewals involves the whole business of satisfying customers. The property manager who is successful at renewing leases is usually a man who appreciates that every contact with a tenant is a sales contact, and who remembers constantly that he will shortly be negotiating with all of his tenants for renewal of leases.

Many property managers allow themselves to get into a belligerent attitude respecting the requests of tenants. They fall into the habit of thinking that the public is out for all that it can get, that it is unreasonable. Now, while every person who deals with the public knows that there are some tenants who demand unreasonable service, most tenants are good tenants and most tenant requests are reasonable. For that reason, students of property management are warned against getting into the habit of classifying tenant requests as *complaints*. Rather, the property manager should adopt the Golden Rule as a method of measuring the validity of tenants' wants. In other words, if tenant Jones calls your office and asks that the leaking faucet in his bathroom be taken care of, think to yourself, "If I had a leaking faucet in my bathroom, wouldn't I want it fixed?" As a matter of fact, the tenant who calls about a leaking faucet is actually doing the property manager and the property owner a favor.

A tenant's opinon of a building, and of the property manager, is generally the result of his *experience* over the period of his lease. This *experience* is the net result of all of the various contacts the tenant has had with the janitor, the decorator, and the members of the property manager's organization. Now, since most tenants are reasonable in demands, their *experience* with the building in which they live will be satisfactory if all of these contacts with the property manager or his representatives have been well and efficiently handled. Perhaps the greatest single threat to satisfaction is procrastination on the part of the property manager or his employees. Frequently a tenant will make a thoroughly reasonable request to the janitor of the building who will agree to take care of the matter and then promptly forget about it. The tenant will have to make the same request again, often two or three times. Nothing is more destructive of goodwill.

Equally exasperating from the tenant's point of view is the indecisive property manager who will "think it over," when the tenant would like to know if he can have a new shade in his living room. The property manager who can not make firm and final decisions will never be successful in his handling of tenants. If a request can be handled, then it should be taken care of *at once.* If it is not possible to carry out the tenant's wishes, then the tenant should be told so, firmly and courteously. Very few enemies are made by refusal of requests, but hundreds are made through procrastination.

The real estate manager must recognize that it is impossible for him to become intimately associated with his tenants on a social basis. Such intimacy leads to embarrassing situations with the tenants involved and inevitably convinces other tenants that the manager is *playing favorites*—a feeling which will increase other tenants' demands at the time of lease renewal and will greatly weaken the property manager's negotiating position.

THE ADVANTAGES OF INFORMATION

There are scores of legitimate reasons for the failure of a property manager to renew a lease. If the tenant is moving away from the city, if he has bought a house of his own, if his family has grown beyond the size of his unit, or if there has been a death; these reasons are beyond the control of the manager, and he cannot charge himself with failure in his renewal program.

Under normal circumstances the tenant whose lease is expiring is under no pressure to move. The question of whether or not he will stay is a matter of negotiation. Now, it is important for us to realize that there are very few periods in our economy when leases expire in a stable market. Rentals are either going up or going down; vacancy is either increasing or it is decreasing. The lease expiration, then, is a focal point of bargaining between the tenant and the building owner. The elements of the bargaining are:

1. The question of whether or not the tenant will renew at all
2. The amount of rent to be paid
3. The extent of the repairs and rehabilitation to be done under the terms of the renewal
4. The length of lease term.

All four of these factors are vital to the decisions which must be reached by the property manager and the tenant.

In chapter 19 we shall discuss at some length the development of a tenant credit file in which pertinent information about each individual tenant is systematically recorded. It need only be said here that this file should also contain information which will be valuable to the negotiator at the time of the tenant's lease expiration. For example: Let us suppose that the negotiation is taking place in a falling market, that the rental of the apartment is $200, and the property manager feels that it might be necessary for him to drop the rent to $190 in order to hold the tenant. Let us suppose further that the manager knows that the tenant has a grand piano which will cost $100 to move. It is obvious that the tenant would not risk the payment of this sum in order to save $120 in a year. Or suppose that the tenant recently bought wall-to-wall carpeting. The existence of investments also will be a deterrent factor to moving. This use of information is not encouraged for the purpose of taking advantage of tenants in an unjustified manner. All negotiation over price is a matter in which the participants maneuver for position and in which significant information plays an important role.

This type of information can prove just as valuable in periods of rising prices. Frequently if the manager believes that an apartment is worth $25 more on a renewal, the tenant will plead that the raise is too much and that he cannot afford the full raise, but will settle for $12.50. If, on the other hand, the manager knows that the tenant just bought a new expensive automobile, he will perhaps have a basis for refuting the tenant's claims of inability to pay.

Elsewhere in this text, we shall discuss the market phases of the important element of market influences on the amount of maintenance work to be done under renewals—a factor which is frequently the most important phase of the negotiation. Let it be said here, however, that the manager must realize that the good tenant is a valuable asset, that his wants are usually less than those of a new tenant, that a lease renewal is by all odds the most satisfactory form of maintaining high occupancy and stable earnings.

When to Negotiate Renewals

In most areas where leases are commonly used in residential buildings, there are certain peak expiration dates. In New York, a high percentage of all leases expire on September 30. In Chicago, about 65 percent of all leases terminate on April 30, and nearly all of the balance come to an end on September 30.

In any event, it is desirable for the manager to approach the tenant at least 90 days before the actual expiration to begin the discussions which will lead to a renewal. In some areas it is customary to use leases which contain a so-called *automatic renewal* clause. This clause provides that the lease continues from year to year, unless the lessee notifies the landlord in writing of his intention to terminate at least 60 days in advance of its anniversary.

A ninety-day period is enough time for negotiations in all except the more expensive, larger-type apartments. In this type of unit the tenant is faced with greater difficulties and expense in any possible move and usually likes to have his plans made farther ahead.

REVIEW QUESTIONS

1. What technique has proved basic to success in renting? Describe good technique in renting a five-room apartment in a 50-unit building in a suburban area.
2. How does a property manager get prospects? What factors influence prospective tenants? What is the desired ratio of prospects to various units? Give an example.
3. Define the following: rental, selling, renewal, transfer.
4. Name several types of rental advertising. List in order of importance from experience in the real estate field.
5. How should a manager figure *net cost of advertising?*
6. What are the three requisites of a sale?
7. As a property manager, how would you handle a prospect who comes into your office to inquire for an apartment?
8. When should renewals be negotiated?
9. Name the basic elements of bargaining between tenant and property manager.
10. What is *automatic renewal?*
11. Why is it more important to renew a tenant's lease than to lease to a new tenant?

SELECTED REFERENCES

Fantle, Chuck. "Leasing Can Be Successful If." *Journal of Property Management,* May–June 1974, pp. 126–128.

Kelley, Edward N. "Apartment Marketing: Timetable for Success." *Journal of Property Management,* July–Aug. 1970, pp. 176–186.

Kelley, Edward N. "How to Plan a Successful Apartment Marketing Program." *Apartment Construction News,* May 1971, pp. 109–113.

"Marketing Today: Changing Trends Require New Outlook." *Journal of Homebuilding,* June 1971, p. 46.

Sachar, Roger. "The Art of Merchandising." *Journal of Property Management,* Sept–Oct. 1973, pp. 220–225.

CHAPTER 10

Managing Furnished Buildings

INTRODUCTION

In previous chapters attention has been drawn to the fact as the three-quarter mark of this century is being passed an unprecedented social revolution is occurring in the United States—and, for that matter, in the rest of the world. Literacy and educational opportunities are on the upswing everywhere. Racial barriers are being broken down. People now are more mobile and less subject to the constraints traditionally imposed by the guardians of the status quo.

This revolution is seen in the new materials that man now has and uses, in his new ability to process information, in the sophistication of the systems he devises and employs, and in the immensity of the store of energy to which he has the key. But nowhere are the changes more dramatically seen than in the new life styles that form the structure of modern society. The result: In almost every racial and ethnic social grouping, family life is becoming less well knit.

While this can be seen to some extent in every developing part of the world, it is especially important to consider the phenomenon as it affects the American scene. Three contributing factors are:

1. Prolongation of life through improved health care, the conquering of disease, improved nutrition, and advances in preventive medicine.
2. Youth orientation, reflecting in part the large percentage of young people in the total population, but also arising from the educational enrichments now available to all through TV, schools without walls, community colleges, and continuing education programs. Consequently, young people more and more are becoming decision makers in political and social affairs.
3. Because of advances in birth control, American families are now smaller than heretofore. Because of the automobile and the airplane, they are less rooted to fixed residential and employment locations. Because of urbanization, large segments of the population have become cliff dwellers. And because of the new mores, the idea of a family unit has been broadened to include life styles that formerly would have been considered unconventional and even outrageous.

Small wonder that new sets of rules are needed for the game of life, no matter at what level it is played.

The property manager has to understand the conditions of the generation in which he is working and to keep pace with the shifting sentiments of those he serves—the owners as well as the customers. Let us illustrate.

One might suppose that because of the trends in population just discussed (leading to the prevalence of highly mobile, often childless couples of whom both partners work, "swingers," and divorcees whose children have flown the coop), the market for furnished apartments would be enhanced. This, however, has not proved to be so. Rather, certain trends in the economy have acted to lower the percentage of residential units that are offered on a furnished basis.

These trends have operated in two areas. In the first place, the average American family no longer is financially able to purchase personal services to the same degree as in former years. The "live-in" servant is an anachronism in today's household, as are the gardener, the handyman, and all kinds of service personnel, in the exclusive employ of a single family.

The "do-it-yourself" vogue was not born out of a desire on the part of Americans suddenly to become plumbers, carpenters, gardeners, painters, and home beauty operators. On the contrary, it stems from the simple fact that the housing consumer, by and large, can no longer afford the wages of service people. This situation has had a profound influence upon the pattern of housing. It has been responsible for the popularity of the single-family dwelling and condominiums, since the occupancy costs of such units can be greatly reduced by the contribution of labor by the occupants themselves.

At the same time that "do-it-yourself" economies have been discovered by housing occupants, it has become possible for all Americans to purchase furniture and utility units on installment credit plans, with monthly payments generally less than what landlords would be inclined to charge for equivalent capital services.

Consequently, furnished apartments are nowhere as numerous as they were several decades ago. In fact, the only furnished accommodations now being offered to the renting public are either at the low end of the market or at the very highest. The former are in the "rooming house" category, or in that of the cheap, older, furnished apartment building found in decaying neighborhoods. At the other end of the scale are the "luxury" resident hotels. But even the latter are not being built very much anymore, so few are the people able to afford the high rentals involved.

Finally, from the investor's point of view, an added factor is inhibiting the contemporary development of furnished buildings. The simple fact is that wages are increasing faster than rents. This means that properties which are labor-intensive (hospitals, hotels, etc.) have a built-in handicap. To a lesser extent the same is true of furnished buildings as compared with unfurnished ones. Just as the cost of labor is a restraint on building, it also affects operating, servicing, and maintaining buildings. What is more, the *productivity* of much of this high-cost labor does not reflect the efficiency of concurrent technological developments. As an example, consider that a hotel maid today does not clean any more rooms than her grandmother did in the same amount of time.

Indeed, the rule that underlies this chapter is that the best real estate investments are those with the lowest ratio of continuing or total labor obligation. This rule especially holds in inflationary periods.

TECHNIQUES, ARRANGEMENTS, AND SERVICES

To a large extent the technique of managing a furnished apartment building is the same as that of administering any residential property. All of the problems of the ordinary property are inherent in the furnished building, but they are *augmented* by the additional responsibilities and duties involved in the purchase, maintenance, and supervision of the furnishings and service. Merchandising becomes more complex, personnel more numerous, and tenant service more varied. Likewise, tenant turnover in furnished buildings is much more rapid because of the comparatively greater mobility of the types of families housed.

For the purposes of this text we shall limit our attention to properties in the higher rental range, namely those that offer "full hotel services" and related options. Therefore, some of the following remarks will not have relevance for the management of lower-quality furnished properties.

It should be emphasized that all property management is what might be called a *detail* business. Because this is true, it is necessary for the property manager to realize that the management of a furnished apartment building, involving as it does a great many more details, requires much more rigid control and constant supervision. The reasons for this augmented need for rigid control are to be found in the operation of the several departments of the furnished apartment building which are not included in the typical unfurnished building.

The Front Office

People who live in a furnished apartment building generally do so because they require and expect services which are not to be found in the unfurnished building. Among these services are those rendered by a front office (the hotel term for the office of the building) in which there is constantly an attendant commonly called a desk clerk. His or her job is to sort mail, receive rental payments, act as a clearing house for messages, accept and pay for COD deliveries, record laundry and valet charges, and perform other services for both the manager and the guests. Usually this front office clerk also handles the telephone switchboard and makes all contacts with the guests and the general public.

By virtue of the fact that this desk clerk handles money and a variety of records, he or she should be selected with a view toward ability and reliability in working on the books. It is essential that procedures be established and forms perfected whereby all of the routine operations can be effectively and systematically recorded. A wide variety of such forms have been developed by printing houses and accounting firms that specialize in apartment hotel and furnished apartment operation.

In larger apartment hotels, the front office routine is divided into separate operations, with the desk clerk being limited to the maintenance of room occupancy and guest records, the renting of transient space, and the basic contacts with the general public. In such cases, all financial activities related to guest and public services are handled by cashiers, who collect rentals, post charges, cash checks, accept COD charges, and make change. Where they are warranted by volume of work, these employees are under the direction and supervision of the hotel auditor.

The Telephone Switchboard

Virtually all apartment hotels, and many smaller furnished apartment buildings, contain a telephone switchboard for use in connecting guests with outside telephone facilities and for communication within the building. Even under the most favorable circumstances it is difficult to make the operation of this facility profitable. The only way is to assess proper minimum charges against tenants and to charge a sufficient amount for individual calls to offset the cost of renting the equipment from the telephone company and to defray at least a portion of the attendant's salary. Inasmuch as rates for telephone service are in most cases established by regulation, this source of revenue is often limited.

Since each telephone call going outside the building is an individual transaction, it is vital for the property manager to establish rigid control over the use of these facilities. Charges made by the telephone company are recorded automatically, both as to number and duration. Any failure by the switchboard attendant to make certain that these charges are passed along to the guests therefore results in an *actual out-of-pocket expense* for the building owner. To ensure the efficient operation of the telephone switchboard, the real estate manager must provide himself with a system for continuously analyzing telephone operation at the end of each billing period.

The Housekeeping Department

The other major difference between the operation of an unfurnished apartment building and that of an apartment hotel is found in the housekeeping department.

In most furnished apartment buildings this department is responsible primarily for the care and maintenance of furnishings, including carpets, furniture, furnishings, drapes, linens, etc., and for organization, training, and supervision of service personnel. The usual housekeeping staff consists of a

Sheet No.

TELEPHONE TALLY RECORD

BOOK NUMBERS			Date		
			Balance Brg'ht Forward		
ROOM	EXCHANGE	NUMBER	TIME	AMOUNT	

NOTICE

ROOM_____ DATE_____

M_____

PLEASE INQUIRE AT FRONT OFFICE FOR
- ☐ NOTE
- ☐ PACKAGE
- ☐ TELEGRAM
- ☐ TELEPHONE MESSAGE
- ☐ SPECIAL DELIVERY LETTER
- ☐ _____

A CROSS ☒ IN SQUARE INDICATES THE PURPORT OF THIS ADVICE

SERVICE REQUEST

APT._____

DATE_____

TO_____   TIME_____

KINDLY ATTEND TO THE FOLLOWING:

WORK COMPLETED { DATE_____   COMPLETED SATISFACTORILY

TIME_____   _____TENANT

WHEN WORK IS COMPLETED, RETURN THIS ORDER TO OFFICE, SIGNED.

CHARGE

TO ACCOUNT OF

_____ROOM_____

DATE	ITEM	AMOUNT	TOTAL

REMARKS

PETTY CASH

_____$__

FOR_____

SIGNED_____

DATE_____

FORM 20-81

ALLOWANCE VOUCHER

DATE_____19 __

ROOM NO._____ NAME_____

DEPARTMENT_____ AMOUNT $_____

EXPLANATION_____

APPROVED

_____CLERK

_____MANAGER

FORM 24 - SHERWAY - CHICAGO

Front Office Control Forms

housekeeper, linen room attendant, maids, and housemen. In some larger apartment hotels the executive housekeeper follows the practice of larger, transient hotels and also supervises the decorating crew. In most furnished apartments, however, the decorating crew works either under the chief engineer or directly under the manager.

In addition to her responsibilities for the direction of furniture, furnishings, and service operations, the housekeeper is generally the management's contact with guests regarding service requests.

Control of Furnishings

The furnished apartment building usually supplies its tenants with linens, dishes, glassware, cooking utensils, and bedding. The organization of such supplies, their storage, and inventory control are under the housekeeping department.

In most cases individual apartments are equipped with a standard stock of such furnishings when the guest takes possession. Replacements are made continuously for normal wear and tear, and the stock is checked when the tenant moves from the unit. Any shortages are billed to the guest prior to his departure.

Linen Maintenance

Because linen is such an important part of the furnishings program, special emphasis is placed upon the development of a linen maintenance system.

The principal factor of linen wear is laundering, not use. Of course this is true under normal operating circumstances which do not always prevail. In typical commercial properties linen is destroyed through misuse. For instance, people use towels to shine shoes, remove lip rouge and lipstick, clean floors, razor blades, etc. Constant vigilance by management enables the building to charge tenants for linen so destroyed as soon as the misuse is detected.

The secret of linen vigilance is a well-organized, well-operated linen room properly staffed and supervised. The purpose of the linen room is to provide a storehouse for the surplus linens in the building; to keep a daily numerical check on linen, so as to forestall loss through theft either by tenants or employees; and to supervise the physical condition of linen through detection of misuse and through the prompt correction of evidences of wear.

The principal function of the linen room in protecting the building against theft is, of course, the daily numerical check of linen. The simplest form of such numerical check is the insistence that issues be confined to returns. A maid who is serving ten apartments is issued towel-for-towel and sheet-for-sheet only when she returns the like amount of a requisitioned item. This makes it impossible for tenants to steal linens without detection or for them to hold linens in apartments without being caught. The control must, of course, be positive. The linen room also examines all returned linen so that misused linen may be charged to tenants as soon as it is returned. In order to avoid disputes with tenants, it is well for linen rooms to mark misused linen and to store such misused linen until after the charge has been accepted and paid by the tenant. For example: If on March 10 the maid collects a towel from Apartment 310 which has been spoiled by the removal of lip rouge, said towel is marked with the apartment number and date and set aside until the bill for the charge has been paid by the tenant. If there is a dispute by the tenant of the charged item, the actual towel is produced with the notation of the date it was found, the apartment from which it was removed, and the name of the maid who reported it.

Substantial savings also are obtained through the surveillance of the physical condition of linens returned by maids. Small tears, rips, and frayed edges can be repaired before substantial damage is done to the individual item. Good linen rooms are equipped with sewing machines and are manned by persons able to do a good job of linen mending. In larger buildings, where substantial amounts of linens are used, a full-time mending girl is an actual economy.

Furniture Maintenance

In most instances the maintenance of furniture in an apartment hotel involves these separate steps:

1. Cleaning and maintenance of carpet
2. Cleaning of fabrics on upholstered furniture
3. Reupholstering of furniture, including structural repairs
4. Refinishing and repair of wood furniture

Carpet wear can be caused as much by dirt as by the actual friction of traffic. Since this is true, it is to the advantage of management to set up a routine for vacuuming and washing carpets in public spaces and apartments. A schedule of such systematic cleaning is a part of every well-operated housekeeping department, with the actual work assigned to a houseman. Not only does such a program lengthen the life of the building's carpet, but helps to sustain the beauty and decorative value of floor coverings.

A great deal of the need for the cleaning of furniture fabrics arises out of misuse or improper original selection. Upholstered furniture properly used (not abused) by tenants should not need major cleaning during the style life of the fabric. If the furniture is improperly selected, its use will in fact constitute misuse. For example: In a transient hotel room or apartment the comfortable chair should not have a back high enough for the male tenant to lean his head against—there will be a dirty spot on the back of the chair from the grease which he uses on his hair. Likewise, in transient accommodations, the arms of davenports should not be comfortable for use as head rests. Similarly, the light-colored fabrics in a decorative ensemble should be reserved for the least comfortable pieces of furniture.

In larger buildings management should recognize the fact that furniture requires constant maintenance; and either a regular maintenance shop should be set up for the reupholstering and refinishing of both upholstered and wood finished furniture, or a contract relationship for such work should be established. Such shops, or reliable contract relationships, enable buildings to insure themselves against poor workmanship since in upholstered furniture especially there is a substantial opportunity for "cheating" in furniture construction and maintenance. Just as you never know whether or not a dentist properly fills your tooth, you are never able to determine whether a piece of upholstered furniture is properly rebuilt, unless you have an opportunity to see and judge the quality of workmanship and materials that go into the product.

Maid Service

People who live in furnished apartment buildings frequently are transient. In the case of married couples (or of single people) there is a high percentage of dual employment with the result that guests or tenants require that ordinary, basic housekeeping services be conducted by the building management. This involves the employment, training, and supervision of maids who are engaged in cleaning, linen distribution, bed making, and general housekeeping.

Inasmuch as the character of an apartment hotel's service is largely determined by the effectiveness of its housekeeping, the work of maids is an important part of good management. In areas where these maids are unionized and union membership is required, the recruiting of this type of employee is most frequently accomplished through union contacts. In other cases, the very best source of maids is to be found among the friends and acquaintances of present employees in this category. Because maids work alone in guests' apartments and are hence subject to the constant temptation of thievery, the greatest care should be exercised in the selection and investigation of this type of help. Controls must also be established which will make it impossible for maids to carry out stolen goods.

In well-operated properties supervised by capable housekeepers, standard routines of housekeeping are adopted. Maid work schedules are set up at the beginning of each day assigning each individual maid a certain number of occupied and/or vacant apartments or rooms. The initial training of the maid by the housekeeper acquaints the maid with the practices of the hotel and establishes a standard of cleanliness which is maintained under inspection by the housekeeper or her assistant. This instruction acquaints the maid with the standard equipment which is issued to her for cleaning, tells her what type of cleaning is the hotel's responsibility and what must be left for the guest, instructs her in the most efficient and most satisfactory method of making beds, and assigns the standard linen distribution for the unit involved. This on-the-job training pays dividends in the smooth performance of duties.

It is frequently difficult to attain exact standardization of the amount of time that individual maids will spend cleaning each of the units assigned to them. However, the labor standards of production must be set by the hotel in order that maids' time will be equitably spread over the units involved. Unless such controls are established and maintained, guests will abuse maid-service privileges by arrangements with individual maids under which special services will be performed for the guests in exchange for gratuities.

In normal furnished apartment operations, maid service is expected to provide the following:

1. Making beds and changing of bed linen.
2. Sweeping or vacuuming of carpeted floors.
3. Dusting furniture, emptying ash trays and waste baskets.
4. Cleaning bathroom and kitchen floors.
5. Replacement of soiled linen.

It is to be expected that tenants will take normal care of their units, that clothing will be picked up and hung up, and that dishes will be washed and put away. In cases where tenants fail to take care of this housekeeping, they should be reported by the housekeeper to the manager and remedial steps should be taken. Often tenants simply do not understand what is expected of them.

General Services

In addition to the maid service, apartment hotels and the better furnished apartment buildings provide a variety of personal and maintenance services. The extent, of course, depends on the rental level of the units offered. Bellmen run errands, walk dogs, and handle baggage. Receiving room clerks make deliveries, send out laundry and dry cleaning, and return unwanted merchandise to stores. Housemen (usually working under the direction of the housekeeper) do all of the heavy housework, such as the cleaning of draperies, heavy vacuum cleaning, moving furniture, and the like. And there may be special guards and security people especially for nighttime surveillance. There may be a doorman and a night gate to isolate and ensure limited access to the lobby and elevators. Perhaps there will be safe deposit boxes for the storage of valuables. Dispensers for items like stamps, soft drinks, cigarettes, and other sundries are common, as are (more recently) coin-operated copying machines. Perhaps there will be a launderette service area, or a restaurant and cocktail lounge off the lobby. The possibilities are numerous.

Suffice it to say that residents of high-rental apartments expect—indeed have the right to expect—certain basic services.

THE ECONOMICS OF FURNISHINGS

The fundamental purpose of obtaining the highest possible net return from a given property over the longest possible economic life carries through all of the property manager's operations, including furniture and furnishings. Given a building not already furnished, the manager should always ask himself, "Could this building be more profitably operated as a furnished property?" Likewise, given a building totally furnished, the manager should always ask himself, "Could this building be operated more profitably on an unfurnished basis?" The process of answering these questions involves the economics of the subject.

Among the questions which the property manager must consider are the following:

1. Does the furniture itself represent a sound investment?
2. Is the property likely to have more or less *consumer pressure* if it is furnished?
3. If the property is furnished, will additional services be required, and if so what will be the additional costs?
4. If such services are required, can they *profitably* be combined with the furniture so that furniture-and-services will earn a profit?
5. Does the property lend itself to the creation of *atmosphere rent* through the process of furnishing?

Giving attention to these questions in the order listed above, we are first interested in the financial return on the furniture itself. By furniture we are now speaking of actual items which will be installed in the rented unit, such as floor covering, upholstered furniture, tables, desks, lamps, curtains, draperies, beds, dressers. Whereas we can assign to each individual item a normal length of life, such a process involves computations too complicated for practical use. Therefore, it may be safe to say that the average life of the combination of these items is approximately six years. On that basis we must anticipate that the additional rental attributable to furnishings must amortize the total investment in furniture over the six-year period as well as provide an interest return on the money invested and the maintenance costs.

Suppose we are considering an *unfurnished* one-bedroom apartment on which the rental is $300 per month. Considering that it already is carpeted, suppose we found that we could completely furnish (or refurnish) it for $1,200. Then, if we were to allow 20 percent of the purchase price for maintenance and cleaning of the furniture (that is, $240), and a 10 percent return on our original investment over a six-year term of amortization (that is, $720), we would have a total cost over this period of $2,160 (= $1,200 + $720 + $240). This amounts to a cost of $360 for six years. Now suppose we find that our unfurnished apartment can now be rented as *furnished* for $350 (instead of $300) monthly, the total gain would be $600 (= 12 × $50), and the net gain would be $240 (= $600 − $360). This profit in many cases would make the furnishing program an acceptable venture.

However, before a manager can draw a conclusion from these figures, consideration must be given to how furnishings will affect the market for the building's space. In many areas there is little or no demand for furnished accommodations. In most such areas the furnishing of units cannot be profitable. In other areas the demand for furnished units is approximately on a par with the demand for unfurnished units. In such cases the installation of furniture will do no more than carry the cost of such an installation. However, in still other areas the transient nature of the population may result in a much higher degree of salability for furnished apartments than for unfurnished apartments, with the result that installation of furniture will produce a substantial margin of profit over the actual cost of the furnishings.

In yet other cases, the demand for furnishings in a particular type of unit is exceptionally strong, and unfurnished units of that type cannot be rented without being furnished. For example: It is nearly impossible to rent a hotel room unless it is furnished; it is exceedingly difficult to rent a small one-room apartment unless it is furnished. On the other hand, the addition of furniture and furnishings to a three-bedroom apartment is very rarely, if ever, profitable. Thus a complete market analysis is a part of the technique of determining the economics of a furnished apartment operation. Without an analysis, the property manager cannot reach a sound conclusion.

After the first two steps outlined above have been taken, it is necessary that the manager analyze, and fit into the total picture, the service requirements created by the furnishing program. In most instances people desire a furnished apartment because their attitude toward residence is impermanent. In still other cases, people desire furnished apartments because the pressure of other activities makes it necessary for them to throw off the responsibilities of housekeeping. In such instances tenants for furnished properties require the management of the property to perform maid service and to provide linen. It is necessary for a separate study to determine the economics of such services.

The technique of this latter analysis is rather simple. Let us suppose we have a building containing 200 rooms. The requirement for rendering maid service will be based on hiring a sufficient number of maids to service the rooms, providing and operating a linen room and housekeeper's office, providing a linen room girl to take charge of the linens, inspecting, etc., and employing a housekeeper for supervision. Assuming that one maid can handle twenty rooms and that one linen room girl and one housekeeper will be needed, it is easy to determine the exact cost of the payroll involved. To this cost of payroll must be added a sum equal to approximately 20 percent of the total which will cover employees' insurance, taxes, sick leave, etc. If the building is a hotel with 200 rooms and 200 baths, the cost may be spread equally over the rooms, and the resultant amount per room is the actual cost of the maid service.

If, on the other hand, the building is made up of studio and one-bedroom apartments, it may be found that the costs cannot be spread out and expressed on a "per room" basis, but rather on a time-study of the amount of work required on each type of unit. Such a study is valuable, it may be added, not just to determine the costs of rendering service, but to establish a reference time-allowance for the maids in each apartment.

In buildings where furniture is provided and maid service is available, most of the tenants also desire complete linen service, i.e., bed linen, bathroom linens, kitchen, and dining linens. Here again the cost must be estimated on the basis of:

1. The original cost of three complete sets of linen per apartment (one in the apartment—one on the linen room shelves—one at the laundry).
2. The cost of laundry on each of the items and the frequency they are laundered (towels are laundered daily whereas the practice of bed linen changes and dining room linen may be varied).
3. Allowance for depreciation of linens (this depreciation rate is based principally on the number of launderings—in commercial laundries— which typical quality linens can stand. For example, bed sheets of ordinary quality will last from 100 to 150 launderings. Excellent-quality types of percale sheets will last for as long as 250 launderings. For a rule-of-thumb yardstick, however, one could ordinarily estimate the life of a typical linen setup as six months if laundered on a daily basis).

By totaling all of these costs and by determining the various linen setups required for each type of unit, the exact linen cost can easily be determined.

We are now in possession of all of the data required to approach the problem of furnishings on a cost basis. We also have discussed the manner in which the property manager can arrive at his determination of operating policy.

If it has been determined that the consumer pressure against a particular building warrants furnishings and service, the manager may consider a flexibility of merchandise based upon something less than full furnishing and service. Many prospects for furnished apartments are able to service their own units partially and are interested in allowances made in lieu of so-called full hotel service. For example, a married couple may not feel that they can invest in furniture or linen and are hence interested in a furnished apartment. The wife may be able to do the maid-service work, and would, therefore, be interested in only furnishings and linen service. In the case of two girls living in an apartment, it may be possible for the tenants to make the beds and straighten the apartment each day, yet these same tenants would like maid service once a week for a thorough cleaning. In order to increase the consumer pressure against a given building, the manager should offer the public as wide a variety of merchandise as possible, at as wide a variation in rent schedule as possible.

Therefore, in a building which offers furnishings, linen, and full maid service, it is desirable for the management to work out a schedule so that apartments are offered on one of the following plans:

1. Unfurnished
2. Furnished with furniture only
3. Unfurnished with linen service

4. Unfurnished with linen service and partial (one, two, or three times per week) maid service
5. Furnished with linen service only
6. Furnished with partial service
7. Completely furnished with service

By following the technique of cost analysis discussed above, the manager may work out price variations for each of these types of tenancy. Inasmuch as partial service requires scheduling of maids' time, the margin of profit for partial service must necessarily be greater than the margin for full service.

Labor Costs vs. Rentals

The so-called apartment hotel and the furnished apartment with service have suffered a great deal of economic obsolescence in recent years because *labor rates have risen much faster than rents.* As we have pointed out in chapter 3 this is evidence of the *imbalance* which has accompanied our recent *selective inflation.*

This trend probably will continue as a long-range economic phenomenon. Consequently, we have *discouraged* the adoption of operating programs which contemplate the *increase of labor requirements,* except in extraordinary circumstances.

Atmosphere Rental

People everywhere are susceptible to an intangible element called "atmosphere." In the Pump Room in Chicago or the 21 Club in New York, people gladly pay a substantial premium to buy a hamburger which would cost not nearly as much in a less-prestigious restaurant. Obviously the difference in price is one of atmosphere rather than beef. Tenants also are sensitive to the class of their environment. People will pay handsomely for the place that has "it"—whatever it is.

While it is certainly possible to breathe a certain amount of "class" into an unfurnished building, the opportunities are infinitely greater to upgrade in this way furnished buildings that offer services as well as space. The broader the services, the easier to establish atmosphere. And indeed, the atmosphere may be so ethereal as to be invisible, save to those whose feeling of self-importance is thereby inflated, or the atmosphere may flow from very real improvements.

To illustrate the nature, extent, and profitability of deliberate efforts in this direction, consider the case of a building in which the value of an unfurnished apartment is $350 per month. Let us assume that the building could be furnished and provided with services for an added $250 monthly. It is not inconceivable that, through the application of imagination, creativity, and taste, a manager could obtain $800 per month as rental for the finished product. In such a case, therefore, he would be compensated for his skills to the tune of $200 per month (= $800 — $350 — $250) in "atmosphere" rental.

The exploitation of *atmosphere* by property managers is an interesting avenue to extra profits for building owners. It is rare that an *atmosphere rental* can be obtained for an unfurnished property, since the primary selling points in an unfurnished property are location and space desirability. People who occupy furnished apartment buildings, on the other hand, are less interested in space per se and more interested in those factors which build up prestige for the occupant. Among such factors are furniture and furnishings—both in the public spaces and in the apartments themselves. The ability to furnish buildings in such a way as to increase the margin of *atmosphere rental* is the keystone of success in the operation of furnished property.

Before leaving the subject of the economics of furniture and furnishings, we must, of course, consider the fact that many properties are operated on a furnished basis, but could be operated much more profitably on an unfurnished basis. The occupants of furnished buildings very frequently require services (other than furnishings, maid service, and linens) which are unprofitable. Among these are the maintenance of bellboys, doormen, switchboards, receiving rooms, etc.—the cost of which must be analyzed in the net result of a building operating plan. The same technique of analysis which is discussed above can apply to an analysis of extra cost factors involved. This, plus an appraisal of the effect on the market, of shifting to an unfurnished basis should determine the course of the property manager.

For the purpose of this text, we will assume that we have determined to furnish an unfurnished property. The question will then arise as to what type of furnishings should be installed. Of course, a great deal will depend upon the price range of the property itself. Some buildings are furnished merely for utility—in order to animate space which otherwise might be unsalable, and other buildings are furnished for the purpose of increasing marketability. Still other buildings are furnished because there is a genuine market for furnished accommodations and because there is a possibility of securing the *atmosphere rental moneys.*

Aesthetics

It is not intended that this text should be a discussion of interior decorating from an academic point of view. Property managers cannot aspire to be interior decorators any more than they can aspire to be plumbers. It is important for them to realize that fact, since there is a great temptation on the part of property managers (especially women) to envision themselves as persons of rare skill in the furnishing of apartments. The property manager should be essentially a "reviewer," and his function in providing furnishings should be largely that of determining the amount of money to be expended and the effectiveness with which others spend that money.

The test of artistry in furnishing buildings, and apartments in buildings, is the *salability* of the finished product. Whereas there are some factors which can be said to be universal, the average taste in furniture and furnishings varies substantially. This variation is dependent upon the background of the individual, upon the level of income, and upon the style accents of the moment. The taste of the public, moreover, is in a constant state of flux, depending upon economic conditions prevailing at the moment and upon the current showing of furniture by the style leaders of the industry.

Styles represent an interesting accommodation to the level of the economy prevailing at the time they are in vogue. In lush periods, furniture manufacturers and interior decorators are quick to realize that pocketbooks are fat and that they can create a demand for rare woods, marble, expensive fabrics, and a general sense of luxurious furnishings. But these same manufacturers and decorators will be equally alert to periods when people are not so affluent, and then push styles that more nearly match the economic mood. The same craftiness will mark the merchandising of more than home furnishings.

In furniture, therefore (especially for hotel use), style is more important than quality, especially in fabrics and in occasional pieces. Thousands and thousands of yards of expensive coverings have been torn off furniture frames because those coverings were out of style long before they were worn out. Whereas the style cycle depends a great deal upon economic conditions, our experience would indicate that it is well to plan to recover upholstered furniture and to replace draperies every three to five years. Thus, we do not buy fabrics destined for longer wear because the drop in their style appeal cuts in on *atmosphere rental monies.*

In setting up furnishings, the property manager can rely either on interior decorating advice, rendered generally by sellers of furnishings, or if his operations are on a broad enough scale he can engage a person for that particular job. It is well to experiment with one or more types of furnishings and to expose them to the public's reaction. Very frequently the apartment, which the property manager thinks is the most attractive and most artistic, may not be the one which sells most readily. As we have said before, the test of the effectiveness of the decorative motif is in the speed with which the product is sold and the rental price which it warrants.

In connection with style, it is pertinent to point out that extremes are to be avoided if possible. One should deal in *modified* rather than extreme style forms. For example: During the so-called *modern decorative period* it was a mistake for an average property to use an *extreme modern* type of furnishings. It was likewise a mistake during the period of eighteenth century ascendancy to use an extreme variety of eighteenth century furnishings. The extremes in style are the most ephemeral in value; the *deadest* when the style cycle starts to dwindle.

From the point of view of the aesthetics of furniture and furnishings, it is

APARTMENT DISPLAY

A furnished apartment must convey an atmosphere of good taste and a homelike quality. Note use of accessories to create a look of completeness and utility.

important that the property manager realize that in setting up a furnished apartment he is setting up a complete home. In the sale of unfurnished units, the property manager is selling a unit of space and a set of equipment with which the tenant himself can develop home atmosphere. In the case of the furnished apartment, however, it should be the property manager's aim to create a home which will not only look desirable but which will appeal to the tenant because of its completeness and utility. In addition to beauty, therefore, the manager should give attention to the details which make the prospective tenant feel that all he needs to do is bring in his clothes, and the apartment is ready to be his home.

There is a separate and distinct technique to this creation of "livability" in a furnished apartment. It consists of thorough care of detail, room by room. For example, in the living room there should be pictures, ash trays, small objects of art, a book and a few magazines (placed in the apartment only during the period of show), and the equipment which one uses each day in a home. A vase of artificial flowers on an occasional table is worth far more than the small amount of money it may cost.

In the bedroom each bed should be attractively made and covered with a spread, the closet shelves clean and edged, dresser drawers paper lined. Real, usable coat hangers are pleasing in the closets instead of the usual helter-skelter array of the worthless hangers left by the former tenant. In the bathroom the shower curtain should be hung, towels placed on towel bars, bath mat placed over the side of the tub, glass in the glass holder, and soap in the soap dish if soap is furnished. Likewise, in the kitchen all of the kitchen utensils should be in order; dishes, silver, and glassware in proper place, dish and glass towels hanging on the towel bars. In fact, the entire apartment should be neatly arranged, thoroughly cleaned, and totally inviting.

The furnished apartment affords the property manager the maximum use of creative ability. The average prospective tenant will pay substantially more money for an apartment which is aesthetically perfect than for one which may be as good, but lacks good taste and the homelike quality which we call *atmosphere.* The operation of a furnished apartment building is strictly detail business with the maximum reward for those who pay the greatest attention to the little things which create *plus* values.

Special Problems

The manager of furnished properties faces special problems which differ somewhat from those encountered in most other phases of the profession. One of the problems has to do with personnel. The bonding rate for hotel properties is among the highest for any kind of employment. Especially among front office and executive help are the temptations great, in view of their exposure to the traditional temptations of money, liquor, and sexual encounter. It follows that the manager will want to ensure sufficient supervision to protect against thievery, fraud, and unbecoming conduct.

The purchasing of those items not ordinarily involved in routine property management produces a whole new set of complex problems. Involved are food, beverages, and a wide variety of other goods and services.

In these connections, a final point is that managers who have extensive operations in the apartment/hotel field should centralize those office activities of a related nature.

REVIEW QUESTIONS

1. Describe the function of a linen room. How would you keep your inventory and how would you know when to replace stock?
2. Why are maids important? You need a maid. How would you find one?
3. Discuss ways of keeping your telephone switchboard out of the red.
4. How can a property manager decide—or help decide—whether the property should be operated furnished or unfurnished.

5. What is the main difference between the operation of a furnished apartment building and an unfurnished one?
6. Suggest variations which may be worked out on furnishings and service to increase consumer pressure.
7. What is meant by *atmosphere rental?* Give an example.
8. What would you do if any tenant habitually damaged towels? Explain procedure.
9. What is involved in the maintenance of furniture? State what you would consider efficient operation, taking as an example a two-room unit which has been occupied by the same tenant for the past three years, but is now to have a new tenant.
10. What are the duties and responsibilities of the housekeeper?
11. How would you figure the cost of maid service on a 300-room transient hotel? On a 50-unit apartment hotel, each unit two or three rooms?
12. What job instructions should be given a maid?
13. Describe the *front office* and functions of the front office personnel of an average-size apartment hotel.
14. How would a deflationary swing, if protracted, affect the market for furnished apartments? Compare the case of an inflationary swing.
15. Starting with the resident manager, name the employees and their duties for a 300-room apartment hotel.
16. Contrast the management problems given a situation where 25 percent of the rooms are for transient guests, as against where 75 percent of the rooms are for transient guests.
17. For apartment hotels, what do you think of the idea of reserving certain sections (perhaps entire floors) exclusively for women guests, for senior citizen guests, and the like? Should transient and permanent guests be separated, for example?

SELECTED REFERENCES

"Furnished Units Take Greater Share of Apartment Market." *Apartment Construction News,* May 1969, pp. 22, 24.

CHAPTER 11

Managing the Single-Family House

INTRODUCTION

In former days a man built his house with his own hands, living out under the stars until the job was completed. The pioneer family typically consisted of a husband, a wife and perhaps some of their parents, lots of children, perhaps some onhanging unmarried adults, hired hands and servants, domestic animals and household pets.

As the cities swelled from within and were added to from without by immigration and the processes of urbanization, residential neighborhoods of single-family dwellings developed. Some of these buildings were mansions, some were modest row houses undistinguished except that inside them their owners could enjoy the illusion of exclusiveness as provided by a front and back entrance.

It never has been possible for a young couple to know with confidence what their housing requirements will be some years hence. Nor do they generally have the money in the beginning anyway to pay for the house that will be desired to enjoy the affluence of their later years. Therefore, it was not uncommon to have a room or two for let, in what otherwise were oversized single-family dwellings.

Occasionally a whole home would be for rent and, by one evolutionary process or another, the habit of people renting and leasing homes rather than building and buying them became entrenched. This chapter thus serves as an introduction to the role played today by the property managers in the merchandising and maintenance of single-family dwelling units not occupied by their owners.

THE HISTORY OF SINGLE-FAMILY HOME USE

In the early history of the United States the housing pattern of the country was overwhelmingly that of the single-family dwelling. For several generations the average such dwelling was little more than four walls and a roof. In the comparatively simple economy which prevailed in those early years, the materials which went into houses were self-fashioned. The only real cost of the house was the labor which went into it, often contributed by the occupant.

However, when the house was completed it represented wealth to its owner. It could either be sold for a sum of money or rented for a continuing return on the investment. Because there were virtually no schemes for home financing and cash was scarce, single-family dwellings came to represent a large portion of the then existing wealth. As people moved on to new frontiers or to better accommodations, as they died and left estates to heirs, more and more houses became available for rental. In this period these dwellings were regarded as investment property. Many of the early fortunes were concentrated in such holdings.

In the late nineteenth century, increased density of urban population forced a more intensive use of city lands, and the multiple-dwelling building came into use. At first, this was a simple structure without plumbing, central heating, or any of the amenities which we now associate with the modern apartment building. Large numbers of such units continue to exist in cities such as New York where the so-called "cold water" units still unfortunately plague the city government.

As housing standards improved and cities continued to grow the vogue for multiple dwellings increased to where, in the twentieth century, a high percentage of all urban housing accommodations was found in this category. For a number of reasons, however, the dominance of multiple units as the major medium for housing the urban population of the United States was reduced by the eventualities of the depression of the thirties. The reasons might be summarized as follows:

1. The steadily rising living standards in the country were the result of a phenomenal increase in wages which produced not only higher material costs, but which saw housing change from simple shelter to the inclusion of complex facilities and equipment. The result was that the cost of creating housing increased sharply.
2. Apartment buildings in the twentieth century not only kept pace with the standards of housing cited above, but they offered "services" to the occupants. These included the maintenance of the building, its public spaces and grounds, decoration of interiors, and servicing of all of the new equipment installed. As costs of labor and materials mounted, the rentals obtainable from such apartment units were not able to rise proportionately, for the simple reason that the consuming public could not afford (or were unwilling to make) the payments required to sustain this level of purchased services. It became apparent that the average occupant of housing could only maintain these standards if he himself provided the services which were generally regarded as essential.
3. The federal government, by several actions of the Congress (FHA, VA, etc.), created financing mechanisms which greatly favored occupants of single-family homes as compared with any other type from the stand-

point of the costs of creating and maintaining such accommodations. For example, low interest rates, long periods of amortization, and risk-insurance were made available to the home buyer, but not to the creator of multiple-family structures. Consequently, the housing consumer (by combining self-servicing with financial advantages) found that there was just no comparison in net value between single-family home and apartment living. When added to the deterioration of urban neighborhoods and the universal nostalgia for semi-rural living, the compulsion to live in the single-family house was overweighing.

All of the above is by way of background to the statement in chapter 1, that *these economic changes have virtually eliminated this type of building from the rental market since it is simply not economic to construct single-family dwellings for rental.* On the other hand, however, there are still thousands of houses in the United States occupied by tenants. In many cases these houses are owned by individuals or corporations or government agencies and require professional management. This chapter is included to present an analysis of the circumstances under which the property manager should consider offering a service to such owners, as well as the techniques which should be employed.

THE MARKET FOR SINGLE-FAMILY HOME MANAGEMENT

A very high percentage of the tenant-occupied single-family homes in urban areas are isolated structures owned by heirs of former occupants or by original owners who have moved away. Almost no houses have been purchased by investors during the last 30 years for reasons given above, and—aside from a very few co-operative projects and remaining government holdings—there are virtually no large holdings of single-family houses by owners who desire to offer them for rent.

In the traditional operation of the real estate cycle, each succeeding depression saw the wholesale foreclosure of home mortgages by large lending agencies. Thus, every 15 to 20 years, thousands of houses came into the ownership of comparatively few agencies. In the last depression, for example, the Home Owners Loan Corporation and scores of insurance and financial institutions took possession of thousands of such buildings. Consequently, they were forced to appoint or engage professional management until the buildings were liquidated.

It is not likely that there will ever again be such a concentration of the ownership and management of single-family dwellings. Even in the last depression, many states passed moratorium laws on the foreclosure of houses. It is almost certain that the Federal Housing Administration, the Veterans Administration, the Home Loan Bank, and even the large life insurance companies (most of whose single-family mortgage holdings are insured by one of the agencies named above) would not dispossess distressed home owners in large numbers.

In view of the above, there is little likelihood that management of single-family houses will ever become a large part of the total property management market. For example, it is obvious that management firms cannot with profit handle isolated single houses at the same rate as multiple-unit dwellings.

Whereas each management firm must determine for itself the dollar level of profitable operation per unit of such housing, it is certain that the fees must cover the cost of obtaining tenants when vacancies occur.

To summarize the situation in the market for the management of single-family dwellings, these conclusions should be cited:

1. In a strictly management office, this type of property does not represent a large field for new business. Fees must be well above other types of management, and will only result in profit if a fairly large number of such properties can be brought under management.
2. In a general real estate office—either of the one-man or departmentalized type—it is probably wise to accept single-family house management at a satisfactory rate of compensation under these general assumptions:
   A. The house probably some day will be liquidated, and it is plausible that the manager will be appointed to handle the sale.
   B. Collateral profits may be obtained from insurance, mortgage financing, and rentals or renewals.
   C. The owner of the property may either own other, more profitable properties for management, or he may be a prospective client for other services.

RENTING SINGLE-FAMILY HOUSES

In the typical area in the United States, standard housing for rental has been in a condition of "shortage" almost continuously since 1940. This has been true especially of single-family houses in all but the blighted and near-blighted areas of our cities and towns. The process of renting such units, when vacant, is a great deal easier than it has been in the past. In view of the fact that there is no real prospect in the foreseeable future of a serious oversupply of housing in the country, the standard techniques for space renting discussed in other chapters of this text need no special augmentation for this type of building. To the degree that houses present an unusual problem, the following steps are recommended.

Establishing the Rental

Because most rental rates on tenanted single-family houses are established by owners, who have no real way of ascertaining the true level of rental housing demand, the average house usually is rented at a rate well below its true current value. Even where professional managers are employed, there is a tendency to underprice home rentals. This partly is true because of the higher risks involved in vacancy of single-family houses. In large apartment buildings, managers can experiment with different levels of rentals, since one vacancy more or less is not all-important in gross revenue. On the other hand, houses are either 100 percent occupied or 100 percent vacant—the difference being just one tenant. Moreover, there is always cause for some apprehension over the protection of the physical property during periods of vacancy. All of these factors combine to cause managers and owners to accept offers of tenancy in many cases without adequate exposure to market experimentation.

House rentals should be established, as all other rentals, on the basis of comparability of value and scarcity. Since the unit of merchandise (the house) is rarely ever exactly the same as other houses in the market—in number of rooms, size of rooms, exterior design, grounds, and location—it is difficult, if not impossible, to pinpoint an exact rental based upon comparability. The manager simply must do the best he can within the framework of investigation of the practical economics. Obviously, the limitations of the fee structure in this type of management preclude a major research project to establish the precise level of an individual rental.

Special Lease Provisions

Usage and custom with respect to the rental of single-family houses varies widely in different areas of the U.S., Canada, and Mexico. Certain general differences between house and apartment renting are common enough to include as being standard procedure. In most cases, tenants accept premises with these understandings:

1. Grounds will be maintained according to certain standards by the tenant, including cutting the lawn, watering shrubs, etc. Often the landlord agrees to take care of seeding and fertilizing.
2. Equipment furnished and maintained by the landlord ordinarily does *not* include either the kitchen stove or refrigerator, these being furnished by the tenant.
3. Decorating most frequently is done by the tenant (especially in houses of modest rental) in return for an allowance in rent given only after the work has been done and inspected by the landlord. This practice has grown out of the fact that most occupants of single-family houses to-day—whether they be owners or tenants—do their own decorating because they simply cannot afford to purchase service of this type.
4. Maintenance of specified types (for example, interior work) increasingly is becoming the responsibility of the tenant.

THE MAINTENANCE PROCESS

Management of single-family houses and the fee schedule of income require a different type of internal organization in the property management office than that employed in the general application of techniques described elsewhere in this text.

Houses cannot be managed on a departmental basis, served by specialists in different types of maintenance, unless the manager has an exceptionally large number of homes located in projects. The reason is that today's cost of management personnel prohibits several people using the time to travel to isolated houses to perform specialized tasks. The ideal method of handling this kind of building is for its management to be assigned to one man who shall have complete responsibility for all types of chores. It shall be his duty to handle the showing of the property and its renting when vacant, to supervise all types of maintenance, to provide for all inspections of premises and work done, and to contact and report to owners when necessary. If the management office is organized on an area basis rather than on departmental specialty, then the house should be assigned to individual management men on the basis of location. If the community is small enough so that one man can cover it without too much waste of travel time, it probably will be found desirable to have him specialize in the problems of single-family houses and to handle all that are managed by the office. This management man should be teamed up with another person in the office, whose responsibility it is to take all calls and cover all details for the man who is so often in the field.

Proper representation of the owners of single-family homes requires a system of regular inspection. In properties where more than one family are located, there is always assurance that unusual or important events will be reported by observing parties. In the isolated single-family house, however, the owner is forced to rely totally upon the tenant for the protection of his property. Many cases have been noted in which tenants have destroyed property or have abandoned it and were discovered only after rental delinquency has caused an inspection of the premises. Actually, the field man in charge of properties of this type should be obliged to view the houses periodically.

It is regrettable, but true, that the majority of single-family houses used for rental housing in the United States are improperly maintained and are in a state of almost continuous deterioration. One of the prime reasons for this sad fact is that there is seldom any actual financial plan for the proper reserving of funds for major expenses. Inasmuch as a large percentage of the owners of property of this classification are uninformed, unsophisticated heirs with typical absentee-owner attitudes, such maintenance needs as outside painting, tuck-pointing, new roofing, and major equipment replacement are put off and often completely neglected. Ideally, the managers of such property should point out such eventualities to their clients and encourage their setting aside a certain amount each month in a maintenance and replacement fund. A typical outside painting job, for example, will often take as much as three or four months' gross rental receipts. Unless there is a reserve fund available, many owners never will accumulate sufficient funds to have all of the work done.

In the chapters of this text which cover Tenant Selection and Credit and Collections, we stressed the importance of the careful screening of applicants from the standpoint of their inherent desirability as housekeepers and neighbors, their moral character, and their financial responsibility. These criteria assume a unique significance in the selection of tenants for isolated single-family homes. In multi-unit rental quarters, the landlord is able to preserve the attractiveness of his property by close direct supervision of employees who have charge of the maintenance of grounds, walks, and public spaces. In houses, these chores become the sole responsibility of the tenant. Unless he is a person of cultivated sensibilities and personal pride (and has demonstrated himself to be such in his places of previous residence), his attitude towards his house will be expressed not only in a lowering of its desirability, but in a deterioration of the neighborhood in which it is located. For that reason we would direct the manager's attention to all of the suggested techniques of tenant selection and credit investigation and would suggest that special emphasis be placed on every single point in the screening of applicants for tenancy in single-family houses.

THE DUPLEX OR TWO-FLAT

Although the vogue for the duplex and so-called two-flat buildings, which created hundreds of thousands of units in our urban areas in the period from 1870 to 1930, has been dissipated largely by economic developments, most of these remaining buildings are still occupied. Even though they are owner-managed in almost all cases, property managers often are called upon to represent owners who, for one reason or another, cannot or choose not to manage them themselves.

The original scheme for the construction and sale of these buildings envisaged the owner living in one unit and renting the other at a sufficient profit to offset his own housing costs. Partially this was a return on capital invested and partially it was a reward for services (janitorial, maintenance, etc.) rendered by the owner. When the landlord is incapable of performing these services, either because of disability or physical absence, they must then be taken care of jointly by the occupants or by a person hired out of the proceeds of rents. Only in the very highest rental units is the latter a practical program. Tenants are usually called upon either to divide the chores or to have one tenant assume the responsibilities in exchange for lower rental.

The techniques of handling this type of property and the management problems involved are more nearly those of the single-family house than of the multi-unit residential building.

PROJECTS OFFERING SINGLE-FAMILY HOUSES FOR RENTAL

Although few and far between, a number of large projects of single-family houses, duplexes, or row houses have been built either for rental or co-operatively by private and public agencies in several areas of the country. The management techniques recommended when large numbers of houses are located on one contiguous set of sites are those suggested for income properties. Here departmental operation is possible; the protection of common-interest adjacency is provided, and the dependence upon a single tenant is not so vital. Moreover, renting comparability is much easier to establish, and the all-out risk of vacancy is not present.

REVIEW QUESTIONS

1. What factors caused a reduction in the proportion of multifamily dwelling units in urban areas of the United States?
2. Why is it unlikely that there will again be vast concentrations of single-family houses in comparatively few ownerships and available for rental?
3. Why is it necessary to charge a much higher fee for the management of single-family houses than for other types of income property?
4. Give the reasons for and against accepting the management of single-family houses by a professional management agency?
5. How would you go about setting the rental on a single-family house turned over to you for management?
6. What special lease provisions should go into a written agreement for single-family house tenancy?
7. Why is it difficult to ensure the long-term physical maintenance of rented houses?
8. Should the criteria of Tenant Selection and Credit for single-family houses be more or less rigidly established than for rental units in general? Explain why.
9. Do you believe that tenants in houses should agree to undertake a portion of their own maintenance and decorating? Explain why.
10. Why is there a basic difference between the management of houses in a project than of those individually owned?

SELECTED REFERENCES

Diener, Richard S. "Managing One-Family Houses for Profit." *Journal of Property Management,* Winter 1963, pp. 78–79.

Hasenau, J. James. *Rent—What Every Tenant & Landlord Must Know; With a Guide for House and Apartment Managers.* Northville, Mich., Holland House Press, 1971. 96p.

Mahaley, Walter C. "Residential Property Management: A Valuable and Profitable Service." *Realtor,* Washington, D. C., Oct. 1970, pp. 11–12.

Mahaley, Walter C. "Servicing the Single-Family Residence Profitably." *Journal of Property Management,* March–April 1972, pp. 64–67.

Wright, Henry H. "Management of Single-Family Residences." *Journal of Property Mangement,* Fall 1963, pp. 55.

CHAPTER 12

Managing Condominiums and Cooperatives

INTRODUCTION

In its original meaning the word condominium referred to a joint or concurrent dominion or sovereignty over a country or region by two or more states. The roots of the word as well as of the ideas behind them are of Roman origin. Here we shall be using the word to refer mostly to dwellings (for example, apartment-like units) within a common structure that are individually owned, mortgageable and transferable, independent of the ownership of other units in the same building.

And a cooperative—as the word is used here—refers to a jointly owned and operated corporate enterprise such as a building comprised of a number of residential units. In other words, in the limited senses under discussion, condominiums and cooperatives both are categories of property units of space available for occupancy (as residences or for other commercial/industrial uses). The occupants of the units typically will be the owners themselves. Thus each unit of a condominium will have its owner(s) with ownership in fee simple, while each unit of a cooperative will have its occupant(s) with ownership accruing from and reflecting a specified corporate stockholder's privilege. And, with the form of ownership different in the two cases, differences in the management requirements naturally arise. This is the subject to be discussed in this chapter following the introduction of it earlier in chapter 6.

The unique aspect of the subject under consideration, of course, has to do with the exceptional circumstance that it is only the owners who are clients of the property managers of condominiums, and it is only a corporation that is the client in the case of cooperatives. Merchandising residential space, as discussed in chapters 9, 10, and 11, is a primary function of the property manager who has tenants as well as owners for clients. And the same is true for commercial and industrial properties owned and leased primarily for rental income investment purposes. But in the cases under discussion in this chapter, the management function for the most part is to maintain the common spaces in the condominium and cooperative buildings and associated property, doing this as a service to the associated and incorporated owners once occupancy has been established. While the condominium ownership form to some extent has made the cooperative form less popular with the public in recent years, condominiums are not built except on locations where the land also is owned

215

by the condominium owners. For this reason and others, managers who specialize in cooperative buildings will be having a lot of work to do for a long time to come. Even so, it is clear that most future work opportunities for property managers will be reserved for those who specialize in condominium buildings. This view, is underscored by the fact that currently (1974) condominiums are being built at the scale of 250,000 new units annually! (In this connection, reference should be made to the PUD condominiums—that is, the so-called Planned Unit Development condominiums—where the unit owners also are the owners in fee simple of the land on which the units stand, thereby diminishing the extent of the common property that has a joint ownership.)

Cooperatives

Cooperatives and condominiums, after all, are ordinary buildings from the point of view of their management problems. The only difference between them and rental properties is in the form of their ownership and their tenancy. The sole reason for devoting a chapter of this text to the special problems connected with the management of these properties lies in the *differences* that managers encounter with this ownership form.

Cooperatives were common in the United States long before condominiums in their present form came into being. To a limited extent, cooperative ownership was employed in commercial properties and those occupied by agribusiness, but the most common form of cooperative ownership was found in residential structures.

As explained in chapter 6, a building owned cooperatively is, in fact, owned by a corporation, the stockholders of which are given proprietary leases on the units within the building. Thus, the first significant difference between the management of a standard rental property and a cooperative is that, instead of reporting to a single owner, the manager of a cooperative building has multiple owners. If a proper policy is not instituted at the outset to channel the contacts of these owners with the managers on a systematic basis, the situation could become chaotic.

As is true of all corporations, the cooperative apartment corporation has an elected board of directors which is representative of the owners. It is imperative that this board clearly establish a set of rules under which its building is to be operated. These rules should cover conduct of the apartment occupants and their guests in every possible area—including such items as personal behavior, criteria of occupancy, payment of bills, conditions under which apartments could be subleased and sold, as well as a wide variety of other self-imposed rules. These rules should be proposed to the occupants, and thoroughly discussed and agreed upon at an annual meeting of the stockholders. Penalties should be imposed for failure to comply. Among these rules there should be standards for contacting the management of the property, the method of making complaints, and the items which should be taken up with the building management and with the board of directors.

It can be easily understood that the property manager could be caught in the middle, that is between owners and the rule-making body, if the management were expected to enforce those rules against the occupant. For that reason the enforcement procedure should be handled entirely by the management as directed by the directors.

Generally speaking, the management firm which handles the building also handles the marketing, initially on behalf of the promoters and secondarily on behalf of the tenant owners. This is usually done for a standard brokerage fee, the same as would be charged in the sale of a house. The manager is frequently called upon to consult with the tenant-owner as to the price which is to be asked for a unit to be sold, and the manager's counsel is a part of the service in connection with the resale. The same techniques are used as would be used in the renting of an apartment. The unit should be prepared for sale in much the same manner as a rental unit to make certain that it exhibits its maximum appeal.

Inasmuch as the owner of the building is a corporation, the sophisticated management firm will offer complete corporate services. For example, the management firm can serve as corporate secretary, attend board of directors' meetings, file corporate tax returns, monitor corporate books and records, implement the corporate regulations, and the like. Proper tax forms as well as insurance coverage and audit reports will need to be issued so that all of the owner-occupants will be assured that the corporate details are being properly handled.

Condominium Ownership

The most revolutionary development that has occurred in real estate ownership in the United States in the last two decades is that of the condominium. Entirely new in concept in this country, condominium ownership has been employed in Latin America and western Europe for many years.

Condominium ownership is most widely employed in areas where inflation is a continuing factor. Its spread in the United States has broadened as inflation has increasingly characterized our economy. Virtually every kind of real estate embracing multitenant occupancy can be owned in condominium, including single-family home developments, apartments, commercial buildings, and resort properties, but the ownership concept is more frequently employed in multifamily dwellings. The way it works is this: That portion of the real estate concerned which is actually occupied by the individual tenant is owned by him in fee simple, and that portion of the development which he shares or uses in common with others is owned jointly, or in condominium. Thus, in an apartment building the condominium owner has title to his unit, while the land, foundation, heating and plumbing systems, halls, and entrance ways are

Principles of Real Estate Management

owned jointly by him and the other occupants of the building. The condominium may be mortgaged separately in the same manner as a single-family house, and it is assessed for real estate taxes just as though it were a detached piece of property. That condominium ownership is almost ideally suited for employment in connection with certain types of resort property already has been pointed out in chapter 6.

The shift toward condominium housing in the United States was initially motivated by two factors: First, condominiums were more profitable for developers to build than rental buildings; and second, condominium owners enjoyed the same tax subsidy which had been extended to home owners from the very beginning, namely, the deductability of taxes and interest from income tax payments.

The reason condominiums were more profitable to build was that, under money market conditions prevailing from 1965 on through about 1973, an interest-rate differential prevailed between mortgages made for construction of rental buildings and those for condominiums. For example, during most of this period, mortgages on rental buildings were at rates of 8-1/2 percent to 9 percent, whereas those to condominium owners were only 7 percent to 7-1/2 percent.

Inasmuch as condominiums were sold on the basis of the advantage of owning versus renting, developers were able to take full advantage of the economic implications of the occupancy cost of condominiums versus rental units. Where such an advantage existed, the developer took a share of the savings instead of passing it all on to the occupant, and these savings were substantial. For example, the tenant in a rental unit was entitled to expect certain services which the occupant of a condominium had to provide for himself. Among these were painting and decorating, plumbing, repairs, electrical repairs, and maintenance. While it is true that the condominium owner had to provide these for himself, he at least had the opportunity to perform "do-it-yourself" labor the same as the usual home owner did. On the other hand, the landlord in a rental building was required to buy these services from decorating contractors and plumbing contractors at costs which very often ran up to $15 to $20 per hour. When these savings were added to those which resulted from the deductability of interest and taxes from the owner-occupants' income tax, the savings were substantial and favored condominium ownership.

A second reason condominiums became so very popular in the decade of the 1970s was the onset of substantial *inflation*. In a period of rapidly rising prices, tenants feared that rentals would be raised drastically and hence desired the protection of the ownership of the dwelling units which they occupied. Moreover, the price of houses was increasing rapidly which confirmed their suspicion that they had better buy their unit. Thousands of units were converted from rental to owner occupancy under the condominium form of own-

LUXURY CONDOMINIUM

In its first season, this condominium containing 184 residential apartments was 95 percent sold and operated. Called the Garden Plaza Condominium, the structure is located in Ocean City, New Jersey.

ership during this period. Accordingly, tenants literally snatched up the units from developers, especially for primary homes.

The shift of thousands of tenants from mere rent-paying status to ownership of real estate was bound to have an impact on politics since each of these tenants became real estate taxpayers and hence had a stake in their community instead of being merely members of the tenant class. Whereas ordinarily tenants have paid little heed to the cost of local government, these same people when converted to owners take a great deal of interest and to a degree change the political complexion of local communities.

There are several classes of condominiums based upon the use to which they are put in the residential field (where most condominiums are found). The most popular, of course, are the *primary housing units,* meaning those housing units which are the basic homes of their occupants. It has been in these housing units that the condominium buyer has found his primary benefit, as noted above. The second most popular use of condominium ownership is found in "second homes," most prominently in resort areas such as Hawaii, Florida, and Arizona, and in ski resorts in Colorado and the eastern mountains. Here developers have built multifamily units by the thousands, which have been offered to people who could buy them, occupy them for a part of the resort season, and sublease them to tenants for either part of the season or in off-season periods at rentals which would go a long way toward letting the original owner occupy them virtually free for the period when they were not rented. By renting them, of course, the owner is entitled to claim them as income property and to take tax benefits which enable him to take depreciation as a deduction (in addition to the interest and tax deductions). Recently the IRS has begun to hedge on these benefits under regulations which require that, in order to be a tax deduction, the apartment must be occupied for certain periods and a required amount of total income must be received by the owner. More-over, the developers have been hedged by regulations of the Securities and Exchange Commission which require certain disclosures on the part of the developers.

These development schemes were carried on extensively until the very high money costs of 1974 increased financing expenses to the point that the advantages of condominium ownership were largely dissipated by high interest costs. Even so, it is thought that the condominium surge will persist in the United States—as it has in all countries where inflation has prevailed. Incidentally, all dwelling units in large portions of Europe and Latin America (where inflation has characterized the economy for long periods of time) historically have been condominium in character.

Getting back to the management of such condominiums, it should be added that a substantial field for property management was brought into play by the resort condominiums. In such cases the managers assumed the responsibility for renting the units during the owners' absence, collecting the rentals and, in some cases, profiting therefrom by participation in the actual income received. The advantages to the absent owner/occupant were obvious, for the manager made it possible for him to feel secure in the ownership of a unit which was constantly watched over and cared for by the management.

In some cases this trend was carried to the extreme by creation of the so-called "condotels" where in effect hotel rooms were sold to seasonal occupants on a contract under which the owner would occupy the room for one month out of twelve and agree to sublease his room for eleven months, at resort rates in which the managers participated up to 60 percent in some cases. Obviously in those cases the management provided full hotel service, including maid service and other traditional hotel staff services and amenities.

One of the most profitable real estate ventures in the early 1970s was the so-called conversion of rental units into condominium properties. Alert managers would select successful rental properties which had high occupanies and stable tenancy and would buy these on the basis of their reasonable rental value. They would then offer the units, first to the tenants and then to the general public, at attractive prices which nonetheless would be very profitable to the developer. On the basis of studies made by those who watch this process, the profit made by converters was in the area of 25 percent over the cost of the rental property.

MANAGEMENT OF COOPERATIVES AND CONDOMINIUMS

The manager's responsibility with respect to cooperative and condominium properties is to maintain the integrity of the corporate aims on behalf of the owners and stockholders. And the integrity to be preserved in many cases extends beyond the routine matters of maintenance of the building's appearance and of the physical plant, to include an effort and an intention to guarantee the exclusive nature of the properties involved. A doctors' cooperative building has a purpose which the owners will be reluctant to see compromised by poor management. Likewise, tenancy of condominium residences is a matter to be guarded in the interests of those who remain as units are bought and sold. Such matters require discreet handling by managers.

Services provided by property managers can range between the extremes of offering only a consulting opinion on major questions confronted by the owners of small properties all the way to fully performing all management functions on behalf of owners of large properties. The critical thing is that a detailed management contract be written that defines unambigiously the responsibilities and obligations of the parties thereto. As will be seen, these general remarks have a special relevance to the management of cooperatives and condominiums.

Thus, while a small eight-unit building is not likely to need a full-time manager, the unit owners may be very glad to retain a management consultant on a

CONDOMINIUM CONVERSION

This twin-tower, 8-story apartment building in Chicago's Belmont Harbor area is an example of a building "converted" into a condominium. High occupancy and stable tenancy are important factors to consider when selecting a rental property for its conversion potential.

fixed-fee basis. In other larger cases, fiscal management services may be needed, so that the assessments of the unit owners can be regularly collected, and so that a budget plan will be followed. With very large properties, however, full management services will be needed. In these latter cases, management firms will negotiate for term contracts covering a year or so, in which fees will be based on the number of units involved with a "cost-plus" protection.

The fact of the matter is that with about one-sixth of the 1.5 million housing units currently being built (in the middle 1970s) for condominium ownership, it can be projected that within 20 years more than 50 percent of Americans will be living either in condominiums or cooperatives. Therefore, the rising popularity of these forms of ownership is providing unique opportunities for professional management.

Because the owner occupant of a condominium unit is completely responsible for his own apartment or commercial unit, the manager of the condominium of which it is a part is actually engaged by the owners jointly to handle that part of the property which is owned and held by all in condominium. Depending upon the kind of arrangement which is made, the owner must assume complete responsibility for the management problems which arise in connection with his particular occupancy. For example, he must handle and be responsible for the payment of bills to take care of all repairs, decorating, and work done in his apartment.

Under some circumstances the management arrangement with the condominium contemplates the manager's handling such matters and charging them to the owner occupant. In such cases we would recommend that the manager agrees to act only on behalf of the owner, submitting all items of repair to him for approval prior to contracting for such service.

One of the problems which the manager faces in a condominium is that employees of the condominium are paid by all of the owner-occupants, and hence any service given to one must be given to all without discrimination. The manager should work out the duties of the employees to make certain that all owners are treated alike and that services of an extraordinary nature are either impartially rendered or charged to the individual owner-occupant. Evidence of favoritism by the employees can be a fatal error on the part of the manager who is held responsible for such unfair treatment.

Because many condominiums are found in resort areas where most owner occupants are absent most of the time, the manager must frequently assume the responsibility of arranging to sublease the owner's apartment during such absences. Depending upon the size of the structure and the nature of the unit, this will involve a wide variety of services.

Differences in management requirements between cooperatives and condominium properties arise because of differences in the ownership characteristics involved. In the cooperative, the unit owner has stock in a corporation which entitles him to a proprietary lease, whereas in the condominium the occupant owns his unit in fee simple. More than that, in cooperatives there will be (at most) a blanket mortgage for the entire property, whereas in condominiums individual units can be mortaged only by the unit owners.

Furthermore, cooperative and condominiums, as a form of multiple-family residence, have management requirements that are both similar and dissimilar to those of normally rented apartments. In all of these categories, of course, the manager will be responsible for the maintenance and care of the common areas and for the collection of certain recurring obligations (maintenance assessments in the former cases, rents in the latter). But, in general, the manager has no responsibility for unit maintenance or for maintaining occupancy, even though these are major management functions in cases where income rental properties are involved.

In any case, the management of cooperatives and condominiums is made all the more complicated by the fact that, with owners living on the premises, unintended mistakes and flaws in service will be quickly seen and reported. The result is that more time will be spent by managers per unit space, and more follow-up will be required to meet owner demands. The remedy for this, of course, is to be sure that fees are set in the first place fully commensurate with the cost (plus reasonable allowance for profit) of the services that are to be demanded.

The fact of the matter is that cooperative/condominium management opportunities offer an attractive and impressive business potential for managers who are prepared to specialize in this work. And just as new management opportunities are now being afforded by the increasing prevalence of public subsidized housing (as discussed in chapters 4 and 6), profit is to be realized mainly by those who understand the facts that lie behind these new occupancy arrangements, and by those who take the trouble to write management agreements that are fair to all of the parties thereto. In other words, managers who have complained in the past that their work with such properties as cooperatives, condominiums, and/or public housing has not been sufficiently rewarding most likely would agree that terms could be found for a renegotiated management agreement that would make the rewards more lucrative for them—and at the same time fair to the clients' interests.

Legal Aspects

In 1961 the Congress enacted legislation by which the Federal Housing Administration was authorized to insure mortgages on condominiums in those states where this form of apartment ownership was recognized. And by 1963 some 39 states had passed condominium acts to benefit from this provision. Today all 50 states, the District of Columbia, Puerto Rico, and the Virgin Islands have condominium legislation. Historically it was in connection with the construction (in 1927) of Chicago's Merchandise Mart within a single air space over the tracks of the Chicago and Northwestern Railway that an awareness of the need for a legalized authority was first recognized.

In 1962 FHA drafted a so-called *Model Statute for the Creation of Condominium Ownership,* and while this has not been followed in its entirety by the state laws that were subsequently enacted, its provisions provide insight into the scope and intent of the various present legislative acts. In this connection, it is to be understood that titles such as "Condominium Property Act," "Apartment Ownership Act," "Unit Ownership Act" and "Unit Property Act" all are to be taken as having the same general meaning.

Other definitions deserve attention: the *declaration,* which is the document that creates the condominium development and serves as its "constitution" for the subsequent operation and administration phases; the *parcel* meaning the lot(s) or tract(s), together with the space above or below the surface of the earth where the condominium building(s) is (or are); *property* includes the parcel with all improvement thereon and easements belonging thereto, and especially includes all features (fixtures, equipment, etc.) intended for mutual use by the condominium owners; *unit* is any part of the property designed and intended for independent use by an owner, to which a public access is provided; *common elements* are all portions of the property except the units; and the *unit owner* is the person or persons owning a unit in fee simple absolute.

Obviously, the various state laws provide a frame of reference to protect the public at large, and potential purchasers in particular, against the mistakes and malpractice of overzealous promoters and developers. More than that, it serves to protect unit owners by having their long-range rights and obligations defined from the outset. For example, on the matter of property taxes, it is stipulated that separate assessments are to be made against the unit owners in such a way that there can be no foreclosure against any part of the property except that of a defaulting owner. And with respect to common expenses, it is made clear that all unit owners are to share proportionately in the costs of administration and maintenance and repair of the common elements. Finally, in connection with the termination of ownership of a unit, specific and rather limited ways are clearly specified. These include: (a) owners collectively agreeing to a voluntary removal of the property from the provisions of the local condominium ownership act; (b) failure of a unit owner for one reason or another to provide for reconstruction costs following a casualty loss; and (c) a legal sale of the property.

In the future, as urban areas continue to expand upward as well as outward, it is clear that more enabling legislation will be required to facilitate the creation of larger and more complex condominium developments than are presently on the books. And continuing attention must be directed to finding new ways of financing.

REVIEW QUESTIONS

1. Write an essay about the differences and similarities between full management duties for condominiums, cooperatives, and multifamily rental dwellings.
2. Under what circumstances would condominium owners merely want occasional management consulting services, so-called fiscal management, or full property management services?
3. How is the common space owned in condominium arrangements? In cooperative arrangements? How do these differences affect the work of the property manager (if at all)?
5. Can a property manager offer maintenance services to a condominium unit owner? If so, under what conditions?
6. As a property manager considering an offer from owners of a condominium or cooperative property, how would you write a proposed management agreement? What would be a sensible period for the initial term of the contract? How would you price your services?

7. Contrast differences in the requirements for property management of high rises as opposed to cluster and townhouse types of condominium properties.

SELECTED REFERENCES

Arnold, Alvin L. *Developing a Condominium: Feasibility, Financing, Marketing.* Boston, Mass., Warren, Corham, & Lamont, 1973. 50p.

Associated Home Builders of the Greater Eastbay, Inc. *The Condominium Development and Conversion Handbook.* Berkeley, Calif., 1973.

Cagann, Robert A. "Maximizing the Profit Potential in Condominium Management." *Journal of Property Management,* Jan.–Feb. 1972, pp. 26–30.

California Real Estate Association. *How to Convert Apartments to Condominiums.* Los Angeles, Calif., 1973. 166p.

Clurman, David and Hebard, Edna L. *Condominiums and Cooperatives.* New York, N. Y., Wiley-Interscience, 1970. 395p.

Clurman, David. *The Business Condominium.* New York, N. Y., Wiley-Interscience, 1973. 185p.

Freeman, Roland D. "Who Should Manage the Condominium?" *Journal of Property Management,* Nov.–Dec. 1973, pp. 253–256.

Lanning, J. Clair. "Trouble-Shooting Condominiums with Management Know-How." *Journal of Property Management,* Jan.–Feb. 1972, pp. 31–34.

Murray, Joseph C. "Condominium Success Hinges on Management." *Journal of Property Management,* March–April 1973, pp. 84–86.

Ripps, Saul M. "Low-Income Co-ops Need Professional Management." *Journal of Property Management,* May–June 1972, pp. 106–108.

Sally, William D. "Avoiding the Perils of Condominium Management." *Journal of Property Management,* March–April 1974, pp. 56–62, May–June 1974, pp. 129–137.

CHAPTER 13

Occupancy Agreements

INTRODUCTION

W hat is referred to here as "occupancy agreements" was called *the residential lease* in previous editions of this book. The difference is not one of semantics. By definition a lease is a contract given by one person (the landlord, or lessor) to another (the tenant, or lessee) for use or possession of lands, buildings, etc., for a specified time and for fixed payments. Usually it is implied that the contract is written and binding in the legal sense with respect to the commitments given by the signatories.

An agreement, even a verbal one, carries a legal weight too, and is enforceable within the bounds of the law—to the extent that the law applies and to the degree that the intent is clear. While the intent of all of the clauses of a lease may be clear to some, the intent of some of the clauses will not be clear to all—at least not for all circumstances.

In other words, from the standpoint of the law there is no difference between what we refer to here as an occupancy agreement and what is referred to elsewhere as a lease (e.g., a residential lease), even if attention were limited (as it is here) to written documents. Why then the change in choosing a title for the chapter?

Because of historical connotations, the word lease relates to and is associated with words such as landlord and tenant. And the latter two words, whether properly or not, often relate to and are associated with wealth and poverty—at least in the public's conception. It is as though there was substance to the idea that the landlord is a first-class citizen, while the tenant is something less.

Occupancy agreement thus becomes an euphemism for lease, employed today to soften and diminish any residual antagonism and hostility that may be felt by tenants for landlords.

The pity is, of course, that acceptable euphemisms cannot be found for words like landlord and tenant. To say that one is the owner and the other the occupant or resident misses the point that owners of certain properties (for example, private homes) may also be the occupants and residents of that property. But in today's world of growing social awareness, one is cautioned to be sensitive to the sensibilities of others, especially of the disadvantaged and deprived. Otherwise misunderstandings will arise which can only complicate the work of the property manager.

In the United States over the last several decades there has developed more widespread (if not altogether universal) acceptance of the proposition that all people are equal and have the right to equal opportunity.

Some readers may misinterpret the intent of the above paragraphs as a criticism of the historically conservative view of real estate ownership. On the contrary, the aim has been to remind students of property management that they have both landlords and tenants as clients and customers. In today's world either or both can be liberal as well as conservative—or vice versa. That is, the business of the property manager is only business. And it is good business to have satisfied customers.

Throughout this book the student will see indications that the property manager very often is in the position of arbitrating tenant-landlord disputes. The property manager who favors one side against the other in this traditional confrontation may gain the acclaim of one of his clients, but lose the respect of the other. Since an occupancy agreement (that is, a residential lease as the term is being used here) basically is between landlord and tenant—with the property manager serving mostly as liaison between the two, it is obviously important that the negotiator of the contract refrain from taking sides.

The property manager should continue to remind himself that to many tenants "landlord-owner" are ugly words, just as he should be aware that some landed gentry are prone to view their tenants with feudal disdain. Even so, the relationship between landlord and tenant, as confirmed by the occupancy agreement they both sign, is—when it succeeds—a symbiotic one. The lease, like a marriage certificate, states the binding conditions of the relationship they have both freely embraced. And, if and when later problems develop, a basis is had for mutually selected third parties to ajudicate the dispute.

This chapter is devoted to the subject of occupancy leases. The property manager who doesn't know what they are and what they say is like the banker who is ignorant about interest rates.

The discussion here about leases also provides an excellent opportunity for students of property management to focus on the critical need to develop contractual arrangements that emphasize the mutuality of interests—rather than the historical antagonisms—of landlords and tenants. And if leases at one time seemed to favor owners, the modern trend is for them to be written fully in accord with local law which has evolved to the point that its protection and guarantee of individual rights are quite explicit.

THE RESIDENTIAL LEASE

A lease is most commonly defined as a contract that grants the possession and profits of lands and buildings for a period in return for rent. Whereas virtually any type of property may be leased, we shall concern ourselves here with leases for residential space. This will include houses, flats, unfurnished apartments, furnished apartments, and apartment hotel units.

The prime purpose of a written lease is to establish a record of a contract made between an owner and a tenant or, more properly described, between a lessor and a lessee. It is not necessary that a lease be written (most states require that leases for more than one year must be written), but we will concern ourselves in this discussion only with those which are written.

The reasons for a written lease, providing for the possession of property by a tenant over a definite length of time, are not the same for the lessor as the lessee. If there is a common characteristic of the interest which both parties have in a lease, it may be summed up by the word "protection." Landlords (lessors) desire leases in order to assure themselves of the actual occupancy of tenants over a period of time or, in any event, a liability to pay rent over a designated period. Theoretically, when leases to qualified tenants are in existence, the landlord may be assured of occupancy for the period covered by the lease and need not worry about losses which would accrue if the space were to become vacant.

The tenant, on the other hand, desires a lease primarily because it provides a security of possession for the duration of its term. Without a lease, tenants are theoretically subject to eviction at the whim of the landlord, and therefore cannot enjoy a sense of security in the possession of the demised premises. We say "theoretically" subject to eviction because in certain areas residential tenants from time to time have been protected by laws regulating rental and eviction. In the absence of such laws, the tenant has no other guarantee of possession than the lease.

DESIRABILITY OF TERM LEASES

The use of residential leases for terms beyond month-to-month occupancy is by no means universal in the United States. In some cities the use of a written lease for a term of one year or more is a standard practice. In other cities all tenancy (whether or not on written lease) is on a month-to-month basis. In almost every city, residential units of the very highest rent levels are covered by written leases of a term of one year or more.

From the point of view of both the landlord and the tenant, there are advantages and disadvantages to written leases longer than those involving month-to-month occupancy. From an economic point of view, a term-lease is an instrument whereby a landlord obtains more or less rent than may be justified by the market. In a *rising* market, the lease tends to restrict the landlord's right to adjust his rental upward in line with market movements. In a *declining* market, the tenant is held to a rental which may be above the going rates for comparable space. In most cases the disadvantage of leases from an economic point of view is greater for the landlord than for the tenant, since in periods of rising rentals landlords can *always* be held to the terms of the lease, but in periods of declining rentals typical tenants do not have the resources to pay a rental higher than that warranted by their current incomes.

Of equal advantage to both parties is the reduction of the agreement between the lessor and lessee to an actual written contract. As we shall see in subsequent discussions of the provisions of a typical residential lease, there are wide areas of potential conflict and misunderstanding between a lessor and a lessee. The insistence on a properly written agreement, which clearly sets forth the responsibilities of each in these areas of potential disagreement, is valuable to both parties.

Because of seasonal fluctuation in the demand for residential quarters in many sections of the country, there is also a mutual advantage to lessor and lessee in an annual lease. If it were not for such annual leases, owners might suffer heavy losses from vacancy at certain seasons of the year. For example, in Boston everyone who can afford to take up residence at the seashore during the summer months faces the cost of duplicate residences. To avoid this double charge for housing, large numbers of tenants might give up their city quarters during the summer months and return to them in the winter.

Conversely, tenants in Miami, Florida, who live and work in that city all year, might be evicted during the winter months to make room for transient tenants who would pay a much higher rental. In the former case it is an advantage to the landlord to have an annual lease, and in the latter case it is an advantage to the tenant.

There are a number of disadvantages in a written term-lease for both the lessor and the lessee. If the landlord desires to obtain possession of his own property he is unable to do so until the termination of the lease. On the other hand, if the tenant is required to move from the city or faces a change in family pattern or of income status, he is held to the lease until its expiration.

An additional disadvantage of residential leases for both parties beyond thirty days is the fact that expiration of the lease establishes bargaining between lessor and lessee. This bargaining is a disadvantage to the lessor in that it provides a focal point for the demands of the lessee with respect to maintenance of decorations and equipment. Furthermore, it brings into existence a periodic analysis of rental by both lessor and lessee to the end that one or the other may seek an adjustment.

For instance, in a declining market a tenant whose employment is steady, and whose income is adequate, may be perfectly happy about the amount he is paying for rent. Under ordinary circumstances he might not think of asking his landlord for a reduction. On the other hand, if his lease expires he is apt to analyze his rent in terms of its comparability to other rentals and in negotiation with the landlord feels duty bound to drive as hard a bargain as is possible. Even though the tenant would ultimately seek to establish an equitable relationship between his own rental and the rental currently being charged for comparable units, he might not have so specifically analyzed the market if his attention through the expiration of his lease had not been drawn to the necessity for bargaining.

The same situation, of course, prevails in a rising market. A landlord who was obtaining a satisfactory return on a given building might not be stimulated to raise his rentals at any given time, if all of his tenants were on a month-to-month basis. However, when the leases in the building expire, it is only natural that the lessor will analyze general price movements, occupancy conditions, and tenant income in order to assure himself that he is obtaining the highest possible income from the space.

The advantages and disadvantages of leases thus shift from the lessor to the lessee, depending upon the conditions prevailing in the general economy. The ideal leasing arrangement may be a written document that runs for an indefinite period into the future, and provides for mutual termination depending upon the requirements of the tenant and landlord for protection. Such leases would offer to both the landlord and the tenant the advantages of a written agreement and would not provide the disadvantage of a focal point for bargaining.

GENERAL LEASE PROVISIONS

Standard forms of leases have been adopted throughout the country by real estate boards, building owner groups, and property managers. These forms are designed to embrace covenants which are applicable to the types of buildings leased, as well as to local laws.

Essentially a lease is merely a memorandum of agreement which describes the premises demised, sets forth the term of tenure, and states the amount and method of rent payment. A simple memorandum of this type, dated and signed by both parties, constitutes a valid lease. However, it has been felt necessary because of the complexities of our legal system, to add a great many additional covenants and agreements to cover all possible areas of misunderstanding and dispute.

SPECIFIC COVENANTS

Service

Under the terms of most leases, the lessor covenants to provide services over and above the mere granting to the tenant the right to possess the described space for a stated term. If misunderstanding is to be avoided, the lease should specify the extent and amount of such service. In single-family dwellings the lease should state whether or not the tenant is obligated to take care of the grounds and to do exterior or interior painting; whether he is to maintain equipment, and if so what types; and whether he is to be liable for any and all repairs to the house.

In apartment buildings the lease should describe the janitor service, if any, which is to be rendered by the lessor. It should likewise state whether or not the lessor is to provide heat, and, if so—in the absence of specific city ordinances—the lease should delimit the season in which such heat is to be provided.

The lease should also cover the use of hot and cold water and state whether or not it shall be provided by the landlord, and, if so, for what purpose. In the light of the fact that more appliances are constantly being installed (air-conditioning, for example), the lease should provide for the eventuality of the installation of such equipment by the tenant. If the structure is equipped with elevators, the lease should recite the extent of the landlord's responsibility with respect to operation, and should protect the lessor against possible liability for change in such equipment.

In larger properties where utilities other than heat and water are furnished by the lessor, the conditions under which they are furnished must likewise be included in the lease, as well as provisions for the payment therefor, and the lessor's rights in the event of nonpayment.

Condition of Premises

Almost all leases provide for inspection of premises by the landlord, and the guarantee by the tenant that at the termination of his tenancy he will return the premises in as good condition as when he took possession of them, ordinary wear and tear excepted. This clause usually contains specific prohibitions against alteration, remodeling, etc., without the consent of the lessor. Likewise, it is frequently used to restrict the maintenance responsibilities of the lessor for services and expenditures not covered in the service sections of the lease.

Use of Premises

Virtually all leases provide that tenants will use the premises for a designated purpose. In the case of resident leases, the use of demised premises is usually restricted to the immediate family of the lessee. This prohibits the conversion of space to other uses and likewise restricts tenants from establishing a rooming house or other high-tenant occupancy which will add to wear and tear on the property. Prohibition against illegal use, with termination penalties, is usually included under this proviso. In larger properties where specific sets of rules for the guidance of tenants are in force, this section of the lease usually provides for a termination in the event of infraction. These rules may cover the keeping of pets, use of lawns, storage of goods, and other regulations having to do with occupancy.

Subletting or Assignment

In order that the lessor may be assured of his control over who may occupy the premises under terms of a lease, a covenant is generally included restricting the rights of a lessee to assign or convey the lease without the written consent of the lessor.

Fire Clause

Inasmuch as it is always possible for a building or specific premises thereon to be made untenantable by fire or other disaster, a clause is universally contained which provides for the disposition of the lease in such an event. This clause either provides for the right of the lessor to terminate the lease after the destruction or damage of the premises, or to repair or rehabilitate the premises within a certain specific length of time.

Landlord's Legal Remedies

Among the specific covenants in every lease are those which provide the landlord with what are thought to be adequate methods for terminating the lease estate in real property, for recovering possession of the premises, and for collecting rents and damages. These agreements are usually contained in a series of clauses which deal with re-entry and recovery of possession by the landlord, summary statutory dispossession proceedings, actions to recover rent, provision for attachment to enforce the collection of rent, statutory liens, judgment liens, and other collection remedies.

Whereas a great deal of the matter contained in these clauses originates in the common law, there is a substantial variance in the landlord's rights between the several states. In virtually all states, action taken under these clauses is properly in the field of the law and represents the work of lawyers and not real estate managers.

FURNISHED-APARTMENT LEASES

Furnished-apartment leases do not differ essentially from those covering unfurnished residences except that they contain additional provisions and covenants specifically applying to the furnishings and equipment provided by the lessor, as well as rules for the conduct of tenants in the building in which the apartment is located.

The principal covenant contained in furnished-apartment leases is one in which the lessee acknowledges receipt of the furnishings in the demised premises and agrees to return those furnishings to the landlord in as good condition as when the apartment was leased, ordinary wear excepted. In most cases the lessee further provides to reimburse the lessor for any articles either broken or missing at the expiration of the lease. In some cases an actual inventory of such furniture and equipment is made a part of the lease.

Inasmuch as the services in the typical furnished apartment or apartment hotel are more complex than those in the ordinary residential space, it is essential that service clauses be broadened to encompass all of the services to be provided.

LEASE RIDERS

Because it is the intent of the written lease to cover all possible areas of misunderstanding and disagreement, any covenants to a lease which are not covered by specific provisions of the standard form used should be made the subject of a special rider or exhibit and should be signed by both the lessor and the lessee and made a part of the lease.

Among the most common subjects for such riders or exhibits are special agreements respecting the termination of the lease during its term. In addition, specific agreements as to decorating, repair, alteration, and maintenance are often the subject of misunderstanding, and should be included in the written lease where one exists.

THE MANAGER AND LEASES

Elsewhere in this text we have commented on the fact that, although the manager of a building is employed by the owner of the property, his long-term reputation will be best served by assuming a role of complete fairness in his dealings with owner and tenant alike. It may not be possible for the professional manager to serve *all* owners. Some building owners desire to take advantage of tenants in such a manner that it would be unethical and unwise for the professional manager to agree to such methods.

Since leases are primarily designed to eliminate misunderstanding between lessor and lessee, it is important that the provisions of a lease be understood both by the building owner and the tenants. In any event, it is good public relations for the manager always to ask tenants whether or not they have read the leases which they have signed and to explain provisions the tenant does not understand.

Lease forms are in existence that are definitely unfair to tenants, and which contain covenants that will be stricken by those tenants who are fully informed or who ask their lawyers to review the lease form prior to signature. Other clauses, while not unfair to tenants in the light of the landlord's rights, are frequently stricken by tenants at the advice of their counsel.

In conclusion, the professional manager should not carelessly adopt a lease form merely because it enjoys a wide use but should adopt a form which is in his opinion a thoroughly reasonable agreement and which can be used uniformly by all tenants. The professional manager who seeks to build long-term goodwill should not use a lease from which informed people will remove basic covenants and which uninformed people will sign as a matter of faith. A proper lease form should be suitable to the informed and uninformed; its covenants should be insisted upon.

REVIEW QUESTIONS

1. Why is it important for a property manager to analyze the lease form to be used in respect to his particular properties?
2. What is a *rider* to a lease and when is it used?
3. Define lessor. Define lessee. What is a lease, and for what purpose is it written?
4. List the advantages: (1) to tenants; (2) to landlord when a lease is written for longer than a thirty-day period.
5. List the disadvantages: (1) to tenants; (2) to landlord when a lease is written for longer than a thirty-day period.
6. List the specific points which should be covered in a lease on unfurnished units.
7. What additional points are covered in a furnished-apartment lease?
8. What is the point of written leases if verbal agreements are binding by law? Is it possible to have a written lease that has all of its provisions stated in a completely unambiguous way?

SELECTED REFERENCES

"Checklist for a Residential Lease." *Real Estate Investors Report,* June 1974, pp. 4–5.

"Fire Insurance and Repair Clauses in Leases." *Real Property, Probate and Trust Journal,* Winter 1970, pp. 532–569.

Kratovil, Robert. *Real Estate Law.* 6th ed. Englewood Cliffs, N. J., Prentice-Hall, 1974. 479p.

McMichael, Stanley L. and O'Keefe, Paul T. *Leases: Percentage, Short and Long Term.* 6th ed. Englewood Cliffs, N. J., Prentice-Hall, 1974. 446p.

Thomas, Victor C. "What Belongs in the Residential Lease?" *Real Estate Today,* Oct. 1973, pp. 46–49.

CHAPTER 14

Office Building Analysis

INTRODUCTION

The management of office buildings is a specialization that increasingly commands the attention of broad groups of real estate people. Builders, developers, and owners must plan for meeting the management requirements even before the cornerstone of a new building is laid. And in the best cases management service will have been initiated long before the first tenant has gained occupancy.

In this chapter, attention is directed to the criteria by which existing office buildings can be valued as to the rentability of space and as to the potential rental cash flow that can be sought. By extension, the method of analysis mentioned here also can be applied to the development of new units of space —in new and remodeled buildings alike.

According to a standard dictionary definition, an office is a place, building, or series of rooms in which some particular service is supplied. In this way a room or building in which a person or firm transacts business or carries out stated occupations can be distinguished from shops, stores, factories, and the like.

The American people are no longer heavily preoccupied with the need to grow crops, raise livestock, or manufacture goods. For example, less than 5 percent of the labor force are farmers and less than 25 percent are engaged in manufacturing. Thus, over two-thirds of all workers today neither make nor produce the articles of commerce by which modern life styles are sustained. It follows that many workers now are occupants of office space.

That the demand for office space will continue to mount is sure. On the one side there are growing numbers of people whose occupations must be housed. And on the other, the rising standards of office occupancy create the need for the assignment of larger and larger floor-area spaces for each worker. Thus, a secretary may be given only a few tens to a few hundreds of square feet of working space, while her boss may be enjoying thousands of square feet of luxurious privacy.

Even with the use of the telephone, a large portion of the business conducted today in offices requires physical proximity. For example, lawyers need to be close to courts and clients; security dealers find it desirable to be near banks; banks should be located for their customers' convenience.

As cities grow and as business parallels such growth, this requirement of physical proximity creates a pressure for larger buildings in which more and more offices can be housed under one roof. This need for concentration of commercial activity is responsible for the surface pressure which produced multistory buildings in which thousands of employees might work at exactly the same location with businesses removed from one another vertically rather than horizontally.

We have discussed earlier the development of the multistory building which is commonly thought of as an office building. This type of building, however, is by no means the only type of office building in the country. Thousands of businesses are carried on in ground-floor offices, in two- or three-story buildings where offices are located above stores, in office sections of industrial plants, and in trailers. In fact, a trend that is important to consider is that the downtowns of our major cities no longer offer a balanced life and a wide range of possible activities. The result is that office buildings more and more are to be found in suburban centers. Whether or not urban renewal and city planning endeavors can reverse such trends in the future cannot be forecast. However, there are major programs of commercial building in most cities today.

SUBURBAN OFFICE CENTER

The suburban atmosphere is preserved in the Coventry Green Office Center in Crystal Lake, Illinois. Several separate entrances to the office add to the feeling of privacy without isolation. The entrance in the foreground is to two suites, and in the left background is a directory for another entrance.

MULTISTORY OFFICE BUILDING

An architect's rendering gives a helicopter's eye view of the Centre Square Office Building Complex located in Philadelphia. The trend toward concentration of commercial activity and physical proximity continues to be one of the major justifications for building multistory buildings in spite of the problems inherent in large downtown areas.

FINANCIAL HISTORY

Originally, a very high percentage of the nation's office construction was by property owners who sought an investment yield through an improvement on suitable commercial land. These properties were financed either out of the surplus funds of the owner or out of a combination of such surplus funds and a loan secured by a single mortgage on the building. Those office buildings which were not owned by a single proprietor and built for investment purposes were owned by what we might call "bulk user" occupants and were built by specific enterprises as a solution to their housing problems. Banks, newspapers, government agencies, and large commercial organizations were "bulk users" who frequently erected such property. In some cases this class of owner built a building larger than that sufficient to house the single enterprise, and, to an extent, became an investor as well as a user.

The "split" mortgage, which came into wide use in the twenties, provided a financial background for what we might call the "promotional" building, erected by promoters who desired to take advantage of liberal financing and strong markets. These buildings were often in corporate ownership, and their stocks were widely held.

Analysis of the financial history of office buildings—like other types of construction—indicates a constant long-term increase in construction cost and a concomitant increase in rentals required to sustain investments. Whereas there are still some instances of the erection of "promotional" office buildings (built by risk-taking entrepreneurs as investments), the trend in recent years has been toward institutional ownership—by large corporations, banks, insurance companies, and others whose prime motivations have been their need for space and the desirability of "image" in the mind of the public.

In the quarter-century following the crash of 1929, multistory office building construction virtually ceased in the typical U.S. city. The reason was that the level of office space rentals would simply not support the construction and operating costs of new office structures. During this period, the expansion of commercial space in most areas was accommodated in two ways: first, by conversion of "loft" and other retail or industrial buildings to office occupancy and, second, by the construction of one- and two-story office buildings in outlying areas which could be erected more cheaply than multistory structures and could be located on relatively inexpensive land.

In areas of extraordinarily rapid commercial or population expansion (such as in New York, Miami, Dallas, Los Angeles, and a few other cities), new multistory buildings were finally undertaken. In most cases these properties were erected by so-called bulk users who needed more space, but could not obtain it on rental.

The dramatic rise in construction costs and changes in techniques in the intervening quarter-century—plus the equally dramatic developments in operating costs and equipment—are seen in the character of the new office build-ings. Their rentals range from $7.50 to $12.50 per square foot. Their exteriors are largely glass and metal. High-speed automatic elevators serve "blocks" of floors, and some floors are also connected by escalators (as in multilevel banks). Air conditioning is standard equipment, as is sound control, and high foot-candle lighting. These new buildings have completely changed the con-cept of "Grade A" ratings as applied to office structures and, in many cases, have resulted in a shift of prestige locations.

As we have noted in previous chapters, rental value is established primarily by the comparability of a specific space with all other space at any given time and by the overall relationship between supply and demand. In the new buildings described above, in these structures which are dramatically different from their predecessors, *comparability* is on the "plus" side. Generally speak-ing, rental rates for the first such structure are established on the basis of the production of a satisfactory rate of return on the investment involved. There-after, rental rates in subsequent structures are established on the basis of the success of the first building, augmented by the standard market measurement technique discussed below.

METHOD OF EVALUATION

Since it is necessary that the manager ultimately establish a base rate rental for the property under analysis and for all competitive properties, some objec-tive system of grading office buildings in terms of their respective desirability must be used. One useful measurement of desirability can be established on the twelve criteria outlined below, against which each of the competitive structures can be measured.

In virtually every city of the United States there are one or more buildings which, under an analysis such as we propose, will be automatically classified as "Class A" properties. These "Class A" properties are apt to excel in all twelve of the criteria we have established for the measurement of office building value. On the other hand, there are also "Class B" and "Class C" buildings, which are so rated because of defects revealed when analyzed against these criteria.

It is possible to find two buildings, one of which is rated as "Class B" and the other as "Class C," merely because the "Class B" building is located in a prestige section of a prestige street, while the "Class C" building (identi-cal in all other respects) is located on a less-desirable street. It must be kept in mind, however, that there is no such thing as *permanent* prestige as it relates to a street or neighborhood. Prestige is established primarily by the character of improvements and the occupants. If Wall Street has tradition-ally been the prestige street, but if Park Avenue has all of the newest build-ings and finest tenants, then the prestige address becomes Park Avenue.

Thus it is that prestige and preferences change as constantly as the hemlines in women's fashions.

Appearance of Surroundings

The value of office building space clearly is affected by the appearance of the surrounding land and improvements thereon. Obsolete and dilapidated buildings detract from an area and reduces the value of even the most beautiful structure which may adjoin such buildings. Dirty streets, unsightly vacant land, and tawdry occupancy are likewise deterrents to values. If such land uses dominate an area, it is virtually impossible for any single building to surmount the attending damage.

Contrariwise, desirable surroundings tend to raise the value of the older but less-desirable adjacent properties. The age of office buildings is not particularly important to their prestige or desirability. Appearance of surroundings, however, is always extremely important.

Transportation

Because multistory buildings house hundreds of persons who must come to the offices to work and transact business, the available transportation facilities vitally affect the valuation.

It is not necessary to give a great deal of attention to this factor, since it is highly improbable that a multistory office building would be erected on any location without adequate transportation facilities. The manager's analysis, however, should embrace a review of transportation facilities. The shift of transportation from public carriers to private vehicles has produced an emphasis on parking and accessibility which is increasingly important in determining the desirability of an office building location.

The Building as an Address

Snobbish and class-conscious attitudes are not unknown in the commercial world. Prestige is an important factor in business. To a degree, it can be attained by close association with established businesses which enjoy prestige. A budding lawyer with a keen sense of ambition will want to have his office in the same building with the leading law firms or, at least, on the same street or in the same general area. The financial institution will choose to locate in the most desirable building in the financial district or as close to such a prestige center as is possible.

Further Criteria of Location

The value of an office building to prospective tenants is in part measurable by its location with respect to business facilities. Even though many requirements for proximity of location have been eased by the availability of instantaneous communication, some types of business find it important to be located close to other offices in the same line of business or in collateral lines with which their operation is associated. As an example, insurance companies find it valuable to be located close to companies serving other lines of coverage, and to brokerage offices whose accounts they constantly service. And law firms find it quite valuable to be close to courthouses and in an area centrally located for the better service of their clients.

It is also important in the measurement of office desirability to consider access to financial services. Bank buildings have long had the practical advantage of offering financial facilities to their tenants while at the same time offering the prestige of association with a leading financial institution. This is particularly true of tenants in the investment field, where close proximity to safe-deposit facilities is virtually a necessity.

Proximity to retail facilities, desirable eating places, and various types of service facilities are also important factors in determining the value of office space.

Building Appearance

When appraising the rental value of a specific office building, one must take into consideration the physical appearance of the building. Although it is possible under certain circumstances for buildings of advanced age to maintain a high level of desirability (because of an *excellent* rating in other factors), one seldom finds a "Grade A" office building with an exterior appearance indicating a high degree of obsolescence in either design or condition. Buildings, like clothing, have style. If the exterior of a building is in conformity with the current style trend in high-grade buildings, then its age need make no great difference, provided that the property is obviously well maintained.

Building Lobby

Important factors in grading the desirability of an office building are the appearance, style, character, and lighting of its central lobby. The entrance of any building (whether commercial or residential) is in a sense the *setting* in which the tenants' business is conducted. The lobby will not only be rated on architectural quality and the effectiveness of illumination, but upon the character established by the management of the property. Poor management may be indicated by a lack of cleanliness and proper maintenance or by occupancy which does not bespeak a high character of tenancy. Unsightly newsstands, or a badly operated cigar stand, can markedly lower the quality, or *setting,* of an otherwise attractive lobby.

Building Elevators

Since vertical transportation is vital to the modern multistory office building, the character and quality of elevator equipment and service are extremely important in the measurement of overall desirability. The first factor in the

grading of elevators and elevator service is the *location* of the elevators themselves within the building. If it is necessary for tenants and the general public
to walk a half block after entering the main entrance of the building in order
to arrive at the banks of elevators, tenants will grow weary of occupancy and
will tend to lower their appraisal of the value of the building's space. This is
particularly true when tenants must retrace their steps in order to get to their
individual offices after arriving on their own floor.

A second factor in the appraisal of elevators and elevator service is the
appearance of the elevator entrances, cabs, and operators. If the cab is modern
in styling, adequately illuminated and ventilated, is serviced by a well-
groomed, smartly outfitted operator, and is equipped with well-maintained
floor covering, then the appearance of the elevator is judged to be excellent.
Any deviation from a high level of visual desirability in any one of these factors
tends to detract from the space value of any office building.

The third criterion by which the public measures elevator service in an office
building is the *newness* and *operating facility* of the equipment. The public
tends to grade a building on the quality of the elevator equipment. Automatic
hatchway doors and signal-control elevators of high speed are the standards
by which elevator equipment is measured.

Speed in elevators from a tenant's point of view does not necessarily mean
the rate of travel of the elevator in feet per minute, but rather is the interval
between the departures of elevators from the ground floor and from the several
floors in the building. Elevator service which provides an elevator at each floor
in each direction every 25 seconds at an elevator speed of 600 feet per minute
is superior to elevator service at 800 feet per minute where the interval between
cars is 50 seconds.

Needless to say, the appraisal of elevators should include the hatchways and
entrance doors on all floors.

Building Corridors

As with the lobby, the avenues to individual offices are appraised in terms
of physical desirability. Floors and floor coverings, corridor walls, entrance
doors, and illumination are basic factors in this comparison with current styles.

Office Interiors

Arriving at the office itself, the tenant's appraisal of the desirability of office
interiors begins with the possible layout afforded by the space. This means the
number of windows and the view and light afforded, the depth of the office
from corridor to wall, and the width of the office between supporting columns.
Although we shall discuss these factors of design in connection with the
detailed appraisal of interior space, the *layout* possibilities generally afforded
by the building are an important factor in its overall desirability.

OFFICE INTERIOR

The general office layout of the First National Bank Building in Memphis is that of a formal arrangement with all desks facing the same way in straight rows from one side to the other. (Photo by Alexandre Georges)

OFFICE LOBBY

The spacious reception area of the law offices of Jenner & Block on the 43rd floor of the One IBM Plaza building in Chicago is typified by attractive lighting and high quality of decoration.

In addition to factors of layout, the tenant is interested in the quality of decoration, interior wall finish, light fixtures and illumination, radiators, washing facilities, and ceiling height. All of these will be judged by their conformity, or lack of conformity, to the theoretically ideal office interior, which is generally represented by the *best* building in town. In the final analysis their value is judged on the basis of comparability, as is true in the case of most space.

Tenant Services

Aside from the elevator service, which has been specifically discussed, the renting public measures office building desirability from the point of view of the quality and adequacy of the various services which either are included in the rent or are obtainable from the building. Among the more important of such services are office cleaning, janitor service, protection services, and general response to service requests. Many office buildings have auditoriums or meeting places which can be rented by tenants on an "as used" basis. These, and the charges made for them, are noted carefully by the prudent tenant who is shopping for office space, or who is determining the wisdom of remaining in a particular office building instead of moving. Often these "extras" are the deciding factors that tip the scale.

Management

The reputation of a building's management is a measurable factor in the value of its space. Business houses are sensitive to the quality of management and its influence on the overall desirability of the building, and to the efficiency of the services rendered. The level of maintenance is an extremely important factor in any building's desirability, but is particularly vital to individual businesses.

Building Tenancy

In discussing the value of a building as an "address," we introduced the thought that office buildings are rated by the public on the basis of the prestige of address. This prestige is, in a large measure, of course, established by the surroundings, transportation, physical appearance, equipment, and maintenance. But it is also produced by the character of the tenants who are known to be occupants.

Commercial buildings are rated by the size, financial standing, and general reputation of their tenants. Professional buildings are rated according to the standing and reputation of the professional men who have their offices there. Financial buildings are frequently rated by the prestige of the bank which may be located on the lower floors or by the character of the financial institutions which are housed in the property. Thus, in any appraisal of office building space value, one must study the tenancy list and establish its value as a prestige factor.

VALUING INTERIOR SPACE

The above factors enable the analyst of buildings to establish the comparable value of the property as a whole to other office buildings in the community. In so doing, a "base rate" for the property can be established.

PRESTIGE BUILDING APPEARANCE

Looking down the winding Nicollet Mall, pedestrians see the Northwestern National Life Insurance building in Minneapolis with its Yamasaki-designed, pillared-architecture surrounded by trees, shrubbery, and flowers.

By *base rate* we mean a price per square foot which refers to the building as a whole and is an expression of its current value in relation to other buildings which have been appraised. For example, if the best building in the business community has a base rate of $7 per square foot per year, and if after the application of the rating measurements above, a building under analysis is rated somewhat inferior to the best building it may be given a value of $6.25 per square foot per year.

Two Chicago building managers, Leo J. Sheridan and Waldemar Karkow, have perfected a formula for spreading a rental schedule over an office building once a base rate has been established by study of the comparable status of the property. Under this formula, the base rate of an individual property is the value of a typical eighth-floor bay on a street front. By *typical* is meant an office bay containing two windows and having a depth of 25 feet from window to corridor and a width of 16 feet between columns. Adjustments in this base rate are made for increased depth or greater shallowness, for increased width, for elevation within the building, for corner influence, and for the exposure.

For example, if the base rate of a building for a typical bay on the eighth floor is found to be $6 per square foot, an identical space on the fourteenth floor would be higher in value *solely* because of being on a higher floor. If there happened to be a setback in the building, which produced a shallower office on the fourteenth floor (and hence a greater proximity of the space to the window area), an additional increase would be made. Similarly, if on a lower floor the depth of the office was 35 feet rather than 25 feet, a deduction would be made because of the quality of the space.

The Sheridan-Karkow formula can be obtained for study by individual students through the National Association of Building Owners and Managers. Although it does not represent a universally accurate system for the spreading of rental values over individual properties, it is unquestionably a good device for such procedure and is well worth careful attention.

REVIEW QUESTIONS

1. What is meant by *base rate* rental? Give an example.
2. How are the following buildings rated for prestige—financial, professional, jewelers? Justify your answer.
3. What is the Sheridan-Karkow formula? When would you use it? Give an example of its use.
4. What is meant by *physical proximity,* and how does this affect the office building?
5. Name the points of importance in appraising elevators in an office building.
6. What is meant by a *promotional building?*
7. Upon what points would you grade a building lobby?
8. What twelve points would you check in evaluating the desirability of an office building?

9. You have a vacancy in an office building which is occupied 80 percent by wholesale jewelers. You are approached by (A) a luggage jobber, (B) a furrier who sells at retail, and (C) a wholesale optical concern. You have no present tenants in the classifications of A, B, or C. All need the same amount of space. What are the desirable features your building possesses for each? Solely from the standpoint of business classification, which would you consider most desirable to you and why?

SELECTED REFERENCES

Building Owners and Managers Association. *Office Building Experience Exchange Report.* Chicago, Ill., published annually since 1920.

"Creating an Office Building." *Buildings,* June through Dec., 1967 issues.

Hanford, Lloyd D., Sr. *Analysis and Management of Investment Property.* 3d ed. Chicago, Ill., Institute of Real Estate Management, 1970. 178p.

"How to Analyze Office Space Demand." *Mortgage and Real Estate Executives Report,* Sept. 5, 1972, pp. 1–2.

CHAPTER 15

Managing the Commercial Building

INTRODUCTION

In the previous chapter we dealt with methods of appraising the comparative values of office building space as a step toward the setting of rentals. In this chapter we shall talk about the larger questions of merchandising and managing commercial buildings—i.e., office buildings, combination store-and-office buildings, and retail store buildings. In the following chapters devoted to the marketing process, further ideas pertaining to retail stores and to various special-purpose buildings will be presented.

Some Modern Trends

In the past decade, institutional developers of office buildings designed primarily for their own corporate offices, but also for investment, have often declined to make much ground-floor space in their buildings available for tenancy. Chicago examples are the IBM Building and the Dirkson Federal Building. In other major cities the trend is the same. Apparently it is felt that tenancy would detract from the institutional image created by the building. There are two disadvantages, however. First, the owners sacrifice the very considerable income that would flow from the added tenant rentals. And second, the elimination of the traditional stores robs such institutional buildings of life and action during the evening hours and on weekends and holidays. The result: central business districts have become less and less animated except during the normal daylight working hours, and therefore increasingly subject to the blights of criminal activity.

In any case, it should be mentioned that, because of the cost of office building construction today, the cash flows in the early years of occupancy are usually insufficient to provide for an adequate return on the investment. Therefore, major buildings require subsidies for these early years.

That fact is having a profound influence on real estate ownership, as already noted in chapter 6. For the most part, individual entrepreneurs no longer construct the major central-city, multistore buildings. Instead, they are being replaced by institutions such as banks, major corporations, insurance companies, and the like. And the traditional developers—no longer able to compete with the corporate giants who dominate the major urban markets—

CORPORATE OFFICE BUILDING

The IBM building in Chicago was designed primarily for its own corporate offices. The trend in latter years has been for major structures to occupy half city blocks and often full blocks. Note the landscaped plaza in foreground.

are left to concentrate their efforts in the outlying regions (for example, around airports, regional shopping centers, and other free-standing locations).

Finally, as another expression of modern trends, many major structures in the central business district today are built to occupy half or all of a city block. In part this is a response to zoning requirements for the ground area to be proportional to the height and overall size of the building. Not only do pedestrians occasionally want to see the sky from the expanse of a landscaped plaza, but the institutional owners of skyscrapers are glad to pay for the extra ground space which enhances the visibility of imposing corporate headquarters. In addition, economics dictates the desirability of constructing bigger and taller buildings, so that the burden of institutional subsidization can be minimized.

MERCHANDISING OFFICE SPACE

Throughout the period for which occupancy statistics are available on the nation's office buildings, the managers of such properties have been faced with problems of space merchandising. Although in some buildings, 100 percent occupancy has been recorded for brief periods, the level of general business activity over the long term has failed to support a demand sufficient to utilize all of the country's office space. Moreover, the dynamics of office building construction have been such that, when a point of high average occupancy is reached, new structures are built, thus introducing new units.

The problem of renting office space in periods of "normal" business activity entails a program of obtaining prospective space users, creating a desire on their part to investigate the available space, facilitating the prospect's inspection of the space, demonstrating the adaptability of the space to the prospective client's needs, establishing in the prospect's mind a conviction that the space represents good value, and inducing the prospect to exhibit preference for the space by closing a lease arrangement. From a purely operational point of view, the renting of office space also requires a substantial amount of planning by the managers so that expansion and contraction of his tenants' requirements can be accommodated without major expense. There is also the matter of space preparation for exhibit to prospective tenants, as well as for tenants who have concluded leases.

Naturally, there is a great advantage in appointing the manager of a new building as early as the first announcement of the construction plans. In this way he can acquaint himself with every detail of the structure as it is being erected, and he can initiate and launch the promotional campaign that will serve to maximize the initial occupancy level. Although typically the prospective tenant in the average American city is not educated to the leasing of space prior to its being available for inspection, a considerable amount of effective work can be done by the manager during the construction of the building.

If the property is being put up by a prestigious institutional owner (such as a bank, an insurance company, or a major commercial corporation) it is probable that the owner alone will influence a substantial number of tenants to locate within the building. For example, the owner undoubtedly will have connections with a law firm, an advertising agency, or any of a number of other firms that can be persuaded to become tenants. All such prospective tenants should be placed on the initial list of prospects and extended an invitation to join in the original tenancy of the building. A list should also be prepared of other logical prospects who likely will be influenced by the location and other advantages of the proposed property. Courtesy calls, for example, can be paid on such prospective tenants—not with the hope of closing a deal with them in advance of the opening of the property, but rather to acquaint them with the advantages.

During the construction of the building certain occasions can be seized upon for publicity purposes, such as ground breaking, and the so-called topping out ceremony, frequently held for tall buildings. Finally, the official opening of the building should be marked with a reception to which the friends, clients, and prospective tenants of the owner should be invited to inspect the new property and its spaces.

Obviously, literature describing the new building and its facilities should be prepared in attractive brochure form. These can then be followed by "point-of-sale" printed matter such as floor plans and instructions to new tenants.

Obtaining Prospects

In earlier chapters we noted the essentially gregarious nature of commercial enterprises. Proximity of location often is a distinct advantage to businesses in allied lines. In almost every city large enough to support more than one or two office buildings, this classification of tenancy results in certain buildings being especially attractive to lawyers, while other buildings may be devoted to insurance companies, financial houses, and other distinct categories.

Many real estate management firms which specialize in office space management create and maintain a list of expiration dates of tenants' leases. As much as a year in advance, the space salesman of the management firm is alerted to the expiration and solicitation is begun. Most office building tenants start thinking about their quarters long in advance of the expiration of their lease. The larger the tenant, the more lead time required for solicitation. In very large firms, contacts are made as much as three to five years in advance of the actual date when action must be taken.

The office building manager must set about obtaining prospects for his space. The first step in the formulation of a rental program for an office building should be an analysis of its suitability for specialized use. In some cases this specialized use will have been established prior to the manager's assumption of the administration of the building. If the building houses a bank and is located in the center of the financial district, it will undoubtedly be largely tenanted by brokerage houses, investment companies, corporation lawyers, and grade-A commercial establishments. If the building is directly across the street from the principal court house, it probably will attract lawyers, court attachés, and mortgage firms.

Whenever a concentration of one type of tenant is indicated, the manager should take steps to see that centers of attraction are established in his building. For example, lawyers find it extremely desirable to locate in the same office building which houses the local bar association or in which there is a good law library. Financial institutions find it extremely desirable to be located in a building in which there is an adequate vault facility. Insurance brokerage firms prefer to be in properties which house branch offices of national corporations.

The desire of like businesses to be together is not restricted to the practice of law, the sale of securities, or the underwriting of insurance, however. In larger cities virtually all types of commercial activity tend to congregate. Certain buildings house jewelers, others are centers of mercantile trade, and still others are principally occupied by contractors. Once any building has been established as a center of a dynamic field of activity, the consumer pressure against the building is stabilized. For that reason, one of the first steps in the analysis of the potential market for an office building should be to determine whether or not it is logical for the building to serve a specific field of enterprise and, if so, what steps can be taken to attract either a large, single, dominant enterprise in the specialty or some center of attraction comparable to a law library in a lawyers' building.

It is, of course, impossible for every building to become the headquarters for a particular type of business. In most cities, the number of individual firms in any one specialty is hardly large enough to fill an office building. The same principle of market analysis, however, should be applied anyway. It might be assumed that every individual, firm, or government agency in the community is a logical prospect for any office building, although certainly a given building is more desirable for some potential space users than for others. If this is true, the manager should devote his selling effort to those prospects who are the most logical users of his space and, therefore, with whom his selling efforts would have the highest potentialities of success. The preparation of prospect lists is as much a qualitative as a quantitative task.

Arousing the Prospect's Interest

In the normal course of events a certain number of inquiries for space will come to the office building manager, either in the form of telephone calls or written requests for information, or as prospects who actually come to the manager's office asking to see and to be quoted prices on space. Except in abnormal periods, or in buildings which enjoy unusually high specialized consumer pressure, the voluntary inquiry of prospects is insufficient to maintain 100 percent occupancy. A substantial portion of the renting activity must be generated by the building management through solicitation.

Since it is inconceivable that a prospective tenant would rent space sight unseen, the first objective of the office building solicitor is to arouse the interest of the prospect sufficiently to get him to come and look at the space for sale. Generally speaking, the principal arguments which can be used by a solicitor to arouse the interest of an otherwise disinterested prospect are the following:

1. *Price advantage:* All well-managed businesses are continuously interested in improving net profits. If the solicitor of office space can indicate a substantial price advantage in an alternate location which meets the requirements of the prospect, he can be certain of arousing sufficient interest to provoke at least preliminary action.

2. *Increased efficiency:* If the solicitor can demonstrate to a prospect that by moving to another building the prospect will materially increase efficiency, he is again almost certain of getting results. Increased efficiency is merely another form of price advantage, yet it is a somewhat different approach and broadens the opportunities for prospect response. The promise of increased efficiency by the solicitor should be implemented, if possible, with plans and layouts demonstrating to the prospective client just how the new location increases efficiency. This demonstration of the adaptability of space is a particularly potent force in arousing the prospect's interest. For example, experience shows that the payroll in the average office building space is more than ten times the rental. Thus, if the tenant can increase efficiency by 10 percent in new, better-designed space, the savings may be greater than the gross rental. It means that, in effect, a higher rental for efficient space is actually *cheaper* than a lower rental for inefficient space.

3. *Increased prestige:* The preceding chapter discussed the factor of *prestige* as one of the important value determinants in office space. Careful analysis of prospects will indicate those businesses which can benefit the most from increasing the prestige of their location. Effective exposition of this value to a qualified prospective client should produce an active interest.

4. *Economy:* The reference to price advantage above envisions *comparable* space at a price advantage. Solicitations based upon *economy* refer to lower-priced space, not necessarily comparable to that presently being occupied by the prospect. For example, many businesses are located in

so-called Grade A buildings in prime commercial locations, but could just as well be located in much less expensive space in a different type of property. In a following chapter we discuss the conversion of loft buildings to office space. Especially in periods of declining general business activity, the proper selling of *economy* space often is highly productive.

To summarize, the solicitor should not call on the prospect until he is familiar with the business being conducted, the customers of that business and all the details that can be found out in advance about the prospect. He should be prepared to discuss in depth the advantages of his building's location (if, indeed, these advantages exist) to the conduct of his prospect's business, and what the advantages are in terms of access to transportation for the customer's client and to shopping, etc. Obviously, having parking available will help attract desirable employees. And then there is the matter of security. Special personnel should be assigned for the protection of tenants' goods and to control access to the building after normal business hours. Similarly, the exits of the building should be controlled, to monitor persons departing with packages and equipment. The corridors should be patroled to prevent unauthorized solicitation. With these controls we are left with other questions. What amenities are available within the building? Clubs? Restaurants? Personal services (barber and beauty)? Shops?

If the manager's building does not happen to have a prestige address, then it may be appropriate to discuss the economy of operation. Many businesses that operate on small profit margins are vitally interested in holding their office costs to the lowest possible levels. Where such objectives seem important to the prospects, the managers should be prepared to explore them in detail.

Harking back to our general discussion of the rental of residential quarters, the same advantages of pointing out value factors pertain to selling office space.

Personal contact is the only truly effective method of soliciting office space. Although *inquiries* for space can be provoked through advertising, the real action-getting sales work is done by personal solicitation.

Facilitating Space Inspection

The office building that is actively soliciting new tenants must be prepared to receive the prospect who comes unannounced, even though the solicitor will try wherever possible to encourage the prospect to telephone him before coming to the building to examine space.

It is vital to the sales effort that the personnel in the office of the building be acquainted with the prospects who have been called upon by the solicitor. Then, when a prospective client presents himself in the absence of the solicitor, the person in the office whose duty it is to show the space will be prepared. The prospect's needs can be discussed intelligently, and he can be shown space of the type which is suitable for his requirements and most likely to interest him.

In buildings of substantial vacancy the management should set up for exhibition purposes a *model* office or several model offices. In cases where it is impractical to erect such model offices, the management should make arrangements with tenants whose offices are attractively laid out and decorated, so that prospects may be shown finished space. It is fundamental in any kind of merchandising to display products for sale only in their most attractive form. The exhibition of vacant and unprepared office space to prospective clients represents poor merchandising.

Establishing Value Conviction

Once the interest of the prospective office tenant has been aroused sufficiently to cause him to examine the space for sale, and once its adaptability to his needs has been clearly demonstrated, the remaining selling effort must be concentrated on establishing in the prospect's mind a conviction of the value of purchasing that specific space.

There are two principal techniques of establishing such a value conviction. The first is the employment of a thorough and adequate competitive analysis, whereby the prospect is convinced that the space in question represents a wise purchase in the light of available choices. The second technique is that of completely enumerating the value components to reduce sales resistance. This latter technique depends on a thorough exploitation of the advantages of purchase, as measured against all of the criteria which could possibly be applied by the prospective tenant.

OFFICE BUILDING MAINTENANCE

Many phases of maintenance in office buildings are identical with other properties. The principal areas of maintenance unique in office building operation are concerned with elevators and with the cleaning and alteration of space for tenant use.

Elevator Operation

The problem with elevators in office buildings is to ensure good service. Unfortunately, management is usually not in a position to dictate the number of elevators originally installed in an office building or in the design of the elevator equipment. All too frequently, the builders of office buildings fail to provide adequate equipment. (This underscores the importance of management participation in advance planning of new structures.)

Generally speaking, office buildings are taller than residential buildings with elevators. As a result, the mileage traveled by a typical office building elevator is considerably greater and the elevators require much more constant, more vigilant maintenance. Moreover, in residential buildings elevators are operated only when there is a call for service, while in office buildings elevators are moving up and down the shaft in *anticipation* of service calls.

The two principal problems are maintenance of a satisfactory schedule providing for a minimum of time between available elevators, and the satisfactory movement of the public during peak traffic hours. As noted in the previous chapter, tenants are apt to judge the character of elevator service by the length of time they are required to wait. The only method available to management to establish the minimum interval between elevators is that which provides for the regular dispatching of elevators both from the ground floor and from the top of the shaft.

With the advent of fully automatic elevators in virtually all but the oldest buildings, the elevator starter actually has become a building receptionist and information officer. In buildings that have multiple banks of elevators, such a person is usually provided for each bank of four to eight elevators. In many larger buildings there is a man stationed who is really the building reception officer and who directs people to different elevator banks and provides them with general information. In the very large structures an information booth is established at the entrance to the building to dispense such information.

There surely is as much difference between the performance of these receptionist-starter-information people as between buildings. In some cases they are alert to the public and attentive to their needs; in others they are merely lolling around having conversation with their friends or the staffs of the various tenants. Obviously the difference in performance is due to lack of training. These people should be taught that they are valuable representatives of management and that their performance does much to give a building a good or bad image.

Building Cleaning

The cleaning problems of office buildings differ from those found in other types of buildings. The relatively heavier traffic in office buildings produces a much greater need for cleaning activity in public spaces. Thus, the bulk of office building cleaning activity must be carried on at night.

A great many office buildings in recent years have turned over their cleaning problems to specialized contracting firms.

The cleaning of public spaces in office buildings is principally carried on at night by the members of the night crew, but an adequate staff of day janitors and cleaners must be maintained to safeguard the cleanliness of the property at all times. Daytime cleaning activities principally involve the cleaning of lobby floors, elevator cabs, front walks and entrances, and special areas and windows. Since the principal cleaning crew works on a night shift, only those cleaning activities which must be done during the day should be handled by the day crew.

Historically, night cleaning in office buildings was started after 11:00 P.M. and carried through to completion. It was done by employees of the building itself (mostly women) under the direction of a night superintendent. In recent years, however, there has been a shortage of such workers. The practice of contracting for union-affiliated night cleaning with companies specializing in that field has grown appreciably.

Building Alterations

Office spaces are custom-designed to meet the requirements of commercial tenants. These requirements call for a wide variety of interior design and equipment and in the larger buildings necessitate the constant service of building trades mechanics.

The question of "who shall pay for tenants' alterations" is one which depends to a large degree upon the level of supply and demand. During the course of an *upswing* in the demand for office space, when price trends are strong, building operators unload as much of the cost of operations as possible on the tenant. In times of high vacancy and a weak market for office space, building management is increasingly willing to make alterations to attract desirable tenants. However, there is an underlying trend toward the universal adoption of a policy that tenant alterations should be done at the expense of the tenant. This is indeed a logical trend, since the requirements of various types of tenants differ greatly, and therefore the alteration costs have no direct relationship to the square foot rental charge.

Regardless of who bears the expense of alteration, we are interested here in the methods of handling alterations. In small office buildings, where the volume of alteration work does not justify the permanent employment of building trades mechanics, outside contractors are brought into the building from time to time to make alterations in accordance with plans and specifications developed by the management. In larger buildings, where electricians, carpenters, and plumbers are employed on a full-time basis, the work in various specialties is carried on by the building crew. Except in the case of extremely large buildings, the masonry work involved in the construction of tile partition walls is done by an outside contractor.

As the standards of housing for American business reach higher and higher levels, the complexity of office building alterations is increased. These higher standards involve the installation of more adequate lighting equipment, sound control systems, air-conditioning systems, additional toilet facilities, and—in an increasing number of instances—cooking, refrigeration, electric typewriters, recorders, mimeographs, and recreational equipment (e.g., saunas, wet bars, and game rooms). The heavier use of office machinery requiring electric power combines with these other factors to increase constantly the loads on original office building equipment, in many cases to a point where entirely new electrical systems need to be installed. All of these factors focus on the need for greater control of physical operation in office buildings and increased technical know-how on the part of building staffs.

ORGANIZING THE STAFF

The operating organization of office buildings under the manager is usually headed by several major operating executives. The chief engineer is responsible for the physical plant and equipment—the heating plant operation, the plumbing system, the electrical system (including elevators), and the maintenance of all equipment. The second executive operating under the manager is usually known as building superintendent. His area of responsibility includes all cleaning activities, alterations, decorating, and services to tenants. The building superintendent and the chief engineer are day employees. The night crew is under the direction of another executive usually described as assistant superintendent or night superintendent.

Members of the day crew in the typical office building are usually men. The night crew is composed of both men and women, with men performing the heavy tasks involved in public space maintenance, and with women employed almost exclusively for the cleaning work in tenant spaces. In larger properties one of these night cleaning women assumes direct supervision over all of the female employees and is usually known as the forelady. She works under the direction of the night superintendent, and her duties embrace recruiting and training female personnel and inspecting cleaned spaces.

Protection Service

Office buildings in large metropolitan areas increasingly are finding it necessary to employ a quasi-police staff, working either directly under the manager or under the general superintendent. The problems of traffic at front entrances are increasingly complex, and the services of doormen, who are also special policemen, frequently are employed. Office building tenants are entitled to protection from itinerant vendors, from petty thieves, and from moral delinquents.

OFFICE BUILDING ACCOUNTING

One of the most comprehensive systems of accounting available to any type of building has been developed for office buildings by the National Association of Building Owners and Managers. It is available on request to students and managers, so it is unnecessary to include in this text a specific discussion of office building accounting. There are tremendous benefits to be gained by standardization of accounting procedure. The manager or management firm that procures this standardized accounting manual will be able to compare results with other members of the industry and measure operations against uniform standards.

MAINTAINING STORE PROPERTIES

It is a common practice in the United States to lease store buildings on terms which provide that the tenant, or lessee, will assume responsibility for maintaining the interior of the space leased, with the landlord being responsible only for the maintenance of the roof and the exterior of the property. This means that the tenant will provide fuel and operate the heating plant, will maintain the store front, do all necessary decorating and interior alterations, pay for his water and utilities, install electrical or mechanical equipment, and provide his own janitor service. Thus the maintenance of store properties is concerned largely with the exterior of the building and involves techniques which are discussed elsewhere in this text.

RENTING STORE PROPERTIES

In other chapters, the techniques of retail location and establishing store rentals has been presented. The real estate manager's responsibility extends beyond these analyses and is aimed at maintaining as near 100 percent occupancy as is possible. This involves special selling techniques as they relate to store rentals.

There is a substantial difference between renting store space and leasing residential properties. In the case of a vacant store, the problem of the manager is not simply that of finding an occupant, but of finding a tenant that can establish in the vacant store a business with the greatest chance of success. The problem involves substantial creative activity on the part of the manager, who must first analyze the location in terms of its merchandising potentials, and then must seek a tenant who will be interested in starting a business in that space to meet the indicated demand. In other words, it is not only a question of finding a tenant who is willing to lease the store, but of representing the owner in determining that the tenant will also contribute to the success of adjacent stores which already might be occupied, and will itself be a success. A business that fails perforce is a tenant lost.

After the manager has determined the potential of the location by application of the techniques of analysis represented in chapter 13, his problem is one of locating prospective tenants in the indicated field of endeavor. Although advertising and other sources of prospect production are available to the managers, there are comparatively few store tenants. The ones that are available may not be interested in the line of business which the manager feels has the highest likelihood of prospering. Where difficulty is encountered in finding likely prospects, the manager must plan a campaign of solicitation and personal interviews designed to uncover likely users for the space. In addition he should conduct an actual search among store operators who may be in the same line of business at inferior locations, and who therefore may be attracted to the manager's vacant store. Often such prospects are identified through various trade organizations or specialized industries. For example, if the manager's analysis indicates that a tavern might be successful in a vacant store, one of the best sources of prospective tavern operators is the local brewery or beer distributor. Here the manager finds an ally in the rental of his space since the local brewery is interested in establishing an additional outlet for its product and is anxious to find a user who will be successful in the tavern business. The same type of prospect source exists in most other lines. If a beauty shop is indicated, schools of beauty or culture or manufacturers of beauty shop equipment are proven sources of prospects. Leading chain organizations are likewise sources for prospects in their area of store specialty. An additional source of prospective store tenants is to be found by the analysis of the store occupants within the area who may be inadequately housed or for whom the vacant store may offer a superior location.

Once the store prospect has been found, the technique of renting such properties is the same as that employed in any other renting. The problem of the salesman is one of proving sufficient value to warrant a favorable decision on the part of the prospect. In store renting, these values are principally concerned with data designed to show the prospective store tenant sound and logical reasons why his proposed enterprise will meet with business success in a specific location. The greater the manager's ability to indicate such potential success, the more likely he will be to procure a suitable store tenant. In the final analysis, the store tenant can only be an asset to a building owner if he meets with success; hence the manager's skill is one of deciding what line of business will do well in the location and what man, woman, or firm has the greatest chance to succeed.

SHOPPING CENTERS

In earlier chapters we discussed the decentralization of urban populations from the center of towns and cities to their periphery. Universally this decentralization of individual citizens was closely followed by the decentralization of retail stores from which these citizens procured their essential goods and services.

Initially these retail stores were so called strip stores, which were located along principal thoroughfares in the outlying areas. However, in more recent years these "strip stores" served by public transportation (streetcars and ultimately buses) were replaced by so called shopping centers. In our definition, a shopping center is a cluster of retail stores in a single development, complete with off-street parking provided as a part thereof. There are a number of types of shopping centers to be found in urban communities, as described in the following paragraphs.

Convenience Center

This is generally the smallest of the shopping centers and is usually found in neighborhoods. Its purpose is to provide convenience goods, those goods which are purchased with greatest frequency by consumers. Since they are consumed on a daily basis, the need for them recurs and is constantly reestablished. The retail businesses most likely to be found in convenience goods centers are grocery stores, meat markets, bakery stores, delicatessen stores, and drug stores—all of which have been combined in the modern supermarket that now replaces the traditional "corner store." Many convenience goods shopping centers also have hardware stores, small appliance stores, greeting card shops, barber shops, beauty shops, book stores, novelty shops, and the like.

Community Shopping Centers

This type of center is somewhat larger and includes more stores than the convenience goods center. Whereas, in typical urban communities, the convenience goods center is designed to serve a *neighborhood,* just as a grammar school serves a neighborhood, the community shopping center is designed to serve contiguous communities, just as a high schools may serve more than one community.

Because community shopping centers have larger trading areas embracing a large population, they are able to support retail stores offering a much wider selection of goods and services. These centers usually offer a limited selection of so called shoppers' goods, those goods that are purchased with reasonable frequency although not necessarily on a daily or weekly basis. Examples are apparel stores, speciality shops, jewelry stores, stationery stores, and perhaps a savings and loan association and a bank. The community shopping center is usually in the order of 1,200,000 square feet of retail space or larger and may have as many as 100 stores.

Regional Shopping Centers

These are the modern "super shopping centers" which usually contain one or more department stores and scores of stores which deal in primary shoppers' goods. The trading area embraces several communities with a combined population exceeding 150,000.

Once these centers have been built at a given location, they almost inevitably attract supporting facilities such as furniture stores and major appliance stores which usually cannot afford the per square foot rentals of the regional centers because they require more space than can be paid for its occupancy. In addition, as noted elsewhere in this text, outlying office buildings are usually attracted to the regional locations because the employees which they must recruit enjoy the amenities to be found in the regional shopping centers. More than likely, a regional shopping center will also attract one or more motels.

The regional shopping center today virtually duplicates the central business district of the metropolitan area and offers major competition to the so called downtown department store. The more modern regional centers boast as many as five department stores and are built in a single complex revolving around inflows, heated and air-conditioned malls, surrounded by thousands of parking spaces.

The management problems of shopping centers become more complex with the increase in size of the center. The techniques of managing convenience goods centers are practically identical with those of managing small complexes of retail stores located along street frontages. The only additions in such areas are management responsibility for snow removal and the maintainance of common areas. As the size and complexity of the centers increase, however, the management problems likewise become more complex.

Many community centers and virtually all regional centers have organizations composed of tenants and designed to boost the local group interests. Generally speaking, these tenant organizations are charged with the responsibility of operating and maintaining the parking lots, staging promotional events and advertising them, and arranging for holiday decorations, floral displays, art shows, and other featured affairs. These organizations are frequently run by the property management firm as a part of the responsibility for the center's management. Obviously, the largest centers require management which is highly skilled in marketing and retail merchandising as well as sales promotion. As a matter of fact, the tenant organizations in the very largest centers are comparable to associations of commerce in smaller cities.

From the time that the first shopping centers were built, the pattern of their development has changed considerably. The original convenience goods centers were generally built by land developers who reserved spaces on residential tracts for such convenience goods shopping. As the size of the centers increased, community centers were generally promoted by finance-oriented real estate or mortgage interests. As might be expected, regional centers are now developed by department store organizations acting through their real estate subsidiaries and by highly sophisticated finance-real estate developers specializing in the art. Great attention is paid to the merchandising mix of tenants' wares and to the skills that go into shopping center planning. Locations are selected which assure these major centers a supporting population with adequate transportation access to the center.

Because major shopping centers require large tracts of land, these centers must be planned well in advance of the crystalization of land use and popula-

REGIONAL SHOPPING CENTER

The modern regional shopping center such as the one illustrated above may be built in a single complex revolving around inflows, heated and air-conditioned malls, and embrace thousands of parking spaces.

tion in outlying areas. The economics of such centers dictate that the land must be purchased while it is still relatively low in price so that large areas can be acquired. One of the objectives of the developers of major centers at the present time is to acquire sufficient land, if possible, not only to provide for the center itself, but to take advantage of the land values it will create. A popular concept is to surround the center with multifamily dwellings which also will be owned and controlled by the developer of the center.

It is obvious that the scope of these larger projects is such that their management has become a specialty. Center property management firms have earned national reputations in this field and individual project. And many managers have likewise determined to devote themselves exclusively to shopping center management as a lucrative specialization.

REVIEW QUESTIONS

1. Could you expect to keep your building 100 percent rented in a normal period through unsolicited inquiries for space?
2. Of what value is knowledge of *adaptability of space* in contacting a prospect?
3. How important is the preparation of a list of prospects for the rental of office space? Explain.
4. What methods would you use in handling alterations and details involved on the premises of a new tenant? What methods on the premises of a tenant who had been on the premises for ten years?
5. How would you arouse the interest of a prospect you contacted who had expressed no previous interest in your building—in fact you "dug up" the prospect because you wanted him in your building?
6. Give two specific ways of convincing a tenant to lease a particular space.
7. What do you consider the most effective means of approach to a customer-renter?
8. Define the responsibilities of the chief engineer. Those of the building superintendent. Those of the night superintendent. Of the forelady.
9. What are the principal problems of elevator operation in an office building?
10. What is meant by the *economy appeal* in office space rental? The *prestige appeal?* The *efficiency appeal?* Give an example of each.
11. Describe an elevator dispatching system in an office building.
12. What is meant by *conviction of value?*
13. When should a tenant be expected to pay for his own alterations?
14. You lease space to a store owner. What are his maintenance obligations?

SELECTED REFERENCES

Carpenter, Horace, Jr. *Shopping Center Management.* New York, N. Y., International Council of Shopping Centers, 1974. 196p.

David, Leo. "The Dollars and Cents of Office Building Management." *Journal of Property Management,* May–June 1969, pp. 122–129.

Gay, Walter N. "Management and Opening of a New Commercial Building." *Journal of Property Management,* Nov.–Dec. 1967, pp. 275–277.

Harding, Richard D. "The Management of New Office Buildings." *Realtor,* Oct. 1973, pp. 8–9.

HUAC Guide for Commercial Buildings. Cedar Rapids, Iowa, Stamats Publishing Co., 1971. 96p.

"Marketability of Office Space." *Buildings,* July through Oct., 1970 issues.

Urban Land Institute. *The Dollars and Cents of Shopping Centers.* 1972 ed. Washington, D. C., 1972. 228p.

CHAPTER 16

Retail Store Locations

.

INTRODUCTION

The renting of a store facility involves considerations different from those encountered in the merchandising of office or residential space. Retail stores taken together form a special category of great importance. The management of them is accordingly a highly specialized activity.

A store is a place where people can buy whatever it is that they want, whether it is needed or not, and also a place where people may be sold things they don't want—whether needed or not. A giant department store is only bigger but not more of a store than is a neighborhood drugstore. And while the property manager of one most likely will not be the manager of the other, both confront problems of the same sort.

The field of commerce in a sense can be divided between those who sell services and those who sell products. Those who sell products, especially retailers, need space for display. The level of business for a seller of goods may be said to be roughly proportional to the available display *space,* while the seller of services' level of business is proportional to the available *time.* For example and at one extreme, the accountant who keeps the books of a number of small businessmen needs no space at all since he travels from office to office and from store to store in making his monthly rounds. The number of clients he has depends only on how long (and how fast and efficiently) he is prepared to work. But, other things being equal, the cash flow of the merchant of a store is to a very large extent a function of the amount and quality of the space occupied by his business.

Property managers who deal with the proprietors of retail establishments, if they are to succeed, must understand the special dependence of their clients on meeting the requirements of adequate and well-situated space. Of course, a wholesaler may need ample space too if warehousing is involved, but to the extent that his business is one of exclusive distributorship, the customers will come to him whatever the location. And his merchandise will be displayed only as samples, or just through catalogue descriptions.

Location is important to those people engaged in the rendering of services such as members of the real estate, legal, or medical professions. The spaces they will lease must be adequate for their activities. The 50th-story office suite of a new skyscraper will be chosen by a law firm (who want the view and the freedom from lobby and street noises), while the ground floor will be preferred by the building's drugstore. More than that, the law firm will choose a space roughly proportional to the number of their employees (weighted, of course, in accordance with the notion that executives need more unit space than office boys), while the retail store will require a space roughly proportional to the number of customers per day who enter the premises to browse and/or to buy.

Not only do retail stores require display space at a prime location accessible to potential purchasers, but usually there must be an inventory. Those in business selling services alone have only their time involved, but merchants must invest hard cash in stock as well as commit their productive hours. Perhaps this is one of the reasons that statistics collected by the Small Business Administration all point to the chancy nature of businesses which involve investments in inventories.

But it is not only the new businesses that so often fail. On the contrary, the remarkable thing is that established businesses involved in merchandising products for which there is an acknowledged public demand can also fail. Perhaps a new branch store is being established or the central store is being given a new home because of a desire for expansion or relocation. Established businesses can fail just as new ones can, especially when heavy inventory costs are involved.

The point being made here is that *location* is paramount. The merchandiser who wants to establish a store must respond carefully to what the feasibility study indicates is the best location for his establishment. In other words, the store merchant—already burdened with the prospect of a heavy inventory cost—cannot afford the disadvantage of a poor location.

The merchant must shop around to optimize his chance for success. His guideline should be the indications of the feasibility study he has authored or purchased. The point is the merchandiser needing space goes to the open market and chooses—whether wisely or not—to occupy one of the several spaces to which his attention is drawn.

Retail store location is a matter of vital concern to the renter of space. Obviously he wants the best, and, to a degree at least, is free to search out and choose from those sites which the current market offers. Store location also is a matter of great concern to the property manager. Since he will usually be working on a percentage basis, if he satisfies an owner, he will be satisfied himself.

The manager must carefully select that particular renter for whom the space is best suited in quality and location. Nothing is gained but trouble in renting space to the customer which is ill-suited to his needs. The short-term occupancy will inevitably be followed by a longer-term vacancy. This is because the reputation attached to a location suffers when there is a history of foreclosures. More than that, a business that fails will be harmful to the businesses in the adjacent locations under the control of the property manager.

Tenant selection involves much more than accepting the first customer who is able to pay. When the tenant is a retail store proprietor, the property manager must base his selection on the belief that the new tenant fully meets the requirements of the renters indirectly as well as directly concerned. The property manager controlling two or more contiguous units of space should not risk the loss of established tenants just to enjoy an uncertain revenue from an untried tenant. On the contrary, the new tenant must not be accepted, unless analysis shows both that he has the chance to succeed in the location under question and that his business will be compatible with those of the neighboring businesses.

EVOLUTION OF RETAIL ESTABLISHMENTS

Retail establishments play an important role in the economy of the nation. Their basic function is to act as a means and a focus of distribution where goods manufactured in many areas of the country can be brought together, to be distributed to the consumer public. Without retail stores it would be virtually impossible for consumers to supply themselves with the goods requisite to living. It would be equally difficult for the manufacturers of the country to find outlets for the goods they produce.

In the early history of United States communities, when most of the labor of citizens was required either to grow sufficient food to sustain life or to provide for the protection for those so engaged, the retail trade of the community was carried on in a single outlet in which goods of every type and description were assembled under one roof for the shopping convenience of the area's inhabitants. This type of store—the general store—still exists in isolated communities.

As our cities grew, and as a greater and greater percentage of our people were engaged in industrial pursuits, the volume of goods available for distribution required additional retail outlets. In place of the general store, then, there grew up a series of retail establishments which came to specialize in one or another type of goods.

The earliest specialization brought a separation of food products from the general store, leaving the latter to handle all other types of merchandise. This amoeba-like process was repeated again and again, as the productive capacity of the nation and the steadily increasing standard of living brought a greater wealth of goods into the market.

In the United States today, stores are classified into groups such as food, apparel, general merchandise, household furnishings, building materials and hardware, restaurants and drinking establishments, and automotive services.

Because of our complex distribution system, each of these classifications of stores contains many subclassifications. For example, in the food group we find food marts, grocery stores, butcher shops, bakeries, delicatessen stores, fruit stands, vegetable stores, etc. In the apparel groups we find women's ready-to-wear, lingerie shops, blouse shops, men's wear, shoes, specialty shops, sportswear, etc.

In the early development of our major cities most retail units were located in the core of the community, the so-called *downtown* area. The major units in these downtown areas were the dry-goods establishments which stocked the fabrics, threads, and notions from which the typical housewife made the clothes for the family.

As communities grew and transportation systems were installed, the termini of these transportation systems were invariably in the downtown area, and this shopping center continued to be the major area of retail trade. With the advent of a broader variety of goods, the original dry-goods establishments took on additional departments to handle the new specialties and ultimately came to be known as department stores. It is important for us to recognize that major department store units in the nation today were the result of an *evolutionary* process, in which types of goods were added as they came into broad use. Looking at department stores as they now are, it is difficult for us to appreciate the fact that not many decades ago such departments as cosmetics, ready-to-wear, sporting goods, beauty shops, etc., were not in existence.

The continued growth of cities, and the greater concentration of shoppers in the downtown areas, which were the termini of local transportation systems, brought the need for larger and larger department stores. In the process, these stores increased their facilities, broadened the selection of merchandise, and, because of their enlarged purchasing power, enjoyed tremendous advantages in offering competitive values to the shopping public. Most urban department stores became virtual museums for the display of attractive merchandise, and no little part of their appeal centered on the surroundings in which their goods were displayed.

During this period of our urban growth, some retail units were established in neighborhoods, principally to provide the daily necessities for residents of the outlying areas. These units were chiefly in the food groups and were invariably small shops, operated by proprietors who depended for their livelihood on the trade of the population in the immediate vicinity of their stores. Locations were selected on the basis of pedestrian traffic, usually at points of concentration of such traffic along the routes of the transportation then in use.

With the advent of rubber-tired surface transportation, which for the first time liberated public conveyances from the rigid pattern of tracks and provided individual shoppers with a means of transportation along routes of their own choosing, the entire pattern of retail shopping in the United States was radically changed. When combined with the impact of electricity upon our urban commercial and industrial structure, these new technological improvements brought into being the decentralization trend which we call urban.

URBAN DECENTRALIZATION

The term *decentralization,* when applied to urban areas, means simply the decline of the dominance of downtown areas in the commercial and industrial life of the community. All of our cities had grown outward from these downtown centers. The pattern of this centrifugal growth depended a great deal upon the topography of the area and upon the natural location. Generally speaking, however, cities took one of three shapes:

1. The *square* city grew up on the plains and was the development of a town around a central square. These cities grew about the same distance in each direction, with the growth influenced only by the transportation media employed. Indianapolis, for example, might be called a *square* town. Others are Denver, Dallas, and Akron.
2. The *fan-shaped* city was originally located on the shores of a lake, ocean, or river. The centrifugal growth was restricted to the area behind the natural barrier, with a *fan-shaped* development being inevitable. Cities such as Chicago, Cleveland, Kansas City, and St. Louis are of the *fan-shaped* design.
3. The *rectangular* city, where peculiar geographical or topographical conditions prevented growth in two directions, but encouraged growth in the remaining two. Manhattan Island is a typical example of the original *rectangular* shape, and its counterpart at the present time is Birmingham.

Prior to the widespread use of electricity and rubber-tired vehicles, this constant expansion on the periphery of our cities was almost entirely residential. Aside from neighborhood retail units, the commercial and industrial activity of the city was concentrated in the downtown area or in the immediate vicinity. With the growth of railroads, industrial plants were increasingly located along the main railroad arteries, usually as close to the central city as possible.

The rubber-tired vehicle and the transmission of power through electric wires liberated both the individual resident and industrial enterprise from the rigid traffic pattern established by rails. Residents of our cities were free to move in any direction, as they chose. Industrial plants no longer needed to be close to the sources of power generated by steam and within areas served by railroads but could locate virtually anywhere that electricity and roads were available.

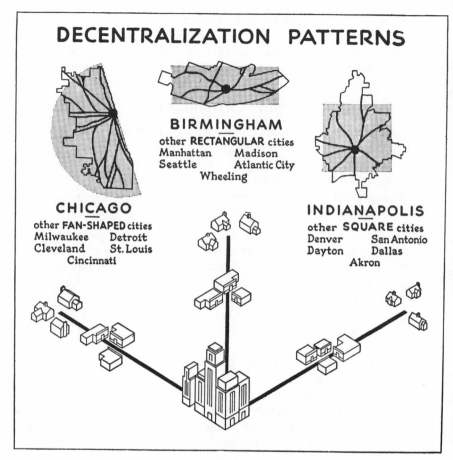

DECENTRALIZATION PATTERNS

BIRMINGHAM
other **RECTANGULAR** cities
Manhattan   Madison
Seattle   Atlantic City
             Wheeling

CHICAGO
other **FAN-SHAPED** cities
Milwaukee   Detroit
Cleveland   St. Louis
          Cincinnati

INDIANAPOLIS
other **SQUARE** cities
Denver   San Antonio
Dayton   Dallas
          Akron

DECENTRALIZATION PATTERNS

The above illustration shows the three basic shapes of cities and illustrates the reason for the relationship between the shape of a city and the operation of decentralization in retail merchandising.

Commercial enterprises—especially retail stores—primarily designed to serve the consumer public, tended to be located as close as possible to mass markets. Thus the new trends, which had changed the movement of residents (consumers), furnished a background for a new pattern of retail distribution. Decentralization of retail units, however, was dependent upon other factors which have played an important part in the process. These had to do with the emergence of the mass production and mass distribution economy.

At the end of World War I the techniques of mass production which had grown out of that war effort were widely adopted by industry. The Ford Motor Company developed a system of manufacture, known as the *production line,* in which the product was built in a series of operations as it moved along on a conveyor belt. This *production line* technique brought into being the modern industrial worker, and integrated men into the giant machines which fashion the industrial products of America.

Production line employment resulted in the increased importance of the operation as a whole and reduced the importance of individual skill. Since more and more industrial products in the United States were manufactured under this system, there developed a tendency toward the grouping of workers into standardized individual performances, with the result that the rates of compensation were likewise standardized. Thus, there emerged a large group of workers whose compensation was almost identical and who came to represent the mass market.

A natural concomitant of mass-production methods is the mass-produced article. In the early history of the country a man who smoked cigars bought them from a local manufacturer. The brand of cigars which the consumer enjoyed could be bought *solely from this company.* In order to obtain an additional supply of these cigars the buyer would have to *return to the source* of manufacture. The same situation prevailed with other types of goods and included the products of tailors, dressmakers, druggists, shoemakers—in fact, with but few exceptions, it was characteristic of the production of all goods.

Mass production, however, introduced technological improvements which gave mass producers a tremendous advantage in costs of production and, hence, in their ability to attract the patronage of the consumer public. The advantage of mass production brought rapid growth to mass-producing firms and the volume of goods which they manufactured for the public. The man who smoked cigars now smoked a White Owl, a Robert Burns, or another of the nationally known, universally distributed cigars. He could buy these cigars almost anywhere, and he was no longer required to seek out the source of their manufacture. The emergence of standard brands brought an identical quality of merchandise which might be obtained at many different points and, as we shall see, provided the background for the operation of the trend which we call decentralization.

The actual working process of decentralization involves what might be termed *trade interception.* This term merely describes the technique of locating a point of retail supply between the *market* for the goods and the present *source* of consumer supply. For example, suppose you are a user of Florsheim shoes. Your place of business and home are located five miles from the downtown area in which a Florsheim store is located. Florsheim shoes are distributed nationally, and the retail purchase price in any one establishment is identical with that in any other establishment. Suppose further that a new Florsheim shoe store is opened in a location *between* your home and place of business and your former source of supply of Florsheim shoes. Why should you travel five miles to buy a pair of Florsheim shoes when you can buy an identical pair of shoes at an identical price by going one-half the distance? The location of the new Florsheim shoe store between you (the market) and the original shop (source of supply) is called *trade interception.*

This process can be applied in any instance where a market for standardized products at standardized prices can be separated from its current source of supply by the location of a *new* source of supply which is *more convenient* to the market.

Whereas the decentralization of *industrial* establishments in metropolitan areas has been motivated by different factors, its implementation has been virtually identical. The financial breakdown of mass-transportation systems in cities prevented the development of surface lines, elevated, and suburban railways capable of handling the rapidly increasing population. The availability of private (automobile) transportation, and the selectivity of motor bus routing, made it desirable for industrial plants to move into peripheral areas where labor could be more satisfactorily recruited and land more economically purchased.

The growth of production line techniques and the advancing costs of labor, likewise, made it desirable for industrial operations to select ground-floor plants. This required large parcels of land which were not available in central city areas. The use of trucks for the transport of goods and the employment of electric power liberated industrial concerns from the confining influence of railroads. The resultant movement of industrial concerns to the periphery of the city stimulated further residential decentralization on the part of consumers and, hence, tended to enlarge the markets which lay further and further from the traditional sources of supply.

The wider use of automobiles for transportation was not alone responsible for the major trend of decentralization but served to implement a revolution in such retail trade that had always been conducted in outlying areas.

Before giving attention to this change in outlying area merchandising, we must understand and appreciate the fact that the technological and inventive skills of enterprisers in the United States had produced a wide variety of goods which were coveted by society as a whole. The budget of the typical family prior to 1900 was concerned principally with *food, clothing,* and *shelter.* As our economy developed and a broader selection of goods was made available, the family budget was enlarged to embrace such things as automobiles, radios, cosmetics, and a host of other items. Moreover, whereas prior to the turn of the century the home had been the scene of the manufacture of most women's and children's clothes, had been the center of food processing and baking, and had been the workshop in which laundry and cleaning had been accomplished, the typical family in the mass market now purchased clothes ready-made, bought bread in bakeries, and patronized laundries.

This wealth of purchase opportunities produced a strain on the individual family budget, in which buyers became acutely price conscious and in which merchandisers sought a more effective level of competitive effort. Paralleling these trends, the costs of labor mounted sharply as workers were organized and the economy expanded. It became obvious that in order for retail units to survive, it would be necessary to operate on reduced margins of profit and at the same time pay higher wages. This meant that relatively less labor would need to be employed in relation to the volume of goods handled by retail establishments.

The first action to overcome these trends was taken in the retail food industry on the neighborhood level. Chain units had already been established where the buying and processing for many individual retail outlets had been combined through joint retail ownership. It now became necessary to combine these retail outlets into larger establishments serving wider areas. In order to attract buyers from such wide areas to a less convenient outlet, it was necessary to establish prices which would serve as successful lure. By increasing the size of individual retail units and by raising their appeal through lower, more-attractive prices, food stores were able to benefit from increased volume at given locations. The logistics of distribution to these units were simplified and economies were effected.

Perhaps the key to the idea of the supermart, however, was the introduction of so-called self-service. By passing on to the consumer the labor involved in selecting and gathering merchandise to be presented at a central check-out point, the food merchandiser greatly increased the productivity of the labor employed in the establishment and thus produced a major saving.

This same trend has been seen to operate in other types of units. Already the corner drugstore is giving way to the large super drug unit. Other small operations are being influenced by the same forces, and a trend toward a pattern of fewer, larger retail units throughout the country is firmly established.

URBAN RECENTRALIZATION

The term *recentralization,* when applied to urban areas, means the process of the revitalization of the central business district in the core city of the major metropolitan areas of the United States.

Whereas the process of *de* centralization is still going on as described on the preceding pages, a counter trend called *re* centralization has been identified and is operating to an increasing extent in most of the nation's metropolitan areas. It is likely that urban populations in the future will continue to be deployed over larger land areas, but that their reasons for selecting their places of residence will be altered somewhat from those which have prevailed over the past half century.

Under the influence of both voluntary and government-inspired urban redevelopment, new residential structures of imposing size have been erected in the very centers of our major cities. With few exceptions, these new buildings have commanded higher rentals and have experienced higher occupancy than the average of competing facilities in their respective areas. In consequence of this impressive record, more and more builders and developers have found it profitable to create additions to this supply of new, centrally located housing.

Up to the present writing, these new residential buildings have exhibited certain definite and rather limited characteristics. Most of them are multistory, fireproof buildings designed to rent (or as condominiums, sell) in the "luxury" categories. A very high percentage are located on *premium* sites. Many of them concentrate their merchandise in small units, containing no-bedroom, one-bedroom, and two-bedroom apartments almost exclusively. As might be expected in view of the size of these units, their occupancy comes almost entirely from the adult population, with emphasis on older couples whose children have married and who have given up single-family dwellings; childless couples, a high percentage of whom are both employed; unmarried young men and young women who have found agreeable partners with whom to live; and single persons whose incomes are high enough to support these rentals for small units.

The fact that "luxury" rentals are obtained for units in these structures does not necessarily mean that all of the occupants are in high-income brackets. For example, a married couple, both of whom are employed, can afford to pay $300 per month for a one-bedroom unit if the husband makes $900 per month and the wife $450. In today's employment markets, these are modest wages. Similarly, two young women who are employed as secretaries at $125 per week each, can jointly easily afford an efficiency apartment that rents for $200 per month.

To a degree, the residential recentralization which is taking place in an increasing number of urban areas is a part of the reemergence of central business districts as the centers of urban employment. While retail trade has been deployed over the entire metropolitan area, there has been a net increase in the activities downtown associated with government, the professions (outside of the medical profession), general commerce and finance, and special aspects of recreation and culture. More alert cities with capable business leadership have organized to combat decentralization through a program of planning and improvement which, it may be forecast, will see central business districts more vital in the next two decades than in the past two.

When we view the history of cities as they have flourished over the centuries, and when we note the degree to which the world's population is today being urbanized, there is little doubt that a meaningful proportion of all city dwellers will continue to reside and conduct their business in the core of their communities.

LOCATION CRITERIA

The single object of store location is the placing of a retail establishment in the spot at which the proprietor can do the largest volume of profitable business. The factors determining that any given spot will serve such an objective are mainly concerned with an analysis of traffic, either present or potential.

Prior to discussing the measurement of present and potential traffic in terms of its impact on the value of a retail location, we should understand certain basic facts about the habits of shoppers. Aside from shopping for pure necessities, notably food and household essentials, shopping is essentially a *multipurpose* activity touching in many cases on recreational needs. The woman who goes to a shopping center almost always plans *several* purchases, not just one. If she buys a dress, she may also buy a pair of shoes, a handbag, a necktie for her husband, and some underwear for the children. Thus there is virtue, from a store-location point of view, in the juxtaposition of several establishments where these various wants can be accommodated. This was the original virtue, and is the sustaining value, of the department store where many such purchases can be made under one roof and under one merchandising policy for maximum convenience to the shopper.

Prior to widespread decentralization, downtown department stores enjoyed a tremendous advantage in this respect, since they were not only able to offer the broadest selection of merchandise in most agreeable physical surroundings, but, because of their tremendous purchasing power, they were able to offer goods at a substantially lower price than could the individual merchant who had far less purchasing power and a substantially lower potential volume of business.

The advent of discount houses, cut-rate stores, and other chain units specializing in various types of merchandise, as well as the entrance of the great mail-order houses into the retail business, produced a situation where smaller mobile units could offer merchandise on a basis competitive with the large downtown units, in locations of much greater convenience to the mass shopper. It was obviously advantageous for such units to locate together so that there might be women's ready-to-wear, men's wear, millinery, etc., within the single block, area, or section, thus accommodating the multipurpose nature of the shopper.

When the individual merchant is faced with the problem of locating his store, he seeks, if possible, to place the unit in a spot at which a volume of consumer traffic is already in existence. If a nucleus of stores (a trading center) has already been established and if a vacancy is available, or if land is available on which a new building can be erected, then the merchant will by analysis seek to estimate the volume of sales which he can wring from the existing traffic. He will measure this potential volume against the rental required and determine whether or not a location in that spot will result in a profitable operation. To do so, he must not only measure the volume of the traffic which exists, but must gauge that traffic as a market for the particular type of goods he wishes to offer.

A volume of pedestrian traffic does not in itself necessarily represent an attractive situation for every retail unit. Traffic must not only be qualified as to *volume,* but must be qualified, as well, as to *attitude.* For example, in major cities commuter railroad stations emit thousands of persons each morning. In front of, or adjacent to, these terminals, there may be extremely heavy traffic, which is not necessarily a large potential for prospective store proprietors. This traffic is in a hurry, is bent either on getting to the office in the morning or, on the return trip, getting home to dinner. Locations on such heavy traffic arteries are seldom good for general retail operations, are almost entirely confined to flash purchases such as last-minute buying of liquor, groceries, flowers, etc. In order to be valuable to a merchant, traffic must be in a *shopping* mood, must have come to the location primarily for shopping purposes.

ENCLOSED MALL

Randhurst Center in Mt. Prospect, Illinois combines established retail names, main aisle merchandising units, and such artifacts as pools to attract shoppers.

If it has been determined that a volume of pedestrian traffic at a given location is essentially *shopping* traffic, further qualifications of the traffic may be made by traffic-count analysis and by a study of the adjacent facilities and the type of purchases made there.

Suppose one is locating a men's shoe store. Two locations are presented. One of the locations enjoys an average pedestrian traffic of 1,000 per hour, and the other has only 600 per hour. Analysis may indicate that of the 1,000 per hour traffic in the first location, 850 are women and that all of the stores adjacent to the first location deal in women's goods. In the second location 400 of the 600 per hour pedestrians are men, and the adjacent facilities are largely devoted to the wants of men. It is, of course, obvious that the men's shoe store should be located in the second location.

The characterization of pedestrian traffic is not only a matter of the sex of the traffic but likewise one of determining the purchasing level as evidenced by the quality of merchandise available. It is usually poor merchandising to locate a quality store in a mass-market shopping area, or, conversely, to locate a mass-market store in a sparsely populated quality shopping area. We do not say *always,* since there are exceptions to this rule, based on a study of traffic.

CREATING CONSUMER TRAFFIC

As we have pointed out, consumer traffic in cities in the United States was at one time created by natural concentration of buyers at the termini of mass transportation systems, or by neighborhood concentrations which were brought into being by purely local traffic patterns. These also were influenced principally by extensions of the transportation systems.

Aside from the build-a-better-mousetrap theory, which enabled a few isolated merchants to cause a crowd to beat a path to their door, retail locations were established by consumers rather than merchants. If a storekeeper desired to do a large volume of business, it was almost necessary that he pay the rental required for a location in an established shopping center or on its periphery. At that time, the rental of a store was not so much a matter of a return required by the landowner on the investment in his building as it was the payment for a franchise granting access to a given buying traffic. The desirability of the traffic in large measure governed the amount paid.

With the emergence of chain stores, which enjoyed a national reputation for quality and price of product, and with the widespread use of newspaper, radio, and TV advertising, as well as with the increased mobility of consumers due to the use of automobiles, it became possible for certain types of retail establishments, either alone or in combination with others, to locate stores on the basis of *potential* rather than *existing* traffic.

Increasingly, large departmentalized stores such as Sears Roebuck and Company and Montgomery Ward and Company, whose names are known to virtually every American and whose reputations are firmly established, have constructed stores in locations which heretofore had no retail value whatsoever. These institutions have relied upon advertising, coupled with reputation and implemented by adequate parking facilities, to attract a volume of buyers to locations which were entirely established by the *pulling power* of the units themselves. Invariably the opening of such a unit by either of these major establishments has resulted in immediate store developments on adjacent property, where proprietors sought to take advantage of the traffic which the unit had *created.*

The creation of brand-new trading areas was not accomplished solely by these merchandising chains but has been accomplished by other nationally known units acting in consort with allied lines. Promoters of new trading areas will develop a representative group of prospective store tenants who agree to sign leases on new shopping centers, when their analysis of the trading areas to be served has satisfied them that a combination of retail outlets can successfully draw upon the trading area for a satisfactory volume of business.

TRADING AREA ANALYSIS

In chapter 7 we discussed *neighborhood analysis.* In defining the term *neighborhood,* we indicated that a neighborhood in Alaska might embrace hundreds of square miles, whereas a neighborhood in Chicago or New York might only be a few blocks. The same variation in size may be applied to the term *trading area.* For instance, the trading area of Marshall Field and Company's downtown store in Chicago embraces several states. On the other hand, the trading area of Marshall Field and Company's Evanston (Illinois) store embraces much smaller territory. And the trading area of Marshall Field and Company's Lake Forest (Illinois) store is smaller yet. The fact is that all of the customers of the Lake Forest store live within the trading area of both the Evanston store and the downtown store.

As we shall use the term, *trading area means the area from which an establishment draws its customers.* The size of the trading area of a retail establishment depends upon a number of factors—all of which might be summed up in the single term *competition.* We have said that Marshall Field and Company's downtown store has a trading area embracing several states. This is true because it is a unique establishment in those several states, and for certain types of clients and merchandise it has restricted competition.

In the mass-production and mass-consumption society that we have been discussing above, it is improbable that any retail trading center will ever enjoy a trading area that overlaps another area that can *more conveniently* be served by an identical set of outlets, offering equally attractive merchandise at equally advantageous prices. By this we mean that if you are the patron of an Atlantic and Pacific Supermart, which is one mile from your home, it

OLD ORCHARD SHOPPING CENTER

The Old Orchard shopping center in Skokie, Illinois consists of 92 acres with 1,030,000 gross square feet of building area including 60,000 net rental space in the Professional-Medical Building.

A PAUSE TO RELAX

Most modern malls contain ample seating areas as well as such pleasing landscape effects as trees, shrubs, or flowers. Such amenities are often the key to a successful trading center that desires to attract us many consumers as possible.

is highly improbable that you will begin to patronize an Atlantic and Pacific Supermart three miles from your home—unless the second is located *on your way* to and from someplace you visit anyway (assuming that both have the same merchandise, prices, customer service, and parking facilities).

In most cities the dominant traffic pattern is represented by the movement to and from *downtown.* Although decentralization has made a substantial difference in the traffic patterns of such cities, the downtown areas are still dominant and are a major factor in population movements. It is inevitably true that traffic will not move *backwards* to patronize a trading center. *Trade interception* is a literal term and describes the process of intercepting business en route to its normal source of supply. Most trading areas, other than downtown trading areas, are fan-shaped and extend a great deal further back of the trading center than in front of it.

In the light of the above, the analysis of potential trading areas represents a study of the traffic habits and purchasing power of the people living within the area under analysis as well as the competitive facilities in existing trading centers now serving the area.

Given a prospective store location to analyze, or an existing building to manage, the property manager should obtain a map of the community on a scale large enough to show all individual blocks. If the purpose of his analysis is to determine the suitability of the location for a *particular kind* of enterprise, the location of the subject site should be fixed on this map and the potential prospective use (type of tenancy) should be noted by the manager.

The next step in the analysis involves the manager's finding out the location of all currently operated competitive enterprise. For example, if the object of his analysis is to determine whether a food store will be successful at a given location, the map should show all competitive food operations. Each of these competitive units should be classified as to type. Small independent neighborhood food stores should be marked on the map in one type of symbol, standard chain units in another type of symbol, and supermarts (whether independent or chain) in a third type of symbol. Notations as to parking and probable volume should likewise be made.

After these competitive operations have been spotted, the map should be marked to show the principal traffic arteries for private transportation and to show all transportation lines serving the area.

The manager will, of course, have in mind the type of unit proposed to be located on the subject site—as to whether it will be a neighborhood independent store, a standard chain, or a supermart. He will also be familiar with the general competitive position of his prospective tenant, i.e., the type of merchandise offered, the price advantages, the facilities of the unit itself, and the level of the prospective tenant's goodwill.

An experienced manager, thoroughly conversant with the type of population and the traffic patterns in the area, will now begin to see the potential limits of the trading area of the subject site. He will know that, unless the traffic pattern indicates a natural concentration of traffic movement in the area of the subject site, the pattern of the trading area will be established by competitive outlets. In the absence of a traffic-pattern advantage, the subject site *will pull from that area which lies closer to it than to other competitive establishments of equal pulling power.* In the case of the food store location, the manager will draw a boundary line on the map to show the trading area thus formed.

If the situation warrants further study involving the measurement of the potential consumers located within this bounded area, the manager should procure a copy of the latest available census and identify the census tracts which lie within this area. From an analysis of the data contained in the census,

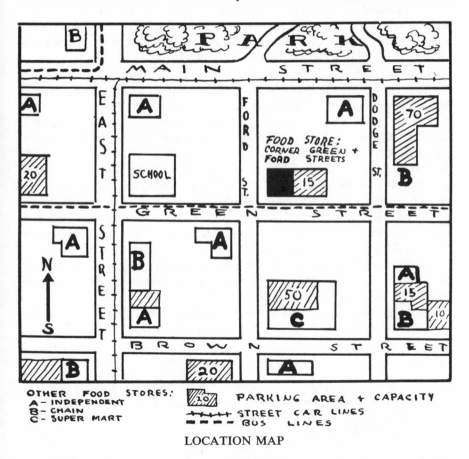

OTHER FOOD STORES:
A - INDEPENDENT
B - CHAIN
C - SUPER MART

PARKING AREA + CAPACITY
STREET CAR LINES
BUS LINES

LOCATION MAP

he will be able to learn something of the number of families located in the area, their composition, and their economic status. If the census has been made obsolete by rapid growth of the area concerned, then the manager will find it necessary to study this growth in terms of new housing facilities created since the date of the last decennial count.

We have discussed above the analysis of a trading area from the point of view of determining its value to a single prospective space user. It is a fact that the size and shape of the trading area of any given location will vary with the type of tenancy, both as to the kind of merchandising unit involved and its competitive position. Thus, the trading area of a sewing machine store may be considerably larger than that of a food store located next door, since the next nearest sewing machine store may be a number of miles away, whereas the next nearest food store may be within a few blocks. Moreover, the trading area of an independent neighborhood food store may embrace a total of twelve square blocks, whereas the trading district of a food supermart operation *on the same site* might embrace twelve square miles.

If the manager is given a prospective shopping development or an existing group of stores to manage, he must gear his analysis of the trading area for each of the individual units to the single unit which has the largest trading area. For instance, if six retail stores are located in a single commercial building and one is a food supermart, the buyers who come to the food mart automatically become potential customers for each of the other five units. Similarly, if a sewing machine store is located in this group, the food mart will benefit from being adjacent to the sewing machine unit and may well attract potential customers from outside of its normal trading area. In this latter case, however, the infrequency of visits to sewing machine stores as compared with food stores would make the tenant of the former the beneficiary of the food mart's pulling power.

The most successful trading center is that which enjoys the highest level of competitive pulling power over the widest possible area. The volume of retail business done in any trading center depends almost entirely on the size of the trading area which can be developed. By size, we do not necessarily mean area, but rather *the number of potential consumers embraced.*

REVIEW QUESTIONS

1. What is meant by *square, rectangular,* and *fan-shaped* cities? How do they arise?
2. What occasioned the rise of today's so called *super-food store?*
3. Describe the early retail outlet and its transition to today's retail outlets, particularly the department store.
4. What is *trade interception?* Give an example.
5. How would a property manager analyze a specific store property as to its location value?
6. What is *decentralization?* How did it come about?

7. Suppose your client wanted to open a lingerie store. You offer him location "A," where the traffic count shows 700 pedestrians per hour, 300 men and 400 women. You also show location "B," where the traffic count is 400, 100 men and 300 women. Which should he take? What other location factors would he want to know?
8. What is the object of *store location?* What is meant by a *multipurpose shopper?*
9. In seeking a location, what does a store owner or merchant consider of greatest importance?
10. What effect has the opening of outlets by concerns such as Sears or Wards had upon the *outlying location?*
11. Define a *trading area.* How does it differ from a *trading center?* What makes a *trading center* valuable?
12. What is *urban recentralization?* What are its characteristics?
13. In what sense is there a coincidence of interests between the property manager and store proprietor on the question of location? In what sense do the interests diverge?

SELECTED REFERENCES

Applebaum, William. *Store Location, Strategy Cases.* Addison-Wesley, Reading, Mass., 1968. 164p.

Gruen, Nina J. and Gruen, Claude. "A Behavioral Approach to Determining Optimum Location for the Retail Firm." *Land Economics,* Aug. 1967, pp. 320–27.

Kane, Bernard J., Jr. *A Systematic Guide for Supermarket Location Analysis.* Fairchild Publications, New York, 1966. 171p.

Kaylin, S. O. "Selecting the Best Site for a Shopping Center." *Shopping Center World,* June 1973, pp. 38–41.

Nelson, Richard R., Jr. "Eight Principles of Store Location." *Real Estate News,* p. 603, July 1962.

Tucker, Grady. "Site Selection for Suburban Shopping Centers." *Real Estate Review,* Summer 1974, pp. 70–76.

CHAPTER 17

Setting Store Rentals

INTRODUCTION

Setting a store rental is that step in merchandising where the property manager seeks to find the balance between the owner's valuation of his property and what a willing buyer will pay. In other words the law of supply and demand prevails (unless, of course, there are rent controls in effect). More than that it must be realized that for each unit of retail store space there may be more than one buyer willing to meet the owner's minimum demand, and one of these buyers may be ready to offer more than the other(s). In this case, the property manager plays the essential role of maximizing profit by searching for what might be called conditions of preferred occupancy. Thus, each space can be thought of as being more suitable for occupancy by one potential tenant as compared with all others.

In this chapter we shall be often (but not exclusively) speaking about the setting of store rentals in shopping center complexes such as the neighborhood, the community, the regional, and more lately the super-regional types. Shopping center volume of business in the USA has almost doubled in the last ten years (in fact, has exploded from an almost inconsequential volume over the last two decades). Today statistics show that almost 50 percent of retail business is carried out in these shopping centers. It is interesting to note that this figure includes retail car sales as part of the total, even though cars generally are not sold in shopping center locations (but at most on adjacent lots). Of course, most large shopping centers are only accessible by car. The retail car sales figure reflects the purchase of a "second" car in order to make the facilities of the shopping center available. This is just one more indication that the future importance of shopping center situations is guaranteed.

Most shopping center store spaces are rented on the basis of five-year leases (for the smaller shops) to 25-year leases (for the major stores). Percentage lease arrangements usually apply according to a formula that guarantees a fixed minimum rental up to a point where the tenants' gross income from retail sales exceeds a certain amount. After this point is reached, rentals become set as a predetermined percentage of gross revenue; the shopping center owner-promoters become de facto partners with their tenants. In the next chapter these aspects of percentage leases will be discussed in detail.

Establishing Rent Levels

Here we simply wish to establish the guidelines that are commonly followed by property managers in setting the level of store rentals. In all cases, whether one is dealing with shopping center tenants, or store tenants in downtown buildings and/or the strip commercial centers in the various neighborhoods, the owner interests are confronted with the following boundary condition: For each store space there will be associated a debt service cost, a certain operating expense, and the expectation to receive a fair equity return on invested capital. The sum of these three values then fixes the minimum rent the owners are prepared to accept on a break-even basis. In shopping centers and premium downtown locations, this minimum rental expectation will tend to average around $7 per square foot per year. The value, of course, will be lower in remote (especially declining) neighborhoods.

The figure just quoted does not mean, however, that every tenant in a particular complex will pay the same base rent. On the contrary, certain locations in every complex can be regarded as premium space, and certain categories of tenants can be identified as willing and able to pay premium prices. Thus, if for the entire complex the average rental must be $7 per square foot per year, for every minor space that may be rented at a $4.50 level there will be other premium spaces that rent at a higher-than-average level (say, for $20 per square foot per year).

The price of a given area within a building is in the final analysis established by the factors of supply and demand which make up the competitive market. There does not appear to be any basis for a relationship between the physical cost of the erection and maintenance of space and its current selling price. If such a relationship prevails at any time, it is largely a matter of economic accident. On the contrary, as we have seen in our discussion of the movement of the shifting fulcrum called *normal* in the long-term operation of the real estate cycle, the whole rental market tends to move upward in sympathy with the declining purchasing power of the dollar and with the increased construction costs of buildings.

Space versus Franchise Rental

There are various techniques of establishing the level of rent for a retail operation. The first of these involves what we might call *space* rental. If, for example, Sears Roebuck and Company determined to build a retail store in a location never before used for retail purposes, their rental will be fixed by the cost of the land purchased, the construction cost of the building with which the land is improved and the depreciation thereof, as well as the cost of maintaining the finished property. If this works out at "X" dollars per square foot, then "X" is a purely *space* rental, and the wisdom of the program must be analyzed from the point of view of a belief that a store so located can produce "X" dollars of sales per square foot—said sales being sufficient to justify the investment involved.

In most instances, however, retail rent values are not merely space rentals, but are of a second general type which we shall call *franchise* rentals. In the case of this type of rental valuing, the price of the store or retail location is not in a direct relationship with the space involved.

Let us take the case of a cigar stand on the main floor of an office building. This retail location in all probability will embrace only a very small number of square feet. The space itself, on a mere *space* basis might be worth only $5 per square foot. On the other hand, the prospective tenant of the cigar store is not motivated merely by the desire to rent a small given area. His interest in establishing tenancy arises out of the fact that the space represents a *franchise* to do business with the hundreds of potential cigar counter customers, who are brought to the building each day and who represent a unique potential consumer pressure in favor of this type of business.

The same element of *franchise* may be said to exist in a retail unit located in an established trading center, in which adjacent units have established a large volume of consumer traffic. If this volume of consumer traffic represents a high potential to a prospective store tenant, then his leasing of the store is not based on an abstract desire to possess a certain area of floor space, but rather results from a desire to participate in this potential business volume. It is the *franchise,* then, that establishes the value and not the space. This franchise is a characteristic of the *land* underlying the store building and is not a quality of the improvement. A prospective tenant, who merely needs *space* accommodation, rarely will pay a rental higher than can be justified by an adequate return on current construction costs plus simply satisfactory land.

The student of retail location values must appreciate that the major objective of a commercial tenant is to do a volume of business. This volume of business must come from the consumer pressure established by the traffic concentration. Now, it is true, of course, that traffic may be concentrated at a given point as a result of a number of motivating factors. In retail establishments, advertising, for example, is merely a means of increasing traffic at the point of sale.

A prospective store tenant, analyzing a location from his own point of view, must appraise the value of consumer traffic in terms of its cost. He may decide that it is not necessary for him to pay a high rental in order to provide a satisfactory traffic volume, because he may feel that the expenditure of a somewhat lesser amount on advertising will produce customers for him at a lower per-head cost. In the case of large national chains, the operators may decide that their goodwill (which may be defined as the net result of all previous advertising and public experience), when added to their current advertising, will more than offset their being away from the so-called 100 percent locations, and make it unnecessary for them to pay a *franchise* rental.

In the typical instance, however, the student of retail location and space value will find that, with but few exceptions, the lowest cost method of placing a business in a position to enjoy a high volume of consumer pressure is involved in franchise rentals. Most prospective tenants must pay this type of rental to attain a high sales volume.

In recent years, retail space valuation increasingly has been established on the basis of a fluctuating franchise payment basis, known as the *percentage rent*. The techniques of percentage leasing are discussed in detail in the next chapter, but we shall give attention here to the theory under which percentage rentals have been established.

The percentage lease is a means of continually adjusting the *franchise* value of a given location in terms of its business worth to a retail merchant. Under the *percentage* lease, the landlord, to a limited extent, becomes a partner of the tenant. If the tenant's business is good, then the landlord's rental is high. If the tenant's business declines, then the landlord's income declines. We must not suppose, however, that the percentage lease is a solution to the manager's responsibility to produce the highest possible net revenue from the store property. In the first place, a percentage lease in order to be satisfactory from the point of view of the landlord must be made only after the following factors have been given consideration:

1. *The type of business which is scheduled for the occupancy of the store must be that which has the best chance to do the highest possible volume under the most favorable percentage terms.*

   It is not enough for the manager to feel that he has done a good leasing job when he has installed a tenant in a given location at a percentage rental which is in line with the usage for that type of tenancy. For example, let us say that a store has been leased to a tavern at a rental of 8 percent. The store is occupied and the percentage is in line with that ordinarily paid by taverns, and the manager may well feel that his problem has been solved satisfactorily. On the other hand it may be that the highest potential use of this store is not for a tavern, but rather for a men's clothing store in which an established percentage rental of 6 percent would produce a substantially higher net income.

   Thus, it is the manager's responsibility to subject all retail space to constant analysis as to the type of tenancy, in order to be assured that the maximum income is being obtained.

2. *The leasing of space on percentage to a given tenant does result in a limited partnership. At least the landlord's rental income will depend to an extent on the tenant's ability and resources.*

   If the operator of the store is an alert and resourceful merchandiser, with adequate financing and aggressive methods, then the income of the landlord will be substantially higher than if his tenant in the same line of business lacks the ability necessary to produce at the highest potential level.

It is obvious that it is the responsibility of the manager constantly to scrutinize the operations of his tenants on a percentage basis, in order to assure himself that they are doing a satisfactory job of merchandising which will result in the maximum sales volume.

3. *A third type of space valuation, and one which has only occasionally been adopted, is that in which the value of the space is established on net revenue of the lessee rather than on gross revenue.*

This unique form of lease has thus far been used in cases where the space rental is virtually nil, and the franchise rental is highly questionable.

A case in point is a recent bank lease in a large midwestern city. A large multistore office building had originally been designed to accommodate a major bank. The entrance to the property featured a stairway to large banking rooms, and it was not practical for these quarters to be used in any other way. The bank for which the space was designed no longer occupied the space, and it was vacant. Obviously, the only prospective user would be a *new* bank. It was equally obvious, however, that no new financial institution at the outset could afford a space rental which would give the owners of the building an adequate return on their investment. Moreover, in the light of economic trends, it has been determined that percentage rentals are not equitable for banking institutions, since the fluctuation in the gross deposits in the banks tends to produce rentals which are either too low or too high in relation to space values.

In this instance, a lease based on a percentage of net profits of the financial institution was an equitable solution. The landlord concluded, after study, that the personnel of the proposed institution were satisfactory to him, and that he was willing to base his rental on their chances for success. His space was valueless without such a tenant, and in order to make the proposed enterprise attractive, it was necessary for him to offer the inducement of proportionate rent.

In the opinion of some, this type of lease will find increasing acceptance over the ensuing years and will be a solution to the space merchandising problems of many special-purpose types of buildings.

FIXED DOLLAR RENTALS

In many secondary store properties, the value of store space cannot be established by *space rental* computation or by a fluctuating *franchise*. As we have noted above, there is no necessary relationship between the capital invested in building space and the competitive rent value at any given time.

Moreover, there are certain types of tenants for whom percentage leases are impractical, either because it is too difficult for the tenant to maintain adequate records of sales or because of the probability of fraud on the part of the tenant. In such cases, the solution is the establishment of what we call the *fixed* rental which contemplates the tenant paying a certain number of dollars in rent each month over a mutually agreed upon period of time, regardless of the volume of his business.

Here, the method of determining rental requires the study of the competitive value of the space and the adjustment of that competitive value for the franchise factors applicable to the individual tenant. Let us illustrate by taking a twenty-foot store in a secondary outlying development in a block containing ten stores. Let us further imagine that this store is vacant and that within three blocks there are also two other vacant stores of like size. Let us further assume that there is no substantial franchise differential between any of these stores in terms of traffic volume.

Given store "A" the manager should, of course, determine the rental on vacant stores "B" and "C." If he finds that they are priced at $200 and $225, he can conclude that the basic competitive value of his own unit is somewhere in that range. On the other hand, let us further suppose that vacant store "A" is located between a specialty grocery store and a specialty meat market. If a prospective tenant comes along who wishes to open a shoe repair shop, store "A" will be valued on a strictly competitive basis, keeping in mind that its traffic is no greater than that to be found in front of stores "B" and "C."

On the other hand, if the prospective tenant is a bakery, store "A" assumes a somewhat different value, since the location of a bakery between the grocer and the butcher enables the baker to take advantage of specialized traffic and, further, affords the opportunity that the location of a bakery in the vacant unit may tend to increase this specialized traffic volume, since it will round out the food facilities. In this case the manager may be justified in asking an additional 10 percent above the space value as a *franchise* rental.

The valuation of fixed rentals is thus accomplished by twofold analysis—by the study of comparability and by estimating potential volume for the individual user.

In addition to fixed dollar rentals, store leases often contemplate variable rentals in which the charge for space is linked to some factor other than a stated dollar amount per unit of space. The most widely employed of such variable rentals is the percentage lease, which is discussed in detail in the following chapter. Another provision for variable rental is one in which the amount to be paid for the space is scheduled to fluctuate with the movement of the Bureau of Labor Statistics' Consumer Price Index. This index is the successor to the so-called cost-of-living index and is designed to reflect broad movements in price levels. In some such leases, specific increases and decreases are called for when the Consumer Price Index rises or falls by a certain amount. In other leases, provision is made for cancellation of the lease (by one or both parties) in the event the Consumer Price Index moves beyond certain limits during the lease term. The principal aim of these provisions is to prevent undue hardship on either the landlord or the tenant in the event inflation or deflation goes beyond certain stated bounds.

DETERMINING LEASE TERM

One of the problems which constantly faces the manager in connection with store rentals is that of deciding the length of term of store leases. We have commented elsewhere in this text on the fact that the property manager is constantly forecasting values when he determines upon the tenancy of a given unit and when he sets the term of leases.

There are several criteria for the determination of the length of store leases against which the manager must measure his decisions. In the first instance, the length of term will depend upon the current position of the economy. If the lease contemplates a fixed rental, the length of the term will depend upon the manager's conclusions as to whether or not a monetary trend over the contemplated lease period will be *inflationary* or *deflationary.*

In inflationary periods the manager must favor short-term arrangements, since he must protect his owner against the vitiating effects of higher general price levels. If the trend is deflationary, then the manager's decision should favor longer terms, in order that the owner may take advantage of higher purchasing power. It must be said in this connection that in the final analysis the objectives of the manager should be to represent both parties to the lease in such a manner as to establish an equitable relationship.

Even in the case of fixed rentals, it is impossible for a lease to be established under which the tenant will be required to pay more for a store than can be earned by the store. Long-term leases in deflationary periods are not a guarantee that the store tenant will pay the rent required, and unquestionably in times of serious depression, adjustments will need to be made. On the other hand, long-term leases in inflationary periods are distinctly harmful to owners. The same tenant who will demand a decrease in rent in deflationary periods (and who will get it if he can survive only by such a reduction) will not allow the owner to renegotiate a lease upward under any circumstances.

There are other long-term trends which the manager must analyze in drawing his conclusions as to the length of store lease terms. These have to do with the fluctuations of percentages, the values of property, the costs of maintenance, and taxes.

From the tenant's point of view, requests for long-term leases arise out of several motivations. In the first instance, in order to occupy the premises and to prepare them for the conduct of his business, the tenant may be required to make a substantial investment which he will need to recapture during the term of his lease. Quite naturally he will be anxious to have as long a term as possible over which to amortize his investment.

Conversely, the manager will feel that such a long-term investment might jeopardize the owner's position in the event that economic trends produce conditions under which a more favorable lease might be made. Where this feeling on the part of the manager is based on strong indications, arrangements can frequently be made under which the lease may be terminated at stated dates by reimbursing the tenant for proportionate amounts of his original investment, depending upon the amount of unexpired term at the time of the termination.

It is natural that a store tenant who establishes a business in a unit of space, and who spends a number of years building up goodwill for his business, will balk at any arrangement whereby the landlord has the right to put him out of business by refusing a lease renewal. Among good merchants, this is a constant motivator for long-term leases. The manager should have no reason to dispossess a successful tenant, since the space involved theoretically should be worth more to the successful, tried merchant than to a prospective tenant. Nonetheless, it is the manager's responsibility to see that the property owner obtains an equitable share of the business volume done by the tenant, even though that volume is principally the result of the tenant's individual effort.

The ideal solution to this divergence of interest is the development of a fair relationship under which the tenant feels certain that he will not be taken advantage of by the landlord at the expiration of comparatively short-term lease periods.

There is still another reason for the anxiety of tenants to have long-term leases. This involves the valuation of the store in case of sale. From the tenant's point of view, he wishes a long-term lease so that, if it becomes necessary for him to sell his business, he can offer the prospective buyer the security of such a lease. This is a perfectly natural and legitimate desire.

From the property owner's point of view, this valuation of security is not a right of the tenant, but rather a right of the landlord, and here again it is necessary for the manager to effect an equitable compromise. If a long-term lease is to be used by a tenant to profit by the sale of his business, then the landlord should share in such profits.

An important consideration in determining the length of a lease term, especially in the case of fixed dollar rentals, is the trend of population in the trading area of the store. In highly developed, stable areas, this is not so important as in regions of rapid growth. A steadily greater number of consumers inevitably produces increased sales volume and hence higher rental values. Short-term leases are favored for new, expanding neighborhoods.

REVIEW QUESTIONS

1. What is meant by leasing on "net revenue"? When might such an arrangement be made? What might influence the manager to lease under this method?
2. You have a location in a spot with a high rate of traffic and want to lease on a *franchise rental basis.* What would this type of lease be based upon, and how would you figure the rental?
3. Is the upward or downward movement of the rental market affected by any social or economic trend? Explain.
4. What is the *fixed rental basis?* When is such a lease advisable? How would you arrive at the amount?
5. For how long a period of time should a lease be written?
6. Why would a tenant request a long-term lease from you? Under what conditions would you be wise to grant it?
7. Define *space rental.*
8. When is a short-term *fixed rental* lease usually written? Why?
9. Given the remarkable growth of shopping center modes of retail merchandising, what do you foresee happening with respect to minimal shopping center rentals in the future?
10. What sort of rental arrangement would you—as property manager—propose for the rental of a doctors' office in a shopping center location? Does a percentage lease make any sense in such a situation?

SELECTED REFERENCES

Beach, Douglas. "High Rents Prompt New Leasing Strategies." *Buildings,* Dec. 1970, pp. 44–48.

Peterson, Eric. "Franchisees: Vital New Tenants for Shopping Centers." *Shopping Center World,* May 1973, pp. 78, 80 +.

Urban Land Institute. *Dollars and Cents of Shopping Centers.* 1972 edition, Washington, D. C., 1972. 228p.

CHAPTER 18

Commercial Leases

INTRODUCTION

Commercial properties were referred to in chapter 1 as comprising places, often but not invariably open to the public, that exist for the transaction of businesses of one sort or another. Specifically included were offices, retail establishments, recreational facilities, and other special-purpose enterprises which are highly individualistic in design and not subject to categorical use. Residential properties are where people live, and industrial properties are where articles of commerce are fabricated or distributed (wholesale establishments). Commercial properties, therefore, are where things are sold (retail stores) and services rendered (offices, restaurants, amusement centers, and the like).

Properties like museums, libraries, and governmental and educational institutions exist to serve public needs and interests. The distinction is, of course, that commercial establishments are profit-oriented whether with respect to goods that are sold or services that are rendered.

No part of the world is wholly black or white. For example, hospitals may have almost any character allowed by the prevailing local laws and range in specific instances from self-serving (profit-oriented) to public-serving (Red Cross) and cost-free institutions. More than that, there are categories of fully profit-oriented commercial properties—such as hotels/motels—that arbitrarily but sensibly have been excluded from this book.

In the present chapter, however, we make no pretense of covering all aspects of the character of commercial leases by which property owners rent space to commercial tenants. Even with the delimitations already mentioned, the spectrum of possibilities is too large to present more than an overview. Complicating factors arise when tenants themselves share in the ownership or when tenants provide for their own (and often nonprofessional) in-house management.

A major distinction first mentioned in chapter 14 can be introduced at this point. On the one side there are the proprietors of commercial buildings whose revenue depends mostly on the total space occupied, for example, retail stores. Space is needed for display of merchandise before the eyes of the potential buyers. Net income is easily identifiable as the difference between sales and the sum of the cost of inventory plus operating expense. However, the gross income in any particular case depends upon a host of factors such as merchandising skill of the seller, the public demand for the product, the competitive advantages associated with the sales location, the exclusiveness of the franchise, store hours, and the like. The main point is that owners of establishments such as retail stores are oriented to think in terms of gross income—since, with this number established, net profits fairly easily can be anticipated.

Commercial properties such as stores whose level of business depends mostly upon space, are the ones that can afford to have their rentals pegged to gross income.

On the other side are the tenants of commercial businesses engaged in rendering public or corporate services for profit. These include the professional firms (lawyers, doctors, accountants, etc.) as well as the various business firms (corporate offices, etc.). The firms may be large or small, incorporated or not, and involving partnerships or not. By and large, however, the services that are rendered are *time*-rather than *space*-oriented. Location may be important too, either to enhance the flow of business, or for prestige and public image, or simply to serve the personal convenience of the office workers and their clients. The fact remains that the level of office business rather than the amount of space occupied reflects how much time is spent by the various workers in their service-rendering activities.

Obviously each office needs space which is roughly proportional to the number of workers. The space demand is not related to the extent of an inventory of merchandise, nor to the flow of customers in and through the establishment. Since the gross income earned by office-based enterprises is not wholly space-dependent, offices should be rented by owners differently than are retail store spaces. It clearly follows that office-space leases in general will be distinctly different in character from store-space leases, and that still other hybrid lease arrangements of an intermediate character will be encountered in the renting of various special-purpose commercial space.

In all cases, of course, the owner interests will be exerting pressure in the direction of maximizing rental income. While these interests may be satisfied with a break-even revenue when the markets are depressed, and while exceptionally they may even be willing to sustain small losses rather than the larger losses sometimes associated with prolonged vacancies, generally they will be looking for whatever profits the market will bear.

The property manager in serving the owner interests, therefore, has the task of finding willing and able-to-pay tenants who will agree to what may be called mutually favorable terms. We shall talk at length about the so-called percentage lease arrangements that are so commonly employed in the rental of store spaces. And, finally, we shall refer to other types of leasing arrangements, particularly those commonly employed in the rental of office building spaces. In other words, we will present an overview rather than a detailed analysis.

THE PERCENTAGE LEASE

In our discussion of residential leases in chapter 13 we pointed out that when premises are let for a year or more at a fixed rental, it is always possible that the building owner will get *more* or *less* for the unit of space than it may be worth, depending upon the trend of the market. Admittedly, the value of residential space fluctuates less rapidly than the value of commercial space. Thus, the inequities which may arise in long-term commercial leases can be a great deal more serious than those in residential leases.

The obvious answer to this threat to the fairness of an established rental is to make short-term leases in order that rental adjustments can be made frequently in accordance with the market trends. For many reasons such a solution of the problem is unsatisfactory for both the landlord and the tenant. In the case of the landlord, he is faced with possible tenant turnover and with the associated loss through vacancy and remodeling expense. From the tenant's standpoint, short-term leases are a threat to security of occupancy, investment in goodwill, and the preservation of equity in store fixtures.

To provide a solution to these mutual problems and to create a lease which can be written for a long term without giving a market advantage to one or the other of the parties to the agreement, the so-called *percentage* lease was devised. Under the terms of such leases, a relationship is established between the volume of business done by a given type of merchandising unit *versus* the space value of the unit as established by the general market. This relationship is expressed in the form of a percentage, and the future rental of the space is set at that ratio for the term of the lease.

There are many who question the right of the owner of a building to participate in the gross revenue of tenants. In other words, it is sometimes held that at least a portion of the tenant's revenue comes as the result of purely personal or corporate effort and not by virtue of the value of the real estate in which the enterprise is being conducted. Although this feeling is founded on fact in many cases, the rights of the property owner are such that he can, at any time, deny the tenant the possession of the space or, in the absence of a lease, can raise the rental by an amount which he (the landlord) feels is justified by the volume of business of the tenant. Acceptance of this concept by the majority of tenants has brought the percentage lease into wide use.

TYPICAL PERCENTAGE LEASE COVENANTS

In form and basic content, the percentage lease contains the essential covenants which were described as being a part of the residential lease. The major difference lies in those clauses which describe the amount of rent to be paid, and in certain agreements which are designed to clarify the objectives of the instrument. Those covenants, having to do specifically with the amount of rental to be paid under the lease, will be discussed later in a separate section. For the present we shall concern ourselves with other provisions usually found in percentage leases.

Records and Accounting

If the rental to be paid for the space demised is to be based upon the volume of business done by the lessee, it is axiomatic that the method of recording and accounting for such sales be a matter of agreement between the parties to the lease. Well-drawn percentage leases contain stipulations on how the records of sales shall be kept and at what periods they shall be audited. In some cases the type of cash registers is specified. Several such machines are invaluable that compile what is called *non-reset total*. These machines cumulate all sales rung up on a permanent meter which can be read by the owner, or his representatives, at any reasonable times.

Provision is generally made for the owner to examine the books and records of the lessee at reasonable times and for the owner's right to have an audit of such books made by his own auditor at his own expense whenever he may feel that there is error in the audit furnished by the tenant. For example, in some large shopping centers all tenants are advised that, on a certain annual anniversary date, at least some of them will have their books subjected to an external audit. The other tenants will then be charged on the basis of their own audits. Tenants soon find out that to cheat in such a system where they are subject to random but periodic external audits is like playing a game of Russian roulette.

Protection against fraud on the part of the tenant is provided either by punitive measures in the form of penalty rentals or by the right of the owner to recover possession of the premises.

Settlement Period

It is possible to write percentage leases so that the percentage settlement must be made daily, weekly, monthly, quarterly, semiannually, or annually depending upon the nature of the business and the character of the tenant. Some provision must be made as to when the percentage rental shall be paid and for what period.

As noted above, the determining factors of when the rental shall be computed and paid are the character of the tenant and the nature of the business. In cases where the character of the tenant is in question or the tenancy arrangement is impermanent, the period of computation should be short and the payment immediate. An extreme example would be the leasing of space to an itinerant purveyor of refreshments for the duration of a state fair. In such a case the rental should be computed and paid daily. On the other hand, where the character of the tenant is above question, the determining factor is the nature of the business.

Some businesses are subject to wide seasonal fluctuation. Take the jewelry business. In normal times, a high percentage of the typical jeweler's business is done between Thanksgiving and Christmas. If the jeweler happens to be paying a minimum guarantee (see below), it might be unfair to compute his percentage rental monthly. In such cases, leases should provide for an annual computation with the payment period due shortly after the peak period of the tenant's activity. On the other hand, a restaurant in a commercial area does not experience a marked seasonal fluctuation in trade, and the settlements can be made monthly as well as annually.

Hours of Business

In most lines of business, volume can be drastically affected by the hours in which the business is operated. The *normal* hours for each individual type of business are usually established by the customs followed by local merchants. In drugstores, for example, usage dictates that hours range from 8:00 or 9:00 A.M. to 11:00 or 12:00 P.M. Suppose, for example, that a manager leased a store to a druggist on a percentage rental, and the tenant—feeling that he could earn a satisfactory living by restricting his store hours from 9:00 A.M. to 7:00 P.M. —failed to keep his place of business open during the *normal* hours. The manager would be unable—in the absence of a specific lease clause providing the hours during which the druggist was to operate the store—to insist upon longer hours. The owner of the building would be denied an opportunity to obtain the maximum income expectancy from *normal* hours of business operation.

The changing pattern of retail distribution that has marked the past several years has called for substantial alteration in the hours of store operation. It is now standard practice for downtown stores to remain open one or two nights each week. Outlying shopping centers feature evening store hours on three or more evenings per week with many large, drive-in centers requiring evening operation six nights per week. The current widespread Sunday operation of supermarkets and major drug outlets, in our opinion, presages broad acceptance of Sunday store opening in the years to come. In the light of these trends, it is important that leases provide for competitive operating hours.

In this connection it may be added that the arrangement which is now a common part of agreements between major shopping center promoters and their tenants is one that binds all tenants to be adequately staffed and fully stocked during all agreed-upon shopping hours. While minor violations of these provisions may be tolerated from time to time (as in the case of a store owner who wants to honor certain state as well as national holidays), property managers are conditioned to instigate legal proceedings against tenants who

flagrantly violate the committment to maximize gross income by staying open
during the agreed upon hours.

Advertising and Promotion

As an added protection against business lethargy on the part of tenants,
percentage leases frequently contain covenants specifying that the store proprietor shall spend a certain percentage of gross revenue, or a certain flat sum
of money, each month on advertising or promotion. This is especially important in those lines of business which depend heavily upon advertising (motion
picture theaters, for example), as a means of attracting a daily volume of
business.

Exclusion of Competition

In some cases a building owner or manager is warranted in granting a lessee
the exclusive right to sell certain types of merchandise or to render certain
types of service within the building controlled by the manager or landlord.
Whereas most tenants will request such exclusive provisions, the question of
whether or not they are to be granted is a matter of logic and analysis of the
market. In a few instances, the answer to this question is obvious. For example,
the request of a barber, or a beauty shop operator, in an office building that
he or she be given the exclusive right to operate in that building is reasonable
and one that (usually) should be granted.

On the other hand, if one owner happens to control a block of stores in a
good retail location and if a request is made by a prospective tenant that he
be granted the exclusive right to sell foodstuff in that block, then it is likely
the request should be denied—especially if analysis indicates that the block
will support two successful food establishments. It is not necessary that both
food establishments serve exactly the same market. One might be a food mart
while the other might be a delicatessen. In most cases, requests for exclusive
rights over certain types of merchandising are dangerous to the interests of
the building owner and should not be granted (unless, for example, the prospective tenant is prepared to pay for his exclusiveness with a premium rental).

Space Maintenance

Long-term percentage leases frequently outlive styles of improvement and
facilities for merchandising. Where leases are granted for longer-than-normal
terms, provision should be made for the modernization of the lessee's fixtures,
store fronts, illumination, and equipment. Such provisions are extremely important for the maintenance of public acceptance for an individual store and,
in many cases, for an entire shopping area.

WHEN TO USE THE PERCENTAGE LEASE

The only possible excuse for the *granting* of a percentage lease *by the lessor* is the writing of a long-term agreement. It is always comparatively easy to establish an equitable rate of rental for short-term commercial tenants. In such cases there may be no need to compute the rental on the basis of the tenant's gross revenue. Neither the landlord nor the tenant needs protection against future victimization by adverse trends of the market when the term of the lease is one year or less.

It should be a basic rule that percentage rentals shall be established only on leases in which there is to be a long term or on leases when the *landlord* or the *manager* desires percentage rentals, either because of a belief that there will be economic changes within a short period or because of an inability to satisfactorily estimate the value of an untested space.

Percentage leases should be made only with tenants of unquestioned honesty. The manager should trust his fellowman, but he should not put tenants in a position of temptation. Individual merchants in relatively small operations do not need long-term leases. Their investment in fixtures and alterations seldom justifies such protection. Moreover, there is no real method by which the landlord can assure himself of the maintenance of adequate or accurate records.

SETTING RENTALS IN PERCENTAGE LEASES

Once it has been determined that the manager should enter into negotiations for a percentage lease, the question of setting the rental must be determined. There are a number of alternative possibilities which should be considered.

1. Should the lease be a *straight* percentage or a *minimum guarantee?*
2. Should the percentage be graduated on varied levels of business volume, or should the rate hold, regardless of volume?
3. Should there be a maximum, as well as a minimum rental?
4. What percentage of gross revenue should be used for a fair and equitable computation of rental?

Examining each of the above questions from the point of view of analytical reasoning, we find that through analysis the right method of percentage charge often can be determined for each specific case.

Straight Percentage versus Minimum Guarantee

Let us first define our terms. A *straight* percentage lease is one in which the rental to be paid is solely related to the volume of business done by the tenant. Theoretically, if the tenant did no business whatever, he would not be required to pay any rental. If his business went to astronomical heights, the same percentage would be paid on the last dollar of gross sales that was paid on the first dollar.

A *minimum guarantee* is an amount of rental that the lessee agrees to pay, regardless of how poor his business may be. If he did no business whatever, the minimum guarantee would be payable; thus the property owner can be sure of a specific monthly minimum rental.

Straight percentage leases—even where they contain all sorts of protective clauses—are obviously dangerous for the property owner. At best they represent a gamble on the honesty, ability, and stability of the tenant. They can be made only with the very highest type of tenant, that is, one with an excellent reputation, proved ability, and proved successful merchandising acumen.

The only real excuse for making a *straight* percentage lease arises out of individual circumstances. Suppose, for instance, that a national chain organization is interested in coming into your town. Assume that you own a suitable building site which you have held for some time and upon which you are losing money—both in interest on the amount you have invested and in the taxes which you are paying out each year. Now the national chain organization comes to you and says that they will lease a store building for a period of fifteen years at a *straight* percentage of 5 percent, provided you construct a suitable building on your land.

Let us imagine that you examine the possibilities of this particular chain store in your community and are satisfied that they can do a volume of business on your location sufficient to produce a rental which will yield you 10 percent on the amount of your investment in the land and building, after amortizing over the life of the lease 50 percent of your investment in improvements. For fifteen years you will obtain a 10 percent return on your investment (as contrasted with your present loss on the land), and at the end of the term you will own the whole site, subject only to a 50 percent loan on the improvement. In most periods (but not necessarily in an inflationary period), such a gamble would be a desirable program, *provided that the merchandising organization was top level.* In other words, the *straight* percentage lease should only be considered when the opportunities for return on investment are *higher* than normal and when analysis indicates to the property owner that the lessee is capable of a successful operation.

Minimum rentals are contained in most percentages leases and represent a guarantee to the property owner that, regardless of tenant business volume, income from the space demised shall not drop below the level of the minimum.

Now the student must draw a distinction between a percentage rental and a *partnership.* In the case of a *percentage* rental, the property owner is *trading* a sliding-scale rental in return for a long-term security on the part of the tenant. It is a known fact that when business volume rises, profits increase at a much faster rate than gross revenues. Thus, even though the landlord benefits from increases in business, the tenant benefits to a much greater extent. Since the tenant has the right to accelerate his profits under maximum conditions, certainly the owner of the property is entitled to minimum protection.

Establishing the Minimum Rental

How much shall the minimum rental be? In the last chapter on "Setting Store Rentals" we pointed out that the basis of store rentals is the expression in dollars of the level of supply and demand as applied to a given unit of space. A store property is worth what someone will pay for it at any given time. The value, however, is a *current* value—at least in terms of the period covered by the offer.

In a percentage lease, the prospective client is proposing that future rental shall be determined by the volume of business which he is able to do in the period covered by the lease. He is to take and hold possession of the space on the basis of that relationship. The owner, on the other hand, has a unit of space which he can sell currently (for a shorter period) at a certain level. Why then should the owner enter into a lease which is a *gamble* on the future and at the same time suffer a discount for the present?

Minimum rentals—in theory at least—should be equal to the *current* value of the space leased. Any deviation from the current value shows the manager's willingness to gamble on *higher* rentals in the future.

To illustrate the point, let us assume that we are the managers of a store on Main Street with a *current* rent value (for any one of a number of businesses) of $100 per month. Let us suppose further that the neighborhood in which the store is located is a dynamic area of rapid growth. We have an opportunity to rent this store to an independent merchant for $110 per month on a two-year lease, and we also have a chance to rent it to an aggressive chain store organization on a satisfactory percentage with a minimum guarantee of $90 per month for a five-year lease. Which shall we choose?

To answer this question, we must carefully analyze the present and future markets for the type of goods handled by the chain organization. If we are able to conclude that the market for the chain store's product will produce a rental in excess of that paid by the independent merchant (on any renewal of his lease), we will accept the former's offer. We are merely fulfilling the obligation of the property manager, i.e., *to obtain the highest possible revenue over the period of management.*

The Combined Minimum Rental and Percentage Lease Formula

At the present time it is becoming quite popular for owners and tenants to find a formula that combines the advantages to each of a fixed minimal monthly rental with those in which rental is figured as a fraction (that is, a percentage) of the merchant's gross income. For example, suppose that an annual minimum rent has been set which meets the owner's requirement to have an adequate return on his investment after expenses have been paid and which is a reasonable amount for the tenant to pay, even in a bad sales year. By one popular formula, this annual minimum rental (say, in a particular case we are talking about $12,000) is agreed. The annual gross is (say, $250,000) multiplied by the agreed percentage lease fraction (by 0.06 as reflects a 6 percent of gross figure for the case at hand). The resulting number (in the cited example: $250,000/0.06 = $15,000) then represents an amount, A, to be interpreted in the following way:

1. If A is larger than the agreed minimum rental, then the owner is due to receive that amount (6% of $250,000 or $15,000); or
2. If A is less than the merchant's agreed annual minimum rent, then the owner is due to receive as rental only the pre-agreed amount ($12,000).

ESTABLISHING THE RATE OF PERCENTAGE

In recent years, property managers have tended to accept as a basis of negotiation certain tables of percentage rentals suggested by various agencies. Such a table is presented on page 306.

Many will feel that the acceptance of such tables is the route of least resistance. It is not the path of conscientious representation of the property owner but just a rule of thumb. Whereas such tables may be accepted as *averages* for enterprises of the type commonly encountered in negotiation, each individual case must be analyzed in the light of the pertinent facts.

The objective of any business enterprise is *profit,* not *ratio of profit.* If you were the owner of a drug chain and had the opportunity to rent a space which could produce $100,000 a year net profit as compared with a space which would produce only $75,000 a year, your interest would be concentrated upon the former location. Now let us suppose that your $100,000 profit could only be obtained by paying a percentage rental of 4 percent, as compared with a rental of 3½ percent for the location, producing $75,000. Which would you choose? The answer is obvious.

The rate of percentage that applies to a given location for a given type of business depends upon negotiation. Merchandising organizations (primarily interested in *net* profits) will pay higher percentages for stores in which they can be sanguine about earning higher profits. The problem of obtaining higher percentages, then, is one of convincing prospective tenants that net earnings will reach the levels which are indicated by the manager. This conviction depends upon the adequacy of the data introduced into the negotiations.

Although few will advocate the blind acceptance of standard tables for the arrival at percentages applicable for different lines of business, averages may be accepted to be used as points of departure in percentage lease negotiation.

In these connections, the student will be interested in how precisely the numbers are assigned in constructing a table of percentage lease ranges. Curi-

CONDOMINIUM SHOPPING CENTER

A lease insurance program was established to help finance local Willingboro, New Jersey merchants who wished to locate in Country Club Plaza, a condominium shopping center having 22 stores and shops. Merchants were given the opportunity to either purchase their stores outright or lease space with an option to purchase the store for $1 after a 15-year lease expires.

NATIONAL PERCENTAGE LEASE TRENDS

	1950	1960	1970	1974
Art Shops:	8–10	6–10	6–10	6–10
Curios	8–10	6–10	6–10	5–10
Gifts	7–9	5–9	6–10	5–8
Handicrafts-Linens	7–10	6–8	5–10	5–7
Automobile Dealers	2–4	1½–3	1½–3	1½–3
Automobile Accessories	4–8	2–5	3–5	2½–5
Automobile Parking	40–50	30–60	40–75	40–70
Barber Shops	10–12	8–10	6–10	8–10
Beauty Shops	10–15	8–10	6–12	6–10
Books and Stationery	8–11	5–8	4–10	5–8
Business Schools	10–14	9–12	10–15	10–15
Candy and Refectory	8–12	5–8	6–10	6–10
Cigar Stores	5–8	5–8	4–10	6–10
Department Stores	3–4	2–3	1½–4	2–3
Discount Department Stores	N.A.	1–2½	1–2	1–2
Drugs-Independent	6–8	3–6	3–8	4–6
Drugs-Chain	3–6	2½–4½	2½–5	2½–4
Drugs-Prescription (Medical Buildings)	8–12	5–10	5–10	6–10
Electrical Appliances	4–7	2½–5	3–6	3–6
Five and Dime Stores	4–6	3–6	3–6	3–5
Florists	8–10	6–10	6–10	7–10
Fountain and Lunch	8–10	5–8	4–10	5–8
Furs	6–10	5–9	6–8	6–8
Furniture	4–8	3–7	3–8	4–6
Garages—Storage	30–45	30–50	30–65	40–50
Oil-Gas Stations (per. gal.)	1¢–1½¢ per gal.	1¢–1½¢ per gal.	1¢–2¢ per gal.	1¢–2¢ per gal.
Grocery Stores:				
Independent	2–4	1–3	1½–5	1½–3
Chain	1–2	¾–2	1–2	1½–2¼
Supermart	0–1½	¾–1½	½–2¼	1–1¾
Haberdashery	6–10	5–10	3–10	5–8
Hardware	5–8	3–6	3½–6	3–6
Hosiery	6–8	6–8	6–10	6–8
Jewelers	8–10	3–8	4–10	6–10
Lingerie	6–8	5–8	3½–10	6–8
Liquor Stores	6–8	3–8	4–6	3–6
Men's Clothing	5–8	4–8	3½–8	4–8
Millinery	6–8	6–10	6–15	8–12
Musical Instruments	8–10	3–7	4–8	3–6
Motion Picture Theaters	14–25	8–18	8–15	8–12
Restaurants	6–10	5–8	3–10	5–10
Shoes, Retail	6–8	4–7	5–8	5–8
Shoes, Repairing	8–10	8–12	6–10	8–10
Specialty Shops:				
Sporting Goods	6–8	5–8	4–8	5–8
Luggage-Leather Goods	7–10	5–9	5–10	6–8
Women's Wear:				
Independent	7–9	4–8	4–10	4½–8½
Chain	5–8	2½–6	4–8	4–8

ous to some perhaps will be the idea (in fact, the actuality) that the percentage numbers for the most part are not correlated to geographical area nor to type of business community. If 5 percent leases are offered to liquor stores in Boston, it is likely that the same will be true for Omaha as well. And the liquor store can be in a suburban shopping center or occupying a space in a downtown hotel building.

An inspection of the percentages as representative of the various types of merchandise and retail operations, in fact shows a rather consistant correlation between the percentage figure and the markup (which finally determines the net profit) characteristic of the merchandise and retail operation under discussion. For example, chain supermarkets have a very small markup (usually less than 1 percent) and the accompanying table shows that the percentage lease figure is correspondingly low. Similarly, parking lots (which have hardly any overhead and salary expense) enjoy a net profit almost as high as the gross income; hence the table shows that the percentage lease figure applying to such establishments correspondingly is high.

The relationship just indicated between markup and percentage lease figure is qualitative rather than quantitative. After all, owners want to maximize profit and so do the merchant tenants. But as time elapses, certain patterns develop, and certain ways of looking at matters become established, where even though the advantage in a particular situation may be tilted to one side or another, the practice has become so established that the disadvantaged party in effect pays a premium price for doing business at all. In other words, the table of National Percentage Lease Trends given opposite reflects to some extent the realities of the matter and to some extent the aberrations from a true compromise of the owner-tenant interests as dictated by custom and convention. As for the latter, the rule holds here as elsewhere that owners and tenants alike prefer some business, even that enjoyed under less than favorable conditions, than no business at all.

TRENDS OF PERCENTAGE RENTAL RATES

In chapter 16 we drew attention to the fact that retail units were being forced into higher volumes as a method of offsetting increased payrolls and lower margins of profit. The super mart is an expression of this drive.

Just as a higher volume of sales must be spread over a relatively lower ratio of payroll and profit, so it must be spread over a lower percentage of rental. During the past twenty years, rates of profit applicable to virtually every type of retail establishment have declined appreciably. It would appear that this trend will continue as an expression of the consumer demand for a more-efficient type of merchandise distribution. In the light of this fact, long-term percentage leases with major merchandising establishments are encouraged in the theory that as time goes on these leases will appear more favorable than they do currently.

THE NET PROFIT LEASE

In a number of business classifications, the percentage lease has proved inadequate. In banking, for example, inflation may push deposits upward at a rate faster than the ability of banks to pay rental. Leases that assess rentals against banks in relation to the total of the deposits are forced into renegotiation in order to prevent the banks from defaulting. An example of this kind of situation was given in the last chapter. Here it was known how a bank negotiated a lease on the basis of a percentage of net profits. Now, of course, no manager should make such a lease unless the prevailing conditions preclude the possibility of either a fixed-rental or a satisfactory gross-rental percentage arrangement. On the other hand, where space is vacant and cannot be rented on any other basis, the net profit percentage rent is certainly better than nothing.

FIXED RENTAL LEASES

In the beginning of this chapter we pointed to the difference between store-occupied and office-occupied commercial building spaces. Retail establishments have a business volume related roughly to the amount of space they occupy, and hence the setting of rental arrangements on the basis of a percentage of gross revenue makes sense. But office businesses need space only for the purposes of the work that is done. There is no merchandise to display, nor is the customer volume usually such that additional space is required except for waiting rooms. The time efficiently spent by workers, rather than the space they occupy, is the critical factor. The volume of business is hardly measured by space factors at all, but rather by employee salaries, by owners' profit, and by corporate reinvestments.

For example, a one-man dentist office has a space large enough for a reception room, an operating room, and perhaps also for a laboratory and/or X-ray facility. No matter how many patients may come each day to be served, there will be only one who occupies the dentist chair at a time. The doctor may charge a fairly fixed or standard fee for his services. The dentist, or a doctor, or a lawyer, or an accountant, are not people who will commit a percentage of their gross to rent, nor would they be good risks as tenants to the owner interests on such a basis.

Or another example. An oil company renting office space in Odessa, West Texas, will not accept a lease with terms pegged to the company's overall international corporate earnings. Space is space to them. So much is needed for each employee. While the parent company has the public at large as the collective customer in the global sense, the Odessa office under consideration represents simply a local in-house facility where certain local and regional company operations are undertaken, and the rent is simply an expense of the corporation.

The fact remains that in many—perhaps most—office building situations, space will be offered and rented precisely for what it is—i.e., space. The owner of an office building complex will realize that on the average he must receive a certain amount of rent annually for each square foot. He knows his debt requirement costs, his operating expenses, his taxes and insurance liabilities, and his expectation for return on the invested capital. He also knows about his ambition for a certain recurring and continuing profit, and he is tuned into the market situation.

The job of the property manager acting on behalf of the owner is to set up a rent schedule that reflects the fact that certain spaces in a given office building complex will be more attractive both in terms of other contiguous spaces, and from the point of view of one tenant as opposed to another. A corner office suite in the Wrigley Building overlooking Lake Michigan and the Chicago River would be preferred by most tenants compared with a basement space adjacent to a back-street delivery entrance. However, not every prospective tenant will pay the premium price for the premium view. For example, an advertising agency would be quite ready to pay extra dollars for the preferred location since they want both a prestigious address and a conspicuously affluent decor. But a print shop will be quite happy with the basement location, a bit because of the address and the proximity to customers, but mostly because of the bargain rental that can be negotiated.

In these instances, of course, once the owner has decided on what the average space rental should be for offices in his building, the property manager will distribute rentals for the individual spaces. He will determine on the basis of comparability with competing office buildings what the market will bear insofar as assigning a value to the premium space. In the end, some spaces will be offered at above-average price and some at below-average price, all in ways that guarantee the kind of occupancy where there will be both satisfied tenants and satisfied owners.

In summary, the property manager is like the person who wets his finger to see which way the wind is blowing. He devises commercial leases according to a variety of formulas that in the end maximize the owner's returns—and therefore his also. The guidelines he uses have to do with current market conditions and market practices. For example, corporate headquarters buildings may be constructed that are larger than required simply to create a public relations image of prestigious identity. Owners in such cases will be willing to offer excess space for office rental at bargain prices rather than suffer a higher loss in widespread vacancy. And there are many other variant considerations on which an accommodation is based so that lease arrangements can be set in particular cases between owners and tenants.

In this chapter we have spoken at length about the percentage lease arrangement formula that is common for retail store rentals and the fixed rental arrangement formulas that are applied in many office-space leasing situations.

It is clear after considering these extreme kinds of renting, and after having a glimpse of the equities that hold for owners and tenants in the intermediate cases, that the property manager himself must approach the problems of arriving at workable commercial leases in the very same way that an artist will work in painting a picture. In the end, all that is wanted is a good result. The creative artist does not let himself be bound by outmoded conventions. The fact that the sky is blue does not mean that it cannot be painted yellow for a better effect. And the fact that $7 per square foot per year may be the average break-even rental requirement for space in an office building, or indeed in a shopping center, does not mean that, in the particular case, more (or indeed less) should not be demanded.

REVIEW QUESTIONS

1. What is a good basic rule for the property manager to follow in establishing a percentage lease?
2. What caused the wide usage of the percentage lease?
3. List ways of setting a rental on a percentage basis.
4. How does a percentage lease differ from the usual residential lease?
5. What is a net profit lease? When is it used?
6. What is meant by straight percentage, minimum guarantee, minimum rentals?
7. What are the advantages of a percentage lease to the landlord? To the tenant?
8. Explain the difference between a percentage rental and a partnership.
9. What is a non-reset total? Where is it used?
10. When might you be willing to give a tenant exclusive rights in occupancy for the resale of specific products or services? What is your opinion of such exclusive franchises?

SELECTED REFERENCES

California Real Estate Association. *Commercial and Industrial Real Estate.* Los Angeles, Calif., 1973. 114p.
　　See chapter 6: *Leasing Office Buildings* by Albert J. Auers.
　　See chapter 7: *Leasing Commercial and Industrial Property,* by John B. Allen.

Kinnard, William N., Jr. and Messner, Stephen D. *Industrial Real Estate.* 2nd ed. Washington, D. C., Society of Industrial Realtors, 1971. 655p.
　　See chapter 10: *Industrial Real Estate Leases.*

McMichael, Stanley L. and O'Keefe, Paul T. *Leases: Percentage, Short and Long Term.* 6th ed. Englewood Cliffs, N. J., Prentice-Hall, 1974. 446p.

National Institute of Real Estate Brokers. *Guide to Commercial Property Leasing.* Chicago, Ill., 1974. 96p.

National Institute of Real Estate Brokers. *Percentage Leases.* 13th ed. Chicago, Ill., 1973. 100p.

Practicing Law Institute. *Commercial Real Estate Leases.* New York, 1974. 619p.

CHAPTER 19

Special Purpose Building Management

INTRODUCTION

Separate chapters in this text have been devoted to the management of apartment buildings, office buildings, apartment hotels, and store buildings—the principal classifications in which the services of professional property managers are employed. To an extent, each of these classifications represents a special purpose building. Yet, the market for the use of such properties is sufficiently broad to have caused the profession to conclude that they are general purpose buildings, and they are so known.

Property managers who engage principally in the management of the above types of property are frequently called upon to manage buildings which might be called *special purpose buildings* in that the market for their use is restricted. Since the student of management should have a rudimentary knowledge of the problems involved in at least the broader categories of special purpose building property, we shall devote this chapter to a discussion of such buildings.

It is important to remark in passing that the management of certain special purpose buildings is such a specialized activity that it requires very special training and skills. No single property manager can be expected to be an expert with respect to all of the questions and problems in the various applications. It is only because of the truism, "Property is property," that the specialist in one field can learn from the experience and practices of specialists in other property management fields.

INDUSTRIAL PROPERTY

In chapter 1 industrial properties were generally classified as buildings in which the interiors were unfinished. Such a definition would allow us to classify garages, warehouses, and cold storage plants as industrial buildings. Such a classification would be correct to an extent, although it may be argued that garages would also qualify as commercial buildings. For the purpose of this discussion, we shall define industrial buildings as those that house enterprises engaged in the processing or manufacture of products. This may describe multi-occupancy buildings housing millinery and garment manufacturing establishments, or it may describe large steel mills.

Locating industrial properties entails analysis of labor, raw materials, distribution, and taxes. In order to assess adequately the requirements of locating any type of industry, the manager must familiarize himself with the special problems relating to these four major criteria.

The labor requirements of an industrial property, of course, vary with the nature of the industry. Some industries need to locate in areas where there are known pools of certain types of skilled labor. Other industries can employ unskilled labor and can be located wherever there is evidence of an adequate labor force. Still other industries require female workers and must be established in locations where such labor is available.

The location of industrial plants from the point of view of labor also involves an analysis of union conditions and prevailing, as well as potential, sources of housing—particularly if the industry to be located is an employer of large numbers of workers and if there are several potential sites.

The availability of raw materials is an extremely important factor in studies of many types of industrial location, since the cost of bringing raw materials to the plant is an essential factor in the competitive position of the manufacturer. Many heavy industrial firms require railroad or dock facilities so that they can purchase fuel most advantageously. Other industries require a quantity of water, as well as water of a certain chemical analysis. Virtually all manufacturing establishments are dependent upon power and must be located in areas where there is an adequate supply at favorable rates.

The location of a plant with respect to favorable sources of raw materials, fuel, water, and power must be weighed against the desirability of the location from the point of view of the distribution of the finished products. Today many industries are locating their plants and warehouses close to expressways, interstate highways, and local airports for both local and national distribution. Thus, the analyst of industrial location must be familiar with the distribution processes employed by the manufacturer, the location of his markets, the traffic problems involved, and the overall costs of distribution. It is seldom, if ever, possible for an industry to find a location which is ideal from all of these points of view—labor, raw material, and distribution. Hence, the ultimate selection of a location must represent the most favorable compromise.

So-called industrial parks have come into vogue in recent years. As a practical matter, these industrial parks are merely industrial subdivisions designed to accommodate light manufacturing, warehouses, research, assembly, and industrial office buildings. Virtually all such industrial parks offer land to comparatively small land users (from one to 15 acres) in restricted surroundings. In most cases, the land is sold to users who either build or lease back their buildings. There is almost no occasion for such properties to require the services of a professional property manager.

In the past several years, the requirements of government at city and state levels have resulted in adoption of a variety of taxes and have resulted in a differential in the desirability of locations from the point of view of the individual industry. One of the influences toward urban decentralization has unquestionably been the ability of industry to locate outside of major cities and to enjoy substantial tax savings. Although it is difficult for industries to move about due to the heavy costs of relocation, city and state taxes play an important part in the selection of sites when industries have reached the decision to seek a new location.

MINIWAREHOUSE

Another type of special purpose building that requires management expertise is the miniwarehouse or self-storage unit as it is sometimes called. Specifically, this structure provides a small, safe, fireproof storage unit for the individual or small businessman. Miniwarehouses first took hold in Texas and have been established since then throughout the South, Southwest, West, some Rocky Mountain and Midwest States, and in the Washington, D.C. area.

THE LOFT BUILDING

It is not possible within the limited confines of this book to discuss the problems of every type of industrial property. Moreover, it is improbable that the average student of real estate management will be called upon to manage any of the more isolated categories.

The type of industrial property most frequently managed by the professional property manager is the *loft building*. A loft building may be described as a building of two or more stories, designed for industrial use. This type of property was originally developed to accommodate the needs of small manufacturing enterprises in the period of rail-fixed urban transportation, when employers of labor found it necessary to be close to the termini of transportation systems, and when the distribution of raw materials and finished products was accomplished primarily by the horse and wagon.

For reasons we will consider later, the loft building is now largely obsolete economically, and virtually none of this type of building has been built in the past two decades. Suffice it to say that the original locational requirements of light manufacturing caused almost all loft buildings to be located on the periphery of downtown districts.

The revolution in housing, urban transportation, industrial production, and labor organization which marked the period following World War I resulted in a sharp change in the management problems involved in the operation of loft buildings. As noted in chapter 1, these management problems are not basically different from those found in general purpose buildings, except in the field of space rental. As a result of the changes mentioned above and of the increased numbers of people engaged in commercial activities, loft buildings have been occupied less and less by firms actually manufacturing goods and more and more by quasi-commercial establishments which do not need to be housed in finished office buildings. A large part of this new occupancy consists of printing and allied arts, semi-warehousing and distributive activities, and bulk office spaces.

An additional factor of importance in the changed occupancy of loft buildings has been the sharp increase in the cost of construction of office buildings and the consequent rise in space rental rates in office buildings.

Many logical office space users have not been able to afford the rentals charged by conventional office buildings. This class of tenancy has been forced to seek out less desirable quarters in less prestigious locations.

The loft building located immediately adjacent to the commercial area has proved to be an ideal accommodation for this type of tenant. With minor alterations, most loft buildings can be converted into suitable office space, especially for use by firms who do not require de luxe quarters, or whose business does not involve the handling of customers in their offices.

The rental value of loft building space is set almost entirely by the level of

LOFT BUILDING

A loft building is a type of industrial property rapidly becoming obsolete from a functional point of view for the purposes for which it was originally designed. However, with but small alterations, it presents numerous possibilities for conversion, particularly for firms who require conventional, not de luxe office space.

demand and the quality of the space itself—both physically and in terms of services rendered. In the case of other types of properties, we have studied such value factors as interior decoration, value of tenancy, atmosphere, or rental. Generally speaking, these factors are not considered in any appraisal of the rental value of loft buildings.

When a manager is given a loft building to operate, his analysis of the rental schedules prevailing there must be based upon a study of the competitive market for loft space weighed against the advantages of the building in terms of the locational criteria which we have described above. The rental value may also be influenced to a degree by the services and facilities of the property, but since these are extremely limited (principally to elevators, floor loadings, fire protection, track and dock facilities, and lighting), they are not as important as in other types of buildings.

The principal variant in industrial space rentals is the level of industrial activity and the position of the economy in the business cycle. Demand for industrial production in the past has come in waves. In periods of rising demand for industrial goods (notably wartime), industrial construction lags far behind the demand for industrial space. At such times, rental value of loft buildings, and all other industrial property, increases sharply. As industrial production approaches its peak, substantial quantities of new industrial construction are undertaken in virtually every type of industry, until the amount of industrial space is equal to the gross demand. Moreover, because new industrial buildings are designed to provide greater efficiency for manufacturers than could be obtained in older, more obsolete properties, the total amount of new industrial construction in any period of rising demand is almost always in excess of the increased industrial requirements.

When industrial production levels off and begins a decline, there is inevitably an oversupply of industrial space, and price cutting to attract tenants is as rapid as were rental increases at the outset of the period of prosperity. At such time *alternative use* for industrial properties, particularly loft buildings, is the principal stabilizing influence and the major tool of the manager in solving the occupancy and rental problem. This is a situation where the property manager has the unique background necessary to meet the problem.

OTHER SPECIAL PURPOSE BUILDINGS

In addition to loft buildings, there are a number of other categories of industrial property, some of which were mentioned above. These major categories are: warehouses, cold storage warehouses, garages, truck terminals, foundries, ice plants, material and coal yards, oil storage and shipping yards, and service stations. Almost without exception, these types of property are occupied by a single tenant or owner. However, when any such property is presented to the professional manager for management and rental, the success or failure of his effort will depend principally upon the adequacy of his knowledge. The problems of heating, painting and decorating, exterior maintenance, and mechanical equipment will not be especially new to the property manager. His major concern will be one of merchandising the space as favorably as possible in the current market, with physical maintenance of secondary concern.

The best source of information about these specialized industrial properties is the trade association which serves the industry involved. For example, if you are given a cold storage warehouse to operate, you will find either in your city or elsewhere a trade association concerned solely with the affairs of cold storage operators. These associations always are in a position to furnish a substantial amount of data on the level of current business in the specialty, as well as other valuable information.

The Society of Industrial Realtors is a separate professional group within the orbit of the National Association of Realtors®. Its members specialize in industrial brokerage, finance, and appraisal. Because most industrial corporations completely occupy the structures in which they are located, the role of managers in this type of property is a limited one.

Theater Buildings

The ownership of commercial properties occasionally brings to the professional manager a building which houses a theater. In almost all instances, the problem of the manager in connection with theater space is one of leasing rather than direct operation. Thus, our discussion of theater management will be restricted to an analysis of the principal elements of theater leasing.

Most theaters are leased on a percentage basis, with a minimum guarantee based primarily on a per-seat value. Since conditions in the theater business are extremely volatile, it is pointless to engage in a discussion here of the percentage which should be applied to a typical motion picture theater. Figures may vary from 6 percent to 15 percent, depending upon conditions prevailing in the industry and upon the location and the facilities of the theater itself.

In recent years motion picture theaters have developed a substantial source of income through the sale of candy, popcorn, and confectioner's goods. This revenue should be included in the excess rent which is to be paid by the lessee as a percentage gross. If a theater is rented on a flat seat basis, this income should be considered in establishing the rent level.

In most theaters the lessor is the owner of the air-conditioning equipment and seats. Carpeting may be the property of either the lessee or lessor but is most frequently the property of the lessor. Projection equipment, on the other hand, is generally the property of the lessee, and if projection equipment is included in the lease as supplied by the lessor, consideration should be given in the rental.

In virtually all cases the lessee pays the entire cost of operation in the theater space, including heating, air conditioning, decorating, etc. Moreover, the tenant agrees to completely maintain this equipment.

The changed recreation habits of the American people brought about by general use of television in the home has caused a sharp shrinkage in the number of operating theaters in the United States—both motion pictures and legitimate. This trend has not altered the rates at which theaters are leased but has greatly reduced their revenues.

Mart Buildings

Since World War I, in many larger cities there has developed a new type of property, called the *mart building*. This description is most frequently applied to a multistory, finished interior property which is a cross between a retail arcade and a loft building. This type of property is used principally by wholesalers and jobbers for the display of sample merchandise. Here, only selections are made by the retailer or dealer, and the final order is shipped from another location. Retail or consumer sales are generally eschewed by mart occupants, and in some instances rigid controls are maintained to limit entrance to the mart only to those persons engaged in retailing.

The design of this type of property is usually marked by display windows on all corridors, wide bays, and depth of space. In view of the fact that the space is used principally for exhibition purposes, artificial lighting is generally acceptable. In fact, the demands for comparatively low rental on such space make it uneconomic to use the type of construction in which there is substantial peripheral area.

The management problems peculiar to mart buildings revolve around traffic, renting, and special maintenance. Most such buildings are faced with the problem of occupancy peaks which occur at times when large numbers of buyers are gathered together for special market periods. At such times elevators are crowded, restaurants are overtaxed, and entry control is difficult. In order for such buildings to prove satisfactory, their original design must contemplate these traffic periods and must provide adequate corridor width, elevator capacity, toilet facilities, etc.

Almost all mart buildings were originally conceived and promoted around a nucleus of specialized occupancy. There are furniture marts, merchandise marts, clothing marts, floor covering marts, etc. In order to be successful, these mart properties must serve a broad trading area and must attract a volume of merchandise buyers to the market events which are staged by the tenants. The renting of this type of property involves a high degree of creative ability as well as a high level of public relations skill in establishing basic relationships with the trade groups involved.

The specialized phases of mart building arrangements which must be given

A MART BUILDING

Internationally recognized as the world's greatest wholesale buying center, the Merchandise Mart in Chicago covers an area of two entire city blocks. Total floor area of the building is 4,229,000 square feet or the equivalent of 97 acres.

attention by the management are those represented by the variable nature of traffic and service requirements, the control of entry, and the handling of merchandise arriving for display purposes.

Medical Buildings

One of the largest industries in the United States is engaged in the care and treatment of the sick. From the point of view of the property manager, however, the impact of this industry upon building management is principally represented by the housing of the medical and dental professions. Whereas thousands of physicians and dentists are located in ordinary office buildings in which there is a low percentage of medical occupancy, there has been an increasing tendency for members of the medical and dental professions to locate in buildings either entirely, or largely, devoted to this specialized tenancy.

There are several types of medical buildings. There is the multistory, specifically designed building; the reconverted office building; the neighborhood store building in which doctors and dentists are located upstairs; and the one- or two-story *clinic* type of a specially designed property, which has come into increasing use in the past years.

As in the case of all other special purpose buildings, the principal techniques of property management are the same as those employed in general purpose properties. In medical buildings, however, there are a number of unique problems arising out of specialized tenancy.

The first of these specialized problems has to do with utilities. Doctors' offices require special wiring for various types of therapy which require heavier than normal electric loads. Lighting is custom-designed for the type of occupancy involved and requires custom installation. In dentists' offices the installation of dental chairs imposes problems of water drainage, compressed air, and gas. All of these installations are extremely expensive and are an important element in the higher per square foot rental which must be obtained from this type of occupancy.

The second problem encountered by the manager in medical buildings has to do with space preparation and design for the tenants' use. Most doctors' and dentists' offices are made up of a series of cubicles, involving substantially more construction of walls and partitions than to be found in typical office space. The requirements for ventilation and air conditioning are greater in medical buildings.

The third type of problem unique in medical buildings is the maintenance service required. The normal night cleaning of office space is made considerably more complicated by the layout of the offices and, in some cases, by the necessity for greatly increased cleaning effort. Because of the requirements for extraordinary cleanliness, the decoration of such spaces is more expensive in the first instance, and it is needed more frequently.

The problems of traffic in medical buildings are greater than those in the typical commercial property. In multistory buildings, elevator scheduling is different than in commercial properties, since the peak loads are less, but the all-day traffic is greater. Many such buildings are required to furnish elevator service (as well as heat and hot water) over longer periods in order to accommodate doctors and dentists who keep evening hours.

Parking facilities are considered to be essential in a well-designed and well-operated medical building and thus present an additional problem to the property manager—often one requiring extra personnel so that proper controls may be guaranteed.

Tenant selection is an extremely important phase of professional building management and is covered rather fully in chapter 20.

The leasing of medical buildings is often a complex problem, especially in the larger properties. Doctors and dentists frequently are associated in groups

PROFESSIONAL BUILDING

These dentists' office suites are spacious and well lighted. Extra partitioning and wiring are available on request. Tenancy of the building is limited to professional people.

and require arrangements peculiar to their specialties of practice and professional associations. Many combinations of doctors engage separate employees for service in reception rooms. In other instances, such suites are provided service directly by the medical building as a method of merchandising.

Rental rates established in medical buildings to a large extent can be judged by the value factors and criteria outlined in chapter 14, in which office building analysis is outlined. The market for medical space has in the past paralleled the market for office space but in the future will be influenced more and more by the cost of so-called clinic buildings in which one or more doctors undertake the ownership of the property, principally in outlying neighborhoods.

Many managers believe there are special collection problems related to medical buildings, but most will agree that policies advocated in chapter 22 are as sound for medical buildings as for any other type of property.

Eating and Drinking Places

The most important recreational activity of today's population is eating and drinking. Thousands of buildings in the country are devoted to such use. Here we are increasingly referring to special-purpose structures which may vary from a hamburger hut to a palatial restaurant and bar.

A high percentage of such properties are owner-occupied and managed. However, the turnover and financial fatality rate for such enterprises is high, and real estate managers are often brought in to solve tenancy problems.

REVIEW QUESTIONS

1. What is a *loft building?* By whom are they mainly used today?
2. How would you establish the rental of a *loft building?*
3. How would you determine the rental value of a building which for various reasons had just been converted to a *loft building?*
4. You are given an industrial property occupied principally by pharmaceutical houses. What do you do, knowing nothing about pharmaceuticals?
5. On what basis are theaters usually leased? What is the customary percentage rental range? What factors usually are involved in leasing theater space to the tenant? Who is responsible for heating or air conditioning?
6. A radio concern is seeking a factory location. What analysis should you, as a property manager, make in order to locate this concern properly?
7. What is meant by a *mart building?* What are its identifying marks?
8. What would you do if a price-cutting wave set in on industrial properties, and you had a vacant or partly vacant industrial building to manage?
9. What problems are concerned specifically with the operation of buildings 100 percent, or at least a large percent, in medical occupancy?
10. What management problems are peculiar to *mart buildings?*

SELECTED REFERENCES

Hanford, Lloyd D., Jr. and Kelley, John. "Design, Development of Medical Buildings." *Journal of Property Management,* Jan–Feb. 1966, pp. 6–15.

Hanford, Lloyd D., Sr. *Investing in Real Estate.* Chicago, Ill., Institute of Real Estate Management, 1966. 157p.

Kinnard, William N., Jr. and Messner, Stephen D. *Industrial Real Estate.* 2d ed. Washington, D. C., Society of Industrial Realtors, 1971. 655p.

"New Uses for Old Buildings." *Real Estate Investment Ideas,* March 9, 1971, pp. 4–5.

CHAPTER 20

Tenant Selection

INTRODUCTION

It is clear that the property manager is involved mostly in a business of selling. Variously we have used the words marketing and merchandising, but if he sells nothing or performs no service—he has no business.

Paramount in this process is ownership interests. Owners not only have their own expectations but also the right to demand that these expectations be fulfilled. For example, a dissatisfied owner arbitrarily may withdraw his property from the market rather than offer its use under unsatisfactory rental or lease conditions.

The property manager stands in the middle between satisfactory and able-to-pay customers and the owners who want only to maximize their profit (or certainly, at least, to minimize their loss) on given property investments. The position often is tenuous. If the owner is not satisfied with the manager's stewardship, the latter may be discharged. But if the tenants relinquish occupancy even for reasons beyond their control, the owner again will not be satisfied. It is virtually a case of double jeopardy.

The property manager who is slavish in serving singular owner interests, however, does not always win the race either. Perhaps William H. Vanderbilt could say in his day, "The Public be damned!" But not the property manager, then or now. That sort of attitude, of course, would be counterproductive—as indeed it would offend the sensibilities of thoughtful people.

In other words, the property manager in each case works within a framework where owner interests are brought into harmony with the aspirations of a certain segment of the consumer population which is in the market for the rental or lease of certain kinds of space. And he does his best to bring about an equitable compromise in the historic confrontation between the seller wishing to maximize profit and the buyer wishing to minimize cost.

The property manager's role as arbitrator has more than an altruistic base, however. His own livelihood flows from his ability to arrange for and perpetuate an amicable relationship between the parties involved. On the one side, this means the property manager often is in a position to choose which properties he will manage. In other words, not every owner will offer acceptable conditions, and even the award of tempting side benefits may not be sufficient inducement for a property manager to agree to accept a particular owner's proposal.

On the other side as well, the property manager—as soon as he is assigned to a particular property—also comes into the position of being able to choose the tenants. Theoretically, tenant selection is based on the wish to guarantee that the respective interests of the various parties concerned have been furthered to the optimum. Thus, the renter/lessor will want maximum value for his costs, the property manager will want maximum reward for his services, and the owner will want maximum profit for his investment.

We have used the words *value, reward,* and *profit.* Since for each person these will have a different meaning, the property manager in the final analysis can be satisfied as long as the reward for *his* service is adequate. This assumes the owner is making no complaint and gives evidence that the manager's service is to be retained; it also assumes that the tenants are satisfied with the arrangements. In a sense "profit" to the one and "value" to the other are matters of personal taste. One doesn't have to worry about the owner's profit and the tenant's value so long as there is no complaint about them, just as one doesn't need an umbrella unless it is raining.

Altogether, the property manager finds himself in a peculiar marketing situation. The product he sells on behalf of the owner is not space but merely a specified use of it (limited both in degree and in time); and his customer is not necessarily the first able-to-buy person who happens to come along. This chapter amplifies these peculiarities.

The fact is real estate values are animated by people; real estate is a consumer product. While most owners of buildings feel the main assets of their investment are land, brick, and mortar, there is good reason to believe that a property owner's principal asset is his tenant. The economic value of any building is established by its rental income. This income, in turn, depends upon the stability and desirability of rent-paying tenants.

Among many naive owners and managers, the sole criterion of tenant desirability is rent-paying ability. Certainly the credit rating of a tenant is an extremely important factor in tenant selection. In fact this text devotes the entire next chapter to the subject of *credit and collections.* However, based upon long-term experience, more than 90 percent of all tenants voluntarily pay their rent somewhere near due date—which underscores the need to determine tenants' value from other points of view.

We know for a certainty that there is a tremendous difference in the financial experience of property owners in evaluating tenants. We also know that there is a great financial advantage to real estate owners in long-term tenants versus short-term tenants. It is obvious that the application of criteria other than rent-paying ability is sound operational planning. This chapter is devoted to tenant selection techniques not concerned with rent-paying ability but other measurements of tenants' desirability—keeping in mind that the primary responsibility of the real estate manager is to so administer the owner's property to produce the maximum amount of net revenue over a period of years.

SELECTING RESIDENTIAL TENANTS

Although it obviously is impossible for the real estate manager to make a complete character analysis of every member of a prospective residential family, the process of tenant selection will be facilitated to the extent that certain personal information can be obtained in a form suitable for analysis. Little will be gained by scrutinizing hearsay opinion, or even authenticated allegations, until objectivity and relevance are independently established. Moreover, the whole trend in modern living is to guarantee the right of privacy — as exemplified by the fact that application forms no longer request information about race, religion, or sex. Still, if and when trusted information is available to the property manager and can be interpreted, it should be used.

The right of privacy is a theoretical right fully secured by the Constitution as ratified by a succession of legal precedents. Ironically, in modern times the sophistication of surveillance devices and computerized information processing and retrieval is so great that, even as the courts further uphold the right of privacy, the violation of it becomes all the more simple. While the property manager should not ignore the indications of the commonly available data sources, he should avoid the trap of letting himself become involved in an illegal invasion of privacy or in practices in which some form of antisocial discrimination can be charged.

We shall discuss a number of criteria upon which tenant selection logically can be based in the event the supporting information is available. In many cases, however, the information will not be available. And when nothing can be done about that, the property manager must make his selections taking this uncertainty into account. In any case, experience shows that employing only the information actually possessed is the one to be followed if the best result is desired. The proof of this was suggested at the beginning of chapter 8, where decision theory is introduced as the basis for developing a management plan.

One example out of many will suffice. Given two families in competition for the purchase of the same residential space, let us suppose nothing can be learned to distinguish between these families as to desirability. In this case the property manager would be justified in flipping a coin, or simply in marketing on a "first come, first served" basis. On the other hand, suppose a chance remark indicates a negative factor with respect to one of the families. Then the property manager is presented with a logical basis for selection. To ignore evidence is to court disaster.

In considering the criteria described below, the property manager will realize that in cases in which there is no information (or only partial information), a discounting of the weight of the uncertain criteria will be in order. Remember that if you run a credit check you must have the prospective tenant's permission. Under the Fair Credit Report Act, a rejected tenant has the right to review the file on his credit rating.

Permanence Potential

Just as some workers change jobs frequently, and indeed sometimes because of this, many tenants are continuously moving from one place to another. On the one hand, the frequent turnover in occupancy inevitably creates a greater than normal maintenance expense. In addition, there will be a further loss in revenue because of the vacancy period between the outgoing and the incoming tenant. If possible, therefore, the record of prior occupancy of prospective tenants should be carefully scrutinized.

Some tenant application forms only request information about the present address. This obviously provides less data than the conventional employment application form where the whole history of prior employment is demanded. Given no solid facts about the residence stability of the prospective tenant, the question simply has to be ignored. And the result is that in the long run rents must be set high enough to compensate for the losses incurred by this kind of uncertainty.

That fact is that people—as a part of the modern spirit of independence—resent questions about where they have lived just as they resent questions which seem to challenge the sanctity of their state of cohabitation. In the long run a price must be paid for such independence—and gladly is paid in many instances.

The evidence is compelling that most well-adjusted and stable families actually dislike moving. They will tend to avoid it because they have taken roots in a community, and more so because they have made a thoughtful selection of their location in the first place. In any case, the potential for permanence in occupancy to some extent can be prejudged by considering the present family structure and the predisposition for stability suggested thereby.

It is a complicated matter, not only to know it, but also to explain it even if all of the information is available. In the introduction to chapter 11 we spoke at length about the new mobility of American families. Other things being equal, people simply move around more than they did in the first half of this century. And with travel so easy, "Why not?" some would say. In addition, people do change jobs on occasion, they do outgrow present living quarters (and adversely are outgrown by them as children leave home), they do get divorced and remarried, they do become dissatisfied with circumstances, and their ability to pay does vary with time. Inflations and deflations form chicken-or-egg sequences in the economic cycles mentioned in chapter 5.

In other words, some moves are amply justified and in no way reflect discredit on those involved. In fact some moves even may be applauded by the property manager (as offering a chance to gain entry for a major overhaul and rent increase), and by the other tenants (as good riddance of undesirable neighbors). And so it goes. The property manager can act only on what he knows, but he also can invoke safeguards against the prospect of suspected adverse situations.

Housekeeping Ability

The problem of building maintenance is, in part, at least, a matter of housekeeping. The desirability of any building anywhere is to an extent related to its cleanliness. This applies to tenant quarters as well as to public spaces and grounds. Moreover, one of the main purposes of interior decoration is to assist the tenant in attaining the objective of cleanliness.

A tenant who is a good housekeeper is infinitely superior—from the point of view of the building owner as well as that of neighboring tenants—to the tenant who is slovenly and untidy. The good housekeeper will require a great deal less maintenance expense in virtually every classification. The habits of good housekeeping will automatically tend to protect the building owner's property, for a good housekeeper is one who takes pride in keeping the premises as attractive as possible. She will be the kind of tenant who reports a leaking faucet before it has a chance to discolor the wash basin. She will see that the children do not mark on the walls. She will dispose of garbage before it attracts insects and vermin. She will take pride in the building's public spaces and will do more than her part in helping to maintain the standards of the building.

Strangely enough, the level of the prospective tenant's housekeeping ability cannot be discerned altogether from her personal appearance. Needless to say one cannot include in an application form a request for a prospective tenant's appraisal of her own housekeeping ability. The *only* method available to a manager to judge the housekeeping ability of a prospective tenant is to *visit* the present home of the prospective tenant to inspect its general condition. Of course, this imposes an additional but necessary burden of investigation upon the manager. Therefore, it is sufficiently important to warrant the added effort on the part of the property manager to see that conveniences are provided that facilitate housekeeping.

Child Care

Even the person most sympathetically disposed toward children recognizes the fact that unless controlled, children can be a major source of destruction. Some property owners and managers solve this problem by simply refusing to rent to families with children. Such a policy is to be eschewed, except in those rare instances when the manager can conclude the building in question is not suitable for occupancy by children.

Families with children are normally the most desirable families and are generally stable in tenancy. The wise building manager and owner want such families as tenants when there is evidence that the families lead well-ordered lives. Here, again, it is impossible for a manager to determine from an application form whether or not the parents are capable of reasonable child discipline. This subject in general, however, cannot be a matter of personal investigation prior to the tenancy arrangement. Therefore, in many modern residential properties special provisions are made to accommodate the special needs of, and the problems presented by, children. Game rooms, playgrounds, swimming pools, and the like are examples.

Living Habits

In single-family residences there is usually enough distance between a tenant and his neighbor to prevent the occupants from being an annoyance to one another. In multi-unit apartment buildings, however, tenants live so closely together that any departure from the norm of behavior can result in definitely unpleasant living conditions. A significant and growing percentage of tenant families has one or more members addicted to alcohol. Other families engage in violent argument. Still others turn night into day, staging lusty entertainments which carry on into the hours when most less-swinging tenants are trying to rest for the following day's work. While managers certainly believe in the right of an individual to live his life as he chooses, he should become concerned when one pattern of living jeopardizes the rights of other individuals within a given property.

Laws that protect the sanctity of the home make it extremely difficult to recover possession of a house, or an apartment, which has been rented to a tenant who subsequently turns out to be a nuisance to his neighbors. Tenants who fail to pay rental fees are comparatively easy to evict. Despite this fact, a high percentage of tenant investigation is devoted solely to determine whether the prospective tenant has a record of good credit. On the other hand, because the remedies for nonpayment of rent are clear and those for other deficiencies in deportment are extremely vague, much greater emphasis in investigation ideally should be placed upon other criteria of tenant selection.

It is extremely difficult, for example, to evict a tenant merely on the grounds he is consistently under the influence of alcohol. Yet such deportment on the part of one tenant in an apartment building may completely alter the desirability of the building for other tenants who may be raising families. As is true in the case of other criteria, a manager cannot tell from an application or from an interview whether the tenant prospect is addicted to alcohol. Any adequate investigation of the tenant at one or more of his places of previous residence perhaps would divulge such information. Such an investigation also could bring to light any other difficulties encountered by the prospective tenant's previous neighbors, and might prevent the manager from threatening the welfare of his building's tenants by the acceptance of an objectionable neighbor. However such investigations, under today's conditions, are largely ruled out for the reasons already stated. Living habits, like religious belief, are held to be strictly private matters.

Tenant Compatibility

From many points of view the real estate manager should operate each individual property under his administration exactly as he would if he *owned* the property. If you owned a twelve-apartment building, you would think of your tenants as a small unit of society in whose happiness and welfare you were vitally interested. You would recognize that the personal happiness of each of the tenants is to a degree dependent upon the ability of the group as a whole to be congenial. Whenever an apartment became vacant, you would analyze the prospective tenants from the point of view of potential compatibility with those already in residence. To use a far-out example, if eleven of your tenants were thieves, you would be reluctant to rent the twelfth apartment to a detective. The point is that the effective manager should consider the factor of potential compatibility in measuring the suitability of a prospective tenant for any individual property.

Discrimination

The people of the United States long have struggled with the problem of giving practical substance to the promise of human equality contained in our Constitution. To their great credit they have clung steadfastly to these ideals and—in the past few decades especially—they have made great gains in the direction of their fulfillment. Yet we are still a long way from the realization of these goals in terms of the willingness and the capacity of people to purge themselves of prejudice to the point of really effective nondiscrimination.

The property manager is uniquely embroiled in the cross-currents of this legal, cultural, and social evolution. The reason is that *housing* (along with education and employment) has been a focal point in the confrontation of the forces involved. Various Supreme Court decisions, new federal, state, and local laws have imposed specific obligations on property managers which must be observed in the proper conduct of their business. Thus, it is imperative that members of the profession have a complete understanding of these obligations at the local, state and national levels. They are especially pervasive in the matter of tenant selection, where sensitivity to human rights is directly encountered.

Social Responsibility

It may be argued that the property manager has a social responsibility in the matter of tenant selection. The term social responsibility shall be defined here as the responsibility of the real estate manager to make decisions in tenant selection which result in human equity. This means that the question of *need* for housing shall be taken into consideration, when the selective process involves choice between two prospective tenants.

For example, let us suppose the building manager is operating a property containing one- or two-bedroom apartments. Let us assume further that a tenant in one of the one-bedroom apartments during the course of tenancy has had a child, and the child is now three years old. He has asked to be considered for the first two-bedroom apartment which becomes vacant.

Now let us carry our supposition another step and say that a two-bedroom apartment becomes available. Let us imagine that a friend of the manager who has no children has applied for the two-bedroom apartment. If the two tenants are equally desirable from the point of view of the criteria ordinarily applied for tenant measurement, the manager should give the apartment to the present one-bedroom tenant, since by so doing he is accommodating the family with the greatest need, and at the same time he is serving the broad interest of the community.

Whereas such decisions are sometimes apparently incompatible with the manager's responsibility to obtain the highest possible income from a given property over the remaining years of its life, there are times when social responsibilities transcend the profit motive.

COMMERCIAL TENANT SELECTION

In other sections of this text (notably chapter 15) we have discussed the necessity of analyzing prospective commercial tenants from the standpoint of ability, aggressiveness, and progressiveness. We shall assume that the student already recognizes the importance of these criteria in commercial tenant selection. However, as is true in the residential field, the investigation of prospective commercial tenants should contemplate a measurement of the applicant's desirability from several additional points of view, if the selection process is to achieve its objectives. In the commercial field, the measurement of tenant desirability is not solely concerned with the personal traits of the tenant (since many are corporations or large aggregations of individuals), but is based upon factors growing out of the commercial problem. Hence, direct inquiry into the background of commercial tenants is easier than trying to discover things about private lives.

The more important criteria for the measurement of a prospective commercial tenant's basic desirability are briefly discussed below.

Reputation

In chapter 14 we discussed the fact that the value of office space is in a measure established by the *prestige* of its tenants, and by the human atmosphere which prevails in the building. Whereas no essential qualitative difference between people can be recognized, it is hardly practical to say that they are not subject to environmental influences. In any event, the manager must recognize the impact of the individual reputation of a commercial tenant upon the building in which he has his offices. This reputation must be measured from a personal as well as a professional standpoint, and should be the subject of investigation during commercial tenant selection.

Service Requirements

A prospective tenant may be perfectly acceptable from the point of view of ability, aggressiveness, and reputation and yet be considered unsatisfactory because of unique service requirements. For example, if the prospective tenant is being considered for an industrial building where there are limited freight loading and elevator facilities, and if investigation discloses that the acceptance of this particular tenant would produce a load on these facilities sufficient to destroy their value to other tenants, then perhaps the tenant should not be accepted. The manager must in all cases, make a study of tenant service requirements as a part of his tenant selection process.

Expansion Requirements

Successful businesses are dynamic and are in a constant state of growth. Buildings on the other hand are static, and cannot always be expanded to meet tenants' growth requirements.

In the selection of tenants the manager must be cognizant of the likelihood of their future expansion requirements, as well as the expansion problems presented by present tenants who occupy adjacent space. In many cases it is unwise for a manager to act favorably upon the application of a prospective tenant whose growth pattern indicates that his occupancy will be temporary.

OTHER TENANT SELECTION

The previous discussion of tenant selection techniques has envisioned the application of criteria to so-called *private* property. Whereas most of these criteria are suitable for all types of buildings, separate sets of criteria are being applied to the growing group of buildings embraced by cooperative, mutual, and public housing. In the latter cases, administrators are concerned with income limitations, family structure, housing needs, and other factors peculiar to low-rent housing.

REVIEW QUESTIONS

1. Name the criteria for selection of tenants of commercial buildings.
2. Besides the residential tenant's rent-paying ability, what other measurements should be made by the property manager? List in order of importance.
3. Explain *social responsibility* from the standpoint of the property manager dealing in residential rentals.
4. How would you judge a prospective tenant's housekeeping habits? Of what value is such information to you?

SELECTED REFERENCES

Idler, Herman C. "Rating Your Residents." *Journal of Property Management,* May–June 1971, pp. 134–137.

Institute of Real Estate Management. *The Resident Manager; An On-Site Management Handbook of Multi-Unit, Residential Housing.* Chicago, Ill., 1973, 87p.

Kelley, Edward N. "Ten Rules in Getting Qualified Tenants." *National Real Estate Investor,* July 1970, pp. 48–49.

Lewis, Cynthia D. "Tenant Selection in Federally Subsidized Housing." *Journal of Property Management,* May–June 1972, pp. 102–105.

"Managing Your Apartments: How to Fill Them Up and Keep Them Full." *House & Home,* April 1973, pp. 89–109.

CHAPTER 21

Credit and Collections

INTRODUCTION

Under the present system of building operation, property managers sometimes base their compensation on a percentage of gross rents actually collected. The percentage is a variable subject to negotiation between the property manager and the owner. Of course, occasionally, a property manager will be working for a salary or for a flat fee. More commonly, however, there will be a strong incentive for rental collection by the manager because his income is dependent on actual collections. Even in the case of institutional and public housing properties, collections remain a vital phase of the manager's activities. And, in some cases, he is forced to deal not only with the tenants, but also with those who in particular cases may be involved in providing recurring rental subsidies.

This chapter develops the attending ideas about rental collections and strategies and procedures for collecting successfully. First we must deal further with the question of tenant credit rating, since—as mentioned in the previous chapter—collection problems can be minimized when tenants consistently are selected on the basis of their good credit habits.

Obviously, the building operating costs, taxes, and general overhead accrue inexorably each day a building stands. These expenses are best met out of *cash* income. They will never be paid by promises alone. Since the income of most buildings is generated by the tenant rental collections, it becomes all the more essential that continuous revenues be ensured through careful screening of tenants' credit and through constant vigilance on the matter of current and future rent collections.

The nearly universal practice of collecting rentals once each month (generally on the first day thereof) actually makes the property manager's office a de facto agency for installment collection. This means that the property manager should become a specialist in the highly complicated questions of tenant credit, and in the attending questions of collection technique. Good screening of applicants for rental space obviously will contribute to the eventual success of the ensuing collection programs. But in the long run, through study of the commercially available credit statements, the ability of prospective tenants to pay rentals over a period of months and years theoretically can be forecast. In other words, in any installment buying the initial sale is predicated upon

333

the tendering of a downpayment (i.e., the first month's rent in the present context). It is the meeting of the later installment obligations, therefore, that is of prime concern to the seller (i.e., the property manager).

It is paramount for management to establish firm and definite policies, not only with respect to rental schedules and maintenance procedures, but also with respect to credit and collection policies. Deviations should be allowed only in exceptional cases. For example, it will be reasonable to accommodate a tenant, who says on the twenty-fifth of a month that the rental due on the first of the following month will not be available until ten days later—especially if it is further indicated that a *one-time only* situation is involved. Or, even if the first of the month is the fixed rental-due date, exceptions routinely can be made for the tenant whose payday falls a few days later.

The public at large has been conditioned in many ways to suppose that stated due dates have no binding sanctity. For example, many credit-card arrangements are made to foster deferred payments by customers, since this in the long run brings in additional *interest* revenue. Life and other insurance premiums routinely have *grace periods,* which cannot but undermine the meaning of a due date. Such laxities perhaps can be justified in some business arrangements, but late-payment clauses (regardless of the level of the associated penalty) are counterproductive in rental/lease agreements.

It must be understood why delinquency in rent paying has a different meaning than defaults with respect to other purchases of consumer goods and services. Items like automobiles, furniture, refrigerators, and the like can be repossessed when purchase contract conditions are not met. Similarly, ignoring a credit-card invoice leads to the loss of the deferred payment privileges which the card originally provided. And nonpayment of a telephone bill in the end often leads to loss of the right for future service anywhere else in the country. But the worst a nonpaying renter suffers in many cases is a period of a few weeks (or months) of free occupancy until an eviction notice takes effect, after which new accommodations can be secured according to the renter's cleverness in camouflaging his past nonpayment record.

After all, many examples can be cited of persons who don't own their own private car because of a prior adverse credit rating. But where in America can families be found sleeping under the stars rather than a roof just because they have a bad rent-paying record?

Eventually, rent collections may become largely automated, for example, via direct (so-called check-O-matic) bank account payments, or through use of credit-card schemes. Thereafter, nonpayment of rent would have the same adverse effect on future credit as nonpayment of department store and other consumer goods accounts. In the meantime, the main safeguard that property managers have for their percentage-based income, is to insist on regular (i.e., nondeferred) rental payments. And by "insist" we mean that there should be no idle threats but rather a set of enforceable (and enforced!) rules governing collections.

For example, as standard operating procedure, the management firm could have the established policy that rents are due on the first of each month, that first notices of delinquency will be sent out on the second day, and that eviction notices will be issued for all accounts that are past due for more than a week. Exceptions would be made only with cause and with as little fanfare as possible (lest other renters claim similar rights for deferred payments).

Any favoritism in rent collection is to be avoided at all costs, as is social fraternization in most general instances. The point can be made that the delinquent tenant who has missed one rental payment finds himself in a worsened position, not only for catching up but also for making the next due payment. To carry such a person on credit is of dubious merit with respect either to his long-range interests or to those of the property manager. These are some of the points to be alluded to in the paragraphs that follow. A corresponding point is that with a verification of facts (for example, through a credit check) of the applicant's statements in the initial personal interview, most of the later collection problems can be anticipated and to a large extent avoided.

Many of the specific points made in this chapter refer to residential properties. Questions of credit and collections for commercial and industrial tenants are unique in themselves, but in essence of a simpler sort.

CREDIT AS THE BASIS OF TENANT SELECTION

The ease with which consumer credit can be expanded in our present economy has imposed tremendous pressure upon the typical family income. The current ability to pay is constantly threatened by commitments made against future earnings. The cyclic nature of our broad consumer income makes it almost inevitable that there shall be fluctuation in the monthly earnings of typical tenants.

The credit manager in a commercial establishment must, therefore, carefully scrutinize each applicant from the point of view of his fulfilling his payment obligation in the future as well as at the time of sale. After all, a one-year lease at $200 per month is nothing more or less than a note for $2,400 which the tenant agrees to pay in equal monthly installments of $200. In our modern economy the typical tenant is likely to execute a number of such notes. Undoubtedly, he has life insurance policies on which he makes periodic payments. He probably is buying an automobile on which he must make monthly payments. It is possible that he also is obligated for similar monthly payments on the purchase of furniture, household appliances, clothing, and the repayment of small loans. If his credit is overextended and his income is reduced either through sickness, interruption of employment, or lower wages, one or more of the holders of these time payment notes will soon find his monthly installment in default.

The very nature of human beings indicates that the typical tenant will pay those installments that are being *most seriously pressed;* and that, in the final analysis, he will pay those installments which, if unpaid, would result in the greatest personal inconvenience.

The Source of Income

Most tenants in the United States pay their bills out of current income. It is the experience of property managers who operate a large number of properties that a tenant who loses his job soon will be unable to meet current rent payments, for example within 60 days. The typical American in ordinary times does not have sufficient cash reserve to meet his living costs for any extended period of time, unless he is fortified with a job.

Therefore, the source of tenant income is a most important single phase of the credit investigation. In most cases this principal source of income will be the tenant's current employment. Very few people in the tenant consumer class live on investments. Most wealthy people of the country (who live on investments) occupy *owned* quarters such as single-family homes, cooperative apartments, or condominiums.

Jobs in the United States are by no means uniform in character, either as to basis of compensation or stability of employment. Therefore, the property manager must analyze his prospective tenant's current job from several points of view. The first of these is type of compensation. It is pertinent to determine whether the prospective tenant is paid on an hourly, weekly, or monthly basis. Generally speaking, most stable types of employees are on a regular salary, payable semimonthly or monthly. It is easier for such employees to meet regular monthly payments.

The overwhelming majority of jobs in the United States and Canada are to be found in five categories, as follows:

(a) *Industry*

Approximately one-fourth of all workers typically are employed in manufacturing establishments. Generally speaking, industrial workers experience less stability in employment than other employees—especially those in cyclic industries such as steel, automobile, shipbuilding, and others. Persons in such industries who have low seniority are more apt to face layoffs than are, for example, high-seniority workers in railroads or utility plants.

(b) *General Commerce and Finance*

Employees of retail establishments, banks, insurance companies, newspapers, advertising firms, etc., account for another 25 percent of all workers. Whereas those with the least seniority are subject to separation in slack business periods, the group as a whole is usually one of stable employment.

(c) *Professions*

The historically great scarcity of virtually all professionally trained people has in the past assured them of strong job security. Today, however, with higher educational opportunities broadly available to increasing numbers, conditions of oversupply and overqualification characterize many job markets.

(d) *Service*

The decline in employment of people who either make things (industry) or grow things (agriculture) has been paralleled by a corresponding growth of those in the so-called service industries. Although employment here tends to be more stable than that of industrial workers, it is apt to be less so than in the other groups.

(e) *Government*

Nearly one-fifth of all workers are employed in some form of local, state, or federal government work. This group tends to have the most stable employment of all.

We have not included *agricultural* workers, since this text is primarily concerned with the urban population. Also farmers and their employees do not often live in properties controlled by formal management arrangements.

Weekly income is under greater pressure for current spending, and it is often difficult for tenants to systematically withhold a portion of their weekly pay envelope for their monthly rental payment. If there should be a further trend toward weekly wage payments, it will unquestionably introduce the possibility that rented quarters in the United States typically will be rented on a weekly rather than a monthly basis. Hourly employees are usually paid once each week. They are not likely to be as stable as weekly employees, because an hourly pay rate is generally established for periodic employment.

The property manager is not only interested in the type of compensation of the prospective tenant, and the rate of that compensation, but also in *stability of employment.* This is especially true of industrial wage earners, since the interdependence of manufacturing processes frequently results in layoffs, beyond the control of either the tenant or (in some cases) of his employer. By and large, the most stable type of employment is governmental or institutional. A man who works for the post office, the police department, the local telephone company or public utility, a life insurance company, or a bank is apt to have steady and permanent work. To this Parkinson's Law attests. On the other hand, a man who works in an automobile plant, in the building trades, in the entertainment field, or in an architect's office is liable to have major as well as minor employment interruptions.

Most property managers are familiar enough with employment sources in their own communities to gauge accurately the stability of employment provided by the employer of the prospective tenant. In a sense, this stability of employment is a forecast by the credit manager of the long-term rather than the immediate outlook for prompt rental payment.

In many areas of employment, length of service is in itself a key to stability of employment. In the great railroad brotherhoods, for example (as in many other lines of work), *seniority* governs stability of employment. In depression periods railroads lay off employees with the lowest seniority, and keep those who have been with the road for a number of years. In the worst conceivable type of depression it is improbable that a railroad employee who has been with a road for over twenty years will find himself out of a job. On the other hand, a railroad man, who has been with a railroad for less than one year at the top of a business cycle, is almost certain to be laid off within a few months after railroad volume begins to decline. Length of employment is not only important from the point of view of seniority, but is also an excellent basis for the judgment of overall credit stability. Highly unstable people are often apt to change employment frequently; conversely, steady, reliable people are most frequently found to have a low frequency of job turnover.

A final phase of job investigation relates to the attitude of the applicant's employer with respect to his employees' obligations. So-called *first grade* employers are generally sympathetic to the legitimate claims of the creditors of their employees. Thus, they may be expected to cooperate with a creditor who has a claim on an employee. In periods of depression this often is helpful to the property manager who finds it necessary to proceed legally against a delinquent tenant.

The Tenant's Previous Record

After the property manager has been satisfied with the prospective tenant's employment from the several points of view suggested for investigation, he then must acquaint himself with the previous record of the applicant in meeting his obligations. The very best source of such information is, of course, the previous landlord.

Morality is largely a habit. A man who has paid his bills promptly in the past will in all probability pay them promptly in the future. Therefore, it is vital for the investigation to include *an adequate contact* with the former landlord. By *adequate* we mean a contact which will establish clearly that the person being contacted *actually* has been the prospective tenant's previous landlord. We emphasize this point because there are thousands of instances where false names of previous landlords are given. Property managers too often will confine their investigation to a letter of reference sent to such bogus landlords who in turn will deceptively report that the tenant has paid his rental promptly. The only genuine investigation of a previous landlord is by a *personal visit* to the property involved in order to make certain that the prospective tenant is now in residence there and to be sure that the name of the landlord as given by the prospective tenant is valid.

In most of our larger cities, agencies for credit investigation have been set up which offer several types of credit reports available to property owners. These reports are prepared by the agencies for a fixed fee per report. The property manager can arrange with such agencies for a certain specified type of investigation. It is recommended that, where such investigating services are retained, the property manager assure himself that the investigating agency will *actually visit* the previous landlords of the prospective tenants in each instance. Many property managers have felt in the past that the cost of such investigations was excessive. However, it is false economy to fail to make a proper investigation of a prospective tenant just because either the property manager or owner wants to save the cost.

Among the collateral facts which should be uncovered by the property manager's investigation are those having to do with the prospective tenant's record in the matter of time-payment obligation. These may be investigated through local credit bureaus or through the larger finance companies which handle most time-payment types of contract. Records can also be obtained of any judgments on file (either satisfied or of record) against the prospective tenant.

THE TENANT CREDIT FILE

Many a property manager is mistakenly convinced that his interest in tenant credit will cease once he has made up his mind that the credit of the prospective tenant is good enough for admission into his building. As we have pointed out above, the collection of rent is an *installment* business. In a rapidly changing economy and in a dynamic society, the status of both the group and the individual are subject to wide fluctuation, even in a period no longer than that of the normal tenancy of an individual tenant. Therefore, the property manager's interest in his tenants' credit is *continuous;* he must assume a constant vigilance over the credit status of each family, firm, or corporation in his buildings.

Because the collection of rentals is such an important part of the duty of the property manager, his whole organization should be pointed toward the successful operation of the collection department. For example, the resident manager, janitor, or caretaker of a residential building (who is one of the most important employees in a property management organization) can be told to report to the office such things as when Tenant Jones buys a new car, when Tenant Smith gets a new piano, when Tenant Johnson goes to the hospital, and any other information which might have a bearing upon the tenant's credit status. Such information should be systematically recorded in the tenant's credit file. It may prove of inestimable value on the occasion of a renewal of the tenant's lease or on the occasion of a negotiation revolving about the tenant's ability to pay.

Such information is especially valuable in periods when the rent market is moving either upward (and the property manager wishes to raise rents) or downward (when the tenant may be petitioning for a reduction). These files should also contain records of all inquiries made about the individual tenant's credit. Frequently a department store will call a property manager's office to say that Tenant Smith has applied to the department store for credit. This is a perfectly legitimate request on the part of both the department store and the tenant, but it should be recorded in the credit file so that other sources of credit may be checked whenever the property manager has occasion to re-investigate the tenant's credit status.

It is recommended that the tenant credit file of a property management organization be located in the central office of the firm, if there is more than one office. This will be a safeguard against known instances where a tenant who lived in one building under the management of a certain firm was evicted because of nonpayment of rent, yet moved to another building under the management of the same firm. Such a possibility results from the maintenance of credit files in branch offices, or in individual building offices, instead of in the organization's central office.

It should be an inviolable rule of all property management firms to insist upon the full payment of one month's rent prior to the new tenant taking possession. There is no more truthfully prophetic maxim than "The man who cannot pay one month's rent cannot pay two." If a prospective tenant has difficulty paying one month's rent as his deposit on a new rental unit, he is probably the type of tenant with whom the manager will have trouble throughout the period of his tenancy. This rule is a basic principle of tenant credit and collection and should not be violated in any instance.

Many managers and landlords follow the practice of requiring "security deposits" as an added protection against damage to premises during tenancy or as a further guarantee against rent losses. In some cases this takes the form of an advance payment of the last month's rent on a term lease (in addition to that for the first month). In others it is an arbitrary cash deposit. Certainly, in the latter case, the tenant is entitled to receive a fair rate of interest on sums thus deposited and a fair and prompt return of the unencumbered residual amount.

RENTAL COLLECTIONS

It is accepted policy that rentals—whether for office, store, loft, or residence—be paid in advance. In the case of monthly rentals, the date for payment typically will be the first day of each month. In many cities and communities in the United States, it is the practice of some property owners, and property managers, to have rent payments due on the anniversary of the date on which the tenant moved into the property. We would like to discourage this practice for a student of property management, since it is inimical to the operation of the types of systems which we shall suggest for rent collection in subsequent portions of this text. There is a distinct advantage to the property management firm in having all of its rentals fall due on the first day of each month in the case of monthly rentals and on one specified day of each week, in the case of weekly rentals. Time is of the essence, not only in connection with rent payment, but in collection activity as well.

In spite of all of the emphasis which we shall devote to the delinquent tenant in this portion of this chapter, it is only fair to point out that *most tenants pay their bills and pay them promptly.* In a well-run real estate management office, more than 75 percent of all rentals due on the first day of each month will be paid on that date. More than 95 percent of all rentals due on the first day of the month willl have been paid prior to the fifth day of the month. Any deviation from these averages is probably due to a lack of efficiency and effectiveness on the part of the property management firm rather than to the delinquency of the tenants. It is important that the student of property management realize clearly and completely that tenants will pay their rental with a degree of promptness in direct ratio to the efficiency and effectiveness of the property manager's collection policy.

The second step in training tenants to fulfill their contractual obligations involves the matter of *prompt action* when the tenant fails to pay his rent on the due date. For example, if Tenant Smith is newly arrived and has been cautioned at the outset that the management firm expects its rentals to be paid promptly, then the management firm must keep its word and be stern about rental collections. If Tenant Smith fails to pay the rent on the due date in the second or third month of his tenancy, the management firm must favor him with some type of communication *on the second day* of the month to remind him that his rental was not paid in accordance with his contract. This reminder can be in the form of a notice sent out on the evening of the first day of the month or by telephone on the second day of the month.

If the property manager fails to take such action, the natural result is that the tenant loses respect for his obligation and begins to slip back in the payment of his rental. Tenants are normal human beings, and as such have a natural inclination to procrastinate. There are so many demands on their family income that they will tend to put off those which are least insistent. Therefore, constant and continuous vigilance by the property manager is the keystone of a successful collection operation. Prompt collection action is basic in training tenants to pay promptly.

It may appear that a good bill collector is perforce a man who *hates all "deadbeats."* Whereas this may or may not be true, it is certain that an apathetic attitude on the part of a property manager regarding collections will ultimately result in a poor collection record. The only sound policy for a collector is to collect, and collect *promptly.*

A common failure on the part of management firms is often the result of a shortsighted fear that vigorous collection action will result in vacancy. This is especially true in times of falling markets, when general vacancy may be high. In such periods many managers build up substantial rental delinquencies among tenants rather than *face the true facts* of the situation and take such collection action as will either result in the payment of the tenant's rent or his eviction. The manager must realize that it is better to have a vacant apartment than a unit upon which the tenant is not paying rent. At least in the case of the vacancy, a fractional saving can be made in heat and wear and tear; at least there will be a chance to rent the apartment to someone who actually will pay the rent. In other words, tenants usually will pay their rentals *as they are trained* to pay them, either promptly or in a slipshod fashion.

In recent decades the economy of the United States has changed from a *producer's* and *distributor's* economy to a *consumer's* economy. The employment of time-payment financing (sometimes called consumer credit) is increasingly relied upon in the sale of goods to consumers—not only for so-called high ticket items like automobiles and refrigerators, but also for run-of-the-mill purchases such as food, clothing, and miscellaneous services and intangibles.

The average U.S. family has accepted the precept "buy now and pay later" to an amazing degree. As a result, wages and incomes are committed in advance of receipt. Among immature buyers there is a tremendous temptation to raise living standards *in advance* of earning capacity merely by executing purchase agreements. Thus it was that the Veterans' Administration found most of its mortgage delinquency was due to overspending rather than to any lack of ability of its borrowers to meet their shelter payments. Property managers must understand the priority of the landlord to receive prompt rental payments and must become devoted to the creation of the proper training program to make the tenant realize it also.

There are several methods that will ensure prompt payment by tenants. The first, and most important of these, is a clear-cut *original understanding* between the property manager and his tenants. When a tenant makes application for an apartment, office, or store, the person who takes the application should carefully explain to the prospective tenant that it is the policy of the manager to take immediate action against tenants when rentals are not paid promptly on the due date. This can be done in a firm but friendly manner, and can serve as a warning to the prospective tenant that he will be treated as a delinquent on the second day of the current month. This conversation should be repeated by the property manager or his representative when the credit of the prospective tenant has been approved and when final arrangements are being made for delivering possession of the space involved. In this manner the manager will properly emphasize this point and will save himself the embarrassment which inevitably attends unexpected and rigid collection methods.

The property manager must realize that when a tenant is delinquent in his rental, he is actually *taking a cash loan* from the landlord, because, when rent is due on the first day of the month and remains unpaid, the property owner is furnishing the tenant with all of the facilities and services which were promised only in return for the rental payments. The fact that the tenant does not pay his rental when it is due does not relieve the property owner of the responsibility of heating the unit and paying its pro-rata financing charges as well as its taxes. Thus, the property owner is actually advancing money out of his pocket in order to support the delinquent tenant. When this situation is explained carefully to tenants, they should begin to see their delinquency in a different light.

For example, if you are the manager of a property in which Tenant Smith has agreed to pay a rental of $200 per month and Tenant Smith comes to your office to tell you that he cannot pay his rent, your problem is not just a matter of allowing Tenant Smith to stay on for thirty days without paying rent, but it is really a question of whether or not Tenant Smith is good for a $200 loan. The answer which should be given to Tenant Smith is that if his credit is so poor that no one else in the world will make him a loan, why should his landlord agree to loan him $200?

The property manager will find from experience that *he is not doing a tenant a favor* when he allows him to become delinquent. The tenant should be forced to resolve his financial situation. If he cannot afford to live in a house or apartment at $200 per month, he should settle the landlord's claim and move out. On the other hand, if the tenant's credit justifies his paying $200 per month and staying in the apartment, then he should be able to borrow the $200 from some other source besides the landlord.

Our point is this: In 99 percent of all cases of extended credit to tenants, the extension is unjustified from the point of view of the property manager as a representative of the landlord. Rigidity of collection policy is the only possible basis for a good and effective collection policy. This same rigidity should apply in every case of tenancy, whether it be in the most exclusive type of private residential development or in the lowest-rent type of public housing. In the case of the public housing tenant, if he deserves extended credit, it should be extended to him by a social agency and not by the organization which is already subsidizing his rental. If he becomes delinquent, he will be denying a worthier tenant the right of occupying the unit.

In these connections, it will be clear that society as a whole extends sympathy—and sometimes concrete assistance—to people in trying circumstances beyond their control. The property manager who underwrites the delinquency of a tenant postpones, as it were, the public's recognition of social problems to be corrected by external agencies. On the other hand, members of minority

groups will sometimes claim discrimination in response to landlord inflexibil-
ity; therefore, it behooves the property manager always to invoke regulations
and penalties uniformly.

ESTABLISHING A COLLECTION SYSTEM

At the outset, we must agree that the effectiveness of any system rests
primarily upon the rigidity with which it is followed by the people who make
it operate. Property management is a service profession operated entirely by
individuals with various responsibilities. To say that a system of property
management is good is much like saying that a particular type of airplane is
safe. An airplane is good if it has a conscientious and capable pilot. The best
and finest airplane in the world may be unsafe if its pilot has no skill and no
conscience. Therefore, all discussions of a collection system are relevant only
when it is the dedicated policy of the property manager, or property management firm, to prosecute the dictates of the system *faithfully* and *continuously.*

Now, just as the credit file is the basis of tenant credit, *other forms are the
basis of a good collection system.* These forms may vary in character and design
but basically, they consist of the following:

The Rent Bill. The question of whether or not to send each individual tenant
a bill for his rent on the first day of the month is one of policy fixed by the
property manager. Some of the modern machine-operated systems provide for
the simultaneous printing of a tenant rent bill and receipt form. Many property
managers who operate a general real estate and insurance office like to mail
rent bills in order to enclose collateral advertising. As a matter of fact, however, many will hold that from a collection point of view, it is not necessary
to go to the trouble and expense of sending out rent bills. When tenants are
trained to pay their rentals promptly, they will do so without receiving a bill.
Every tenant knows that his rental must be paid on the first day of the month,
and the nature of his individual budget is sufficient reminder. It is unwise to
let tenants get in the habit of relying on the management firm to provide
reminders when obligation are due.

In the case of buildings in which there are special services of varying
amounts (such as electricity, maid service, laundry, and valet), rent bills are,
of course, a necessity. This is usually the case in office buildings, apartment
hotels, and furnished apartment buildings where there is usually a resident
bookkeeper and where rentals are generally payable on the premises.

The Reminder Notice. The operation of this type of form is explained subsequently herein. Illustrated are certain types of reminder notices, as well as form
letters which may be used as a prelude to legal action.

The Eviction Notice. Whereas there are some differences in this type of form
among states (see explanation of the form's use), the form illustrated on page
351 gives the essential details of the notice that is served on delinquent tenants

against whom suit for possession is to be instituted by a property manager or management firm.

The Form Letter. Certain form letters are helpful in the operation of collection policies. These form letters are not prepared in advance, but are individually typed in each instance in accordance with the language of the form. It is a wise policy for the management organization to create their own standardized letters, instead of having each employee in the property management office compose individual versions. Various form letters covering the collection field are illustrated in the next few pages.

Action Against Delinquency

If the policies recommended above are adopted by the property manager, then it shall be assumed that he is dedicated to the idea that all rentals shall be paid in advance, that monthly rentals shall become delinquent on the morning of the second day of each month, and that weekly rentals shall become delinquent on the morning of the second day of each week. Therefore, we shall envision the property manager taking action against tenants *immediately,* whenever they are delinquent. It is in answer to the question—"What action should be taken and when?"—that we devote this section.

Action in the case of delinquents can be divided into two general categories. The first is organization action—those things which can be done by the property manager or his employees to stimulate rental payment—and, second, legal action designed to guarantee payment of rental or the eviction of the tenant. Let us analyze suggestions for action of both types and the timing of each.

If a tenant is delinquent on the morning of the second day of the month, his account should be the subject of organization activity. This organization activity will take several forms. For example, if an unsatisfactory response is given to the reminder letter, an eviction notice may follow.

Whereas the collection attitude of the property manager has already been explained to the tenant, and the delinquent tenant can therefore expect prompt action against him, it is nonetheless good public relations for the property manager to allow a *reasonable* interlude between the due date of the rental and *legal* action for its recovery. This interval in most cases should be no more than five days, during which time the tenant should be given notice reminding him of his delinquency and promising further action if the rental is not promptly paid.

Most organizations use a type of reminder form as illustrated on subsequent pages. Some managers prefer an individually addressed letter, which can serve the same purpose. The form should be mailed out at the close of business on the first day of each month, so that the tenant will see that his delinquency has been noted by the second day of the month. A routine should be established for the mailing of these reminder notices. It is suggested that this routine be carried through by the accounting department, or by the property manager's bookkeeper, since the basic records or rental collections are the responsibility of these employees.

As an alternative to the written form sent through the mail, the property manager may elect to have the accounting department or the bookkeeper prepare a list of unpaid rentals on the morning of the second of the month. This would allow for the posting of such rentals as might be received in the mail on the morning of the second. When prepared, this list should be placed in the hands of the property manager responsible for the building in which the delinquent tenants reside. He then will proceed to contact these tenants personally, preferably at the place of business of the employed tenant or, if such contact is not practical, by telephoning the wife of the tenant.

Whichever form of reminder practice is followed, the important fact is that the delinquent tenant has been notified of his delinquency immediately upon its occurrence and has been promised that, unless the rental is in the hands of the property manager on or before the morning of the fifth day of the month, the property manager will be forced to take action for collection on behalf of the building owner. We say that action has been *promised* rather than *threatened,* because we believe the reminder can be handled in a courteous and pleasant manner without any loss in impact and firmness. Many people are sensitive about the way in which they pay their bills. Whereas the best way to cure this sensitiveness is to pay bills promptly, it is nonetheless the property manager's public relations responsibility to see that the operation of his collection policy shall proceed with the smallest possible loss of goodwill. This anxiety for public approval, however, should not be carried to the point of a *failure* of the collection system. In the long run, it will not pay the building owner or the property manager to establish goodwill by allowing a volume of delinquency. It is possible to establish and carry through a firm collection policy without losing the respect of tenants. People, in principle, will agree that bills must be paid promptly, and the worthwhile tenant is seldom offended by a well-conducted, firm collection policy.

The laws of most states provide for the serving of an eviction notice by property managers or their agents. These eviction notices are usually returnable in court after a certain number of days have elapsed. In some states eviction notices are returnable after three days; in other states, five days must elapse; in still other states, seven days or more are required.

The operation of the eviction notice customarily goes something like this: The property manager fills out an eviction form similar to that illustrated on page 351. It is customary that this form is made in triplicate—one copy to be served upon the tenant, and one to be filed in court by the attorney representing the property manager or the building owner(s). It is extremely important that the form be filled out *in careful compliance* with the legal procedures specified for such forms, for the reason that frequently eviction

**MODEL
LETTERS**

Downs, Mohl & Company
MANAGERS OF INVESTMENT PROPERTIES

TELEPHONE CENTRAL 6-5606

FIRST NATIONAL BANK BUILDING
CHICAGO 3

JAMES C. DOWNS, JR. C.P.M.
ARTHUR F. MOHL

KENDALL CADY. C.P.M.
WILFRED D. HOWELL

June 6

Mr. John Doe
14 East Smith Street
Chicago, Illinois

Dear Mr. Doe:

Because we have not as yet received your current rental
on Apartment 3-W at 14 East Smith Street in response to
our letters of June 2 and June 4, we have placed your
lease in the hands of attorney, John Jones, with instructions
to take such action as may be necessary.

Our office has been instructed not to accept a rental payment direct from you during the pendency of Mr. Jones'
handling of the matter. Therefore all arrangements must
be made through the office of Mr. Jones which is located
at 154 North Main Street --- Telephone Cactus 6-3821.

Very truly yours,

John Smith.

John Smith

Downs, Mohl & Company
MANAGERS OF INVESTMENT PROPERTIES

TELEPHONE CENTRAL 6-5606

FIRST NATIONAL BANK BUILDING
CHICAGO 3

JAMES C. DOWNS, JR. C.P.M.
ARTHUR F. MOHL

KENDALL CADY. C.P.M.
WILFRED D. HOWELL

June 4

Mr. John Doe
14 East Smith Street
Chicago, Illinois

Dear Mr. Doe:

Our attention has been drawn to the fact that your rental
on Apartment 3-W at 14 East Smith Street for the current
month remains unpaid.

You will recall when your tenancy was originally established
members of our staff advised you that it was our policy that
all rentals should be paid on the first day of the month in
advance.

We assume that your failure to make your rental payment in
accordance with your agreement has been an oversight. We,
therefore, merely wish to remind you that our policy remains
unchanged. In the future we will appreciate your having your
payment in our office promptly on the first of the month.

Very truly yours,

John Smith.

John Smith

Downs, Mohl & Company
— Not Inc. —
MANAGERS OF INVESTMENT PROPERTIES

TELEPHONE CENTRAL 6-3000

JAMES C. DOWNS, JR. C.P.M.
ARTHUR F. MOHL

KENDALL CADY C.P.M.
WILFRED D. HOWELL

FIRST NATIONAL BANK BUILDING
CHICAGO 3

June 4

Mr. John Doe
14 East Smith Street
Chicago, Illinois

Dear Mr. Doe:

Our accounting department advises us that your current rental, about which we wrote you on June second, has not as yet been paid. In the light of our established collection policy it is necessary that we advise you that unless your rental payment is in our office on or before the close of business on June sixth we shall be forced to place your lease in the hands of our attorneys for collection.

If there are circumstances which appear to you to justify your delinquency and would warrant an extension of credit by the owner of the building in which you live, we trust that you will communicate with us at once in order that we may review the situation with you.

We, of course, regret the necessity to take such summary action as is indicated but in the light of your default in your agreement with us we feel justified in so doing.

Very truly yours,

John Smith

John Smith

notices are thrown out of court on a technicality because they were improperly drawn.

When the form has been properly filled out, it is placed in the hands of the person in the property management office responsible for the building in which the delinquent tenant resides. This form is then served upon the tenant. In some states the form actually must be served upon a person who is above a specified legal age and who was found to be in the premises in which the delinquency has occurred. In other states it is possible, if no one answers the door at the tenant's house, to serve the form by posting it on the main entrance of the premises involved. The form usually provides for an affidavit of service, which is filled out by the person who serves the notice, either by delivery or posting. This affidavit is filled out on the copy which is presented to the court.

Under the normal procedure, if the tenant has not brought his rent to the property manager within the specified number of days, the eviction notice is filed in the court by the attorney representing the property manager or the building owner. When the notice is filed in court, the court will set a date for the hearing on the eviction suit and will provide for notifying the tenant that he is to appear in court. When the tenant appears in court, he is generally given an opportunity to pay his rent. The landlord does not always face a legal requirement to accept such rent, yet the operation of our courts is such that if a tenant offers his rent, the judge will usually direct the landlord to accept it. If, on the other hand, the tenant is unable to pay his rent, the judge will usually set a date by which time the tenant must vacate. If the tenant has not vacated by that date, then the attorney for the landlord, or the property manager, obtains a writ of eviction which is placed in the hands of a bailiff who will carry out the court's order. Under the most favorable circumstances, it generally requires 30 to 45 days to evict for delinquency.

As noted in an earlier discussion of Eviction Suits (chapter 2), the laws relating to suits for possession by landlords have been changed in many states to broaden the rights of tenants. Even in cases where nonpayment of rent is admittedly involved, courts are more and more reluctant to evict families. This is all the more reason why action must be prompt when delinquency is encountered.

Other Legal Action

In many states leases contain a clause under the terms of which the tenant authorizes any attorney to confess judgment on his behalf in any court. Once obtained, the judgment may be used to levy against property belonging to the tenant. In most such states, tenants are entitled to a fixed sum of money as an exemption. If they can prove that their total wealth amounts to less than this exempted total, the judgment is useless.

Most residential tenants in the nominal rent ranges do not have sufficient assets to make the judgment clause valuable from the property owner's point of view. Tenants whose employment is stable and whose wages can be garnisheed usually pay their rents. Likewise, tenants with substantial visible assets are also very seldom found in the delinquent column. For that reason, the judgment clause and the suit for rent are seldom practical proceedings.

In several states, there are other possibilities for legal action against delinquent tenants. Most of these involve complicated legal techniques which should only be handled by and under the close counsel of an attorney.

It should be clear to the student of property management that *time is the essence of collection* and that continuing vigilance is necessary if the manager is to enjoy a high percentage of collections.

REVIEW QUESTIONS

1. What is the basis of a good collection policy?
2. How would you arrange to have all of your lessees pay rents promptly?
3. When should rents on *all* properties be due and payable? Why?
4. Name the steps of credit investigation of potential tenants.
5. When does a property manager's concern about the tenant's ability to pay the rent stop?

COLLECTION FORMS

Reminder Notice Number One

DRAPER AND KRAMER,   STATEMENT OF ACCOUNT
Incorporated
2446 East 75th Street
SAGINAW 3763

Chicago,   19

Permit us to call your attention to the fact that our records show your rent unpaid for the current month.

We would appreciate your prompt remittance.

DRAPER AND KRAMER, Incorporated

By

DRAPER AND KRAMER,   RENT PAST DUE
Incorporated
2446 East 75th Street
SAGINAW 3763

Chicago, ... 19....

We have not received your rent for the month of............
....amounting to $...................although it has been previously called to your attention.

As we are required to report at once to the owner, we are obliged to ask for immediate payment.

DRAPER AND KRAMER, Incorporated

By...............................
.... Collection Department
....
......................................Chicago

Reminder Notice Number Two

DRAPER AND KRAMER,   FINAL NOTICE
Incorporated
2446 East 75th Street
SAGINAW 3763

Chicago,..................... 19.......

Your attention is again called to the fact that your rent for the month of....................amounting to....................has not been paid. Being considerably overdue, we must now insist upon immediate payment, or we shall have to take such steps as may be deemed necessary to protect the owner's interests. Yours truly,

DRAPER AND KRAMER, Incorporated

By..

Collection Department

Final Reminder Notice (Printed in red ink)

COLLECTION FORMS

The Eviction Notice

LANDLORD'S FIVE DAY NOTICE

To_____

You are hereby notified that there is now due the undersigned the sum of_____ Dollars and_____Cents, being rent at the monthly rate of $_____ for:

(a) balance of $_____ due for the month of _____ 19 __, and

(b) $_____due for the months of_____ 19 __ through_____19 __ for the premises situated in the City of Chicago, County of Cook and State of Illinois, and known and described as follows, to-wit:

_____
_____
_____
_____

together with all buildings, sheds, closets, outbuildings, garages and barns used in connection with said premises.

And you are further notified that payment of said sum so due has been and is hereby demanded of you, and that unless payment thereof is made on or before the expiration of 5 days after date of service of this notice we shall take action to evict you from the premises.

_____is hereby authorized to receive said rent so due.

Dated this_____day of_____A. D. 19__

_____
Landlord

By DOWNS, MOHL & COMPANY, Agent

By_____

FORM DM 120

Below: Examples of Rent Bills

Telephone Longbeach 9160

The
BRYN MAWR
5550 KENMORE AVENUE
Chicago 40, Ill

To_____

Apt._____

ALL RENTS PAYABLE IN ADVANCE

	Balance	19			
	Rent From	To			
	Telephone				
	Miscellaneous				

Direction: Downs, Mohl & Company

The Embassy
Pine Grove at Diversey
Telephone DIVersey 4440
CHICAGO 14

M_____

*Apt*_____

STATEMENT OF ACCOUNT
FORM 19 - SHERWAY - CHICAGO

Balance			
Rent From To			
Telephone Local			
L. D. & Telegrams			
Valet			
Laundry			
News			
Cash Disbursed			
Miscellaneous			
Total			

ALL ACCOUNTS PAYABLE UPON PRESENTATION

6. Where should the credit record of the tenant be located? Why?
7. Upon what does a property manager base *his compensation?*
8. Would you consider a postal employee or a banker a good credit risk for prompt monthly rent payment? Explain.
9. What should the property manager know about the prospective tenant's record in meeting time payments, and why?
10. What is considered the *most important* phase of investigating a tenant's credit rating?
11. What is considered the basis of a good collection system?
12. When should action against a tenant be taken? Explain.

SELECTED REFERENCES

Hanford, Lloyd D. Jr. "Effective Rent Collection Systems." *Journal of Homebuilding,* Jan. 1970, pp. 84–88.

Institute of Real Estate Management. *The Resident Manager; An On-Site Management Handbook of Multi-Unit Residential Housing.* Chicago, Ill. 1973. 87p.

"Paying Rent with Credit Cards." *Mortgage & Real Estate Executives Report,* Sept. 5, 1972, pp. 5–6.

CHAPTER 22

Tenant and Public Relations

INTRODUCTION

In chapter 20 we spoke of how to select a tenant. An aspect of this chapter is how to find them in the first place and to keep them once they are found. Public relations policy is aimed, at least in part, at giving the manager's firm and the properties he controls a good outward image. Potential customers never will be lost because of a good reputation, and tenant relations are aimed at accomplishing the same thing from within. Established tenants will remain tenants so long as they are pampered and given the attention they deserve.

Big property management firms often will be represented by public relations consultants, just as they may have an account with an advertising agency. In fact, major commercial buildings such as office buildings usually are assigned special public relations representatives either by the property manager or by the owner(s) directly. Alternatively, the management office may employ in-house tenant and public relations specialists to deal directly with the aggravating problems of keeping people with diverse interests and problems informed and satisfied. Also, there may be the need for an employee relations person to maintain harmony within the management office itself (see chapters 25 and 26).

The role of all these people is to listen to complaints against the owners and managers and to correct any mistaken ideas about the intentions of these owners and managers. In the real estate business, of which property management is a part, disgruntled tenants can be a worse plague than a depression.

Although the tenant is not the manager's basic client, he is the customer of the manager's client. He is also a potential client of the manager's organization. If the property manager is also a broker, the tenant may some day buy a home or a place of business. Even if he remains as a tenant, he is a potential customer for the manager's insurance department or for any other collateral service which the manager may offer.

Nothing is more offensive to the enlightened property manager than the traditional landlord-tenant relationship of constant conflict over mutually exclusive interests. It is true that there is a fine point of bargaining at the outset of the landlord-tenant relationship, yet the conflict of interest between the two generally has been exaggerated. By and large, landlords only want a fair return from property consistent with current market conditions. Tenants, on the

353

other hand, are merely concerned with obtaining good value for rent money and with receiving all the services for which they bargained. A large portion of the conflict between the two points of view is avoidable when sound management practices are employed.

The conscientious property manager, who enjoys a modern concept of the broad responsibilities of the business executive, is actually an arbitrator of such conflict as may exist naturally between a buyer and a seller. Since only one pattern of procedure may properly be described as *fair* to both parties, it is possible for the manager to be a representative of both the landlord and the tenant in establishing an equitable arrangement. The successful manager inevitably conducts an educational program in which both landlord and tenant are brought to a realistic understanding of their mutual concerns and objectives. Such a program can be conducted successfully, if the manager's attitude is one of understanding based upon the realities of his liaison role.

A fine point of ethical interpretation is to be found in this relationship. Although it is the manager's duty to see that the tenant is given fair treatment, he cannot purchase the tenant's goodwill at the building owner's expense. On the other hand, he cannot make a record for himself by refusing to accede to the tenant's reasonable requests or by withholding services for the sole purpose of increasing the building owner's advantage.

DEVELOPING A TENANT RELATIONS POLICY

In most cases the classically poor relationship between the building owner and the tenant grows primarily out of mutual misunderstanding. Thus, a sound tenant relations policy should be built upon the manager's insistence on a basic understanding with the tenant on all matters relating to tenancy. The first step toward such an understanding must be taken during the original negotiations with the tenant. As nearly as possible, the results of these negotiations should be recorded in written form and the contents reviewed with the tenant at the time the negotiations are consummated.

In addition to a written agreement covering the fundamental points of the tenancy arrangement, the manager should explain the policies of rent collection to be followed, as already discussed in chapter 21. The manager should review carefully the regulations which govern the building in which the tenant is to be housed, and he should indicate the methods of enforcement of such regulations. Also, the manager should be certain that the tenant understands the maintenance policies of the building and how the maintenance responsibilities are divided between building owner and tenant. The tenant should, likewise, be told how service requests are to be made, to whom addressed, and in which areas they will be acceptable.

There is no substitute for forthrightness in human relations. The manager who would have a successful tenant relations program must learn one lesson and learn it well; namely, that procrastination is ruinous. When a service request is made, the tenant should be told immediately whether or not it will be granted. The most serious mistake made by many managers is accepting service requests they know will not be granted. If a tenant asks for a new window shade under circumstances in which the manager knows it is impossible for him to furnish such a shade, the tenant should be told immediately that the manager is sorry but no shade will be furnished. If the manager will take the time to explain the *why* of the decision, he will take a great deal of the sting from the refusal and will retain the tenant's respect. If the manager merely accepts the request for the window shade and procrastinates, ultimately he will incur the enmity of the tenant. The latter is poor public relations and has no place in well-organized management.

A sound tenant relations program requires more than a realistically sympathetic attitude on the part of the manager. Since many tenant contacts are with managers, maintenance people, janitors, telephone operators, or clerks of the management office, good tenant relations can only result from a training program under which the staff is acquainted with the manager's tenant relations policies. It is a truism that people who deal with the public constantly are apt to become cantankerous; they are apt to conclude from a large number of individual, unreasonable requests that the public as a whole is unreasonable. It is a repetition of the old-time schoolteacher attitude to the effect that after a certain number of years all children turn out to be "pests."

While property managers cannot go so far as to adopt the principle "the customer is always right," *the basis of the personnel training program should be that "the customer is always entitled to sympathetic treatment."* As a matter of fact, the rule of thumb is that 90 percent of all tenant requests are reasonable. If they are tended to properly, the tenant remains reasonable. On the other hand, when tenants' service requests are treated lightly by members of the manager's staff, and when such requests go unheeded for days, weeks, and even months—then the tenant is rightly incensed and the balance of good relations is upset.

Alert management agencies recognize the fact that good tenants are a tangible asset. Good tenants remain in residence, thus avoiding expensive turnover. Good tenants protect the manager's property and thereby minimize the cost of maintenance. Good tenants advertise the building and the manager and are valuable in reducing vacancy losses and selling expense.

Having in mind the values of a solid, well-satisfied tenancy, managers of large buildings—particularly the large project-type properties—make every effort to build tenant goodwill by making life in the project as pleasant as possible. For instance, arrangements are made for children to have supervised play and for preschool care; recreational events are staged and tenant organization groups accommodated. All of these activities represent sound tenant relations, and tend to solidify the earning capacity of the property.

TENANT UNIONS AND COLLECTIVE BARGAINING

In recent years in some urban areas, tenants have banded together to form so-called tenant unions for the purpose of entering into collective bargaining negotiations with landlords. Thus far, such steps have been largely confined to residential property in slum or semi-slum areas. Usually the first move in such a program is the calling of a rent strike in which tenants withhold their individual rental payments as a means of forcing landlords or their agents to the bargaining table.

At the present time there still is no general recognition of the rights of tenants to either withhold rentals or bargain collectively over rentals, maintenance policies, tenant services, or general grievances. Under traditional landlord-tenant law, it is presumed that in the free market a tenant will either pay the rental asked and acept the premises in the negotiated condition or that he will seek accommodations elsewhere. The landlord has had the right to arbitrarily set the terms and conditions, and the tenant has had the right to accept or reject them.

In recent years, however, there has been a broadly increased recognition of the obligation of the landlord to meet certain minimum standards for occupancy. Housing codes setting forth such standards have been adopted by municipalities and other local governments, and their enforcement has been more and more rigidly prosecuted. Yet tenants do not have the right to withhold rentals as a means of forcing compliance with such standards. Under the law the proper governing agency alone was charged with such enforcement.

The law school of the University of Chicago in the fall of 1966 conducted a conference on the subject of the law of landlord and tenant. In the literature announcing that gathering it said:

> Recent efforts to improve the conditions of urban life have made it apparent that the shortage of decent housing for families of low and moderate income presents one of the most pressing problems facing the urban poor. While basically this is an economic problem, the importance of the legal relationship between landlord and tenant cannot be ignored. Although extension of legal services to the poor has brought the promise that tenants' rights can be effectively enforced, it has become clear that often inadequate attention has been given to the substantive law affecting indigent persons. The law of landlord-tenant, developed in a different context to meet different social goals, has in many instances proven unsuited for the needs of modern urban society. If "equal justice under law" is to become a reality for the urban poor, there must be development and change in the substantive law governing the landlord-tenant relationship.

And, as time marches on, the legal machinery is seen moving in the direction called for by the above announcement.

This development and change in the legal background of the landlord-tenant relationship has already begun and undoubtedly will be accelerated in the years to come. In many states, statutes have been enacted which impose a duty on the landlord to put the premises in habitable condition.

In New York City rent strikes by groups of tenants organized by CORE and NAACP resulted in a 1963 circuit court decision condemning rent strikes, but permitting the establishment of a court-supervised escrow for building violations to be repaired out of rents deposited by the tenants. This is still being done.

New York codified this judicial decision in 1965 by enacting two landmark statutes permitting tenants to withhold rent. Under Chapter 909 of the New York State Laws, one-third of the tenants of a substandard building may petition a court for repairs of building violations through a court-supervised escrow. Upon finding that housing violations exist and that the tenants are not responsible for them, a court may order that all rents be deposited with the clerk of the court, and that such deposits be used to remedy the conditions alleged in the petition.

Under Chapter 911 of the New York State Laws, when a landlord has failed to correct all building violations within six months after he receives notice from the city building department, all rent is abated (not just postponed) until such violations are completely corrected. The statute provides tenants with a valid defense against any suits for ejectment or non-payment of rent instituted by the landlord.

In addition to the Speigal Law in New York State, other legislation along these lines is under active consideration in many states at the present time. The trend will deserve close scrutiny by property managers.

In summary, it should be pointed out that tenant organizations are a legal requirement for all subsidized housing falling under FHA Section 236 (subsidized housing) and local housing authority regulations. These are set up to work with management in resolving difficulties arising out of poor management on the one side, and out of nonperformance and objectionable tenant behavior on the other. In fact, it may be pointed out that tenant organizations sometimes are formed even in luxury apartment situations where the weight of a collective voice is wanted as leverage to obtain management action. And, of course, in condominiums and planned unit developments, the owners as stockholders also belong to a de facto organization through which the interests of the residents can be voiced and heard.

Under the somewhat nebulous laws, tenant organizations are obligated to define services that are thought to be lacking, and also to engage in tenant education programs. Often, when the officers of such organizations sit down with management representatives, issues can be arbitrated by compromise without formal legal actions. It cannot be overemphasized, however, that much of the associated difficulty comes from bad management—or at least from misunderstood management. The role of public and tenant relations to avoid these disputes is thus seen to be crucial.

There is no question but that tighter laws eventually will be enacted to guarantee balanced equities between the conflicting owner-manager and tenant interests. Whether the law will someday recognize the right to withhold rents under extreme conditions of provocation is another matter. But welfare departments now have already established their right to withhold their share of subsidization under certain conditions. Society is changing, as we saw in chapter 4 and as we can see by looking out the window.

PUBLIC RELATIONS

Public relations means public knowledge, public approval, public confidence, and public preference. The primary object of a manager's public relations program is to acquaint as many people in the community as possible with the existence of his company and what it does and what it stands for, in every way possible, to encourage public approval of his company and to so mold this approval as to bring his services to the point of preference. Public relations means making friends for oneself and for the organization, and establishing a desire for the product—whether it is an insurance policy, a property, or a service.

The development of a sound public relations program is extremely important to the real estate manager. For instance, in many lines of business it is possible for a well-made, serviceable, and needful product to gain broad acceptance because of its own proved qualities. However, the real estate manager has no product except service, and the entire burden of establishing public acceptance rests upon the personnel of the organization. The very nature of property management requires that client contacts be governed by a high degree of trust and confidence. The business is entirely one of stewardship, and in the final analysis, the business advances in proportion to the reputation of the steward and upon his public relations ability.

Good public relations for the individual is sometimes based on such qualities as personality, honesty, and perseverance. In an organization, a good public relations program is not accidental; instead, it is the result of careful planning and constant vigilance.

Every management organization, and every property manager as an individual, should have a planned public relations program designed to attain for the firm or individual the qualities of public knowledge, public approval, and public acceptance. Such a program should be pointed to the attainment of specific results, and should be based upon preconceived factors and an insistence that such accepted concepts be soundly implemented.

If public knowledge of a manager's existence is to be established among a wider and wider circle in the community, then the manager, junior executives, and all employees should be encouraged to increase their circulation among creditable groups within the community. Moreover, this circulation should be deliberate and calculated to build individual goodwill. Members of the organization should be instructed in the principles of sound attitudes and relationships, and should be aware of their responsibilities as representatives of the organization or firm.

Individuals within the organization should be encouraged to participate in professional activities and to establish themselves as respected authorities in their particular fields. They should be helped to write and speak well and perform activities that will bring credit upon themselves and the organization they represent. Members of the organization should be encouraged to seek and welcome leadership in civic affairs and to perform well the duties in which they are engaged. Frequently, public relations work is harmed rather than helped by those who accept positions of responsibility in civic affairs when they subsequently fail to measure up to the responsibilities involved. Only those assignments should be accepted which can be fulfilled with distinction, adding to the general reputation of the organization.

It is axiomatic that a good program of public relations cannot be carried on by an organization unless each individual in that organization is fully aware of the public relations objectives of the firm and understands that the attainment of the objectives is as important to each employee as it is to the principals.

It is to be assumed that any well-administered organization is regularly assembled in staff meetings for discussion of the firm's problems, and that the public relations objectives regularly will be on the agenda of such gatherings.

Publicity is, perhaps, one of the most effective methods of building reputation. People believe what they read in the editorial and news columns of the newspapers, although they may question the veracity of advertising. Every individual or organization should be aware of this extremely potent force for the creation of goodwill, and should be alert to every opportunity for favorable publicity. One member of the staff of the organization should be responsible for the regular submission of publicity ideas and, if possible, a publicity agent should be retained to scrutinize the operation from the point of view of publicity potentialities.

Although advertising is discussed in the following chapter and also in chapter 9), the advertising of the property manager should be reviewed continuously from the public relations as well as the sales point of view. Often advertising, which is successful from a purely temporary selling standpoint, represents poor public relations and should not be used, even though it may be temporarily profitable. Conversely, the property manager should realize that frequently advertising, which seems to be valueless from a sales point of view, may produce excellent results when considered as a public relations device.

MEASURING PUBLIC RELATIONS

It has been said that the essence of good public relations is a capacity for critical self-examination, a willingness to make changes and the ability to carry out essential changes.

Thus far we have stressed the importance of the property manager's taking time out from his regular routine to be an economist, a personnel director, a maintenance man, and a score of other things. To an extent, all of these developed abilities will be meaningless unless they are placed in a setting of sound public relations. Such a setting requires design of the type which can be created only through critical self-examination. At some point in each day, week, or month, the property manager should take time off to take a critical look at the operation of his business. He should examine himself, his appearance, his attitude, and his effectiveness. He should study each of his employees in terms of fulfillment of their public relations' responsibility. He should scrutinize his office with a view toward making it more attractive, more efficient, and more receptive. He should look at his buildings strictly from the point of view of whether or not they reflect credit upon the organization and whether or not they win public approval and preference.

Beyond self-examination, the manager should take steps to measure the level of public acceptance of his enterprise. If necessary he should employ interviewers for the purpose of telephoning residents in a representative cross section of the community to ask if they have heard about the John Jones Company. A questionnaire should be developed for the telephone interviewer so that, if a respondent has indeed heard about John Jones Company, a further question will be whether the respondent knows the location of the John Jones Company, the nature of its business, its general reputation, etc. Questionnaires of the same type may be used by interviewers in the course of personal visits to homes, apartments, shopping areas, or anywhere the public congregates. Only by such a sampling of public opinion can the manager determine whether or not his public relations program is effective.

In the process of self-examination relating to public relations, attention should be given to the location of the management office. In spite of the old shibboleth about "build a better mouse trap, etc.," people are more apt to do business at locations of maximum convenience. Moreover, a high level of passer-by traffic, whether pedestrian or vehicular, offers a large circulation which can be capitalized upon in the field of public relations.

One of the most important methods of measuring public relations effectiveness is by determining the source of each type of business contact. Agents of buildings should be instructed to ask prospective tenants how they happened to come to the property. Clerks in the office should ask those who come into the office how they happened to select the John Jones Company. If it is found that certain media are pulling well, efforts and expenditure in these media should be enlarged; if it is found that the media are failing to produce desired results, they should be reduced proportionally or discontinued.

The only purpose of critical self-examination is to establish a course of action. It is useless for the businessman to acquaint himself with the deficiencies of his organization unless he is willing to act to remedy the conditions responsible for such deficiencies. Too often, a business operates in a well-defined "rut." Executives and employees fall easily into crystallized routines from which it is extremely difficult to extricate themselves.

REVIEW QUESTIONS

1. Why should your employees be active in civic affairs? What are the individual employee's responsibilities to his firm if given a civic committee chairmanship?
2. What would you say was the objective of a property manager's public relations program?
3. Basically, what does a landlord expect from his property? What does a tenant expect in return for his rent money?
4. What is the value of favorable newspaper publicity?
5. Name a way to measure the effectiveness of your public relations program.
6. Of what value is publicity?
7. What is meant by self-analysis on the part of the property manager?
8. How would you handle a tenant who wanted a storm door put on, and you knew that it could not be done?
9. To ensure good public relations with the tenant from the first rental payment month, what points should the property manager make clear to the tenant in addition to those specified in the lease?
10. The janitor in one of your buildings is quite active in Boy Scout work in the community. Do you as a property manager have any responsibility to him. Explain your answer and how any responsibility would be executed.
11. When misunderstandings arise between the tenant and property manager, what usually is the primary reason? How would you prevent misunderstandings.

SELECTED REFERENCES

Glassman, Sidney. *Tools for Creative Property Management.* Institute of Real Estate Management, Chicago, Ill., 1974. 52p.

Petlik, Michael. "How to Keep Existing Residents." *Journal of Property Management,* Sept.–Oct. 1973, pp. 200–201.

Rose, Jerome G. *Landlords and Tenants; A Complete Guide to the Residential Rental Relationship.* New Brunswick, N. J., Transaction Books, 1973. 288p.

Sally, William D. "Professional Management. The Better Way to Meet the Tenant Movement." *Journal of Property Management,* July–Aug. 1973, pp. 152–157.

"The Landlord Tenant Relationship; Three Management Approaches to Improving the Overall Quality of Urban Housing." *Journal of Property Management,* July–Aug. 1973, pp. 151–163.

CHAPTER 23

Owner Relations and New Business

INTRODUCTION

The basic asset of any business is the goodwill of its customers. In many types of business a large part of the goodwill of individual clients is based on the quality of physical merchandise and/or services, and in the satisfaction in ownership that is displayed.

Real estate management is considered to be a profession by various professional societies—notably the Institute of Real Estate Management—which certify the character, integrity, and ability of its members. On the other hand, real estate management from many points of view can be considered a business. Unlike many businesses, however, real estate management does not involve trading in goods. Building owners are one category of customers of a property manager and are comparable to the clients of a lawyer or the patients of a doctor, in that the major portion of the service rendered is made up of opinion and judgment. The quality of the service provided by a property manager, like that of a doctor or a lawyer, is determined by the breadth of his knowledge and the skill with which it is employed. Unlike the purely professional man, the real estate manager enjoys the freedom of new-business solicitation, advertising, incorporation, and other activities not considered ethical in the medical and legal professions. And tenants are another category of customers whom property managers serve.

A few real estate managers have organized firms that have attained truly institutional status, but most real estate management in the country is conducted by men whose business is based primarily upon personal relations with their clients. Thus recognition of the value of client relations is the most important plank in a platform of successful operation in the field of real estate management.

In the previous chapter, ideas were presented on how a property manager should deal with tenant-customers, and here we will discuss optimal relations with owners. These remarks will provide guidelines for the solicitation of new business and the retention of old.

Anyone who owns a building operated for income is a prospective client of the manager or management firm. However, those persons or organizations most likely to engage professional managers fall into the four groups outlined in the next few paragraphs.

Individuals and Limited Partnerships

Those individuals who are *busy in their own enterprises* regard their income properties strictly as an investment. Most such property owners have neither the time to assume the details of management nor the inclination to take on the often onerous chores of collecting rents, handling rental inquiries, showing space to prospective tenants, listening to service complaints, or supervising maintenance.

The large group of *absentee landlords* do not work or reside in the immediate area of the property they own. They are almost certain to require the services of local managers and are an excellent source of management business.

Syndicates are usually groups of businessmen animated by a desire for either profit or yield who need professional guidance as well as disinterested administration. Often, these syndicates are actually the creation of a management firm which has, as a prime objective, the management of properties owned by such syndicates.

Lawyers represent either living owners or the estates of deceased ones with properties requiring administration. While some lawyers will undertake the management of properties as a sideline, most busy, successful lawyers engage professional management.

Corporations

As noted earlier in this text it is only in recent years that corporations have become common owners of investment real estate. As in the case of individuals, such corporations fall into several major groups. First, there are corporations that own and have the responsibility for operation of income properties but that are not large enough to create an organization for that purpose. These corporations almost always engage the services of professional managers. Second, there are corporations that come into being as the result of the formation of cooperative or condominium properties. In such cases, most of the stockholders are engaged in businesses of their own and have neither the inclination to nor the capability of administering the property in which they have an interest. Moreover, there is an advantage in having an outside management firm, rather than one of the residents, manage the property. Third, there are what we call "bulk users" of space (principally commercial), who erect buildings primarily for the purpose of housing their enterprise. However, either for prestige or future expansion, these corporations often put up buildings substantially larger than their own space needs. As a result, the building not only requires administration, but renting as well. Some such corporations engage individual managers on their payroll to administer their property. Others—the majority—engage management firms for this work.

Financial Institutions

Second only to individuals, the largest market for professional management services is represented by financial institutions. Banks, insurance companies, trust companies, savings and loan associations, mortgage bankers, and investment houses almost inevitably come into possession of properties for administration—either because individual owners name them to that responsibility through trusts and estates, or because of foreclosure of mortgages which from time to time are in default. As has been pointed out elsewhere in this text, acquisitions by financial institutions are apt to be high during periods of recession and depression and low during periods of peak prosperity. At all times, however, financial institutions are excellent sources of property management business.

Government Agencies

In chapters 4 and 6 we discussed government—federal, state, and local—as an increasingly more important factor in the typical local real estate economy and an important prospective client for the property manager. With the present level of federal agency participation in apartment financing, it is inevitable that these agencies will come into possession of properties for management. Given the tradition of private operation of income property, most government agencies will engage the services of private professional managers rather than set up their own management departments. Obviously, it is imperative that property managers be fully aware of and responsive to all government regulations concerning the type of property being managed.

Scores of various agencies in government are from time to time faced with the acquisition of income property. Litigation in the courts is a constant source of the naming of receivers, trustees, and so forth. For all of these posts, the private property manager is indeed a qualified prospect. Thus it is that the alert manager will do well to see that he is acquainted with the heads of local offices of federal agencies and that he is in good repute with the courts having jurisdiction over such matters.

SOUND OWNER RELATIONS

Sound owner relations can result only from well-based original client contacts. This means that in his original solicitation of business, the manager should confine his selling arguments to the services and accomplishments which he is certain can be satisfactorily delivered either by himself or by his firm.

Once a prospective client has been persuaded to establish a relationship with the property manager, that relationship should be crystallized in the form of an adequate management contract, under which the owner agrees to place the management of his building in the hands of the individual manager or management firm. A specimen contract, which has been adopted by the Institute of Real Estate Management, is included in the appendix for the perusal of students. It is not necessary that this precise form be used. But it is essential that all management relationships be covered by a written contract which should clearly point out the following:

1. An adequate description of the property to be managed
2. The exact names of the owner and the manager
3. The rate of compensation to be paid for the management service
4. A clear statement of the responsibility and authority of the manager and any limitations placed upon his operation of the property
5. Provisions for adequate protection to both parties from the risks of agency
6. Length of term of the agreement and termination provisions

While it is essential that an actual contract of agency be executed by and between the owner of the property and the manager, such a contract need not be for a long-term period. As in the case of a lease, there are advantages and disadvantages in a long-term management contract from the point of view of both the owner and the manager. In certain circumstances, the manager is warranted in insisting upon a long-term contract if he is to perform special services for which he cannot be adequately compensated in a short period. Generally speaking, however, the manager should recognize the fact that *business held solely by contractual ties is not sound.* The manager should realize that he must retain his business primarily as a result of the satisfaction of his client, and not because he has persuaded the client to sign a long-term agreement. Even in cases where such a long-term contractual arrangement exists, the manager should treat all of his clients as though they were on a month-to-month arrangement.

Managers who desire to establish sound owner relations with clients whose buildings will actually be managed by subordinates and employees of the manager must at the outset explain to the owner that others will be responsible for many of the details of management. Only by such a frank initial understanding can the manager hope to render satisfactory service to a substantial group of clients. If the manager fails to disclose the fact that he personally does not perform all of the services incident to management of the client's property, he will gradually assume an unconscionable burden and will be in constant jeopardy of losing his business.

Sound owner relations are dependent also upon the client's understanding of the fact that the manager cannot control the basic trends in the economy. Management can do no more than to produce the *highest possible net return* in the light of prevailing economic conditions. In good times it is possible for poor management to show excellent earnings; in bad times it is frequently impossible for the very highest level of management to produce even satisfactory returns.

In chapter 2 of this text, it was emphasized that one of the basic reasons for the manager's analysis of current market conditions is to enable him to demonstrate to clients that he is operating at the highest possible level in the light of trends in the economy. It is obvious that no sound relationship with a client can be enjoyed by a manager whose employment is based on promises of fixed earnings or yields for his client.

MAINTAINING OWNER'S GOODWILL

Opinions of property owners are established in response to two general categories of stimuli. First, there is the owner's personal experience, which grows out of the operating record of the manager and the clarity of its presentation to the owner. This operating record is established through the owner's personal contact with the manager himself, or with members of his staff, and by the communications sent to the owner from the management office.

The owner's opinion about management is also established by what we might call secondary experience, or the type which grows out of the contacts with and the opinions of others as to the character, integrity, and ability of the manager—all of which combine in the factor of reputation.

As noted above, the control of the owner's personal experience with the manager, or the management firm, rests upon the careful presentation of operating experience in the form of the written or printed word, as well as in the careful planning and execution of personal contacts with the owner.

There is a fine point of distinction between too much and too little contact with clients via the written word or printed form. The most important basic written contact between the manager and the owner is the monthly statement of operations. Here the owner receives an exact dollars-and-cents accounting of income and expense, as well as a statement of his net operating income. We will discuss in chapter 26 the preparation of this owner statement and the various forms in which it may be presented. Suffice it to say here that the form of monthly report should be designed with emphasis on clarity as well as appearance.

It is only natural that the owner of a building should be reasonably familiar with its operating potentials and should, therefore, have an idea of an amount which he believes the building should produce each month, subject to seasonal fluctuation. If the owner's statement shows a net operating return equal to this normal expectancy, and if there are no unusual items in either the expense or income classifications, then it is not absolutely necessary to include a letter with the statement. However, experience shows that no such *raw* communication should be addressed to a client without the friendly evidence of personal interest, which so easily will be reflected by an accompanying personal letter. Even if the letter says no more than that the current month was characterized by purely normal operations, it should be sent along with the statement.

Virtually every building experiences individual months in which either income is lower than normal, or expenses are higher than normal, and vice versa. The manager must recognize that the owner's *primary* interest in the monthly communication is to ascertain the level of his net income. As we pointed out above, the owner *always* has a preconceived notion of the amount of revenue which a property ought to produce during a given month. Any deviation from this norm is a subject of immediate concern, and a drop in his anticipated income always comes as a shock.

Because any deviation from normal income is apt to produce in the owner an immediate reaction that the management has *failed,* it is vital that the manager have a plausible explanation for the decline in income. The reasonable client will quickly understand why the amount of his check is below expectations if the explanation of the reasons is clear, concise, and convincing. If, on the other hand, the letter that accompanies the statement is not clear, concise, or convincing, the owner will tend to nurture his disappointment in the management, and his confidence in the management firm's ability to represent him will gradually be undermined.

For that reason it is extremely important that each monthly statement be reviewed carefully by management so that an explanatory letter is prepared to document the factors of income and expense that may have been responsible for a decline in net revenue.

In addition to the monthly report, there are many occasions when managers or management firms believe they must communicate in writing with their clients. Most authorities would say that such communications in writing should be limited as much as possible and should be sent to the owner only when he is away from the city. If he is in town, personal contact, either face to face or by telephone, is much more effective than a written communication. Only when personally in contact with the client can the manager sense his reaction to a question asked or a proposal made. Only in such an interview can the manager be assured that the outcome of the contact has been satisfactory. Wherever possible, such personal contact should be made when the monthly statement shows unusual deviation from the norm and explanation by written communication is difficult. There is no substitute for personal contact; letters should be written only when an interview is impractical.

Our admonition against writing letters to clients on all occasions does not overlook the frequent need for written confirmation of understandings reached with the client. Whenever decisions reached in a telephone conversation or personal interview require a written record, the manager should send the client a memorandum.

In cases where it is impossible to handle client contacts by a personal call or over the telephone, extreme care should be taken in the preparation of letters. Whenever a letter is to be written by someone other than the person directly responsible for the client relationship, the letter should be read carefully by the executive who is most familiar with the client.

In any case, property managers must be alert to the special problems which involved in holding business during periods of general adversity. For whenever the real estate posture is one of lower rentals, higher vacancies, and increased operating expenses, the property manager is in a period in which it is impossible for him to present his clients with an operating record which they will consider "satisfactory." It is a truism that most owners or stockholders tend to regard the value of their property as the capitalization of its most favorable income stream. In other words, the "best" earnings experience quickly becomes the owner's "normal" expectancy.

Since it is inevitable that property owners (whether an individual, corporation, financial institution, or the government itself) will be dissatisfied when the reports of the operation of their property indicate a steadily declining net income, the manager who wishes to keep his business during a real estate downswing must make certain that the owners are steadily assured that the job being done on their properties *is the best that can be done under the circumstances.* This means that the property manager must keep his owners *fully informed* as to the extent of the downswing. Moreover, the manager must take every opportunity to show that his efforts are producing a better-than-average result, even though net income is declining.

Personal Contact

In his personal contact with the building owner, the manager should follow certain basic principles of client relations. The frequency of calls upon the owner is a matter best decided with regard to the circumstances of each particular case. Some property owners turn their buildings over to managers principally because they are anxious to rid themselves of operating detail and wish to be spared all avoidable contacts with the building. Other owners turn their buildings over to managers because they desire to be free of the little details of tenant contact and personnel administration. Still, they desire the manager to visit them frequently.

In the case of the individual property manager whose clients are few enough to enable him to conduct all personal contacts himself, the frequency of such contacts is a matter of individual analysis. He will stay away from the man who wishes to be completely free from responsibilities in connection with his building, and he will visit frequently with the man who likes to know about the progress of his property. In larger organizations where the principal executive cannot possibly maintain all of the client contacts, the business should be organized in a manner to provide an executive who is responsible for client relations in each case. Large advertising agencies, for example, are headed by men known as *account executives*. These executives are primarily responsible for certain of the agency's accounts and supervise all contacts with such clients, whether written or personal. This practice is sound for real estate management firms as well as advertising agencies.

When a new property is brought into the office, it should be assigned to such an *account executive*. The first few times that personal contacts are made between the account executive and the client, the person responsible for acquisition of the business should accompany the account executive, in order that the latter may gradually take over full direction of the account. This account executive, when he has become thoroughly acquainted with the client, can assume complete charge. It seems needless to say that his executive will be responsible for direction of the productive and financial services performed for the client.

It is not always possible to restrict the client's personal relations with the management firm to the individual manager or to the account executive in a larger organization. Clients have a habit of dropping into the manager's office just to see how things are going or to perform some specific errand in connection with their property. As clients, they feel they are important and are quick to judge the management firm by the manner in which they are received and treated on such occasions. Thus, it is important that all employees in the management office should meet as many of the clients as possible, so that when clients do come into the office they are recognized and treated with special deference.

NEW BUSINESS

Whether or not growth is actively pursued, to stay in business even at the same level requires constant solicitation of new business to replace accounts which are lost for reasons beyond the control of the proprietor. This is especially true in real estate management. Accounts are constantly lost through the death of property owners and the subsequent decision of the heirs that the properties should be liquidated. In other cases, clients determine to sell properties to new owners who may have commitments to other management firms, or who may decide to operate the property themselves.

Thus, even if a manager or management firm has a continuously satisfactory relationship with all of its clients, there is a constant necessity for the solicitation and acquisition of new business if shrinkage is to be avoided. It is the ambition of all business to grow, and such growth can be accomplished only when the amount of new business exceeds the atrophy of old accounts.

Years of observation of men who are attracted to administrative positions indicates that there is a natural lethargy among managers with respect to direct selling. Frequently the person who enjoys administrative work eschews sales work. Often the administrator finds himself so involved with the details of management that it is easy for him to procrastinate and put off the calls which must be made if new business is to be acquired. It is important for the student of real estate management, who proposes to establish himself in business either as a proprietor or as a valued executive in a going organization, to realize that there is need for constant self-discipline in the matter of devoting a portion of each day to developing new business.

Every dynamic organization has adopted a definite selling plan under which its executives and employees are required to spend a certain amount of time and effort in new business solicitation. Such a plan should make this kind of sales work as nearly automatic as possible, in order to avoid the pitfalls of natural lethargy.

Methods of Selling Management Service

The single most effective device for selling management service is *direct solicitation.* There is no substitute for the well-planned, carefully conducted personal interview with a prospective client.

The first problem involves the analysis of the market for management service. This means the preparation of a list of owners of properties which the manager feels it would be profitable to manage. Such a list should be carefully checked for accuracy—both as to the identity of the owner and the character of the property involved. It should be maintained continuously as a sales assignment file and rechecked at intervals so that changes in ownership are recorded regularly.

We referred above to a *well-planned* interview with a prospective client. Certainly anything as important as the solicitation of an owner for the management of his property deserves adequate preparation. The manager should know upon whom he is calling and as much about the owner as possible. He should know the building for which he is soliciting management and as much about the building as possible. He should know exactly what he proposes to do with the building, and should be prepared to demonstrate why he would be able to do it. He should be qualified to give his prospect concrete reasons as to why there are advantages in professional management, and why there is a specific advantage in this particular management.

All of this means that prior to making the actual call on the prospective client the manager will learn as much about the owner as he can. He surely will have made a careful examination of the building owned by the prospective client and will have analyzed it to the point of developing reasons for its need of the manager's service. Certainly the manager should also have equipped himself with a well-prepared sales kit through which he can acquaint the pro-

SELLING TOOL

The well-equipped solicitor of real estate management services should carry a sales kit upon which the attention of the prospective client may be focused during the sales presentation. A well-designed sales kit is shown above.

spective client the kind of work done by his organization and its qualifications in the field of management.

The manager who plans a campaign of direct solicitation for new business must recognize at the outset that it is extremely unlikely that the owner of any property will turn over its management as the result of *one* call. The property involved often represents the largest single investment of the prospective client, and its administration is therefore a matter of extreme importance. For that reason the solicitation often requires many calls, much persuasion, and perseverance. The manager must keep in mind that *every building owner is a potential client* and that every contact with a building owner is a potential sales contact. Only through constant and assiduous effort in the area of direct solicitation can a continuous flow of new business be obtained.

In addition to direct solicitation, *advertising* can be effectively employed in the sale of management service. Such advertising is generally institutional in character, designed to build the reputation of the management firm and to increase the community awareness of the existence of a particular organization. Three types of *institutional advertising* have proved to be the most effective.

1. *Display advertising* in community newspapers reaches a wide circulation and, if well handled, builds institutional prestige. It is generally advantageous to run such advertisements on the financial page of local newspapers, although this preference has by no means been demonstrated to be the most effective. When a management firm buys newspaper advertising, it is paying for circulation of which only a small part represents potential customers.

2. *Direct-by-mail Advertising* for new management business has the virtue of allowing a wide range of copy and of being addressed solely to logical prospects. Direct-by-mail advertising is sent only to those persons *who have been qualified as logical prospects,* and who are the actual owners of buildings which have been determined to represent profitable management business. As is true in all direct-by-mail advertising, the care with which mailing lists are prepared and maintained is to a large degree responsible for the success of the effort.

3. *Signs* on buildings and elsewhere are a particularly potent source of new business. Prospective clients are influenced by the judgment of their fellow building owners, and every time they see a building on which there is a sign "Managed by John Jones," it is helpful to the cause of John Jones.

   It seems needless to say that all signs inscribed with the name of the manager or management firm should be carefully designed and meticulously maintained. Nothing is more apt to destroy confidence in the management ability of an organization than a sign which has been allowed to deteriorate and which stands as a testimonial to slovenly management. On the other hand, well-designed, carefully placed, and attractively maintained signs are an extremely effective institutional advertising medium.

In addition to purchased advertising, a carefully conceived public relations program, such as was discussed in chapter 22, is an extremely valuable aid to the sale of management service. The relinquishment of the administration of his own property by an owner is based primarily upon *trust.* In the case of a management firm, this *trust* is most often justified by the owner on the basis of the appraisal of the organization by the community, an appraisal dependent on the general reputation of the firm.

Management Agreement, Fees, and Plan

In the section above where the establishment of sound owner relations was discussed, we have referred to the management agreement as the contractual document that sets forth the understandings about mutual rights, duties, commitments, work responsibilities and obligations between owners and their property managers. Specifically it must set forth those activities that the property manager remains free to undertake on his own initiative, versus those which should be referred to the owner for prior approval such as:

1. Those conditions under which the property manager is free to execute leases with tenants.
2. What about major repairs?
3. Who pays for the advertising?
4. What about the insurance and bank arrangements?

The management agreement which is signed as a confirmation that a new business relationship has been established, becomes the guideline upon which the management operating plan can be referred and based. More than that, the agreement is the key to devising the formula for fixing the rate of compensation. Fees, of course, are by no means uniform throughout the United States, but generally reflect local market situations. On the other hand, the choice between a flat (say, monthly) fee, as opposed to one which reflects a percentage of the gross income for the property, usually depends on whether or not the property manager is involved in a lot of merchandising.

Thus, it follows that with long-term tenants, a management fee easily can be set at a fixed amount. On the other hand, in cases where tenants are frequently moving in and out, the percentage formula makes sense as an inducement and a reward for the property manager who maintains high occupancy. The management pricing questionnaire that is an illustration of this chapter, along with the Management Agreement illustration, will be helpful in this connection. For these, see the appendix.

REVIEW QUESTIONS

1. Give some fundamentals in personal contacts with building owners.
2. How are opinions of property owners usually formed by department managers?
3. Should a property manager tell the owner of a building for which the manager has just contracted that other persons will actually perform the various functions to which the manager has agreed? Justify your answer.
4. What is meant by *normal expectancy* of the owner?
5. Should a manager promise his client-owner specific earnings? Justify your answer.
6. Of what value is advertising in soliciting new business? When would it be used? Name the media you would use to seek new business, and explain the reason for using each.
7. When you take over a property, what agreement should you make with the owner? Should you have a written contract covering these points?
8. What is an *account executive?* Outline his general duties.
9. Your owner expected a $1,000 net income from his building in June, but the monthly statement showed $645. What do you, as a property manager, do about this—in the interest of holding your client-owner?

10. What is meant by a *well-planned* interview in seeking new business? Explain in detail.
11. Is getting new business important, and why?
12. If you were opening a new property management department, what types of people and organizations would you contact to solicit business?

SELECTED REFERENCES

Barton, Stanley. "Guidelines for Assuming New Accounts." *Journal of Property Management,* Mar.–Apr. 1972, p. 80.

Institute of Real Estate Management. *The Real Estate Management Department: How to Establish and Operate It.* 2d ed. Chicago, Ill., 1967, 148p.

Leone, Louis A. "Reporting to the Property Owner." *Properties,* Dec. 1968, pp. 84–85.

"Make Your Management Services Profitable to Owners." *Real Estate Trends,* Apr. 1966, p. 2.

Rosenthal, Howard. "Selling Management." *Realty,* Dec. 18, 1973, p. 77.

CHAPTER 24

Operating a Management Office

INTRODUCTION

U p to this point we have been concerned with those techniques that apply to the operation of buildings. This chapter will be devoted to the administration of a property management office and will discuss the manager's administrative problems in his own business.

The real estate management of the nation is conducted in several types of offices and is carried on by various kinds of organizations. By far the largest volume of property is handled by managers who are *directly employed* by the owners of a single building, and whose duties are concerned entirely with the operation of that building. Many office buildings, hotels, apartment hotels, and other large buildings are operated in this manner. In some cases, the managers of these properties operate on an agency basis, which permits them to accept the management of other buildings or to operate in the general real estate field. In other cases, individual building managers are in the employ of building owners and are paid directly out of the building's funds but are supervised by the executives of a management firm that renders management service to the owners. In most cases, however, the activities of the manager are restricted to the individual property.

The second type of property management operation might be termed the *institutional office*. This would embrace real estate management departments of banks, insurance companies, government agencies, churches, endowment funds, and other types of institutional administration. Generally speaking, the United States does not have the volume of real estate in institutional ownership found in older countries. In England, for example, a very large percentage of urban property is owned and operated by this type of organization.

The third major category of real estate management is the *agency type* of administration, which is carried on predominantly in real estate offices. Here real estate management is a department of a commercial enterprise embracing activities such as real estate brokerage and insurance. In many cases, such offices also conduct a mortgage lending agency.

LOCATION OF THE OFFICE

In those instances where the management of a building is carried on at the building itself, the only problem of location involves the selection of an area for the office of the building—an area providing maximum convenience from the point of view of present and prospective tenants, without using space which has specialized value for other uses. In office buildings, the office of the building manager is usually located on one of the upper floors, because the ground floor space is too valuable. In multistory buildings large enough to contain local and express elevators, the office of the building is usually located on a transfer floor served by both types of elevators.

In hotel properties, the location of administrative offices usually depends upon the size of the hotel. In smaller hotels where it is desirable that the manager have broad contact with the public, the offices should be located adjacent to the registration desk and cashiers' cages. In large hotels, where the contacts with the public are handled by assistant managers on duty in the lobby, the administrative offices are frequently located on the mezzanine floor. In apartment hotels, where there is constant contact between resident guests and the management, it is recommended that the building's administrative offices be located on the ground floor at the point of maximum convenience to the resident guests.

The location of the institutional real estate management office is frequently dictated by the institution itself. In the case of banks and insurance companies, the property management department is usually a part of the central office. In the case of other institutions, it is frequently desirable to locate the management office in one or another of the institution's buildings—preferably in the one closest to the center of the holdings—in order to provide maximum convenience to those who do business with the management office.

The location of the real estate office itself depends essentially upon the character of the specific operation. A ground-floor location is the choice of the largest percentage of the nation's real estate offices—either in store space or in buildings specifically designed and constructed for such use. If the real estate office does a great deal of business with the general public, it should be located as close as possible to the center of consumer activity, because consumer accessibility is important. Since real estate offices cannot pay rents high enough to warrant being situated on major shopping streets, they are usually found on side streets peripheral to the shopping area. In large cities, real estate offices are frequently located on upper floors in downtown office buildings. In such cases, they trade the advantages of more favorable consumer locations for the prestige which accrues from such location.

Many large real estate firms in urban areas operate branch offices as well as a central office. These branch offices are located in one or more outlying neighborhoods to attract and interest additional consumers. For that reason, almost all branch office operations are conducted in ground-floor locations.

Office Layout and Design

The "affluent society" that has developed in the United States has seen the raising of housing standards for business as well as for residences. It is a proven fact that attractive, modern business quarters can be a significant factor in the acquisition of new business. It is also true that the provision of custom-designed offices can represent a genuine saving both through increasing the efficiency of operation and facilitating the recruitment of desirable employees. In the past several years, many real estate organizations have erected their own office buildings in prominent locations. Such building programs have been undertaken not only as desirable investments, but they have added substantially to the owners' all-important "image," and hence to the volume of business.

Although it is not necessary or advisable for the management office to be luxuriously appointed, it should be as attractive as possible and should represent the employment of the techniques which are the manager's stock in trade. Since the use of color is an effective method of merchandising all space, the management office should be artistically colorful and should be a demonstration of the manager's know-how in that field. Likewise, the management office should be properly illuminated, with the lighting not only adequate, but attractive. The furnishings of the office should be simple, in good style, and uniform. And, following modern practice, a tasteful use of decorator plants can be recommended.

The office layout of a property management office should, above all, depict efficiency. All too often, even the casual observer could recommend changes in layout that would obviously be beneficial both to the public and the employees. To a degree, the design of a management office is a reflection of the efficiency to be found in the firm's operations. Office arrangements and procedures, therefore, should be the subject of exacting scrutiny by the manager and his associates. Above all, the layout should accommodate the basic functions of the property management firm.

What are these functions? First, there is the matter of receiving the renting public who present themselves at the manager's office to indicate their desire to rent space in his properties. Provision must be made for the immediate and courteous reception of these prospective clients and for interviewing them in comfort and privacy. Second, there is the accommodation of the needs of the existing tenant who come to the manager's office to pay rentals, to make service requests, or to hold conferences regarding lease and tenancy renewal. All of these are considered by the tenant to be personal and important matters, worthy of consideration and privacy. Third is the reception and interviewing of those persons whose visits are prompted by the maintenance operation of the manager. These include salesmen, contractors, tradesmen, architects, and others. If the manager handles them courteously and efficiently, it will go a long way toward establishing his reputation among a group whose contacts are wide and whose esteem is invaluable. Finally, the office must provide adequate space for its accounting operations in an atmosphere conducive to concentration and accuracy.

It would seem unnecessary to comment on the matter of maintenance. However, real estate management is a detailed business involving the broad use of papers, books, catalogs, collection files, etc., with which desks can become littered. There is a constant temptation for personnel to allow desks to become cluttered with a miscellany of papers, samples, and other debris that is bound to accumulate unless an organization policy is maintained, such as: *desks must be neat and attractive at all times.* It is easy for a client to conclude that an employee is inefficient when his desk is piled high with papers, and when he has difficulty locating those particular papers that have to do with the client's affairs. Neatness should be fundamental in the management office; in fact, it is more important in the case of a property management firm than in almost any other line of commercial business.

Whenever possible, real estate management executives should be easily accessible to the public. Experience shows that the soundest type of management office is one in which all executives occupy desks in the general offices, instead of in private rooms hidden away from the public. Conference rooms can be built to accommodate interviews requiring special privacy.

This is especially true in hotel offices or in buildings where the manager has broad contacts with the tenants. It is a mistake to create an unctuous aura around the individual building manager. Envy is the secret cause of most of the world's dislike, and it is ruinous to the public relations of a manager to create an atmosphere that will result in the envy of his clients.

Office Equipment

We have pointed out elsewhere that the property manager creates no product, has no inventory, and usually has no substantial plant investment. Inasmuch as he has comparatively little equipment, it should be the best obtainable. In the average real estate management office today, the proprietor or the owning stockholders are faced with one of two eventualities—either the cost of operation must be reduced, or the net earnings of the office will decline. In the case where the volume of work is not to be decreased, such lower costs can be accomplished only by a reduction in personnel through increased efficiency. Since it is presumed that in an efficiently operated management office the personnel are constantly busy, their productivity can be increased only by use of modern, efficiently maintained labor-saving devices.

There is no reason that the historical evolution of technological improvements must be restricted to industry or agriculture. Increasing efficiency and lowering labor requirements have been successfully employed in recent decades by banks, insurance companies, and various commercial enterprises. They have also been introduced in real estate management companies, where machines are employed increasingly to replace labor or to substantially increase labor's efficiency. Moreover, these same organizations have benefited from the installation of *machines that sell*—that pay for themselves many times by increasing business volume.

Even in the present computerized era, the typewriter is certainly the basic office machine employed today. It seems trite to discuss the typewriter in a text of management, yet some business executives still are tempted to believe that any machine that prepares satisfactory letters is good enough for office use. But this is not the case.

Typewriters, like other business machines, have been improved remarkably in recent years. These improvements permit better performance—both in the work produced and in the efficiency of the operator. Certainly any real estate or property management executive making an analysis of operations should check his typewriting equipment, make certain that it is the best available and—even more important—that it satisfies the stenographic employees. If a secretary earns $150 per week, a 5 percent difference in her production will pay for a new typewriter in a short period of time.

Electric typewriters are now almost standard equipment in established offices. Where volume of production is a factor, manufacturers claim higher production with lower operator fatigue. In offices that require a number of copies of letters or reports, the power thrust of the electric typewriter enables the typist to maximize the number of copies that can be made in one typing operation. These typewriters also offer type faces that are valuable in interest-provoking advertising pieces and can be used in place of printer's type for direct offset printing.

Dictating machines have been eschewed frequently by both executives and stenographic employees. These whims are understandable—providing the manager can afford to indulge himself and his staff. On the other hand, dictating to a stenographer is a distinct luxury. Use of dictating machines definitely increases office efficiency and makes possible a reduction in required personnel through the establishment of secretarial pools.

From the executive point of view, dictating machines offer the advantage of immediate availability at any time of the day or night. The new electronic dictating machines can be used with either a desk or hand microphone. Dictation can be at a conversational pitch with a minimum of effort. Moreover, the transcribing apparatus now available reproduces the dictation clearly at any adjusted volume by means of comfortable and governable listening devices.

Alert management organizations and real estate offices are making use of portable electronic dictating machines. The portable machine is an excellent aid for building inspectors and executives in making on-the-spot reports when visiting various properties. These portable machines may also be taken to conferences, to the executive's home, and on trips.

The telephone reorder is a very useful attachment for the modern dictating machine. Many commitments are made over the telephone which are later subject to misunderstanding and question. The use of such attachments is extremely valuable to record important conversations. Inasmuch as federal law now requires a warning signal to advise participants that a telephone conversation is being recorded, there is no ethical disadvantage to such recordings. The new, easy-to-file permanent records are especially desirable and make the preservation of telephone conversations both practical and convenient.

Intercoms are step savers for executives and employees alike. Useful in offices with or without telephone switchboards, these intercommunication systems are frequently vital to maximum efficiency. The most common use for such equipment is between the desk of the executive and those with whom he is in frequent contact. Messages can be relayed to a secretary without either using the telephone or having the secretary make a wasteful trip into the executive's private office. By means of a multistation switch, the same time and energy-saving procedure may be followed with other personnel.

Contacts between closely related work stations (cashier and collection supervisor, for example) often require needless trips or constant telephone communication. Such closely related stations can be served profitably by intercoms.

Addressing machines are extremely valuable in every progressive management office, regardless of size. Available in a wide range of prices and capacities, these machines not only save labor, but are an essential part of the mechanized selling effort so vital to steady, efficient business growth.

Among the uses to which such machines are commonly put, the following are the most important:

1. Every management office regularly mails recurring correspondence to certain addresses, e.g., local utility companies, regular clients, purveyors, etc. With an addressing machine, envelopes for these persons and firms may be run off automatically, so that stenographers and clerks do not need to address manually each time a mailing is made.
2. The development of separate files and addressing plates for various types of advertising ensures the uniformity of mailing and reduces resistance to frequent mailing.
3. Addressing machines are often used by the accounting department for preparing rent bills, receipts, and owners' statements.

Stamping, sealing, and mailing machines are being manufactured for every size of business. Ranging from a simple device which "takes the lick" out of sealing envelopes and stamps to the modern motor-driven machines which provide automatic postage, these devices not only eliminate labor and speed up general mailing, but also may be used for direct-mail advertising.

Postage scales are a *must* in any efficient mailing operation. Improperly stamped mail is either a waste of postage or a nuisance to those who must pay for "postage due." Especially in mailing to clients, management offices should make certain that postage is correct. Many a client has been lost because of mismanagement in mailing.

Duplicating machines fill a wide variety of roles in the management office. From the simple mimeograph job to more expensive copying, they are valuable both as labor savers and as aids to selling. Continuity is frequently more important in advertising than either copy or format. Most management offices neglect opportunities for selling by mail, because they believe that advertising must be extravagantly prepared and expensively produced. On the other hand, some offices are growing steadily in management volume as the result of a constant barrage of self-created and self-produced mailing pieces prepared on duplicating machines.

Copying machines are devices which pay for themselves in offices where a number of copies of reports must be prepared for wide distribution. Eliminating the necessity for tedious, labor-consuming retyping, these machines produce limitless numbers of copies with slightly less labor than that required for the original.

Photographic copying machines are available that will produce exact copies for record use and for use away from the office. These machines will reproduce leases, invoices, notes, and other documents for which exact copies are frequently requested.

Microfilm machines are an answer to the problem of record storage, which is increasingly a burden to the real estate office. Many management firms are either failing to retain records that may some day prove extremely valuable, or they are paying rent for space for the bulk storage of such records. Microfilm enables the management office to retain many years' accumulation of important correspondence, documents, etc., in a space smaller than that which would be needed for a few days' papers in the original forms. Moreover, systems and devices for indexing such material are available, and they make it easy to retrieve sought-for papers.

Machine bookkeeping has been adopted almost universally by banks, hotels, savings and loan associations, and every type of business with any volume of accounting. In the field of real estate management, larger offices have replaced hand account-keeping by one or more of the wide variety of mechanized systems available. Offices with more than 300 tenants and 20 clients are logical users of machine bookkeeping. Most manufacturers of this equipment maintain a staff of experts thoroughly familiar with the accounting problems of real estate and property management agencies.

Computers of various levels of capacity and sophistication can be employed in a wide variety of uses in every aspect of the property management field, but especially in the matter of record keeping. Their application and use is virtually a separate science which is both complex and expensive. Suffice it to say here that a property management organization with any volume of business should consult experts in this field for an analysis of its advantages and disadvantages.

Other machinery, such as check-writing and payroll machines, is essential to any program directed to maximum use of the office employees' time. In large offices it is probable that one of the many types of calculating machines will prove a wise investment.

Contract bookkeeping is increasingly available from firms which specialize in computer operation. Banks and other organizations over the country are now widely employing such contract organizations. While they are not yet in common use in the property management field, it is certainly likely that they will be in the foreseeable future.

The creation of efficiency in labor is by no means confined to installation of machinery. Scientific studies have proved that personnel efficiency is vitally influenced by the comfort and design of chairs, the height and width of desks, and the type of floor covering and illumination. Improper seating hastens fatigue and decreases personnel efficiency in the latter part of each day. Desks that are too high cause fatigue through discomfort and often cost the business proprietor in "work hours lost"—more than if he bought new desks.

In large management organizations, one member of the staff should have a background of industrial engineering. The constant critical examination of basic equipment and its operation by the management organization is invaluable.

Office Organization

It is obvious that no single pattern of office organization can be perfected that will apply in all cases because of differences in both type of work assignments and size of operations. The following job descriptions, however, can be used by the one-man operator as a checklist of duties, or they can be studied by those interested in large organizations as a key to various types of positions.

THE GENERAL MANAGER

   I. Responsible for policies
      A. Rates to be charged for services
      B. Commission payments
         1. Amount
         2. Cooperation with other realtors
  II. Development of new business
      A. Direction of new account solicitation
      B. Determination of desirability of new accounts

   C. Institutional contacts
     1. Through clubs, social affiliations, and identification with professional activities
     2. Through publicity in trade journals and newspapers

III. Direction of the business
   A. Supervision of operation cost
   B. Supervision of departmental activities
     1. Reports from department heads
     2. Occasional inspection of properties

IV. Maintenance of morale and motivation of employees
   A. Emanation of confidence and faith
   B. Personal interviews with members of the staff
   C. Departmental and general staff meetings
   D. Demonstration of knowledge of every phase of business
   E. Fair treatment and recognition of good performance

MANAGER OF THE RENTING DEPARTMENT

  I. General supervision of rent brokers
   A. Through daily reports
   B. By sales meetings
   C. Through personal interviews and discussion of the individual broker's work and problems

 II. Knowledge of market conditions and trends
   A. Personal exploration of districts and buildings
   B. Reports from the management department
   C. Information supplied by brokers

III. Supervision of activities in the renting department
   A. Examination of prospect cards
   B. Daily check with listing clerks
   C. Examination and personal approval of earned commission or credit slips
   D. Inspection of units available to rent

IV. Solicitation of new business
 V. Training and motivation of renting department personnel

MANAGER OF THE MANAGEMENT DEPARTMENT

 I. Direction and supervision of activities and personnel
   A. Reports from management men
     1. Inspections
     2. Tenant contacts
     3. Building personnel as to the number of changes in help and reason, and as to the total payroll under supervision of management man

    B. Reports from cashier
      1. Tri-monthly record of delinquency
      2. Number of units vacant
      3. Total rent roll
      4. Gain or loss of business
        a. In units
        b. In rent roll
    C. Reports from service request clerks on number of requests handled, number referred to building staff, and number of orders written to contractors, supply houses, etc.
    D. Reports from purchasing agent on labor costs and commodity costs
  II. Personal examination of owners' statements
    A. Meetings and interviews with entire personnel
    B. Direction of collections and collection policy
 III. Owner contacts
    A. Personal interviews in company of management men
    B. Letters with owners' statements
    C. Frequent communications about matters interesting and beneficial to owners
    D. Semi-social calls to strengthen personal relationships

The managers of the renting and management departments form a sales team for the solicitation of new business. Each makes an analysis of the property and prepares a proposal which may be used for intelligent discussion and planning. The general manager is the promoter and director for the solicitation of new business, but the actual selling is done by the managers of the renting and management departments. (See "The Management Man," below, for duties of the latter.)

THE LISTING CLERK

   I. Preparation and maintenance of the listing book
    A. Securing information from the management department
    B. Securing information from other real estate firms
  II. Maintenance of prospect file
    A. Recording of names and expiration dates
    B. Systematic filing (for later follow-up) of prospect cards
    C. Recording of leads and assignment to brokers

It is essential that the listing clerk be impartial in the distribution of leads to brokers. Any favoritism tends to break down respect on the part of those who think they have been gypped and thus works against the complete kind of cooperation that develops maximum rentals.

RENT AGENTS (RESIDENTIAL)

I. The leasing of units in apartments and of houses
   A. Knowledge of units he is seeking to rent
   B. Diligent follow-up of leads
      1. Telephone inquiries
      2. Recording calls and interviews on prospect cards
      3. Keeping in mind prospect needs so they may be contacted when suitable vacancies occur
   C. Intelligent cultivation of the prospect
      1. Ascertaining his requirements
      2. Inspection of the prospect's home when possible, and recording type of furniture, living standards, etc.
      3. Intelligent selection of units for showing that fit into the prospect's requirements and preferences
      4. Ascertaining what the prospect likes as he is shown available units, and concentrating the sales effort on that particular unit
      5. Resourcefulness in appealing to prospect's vulnerable points—price, love of family, desire for modern conveniences, etc.
II. Cooperation in the solicitation of new business
   A. Observation of competitive buildings and comparisons
      1. Condition of the building
      2. Condition of available space
      3. Accessibility of available space
      4. Price with respect to other units
   B. Personal contact
      1. Owners when renting units in their buildings
      2. Janitors and employees in buildings
III. Promotion of goodwill
   A. Businesslike, well-mannered, courteous, and generous dealings with the public, building owners, and competitors
   B. Reflecting satisfaction with the company and personal contribution to its activities.

THE MANAGEMENT MAN
(Supervisor of Residential Managers)

I. General responsibility for buildings assigned to him
   A. Collections
   B. Cost of operation
   C. Occupancy
   D. Condition of building as to cleanliness need of repair; manners and efficiency of personnel

II. General administration of properties under his supervision
    A. Collections
        1. Based on cashier's reports
        2. Telephone calls
        3. Personal contact
        4. Letters
        5. Five-day notice
        6. Direction of legal action through attorney
    B. Cost of operation
        1. Personal approval of orders for labor and materials
        2. Knowledge of conditions incidental to the necessity of ordering labor or materials
        3. Knowledge of help required to maintain building in first-class condition, and basing of payrolls upon the building's actual requirements
    C. Assurance of occupancy
        1. Keeping units in attractive condition—decorating, cleanliness, improvements necessary to meet competition, maintaining price in keeping with market
        2. Making sure certain buildings are being shown
    D. Maintenance of building—regular inspections, checking personnel
III. Contact with tenants
    A. Personal calls and recording reactions
    B. Personal attention to tenant correspondence
IV. Basic contact with owner
    A. Frequent personal interviews
    B. By advising owner of conditions in building
V. Direction of building personnel
    A. Hiring of janitors or chief janitors
    B. Approval of help hired by chief janitors
    C. Control of efficiency and manners
VI. Renewal of leases
VII. Cooperation in the solicitation of new business
    A. Observation
    B. Submitting ideas for improvement of management of competitive buildings
    C. Assisting the Rent Manager in the analysis of prospective business

THE PURCHASING AGENT

I. Supervision of all purchases by or through the organization
    A. Preparation and maintenance of purchasing outline used by service request clerks

    B. Maintenance of a coefficient of cost and labor commodities

    C. Analysis of products purchased to determine their basic worth with aid of competent building engineers serving in the capacity of a technical advisory committee

  II. Investigation of new building appliances, equipment, and materials

 III. Direction of activities of service request clerks

 IV. Approval of all bills paid for labor and materials

  V. Preparation of estimates of cost of operation for buildings under consideration as new buildings

THE CASHIER

   I. Receive, record, and bank all money received by office

    A. Enter rents on tenants' collection cards

    B. Make out journal entries, cash disbursements, check orders, etc.

  II. Make tri-monthly reports to Management Men covering buildings under their supervision

 III. Billing of special accounts on duo-account buildings

    A. Electric light current and lamps

    B. Special service

    C. Telephone

    D. Maid service

    E. Garage rent

    F. Garage special service

 IV. Check of rent bills and addition of balances, if any

  V. Drawing of building payrolls and janitors' expense slips

SERVICE REQUEST CLERKS

   I. Handle all telephone calls for management men and all telephone requests for service from tenants (Note: These persons should be patient, courteous, and service-minded. They have more contacts with customers than other members of the organization. Their efforts should be checked frequently by calls from the outside, and by listening to their conversations. They should be familiar with all the properties handled by the organization.)

  II. Arranging for disposition of all service requests

    A. Calling janitor at the building

    B. Calling management men

    C. Written order to contractor

      1. Using purchasing outline

      2. Advising disposition to tenant

III. Arranging for the disposition of supply and labor requisitions of the janitor
  A. Obtaining management men's approval
  B. Written order

In the foregoing, we have outlined representative job functions and responsibilities that exist within the context of every management office—large or small. Each particular office, of course, will be characterized by its own arrangements, reflecting the exact scope of the company's business on the one hand, and the presentation style of the proprietor on the other.

As for the size of the management office staff, however, this depends upon three principal factors, namely: the number of tenants to be serviced, the number of clients served, and the average size of the properties involved. For example, the "management man" listed in the outline above is the basic employee of the management company. As can be seen from an outline of his duties, he is in the field during the greater portion of his work hours; hence he needs an assistant who is constantly in the office to handle detail work, take messages, and receive the public. This means that each management man must have a competent secretary with whom he works as a basic team. In the one-man operation, this management man and his secretary constitute the entire staff. Here, the secretary is a combination secretary-bookkeeper and performs all of the chores incident to the accounting operation.

In larger organizations, the management man is assigned a specific number of buildings containing a certain number of tenants. Experience suggests that in the event the buildings are all single-family residences, the maximum number which can be handled efficiently by one management man is approximately 150. Thus he would be handling 150 buildings and 150 tenants. On the other hand, if the average building under his jurisdiction contains 10 units, it might be possible for him to handle up to 300 tenants and this would mean 30 buildings. If the average size of the buildings was 20 units, the manager might be able to handle up to 500 units contained in 25 buildings.

In organizations handling several thousand units of property, it is a workable rule to have a general executive for each five management men. Whereas these suggested work loads are not by any means fixed, they will serve to give the student some idea of the personnel requirements of the management office.

Developing Profitable Management

By far the largest number of people engaged in real property management are direct employees of individuals or corporations. Their compensation is either in the form of a straight salary or is based on a percentage arrangement in some manner related to profits from the building managed. This section of the chapter is concerned with a discussion of those real estate managers who are in the *business* of real estate management and who manage a number of properties on an agency basis for a contract fee. The *profits* from such a management operation represent the difference between the gross revenue received in management fees and the costs of providing the service.

Most management fees are related to the gross income of the property managed. Real estate boards in urban areas generally establish a schedule of fees which are locally accepted as *standards,* but are not universally followed as a matter of practice. These fees vary considerably, according to the sections of the country, but as a round number the fees for most unfurnished residential properties represent 5 percent of the gross rental income. In some sections, managers are paid an additional percentage of expenditure on the theory that additional service is required. In most cases, however, the percentage-of-gross fee is considered to be payment for full management service, and no additional compensation is necessary. The management fee for commercial buildings is often the same as that for residential buildings, except that in large-income properties the rate is frequently shaded as the gross revenue rises. In hotels, the management compensation is a matter of a special negotiation and is usually related to a percentage of the gross rooms revenue plus a somewhat larger percentage of food and beverage department *net* incomes. In all larger properties, the rate of compensation is a matter of negotiation.

Many will agree that the standardization of rates based on gross income is an unsatisfactory, impractical, and undesirable method of compensation. Management service is certainly a professional activity. A standard of professional people everywhere is to relate compensation either to ability or to performance and to shun any form of standardization. It may be assumed that the rewards for ability are to be found in an increased volume of business, but such an assumption is incorrect and explains the willingness of some managers to build a large organization as a pretended measure of his ability.

In recent years there has been an increasing tendency to relate the fees for management service to the *performance* of the manager. In such cases, a minimum fee is agreed upon with the understanding that the manager will participate on some basis in increases in net profits.

At the outset, the operator of the management business should study the costs of operating various types of properties and should accept for management only such business as will be profitable. In many instances, general real estate offices, which offer collateral services, are willing to assume the management of buildings at rates which produce less than satisfactory profits on the theory that the administration of such buildings will at some time produce collateral revenue. If the ownership decides to sell the property, for example, it is probable that the real estate office will earn a brokerage fee. If the mortgage becomes due, it is thought probable that the real estate office may profit from the placing of the new loan. There is also the possibility that the real estate office may write the insurance on the property or perform other services for which additional fees may be charged. This type of reasoning cannot always be applied safely, however, because in certain periods of the real estate cycle the income from other departments of the real estate operation declines to a point where the bulk of overhead must be assumed by the management operation. If a volume of management business has been undertaken on the basis of fees which will not in themselves produce a reasonable profit, the organization will find that it is necessary to raise fees at the most difficult time in the cycle.

The profits from real estate management are by no means uniform, even in identical properties. Unreasonable building owners frequently require amounts of attention entirely unjustified by the level of the fee for management service. Properties with extremely heavy tenant turnover or with poor physical equipment demand more staff time than can be paid for out of standard fees. Properties located in remote areas require large amounts of staff travel time, plus the expense of transportation. Although certainly the manager is bound to expect some deviation from the *norm* of cost, each single piece of business should be reviewed from the point of view of cost of operation, and it should be accepted for management only when there is evidence that it will represent profitable business.

In small towns and cities, the manager faces a limited market, and his energies must be devoted to obtaining any type of profitable business. In larger cities, however, where numbers of large buildings exist, the manager should keep in mind that it is as easy to sell his service on a large property as on a small property. In fact, the owners of larger properties are frequently easier to service than the owners of smaller properties. The former usually have a higher level of business comprehension, make quick decisions, and require little coddling.

The owners of small properties, on the other hand, are apt to be persons whose entire interests are centered in a single property and who naturally will require a great deal more personal attention. In general, the operating expense of the property manager is made up of four principal classifications: rent, payroll, equipment and supplies, and advertising and promotion. With the exception of the single item of rent, these expense factors are instantly controllable and can be maintained in satisfactory relationship to gross revenue. The operating problem is thus one of obtaining a satisfactory volume of basically profitable business and of establishing and maintaining a fixed-level relationship between gross revenue and operating expense.

REVIEW QUESTIONS

1. Why is office equipment important? Give examples to support your answer.
2. What factors are involved in the selection of office location for the real estate manager or management firm? Give examples.
3. What is a *telephone recorder?* Why is it valuable?
4. Name several types of property management. Define each.

5. Suppose you are short of storage space but want to retain your records. What would you do about it?

6. Research shows you that a community is ready for a branch office. Where would you locate your particular office in the community and why?

7. You have an efficient employee; but, paradoxical as it may be, he or she is not a good housekeeper with his or her desk. Should this concern you? Why—and what would you do about it?

8. Give job descriptions: general manager; manager of renting department; purchasing agent; listing clerk; management man; service request clerk; cashier.

9. You are opening a property management office where your manpower must be limited to three employees. Give these three titles, and outline duties you would assign each. Upon what did you base your decision to have three?

10. Your organization handles 3,000 units of property, how many general executives should you have? How many management men? Explain.

11. You are managing a residential property in a metropolitan suburb with a gross income of $24,500 monthly. What is the usual income you could expect for service as the property manager? Explain how you reached your answer.

12. Why are some real estate firms inclined to take on the management of properties which do not pay adequate profits or give an adequate net return? Should this be a common practice? Justify your answer.

13. You are opening a real estate office and you plan to hire only one person to assist you. Name four factors which you must consider in setting up your operation.

14. What are the basic functions carried on in the property management office that should be considered in planning physical arrangement of office space?

15. Some property managers have come to the conclusion that earnings received from the management of properties as diverse as subsidized housing and high-priced condominiums are not profitable. What is wrong with their way of thinking given the fact that these property forms, because of their growing prevalence, are here to stay and need more and more management services?

16. From what you already know about computers, how do you envisage they will be used five years from now—and to what extent?

SELECTED REFERENCES

Beckwith, A. T. "Staffing the Management Office." *Journal of Property Management,* Fall 1961, pp. 26–29.

Casey, William J. *Real Estate Desk Book.* 4th ed. New York, N. Y., Institute for Business Planning, 1971. 341p.

Glassman, Sidney. "Computerized Future for Property Management." *Journal of Property Management,* Mar–Apr. 1970, pp. 93–97.

Glassman, Sidney. *Tools for Creative Property Management.* Chicago, Ill., Institute of Real Estate Management, 1974. 52p.
    See "Operating Statements As They Relate to the Property Manager."

Hanford, Lloyd D., Sr. *The Property Management Process.* Institute of Real Estate Management, Chicago, Ill., 1972. 86p.

"TASC Expands Property Management Services—New Computer Center Revealed." *New England Real Estate Journal,* Sept. 29, 1972, Section 2, p. 18.

The Real Estate Management Department: How to Establish and Operate It. 2nd ed., Chicago, Ill., Institute of Real Estate Management, 1967. 148p.

"What You Need to Know to Build a Property Management Department." *Buildings,* May 1964, pp. 74–75.

CHAPTER 25

Selection and Training of Personnel

INTRODUCTION

It is difficult to think of a profession in America which is not also a business. Musicians, lawyers, doctors, and actors are all faced with the problem of merchandising their services, of promoting demand for their product. In most of these professions the success of the individual is totally dependent upon his or her own action, capability, and value. In the field of property management, on the other hand, the administrator of a management organization depends for his reputation to a large extent upon the service of *other people*—people with whom he works, either as an employer, employee, or associate. A real estate manager cannot work alone. Even if he is a one-man operator, he must have office help. He must have janitors, caretakers, maintenance men, and other service people on call. In few other businesses is there such dependence upon people.

The property manager has no plant, no tools, no inventory, and no merchandise to exhibit. Men and women are the tools, the equipment, and the product of the manager. They make or break his reputation, they hold his destiny in their every contact with the public. Their friends are the manager's friends, their enemies his enemies. For that reason the selection and training of personnel loom large in the success or failure of any property manager or management firm. And for that reason the student should give proper emphasis to the study of methods by which he can protect himself against failure in this important activity.

Judging people, like judging horses or dogs, is a study. In a lifetime one may have seen thousands of horses, ridden scores of them. Yet such a person may know nothing about judging horses. The answer is that some may be not interested in horses beyond their ability to provide a means of transportation over rugged or hilly terrain. But, there are many in the United States who can look at a horse and tell almost exactly how old it is, how fast it can run, how much of a load it can pull, and what it is worth on the market. The reason they can do this is that they think about horses—critically, analytically, and academically. Obviously whoever spends his life among horses would learn about horses from all points of view.

Property managers spend their lives among people in the most intimate sort of business association. Therefore, they must study people, critically, analytically, and academically. They must learn to judge people; to know an introvert from an extrovert, a worker from a drone. Yet, there is certainly value to experience with people, provided you think about them and record your experience in the back of your mind. Bank tellers learn about people, because if they didn't they would soon collect a bundle of bad checks. Men in the customs inspection services at our borders learn about people and can almost smell a smuggler or an illegal entrant. The reason they develop this ability is that they think about people, they record previous experience in their minds, and they develop types of images in their mental catalogues. Some of the best judges of human beings in the world are taxi drivers. They can tell at a glance what kind of a tip you will give them. From such examples, we seem to have basis for a belief that an art of judging people exists. Certainly such an art is vital to the property manager.

There is a dual responsibility in personnel. If you are an employee, you have a responsibility to yourself and to your employer. If you are an employer, you, likewise, have a responsibility to your organization and to your employee. This dual responsibility is the basis of good employer-employee relations, without which there can be no true organization spirit. Mutual benefit is the keystone of all successful human relations. The days of slaves, serfs, and indentured workers are gone. Recognition of this fact is the foundation of a sound attitude for employers and employees.

SELECTION OF PERSONNEL

A job is a blessed thing. To conscientious, hard-working employees, who are distinctly in the majority, a job represents a guaranteed future for family and self. It means security and freedom from want. It makes the difference between happiness and heartache.

A good employee is like a jewel. To the average hard-pressed employer, a good employee means help and comfort, and a good employee brings the peace of reliability and the calm of confidence.

Now, one would think that the establishment of such an interdependent relationship would be the subject of much mature thought on the part of both the boss and the worker. Yet, sad as it is to relate, many employer-employee relationships are established without the care one would give to the selection of a new suit of clothes. The way it usually happens is this. A stenographer walks into an employment agency. She knows shorthand, she can type, she thinks she is worth about $150 a week. She wants a job, period.

Now let's look at the other side of the picture. A property manager wants a stenographer. He calls the agency and says: "I need a secretary. Send over two or three girls for me to interview." Eventually the woman described above walks in. If she looks reasonably presentable and thinks the salary is acceptable, she is hired on the spot. A few cursory reference contacts are made, and a new employee is hired. Two problems are solved. The man has someone to take his dictation, and the woman has a job. There may be ten good reasons why the newly established relationship is unsound, why it cannot possibly last, and why both parties will go through a long period of inefficiency and unhappiness before ultimately parting company. But, the problem of the moment has been solved. That type of hiring is typical of our personnel selection in many of business organizations today!

However shortsighted and anxious the typical prospective employee may be, the employer who seeks to build a sound, successful organization must have a more adequate technique of personnel selection than the mere need of a particular kind of technician or the mere availability of an attractive applicant. There appear to be certain time-tested principles to be followed in the selection of personnel, the most important of which are the following:

1. Whenever a new employee is engaged for a property management organization, the attitude of the employer should be that the person is being hired *for life*. Changes in personnel are expensive, and they contribute to general organizational inefficiency. It takes a good while to effectively train an employee. Each person in an organization represents a substantial investment in time and money. An intelligent employer, therefore, will not engage any employee without considering that the arrangement is completely permanent.

2. An employer's hiring policy should be based upon something more than the simple need for an employee. Moreover, his selection should be made only when he finds that the applicant matches certain predetermined specifications, rather than when he concludes that the applicant is the best of three or four interviewed. For example, if a receptionist and switchboard operator position is open, the hiring official should first establish the qualities of an ideal applicant. An employee in this position should have a pleasing telephone voice and a good memory for voices. Even though it is not necessary that all personnel be physically attractive, it is important that a receptionist should be above average in presentability. A good receptionist must have a pleasant disposition and a real interest in people. She should be the type who enjoys small talk, since she will be talking to people who are waiting for you and it is important that their wait be as pleasant as possible. After these qualities have been determined, then it is important that she be a good mechanical operator, since faulty telephone service is an aggravation to the public, and most of the public contacts of the firm are by telephone, rather than personal.

Specifications of this type should be thought out for every position in the real estate management office. Applicants should be engaged *only when* these specifications have been matched by a person with all of the qualities desired. Perhaps such a hiring policy is more work for the hiring officer, or perhaps it will take longer to find just the right person, or perhaps temporary help will have to be engaged to "fill in" while the permanent employee is being sought. A procedure that represents sound personnel policy will contribute toward the building of a successful organization. On the other hand, the slip-shod employment methods of some business offices merely create dispirited, inefficient, and ineffective associations of people, loosely knit and imper-manent.

FINDING PROSPECTIVE EMPLOYEES

There are several methods of going about finding people to fill positions. The most common of these are employment agencies, *help-wanted* advertise-ments, reference by friends or associates, and outright recruiting. These are means of getting new employees from outside the organization. We must certainly call attention to the resource of *promotion* from other positions within the firm. Strangely enough, many employers overlook the great value of maintaining a dynamic factor within their organizations. Upward move-ment within the operating structure is a fundamental factor in the maintenance of an esprit de corps so valuable in long-term personnel satisfaction. Fre-quently, employers are too lazy to promote people from the ranks. Such promotion means that two people have to be trained instead of one. The new employee must first learn the work of the person to be promoted, and then the old worker must learn the new job. Creation of a hard-hitting, enthusiastic group of people is *not the easiest way,* but it is sound policy.

If there are no applicants available for promotion within the ranks, then the methods first outlined above must be used. In respect to the first two, i.e., employment agencies and "help-wanted" advertising, there is one common objection. Most good employees are now employed and they are happily employed. Generally speaking, the people who read "help-wanted" advertising or haunt the employment agencies in normal times are those who are chroni-cally dissatisfied or who have the constant feeling that the grass is greener on the other side of the street. Their unhappiness in their present job is usually due to their attitude rather than their environment or working conditions. The chances are that when they come to work for you, they will still read the "help-wanted" columns, and they will still haunt the employment agencies. For that reason, we prefer the people who come as the result of reference by friends or other employees, or, still better, the people who are actually re-cruited for employment because they are known to be doing a good job for someone else. In this latter type of contact, the employer has greater chance of finding the person who will exactly fill the specifications for the position which is open.

INVESTIGATING PROSPECTIVE EMPLOYEES

Before discussing the property manager's own techniques of investigating prospective employees, we should point out the existence of professional services available to employers which assist in both the selection and training of new employees. These services offer psychological tests designed to determine the prospective employee's suitability for the type of work under consideration. They also undertake the analysis of an individual's background, with reports on stability, character, and so forth. Specialized services of this kind are being employed increasingly by large firms in all lines of business.

The amazingly lax methods of hiring people that prevail in certain American business offices are paralleled by an astonishing indifference in the matter of investigating prospective employees before they are actually hired. This laxity carries over in many instances to employees after they are members of the organization. For example, we have found numbers of firms who do not keep adequate records on their employees and who do not have data on when raises were given or when people were absent from work and for what reason. It is no wonder that such employers give inadequate attention to the matter of promotion, since they lack the basic information from which to determine which employees are promotable.

Virtually all letters of reference are meaningless. For example, the tendency is for previous employers never to write an unfavorable reply to an inquiry on a former employee. If the employee was at all acceptable, it is the practice of most previous employers to "give him a break" by saying that he was satisfactory. In cases of outright dissatisfaction where an employee was discharged, most former employers simply do not answer the letters. For that reason, we say that letters of reference are worthless in 95 percent of the cases.

The basis of investigation of prospective employees is an adequate application-for-employment form. Such a form should list all of the desired data and should, above all, be a *complete* record of the applicant's employment since he or she left school. Provision then should be made for a personal interview with at least the two most recent previous employers. Most management firms, in looking up prospective tenants, have developed facilities for conducting such interviews and can arrange for this kind of investigation without too much difficulty. In cases where important office personnel are being investigated, it is suggested that an excellent plan is to visit the home of the prospective employee. Much can be learned about a person's desirability from the way in which he or she lives.

In these days, when a large percentage of both men and women employees are married, it is a good plan to interview the wife or husband of the prospective employee. Domestic influence is one of the strongest force in life. A man or woman who is mismated is apt to be a poor employee. The few minutes' inconvenience involved in an interview of this kind can often prevent an unsatisfactory association, which might take months to discover and correct.

EMPLOYMENT APPLICATION
SHANNON & LUCHS COMPANY
Property Management Department

1. Applicant's Name _____ Age _____
Address _____ Phone (Home) _____ (Work) _____
Married (yes)___ (no)___ No. in Family _____
                            (Adults)   (Children)
Social Security No. _____
2. Job Desired _____
        (Res. Mgr., Engineer, Porter, Elevator Oper., Janitor, Charwoman, etc.)
Desire Quarters (yes)___ (no)___
3. Present Employer's Name_____ Phone_____
                 Real estate firm or owner
Address_____
Name of Supervisor or Res. Mgr._____ Phone_____
How long employed at present job_____ Salary _____
                           (week or month)
Reason for leaving _____
Explain Duties _____

Previous Employer's Name_____ Phone _____
Name of Supervisor or Res. Mgr._____ Phone_____
How long employed? From_____ To_____ Salary _____
                           (week or month)
Reason for leaving _____
Explain duties _____

4. Check either "Yes" or "No" to each of the following:
   a. Can you make minor plumbing repairs?   (yes)___ (no)___
   b. Can you make minor electrical repairs?   (yes)___ (no)___
   c. Can you do any painting?   (yes)___ (no)___
   d. Can you do any plastering?   (yes)___ (no)___
   e. Are you familiar with air conditioning system? (yes)___ (no)___
   f. Are you familiar with oil burner operation?   (yes)___ (no)___
   g. Are you familiar with automatic stoker opr.? (yes)___ (no)___
   h. Are you familiar with hand-fired furnace operation? (yes)___ (no)___
   i. Are you familiar with steam heating systems? (yes)___ (no)___
   j. Are you familiar with hot water heating systems? (yes)___ (no)___
   k. Do you hold a D. C. Engineering license   (yes)___ (no)___
      If answer is "yes", what class   _____
   l. Are you a licensed elevator operator?   (yes)___ (no)___
   m. Do you operate a switchboard?   (yes)___ (no)___
5. Attach any additional papers, letters of recommendation, etc. to this application.
Interviewed by_____ First Impression _____
Use reverse of this application for references investigation findings.
If applicant is hired, file this sheet in owner's file.

An adequate application-for-employment form, as illustrated by the above form, should be one of the bases of investigation of prospective employees.

TRAINING PROGRAMS FOR EMPLOYEES

It is not the purpose of this text to discredit the personnel programs of the typical business organization. Yet our broad observation of the normal procedures in the average office we have visited and studied has revealed an abysmal negligence in the matter of training new employees. Strangely enough, the typical business man is not as considerate of the performance of a new associate as he is of his new car. When a new automobile is purchased, it is tenderly broken in for the first several thousand miles. But when the new employee reports for work, he is usually instructed about like this: "Here is your desk. Start right in. If you have any problems, everyone will be glad to help you." Nobody takes the new employee aside and carefully explains the firm's operating policies, ideals, and objectives. The new employee is left to learn his job by himself and to pick up whatever knowledge he can get about how and why the organization functions. Usually he is immediately thrown into his work up to his neck. There is no *break in,* no easing up to the ultimately high speeds of full production, and no five-hundred-mile check-up. It is amazing that employees perform as well as they do. Certainly it is not because of adequate or sympathetic training.

Now, it is not always possible for the chief executive of a busy organization to take the time to properly instruct a new employee in every phase of the new job. But there is no valid excuse for a failure to give that proper instruction. The only way to avoid spending the time is to create shortcuts which will get the same result without the time involvement. For example, in some organizations an employee manual will have been prepared which has been departmentalized to provide written instructions which are given each new employee. These instructions, which are prepared for every job from executive to elevator man, should contain the following information:

1. The general conditions of employment, such as hours of work, holidays, sick leave, and vacations.
2. The policies of the organization as they affect public relations, the employee's attitude, and the employee's future.
3. A complete discussion of the particular job—how it is done and its meaning and importance.

HOW TO KEEP EMPLOYEES

Since employees are the principal resource of the property manager, it is as important to keep trained workers as it is to keep clients. For without the employees, the character of the management service rendered will deteriorate and the clients will soon disappear.

The fundamental requirement of satisfied employees is adequate compensation. Let us agree at the outset that no amount of palaver and backslapping will substitute for a full pay envelope. Too many property managers fail in this responsibility to their employees. They hire additional people in order to increase the business. They charge the same rates for these people as they do for themselves, yet they seek to hire them for a fraction of what they reserve for themselves. In the long run, employees are keen to the ratio of their "split." If they think that the boss is taking too big a cut, if they feel that they are being taken advantage of, they will be disgruntled and that attitude will show up in every contact they make.

Every employer should constantly ask himself this question about each of his workers: "Am I paying Jones just a little more than he could get from anyone else who knows his value as well as I do?" It is axiomatic that an employee should be worth more to his employer than to anyone else. In most cases it is a matter of personnel failure when a man is forced to leave a firm and go elsewhere in order to get more money. It is the result of either lack of fair pay by the employer or a failure to convince the man that the firm has as good a future as that of its competitor. In either case, it is failure.

Cash remuneration is only one aspect considered by today's employee in rating the monetary value of a job. Often of equal importance are so-called fringe benefits which are offered as an added inducement to employment and as a means of ensuring longevity of business association. As taxes on cash wages have increased with earnings, more employees give serious consideration to collateral emoluments. Important among these are provisions for retirement, hospitalization, medical care, group insurance, physical disaster protection, paid holidays, and vacations.

Conceding then that the rate of pay is fundamental, let us look at other methods of keeping employees over a long period of years during which they are happy with their work. There is an old cliché, probably coined by employers, that "money isn't everything." Oddly enough, there is a great deal of truth in that statement. Most people are lethargic about making changes in their employment, especially if they are happy in their work. If they are confident that they are getting fair treatment from their boss, and if they feel that their job is secure, they will be reluctant to take up new work in a new environment for a few dollars more a week or month. In the light of this fact, it is wise for the employer to set up an operating program under which he deliberately sets out *to increase his employees' ties to their jobs.* It is just as sound to point out added values to an employee as it is to a prospective client. Some of these added values, which will result in greater employee satisfaction, are attained by the practices outlined in the next few paragraphs.

Promoting Congeniality (Not Familiarity)

The average person is gregarious; he enjoys the people with whom he is associated. As his friendship for them grows, his reluctance to part with their company also increases. Many successful organizations sponsor the publication of house organs which keep the employees in touch with one another and give recognition to significant service. It is not necessary that a house organ be an expensive, handsomely printed paper. It can just as well be mimeographed if it is carefully and interestingly written.

Another method of promoting wholesome congeniality is through regularly scheduled recreational affairs. Bowling leagues, dinner meetings, golf outings all tend to create traditional good times if they are well planned and regularly held.

Congeniality in human relations is founded upon mutual trust. If you want good workers, trust them. If you have an employee you do not trust, do not make his life and yours miserable by prolonging the relationship. Find out at once and *for certain* whether or not he is trustworthy. If he is not, get rid of him. If he is, decide he is, and throw away your doubts. It is important for your people to *know* that you trust them, for only then will they completely trust you. Without such mutual confidence, there can be no true congeniality.

Inspiring Confidence in the Organization's Future

There is an old shibboleth to the effect that "nothing succeeds like success." For generations our ancestors gave their support to kings because they were somehow symbols of success. There is an expression among local politicians which goes, "nobody likes a broken skate."

Now, all of these sayings apply to employees. They want to be associated with a firm, or an individual, who is *going places,* even if they are not particularly ambitious themselves. They want to feel that their employer will be successful in any kind of business, because one of their basic desires is security. They want to work for and with a man who faces the future with confidence, who is anxious to succeed, who, in short, is obviously ambitious.

No good husband takes his problems home at night. No good employer ever lets his employees know of his worries or ever seems depressed by the turn of events. Such attitudes are infectious. Wherever there is a disheartened executive, it is likely that an entire organization is down at the mouth.

One of the prime elements of this sort of employee confidence can be born out of the kind of treatment the employee gets when he wants or needs time off. If he feels that he will not be paid when ill, he might worry himself sick thinking about it. If he feels that his employer will not allow a reasonable time off for purely personal business, then he will probably lie about his excuses for absence. Very few people abuse privileges. If they do, they are not the kind of people who will be wanted as employees. If they do not, you will never lose by granting their requests. Generosity begets gratitude. A grateful employee will never deliberately do you harm.

Encouraging Personal Development

The old-time Scrooge-type employer was always afraid that his employees would become well known and well respected, that they would steal his business. He subscribed to what he imagined was the *divine right of proprietorship*. Realistic men at the head of property management organizations know that they can stay at the top only so long as their tenure of that position is justified by personal ability. Moreover, they know that since *man* is the basis of management, their organization will be bigger and better if they have a group of well-known, well-respected men, than if they have a group of colorless dolts. There is a satisfaction in leading a pack of greyhounds and no joy whatever in being at the head of a procession of snails.

Every human being has a yearning for significance and is happier when he is able to employ some of his time in activities which tend to lift him from the mine run of people. The employer who recognizes that the first duty of his employees is to themselves does not need to be frightened or depressed. He rather should make certain that in gratifying *their* desire for significance, his employees also add to the importance of the organization. Thus, the employer should send his people into trade and community activities and should give them sufficient time to do a good job on real estate board committees, Red Cross drives, and civic activities. He should encourage membership in professional societies, writing for trade papers, and preparing and delivering speeches. By so doing, he will force himself to act similarly in an outgoing way, to the ultimate benefit of his whole public relations program.

Personal Interest in Employees

One of the reasons politicians go around kissing babies is that it pays dividends at election time. The employer who can stimulate a genuine interest in the welfare of his employees, who can remember personal details about their families, and who is thoughtful enough to render kind little services at times of importance to his employees will build a tight and loyal corps of people.

There are certain times when all people need these kindnesses to round out their happiness—at Christmas, at the birth of new babies, at weddings. At these times there is special significance to kindness. A small present, the offer of a loan, or the expression of sympathy in the right manner is invaluable to human relations. Very frequently people fail to write a note to a person whose mother has died because "I can't think of anything to say; it's so superficial." These people fail to get the whole point of normal reaction. However trite it may be to visit the sick or comfort the afflicted, it is an expression of good will as old as man and a factor in building enduring friendships.

DEALING WITH LABOR UNIONS

Employees in most of the nation's big-city buildings have been completely organized for many years. Generally speaking, the labor unions that represent these employees are old, well-established organizations headed by responsible men. Although, from one point of view, the aims and objectives of these unions are contrary to the interests of building owners and managers, trade unions are a definite part of the American economy, and the ability to deal successfully with such unions and their men is today a major goal of real estate management.

An enlightened point of view for management in connection with its dealings with labor unions is that under which management deals vigorously to maintain labor conditions in line with the general trends of the economy, and to keep its working conditions at the level of the best current practice. This does not mean that management should be a *foe* of labor or that management's aims and objectives should be to keep the price of labor at the lowest possible level.

The relationship between an individual property manager, or an individual management firm, with local labor unions can either be extremely helpful or extremely harmful. Good relations with unions are not necessarily based upon the manager's capitulation to all of labor's demands, but rather on fairness and reliability in all dealings with unions and their members. If good relations exist, labor unions can be extremely helpful in disciplining personnel, recruiting desirable new help, and in settling labor disputes. In the absence of prejudice, the principles of good relations with labor unions are virtually the same as the principles of good public relations in any and every area of business.

REVIEW QUESTIONS

1. Upon what should the property manager's dealings with labor be based?
2. How would you look for a bookkeeper if your present employee resigned?
3. Suggest a method of indoctrinating a new receptionist in her job.
4. What is the basis of good employee-employer relations?
5. Name the principles which should be followed by an employer when employing.
6. What methods would you use in encouraging your employees?
7. What methods can an employer use to see that his employees remain with him over the years? What is the value of low employee turnover?

SELECTED REFERENCES

Beckwith, A. T. "Staffing the Management Office." *Journal of Property Management,* Fall 1961, pp. 26–29.

Draper, Kenneth. "Training Personnel for the Real Estate Management Business." *Journal of Property Management,* Winter 1961, pp. 119–123.

The Real Estate Management Department: How to Establish and Operate It. 2d ed. Chicago, Institute of Real Estate Management, 1967. 148p.

CHAPTER 26

Records, Accounting, Tax Service, Research

INTRODUCTION

There are three general purposes for record keeping in property management: to produce data useful in determining management policy; to obtain necessary figures for the proper filing of tax returns; to control and account for cash and other physical property.

These general purposes may be served effectively by widely differing sets of records or systems. Everything depends upon the size of the management organization, the type and variety of properties, and the individual characteristics of the manager. The exact forms and styles to be used are flexible, but adequate if the basic purposes are served.

Before the nineteen thirties, there were few individuals, or institutions, who owned more than one property. This era of foreclosure brought groups of properties into the hands of single owners or operators. This circumstance, coupled with the natural development of management technique under sponsorship of The Institute of Real Estate Management, provided impetus for improvements in accounting and record procedure. Many firms have made their procedures conform to those originally specified by an institutional client or have set up their own standards.

THE REPORT TO THE OWNER

The primary record to be produced is the monthly report to the owner. All other records are secondary as either necessary to operation of the property or used for interpretation of the data in the monthly report. The monthly report in its simplest form is an *accounting* to the owner of money received and money paid out. The style used by the manager to present this information can be most helpful to the owner, or it can be confusing. The report should logically cover the four principal factors of operation: *sales* (gross revenues billed, occupancy, rental rates); *collections* (cash receipts, uncollected balances, evictions); *operations* (personnel, expenses, purchasing); and *maintenance* (repairs, alterations, physical).

A monthly report for a small property does not present serious difficulty. It should show in detail, and in total, the income from tenants, as well as collections and unpaid balances. It should also list disbursements in classified order, giving details of payee and nature of expenditure. All of this information may by given on one page.

For larger properties, the report should be in summary form (such as Sample Form 1), with supporting schedule (Sample Form 2), or schedules, giving further details in full. The summary readily enables both owner and manager to understand the general results for the month, and any questions will be answered in the accompanying detailed schedules.

Records of Income

Transient hotels have long used the *transcript* system of recording income charged to occupants, and of accounting for unpaid revenues. Its use is almost mandatory for the sake of accuracy in properties housing more than a few tenants. Many *agents* still use the antiquated method of preparing merely a list of names, and amounts collected, with the inevitable result that inaccuracies occur as to periods covered and amounts due.

The transcript is another name for a report of collections. It is a record of the tenants' names and their space identifications (room numbers should be shown). In order to account for all rentable space, all vacant units as well as occupied units are listed on the transcript. It is also a record of the amount of rent (and other charges if any) which accrued for the month, whether paid or not, and it shows amounts remaining unpaid at the month-end.

SHADYSIDE APARTMENTS BUILDING
SUMMARY OF RECEIPTS AND DISBURSEMENTS
MONTH of November

INCOME:	BILLED	COLLECTED
Rentals	$15,300.00	
Other...	600.00	
Total Income	$15,900.00	$15,673.00
OPERATING EXPENSES:		
Janitor and house..		$ 2,340.00
Heat, light and power		2,494.00
Repairs and maintenance		854.00
Administrative		1,863.00
Total (per figure 2)..		$ 7,551.00
NET OPERATING RECEIPTS		$ 8,122.00
OTHER RECEIPTS:		
Fire loss recovery..		$ 478.00
Total Net Receipts..		$ 600.00
OTHER DISBURSEMENTS:		
Fire damage repairs..		$ 529.00
NET RECEIPTS REMITTED		$ 8,071.00

SAMPLE FORM 1

SHADYSIDE APARTMENTS BUILDING
OPERATING EXPENSES PAID
MONTH of November

JANITOR AND HOUSE:

Wages:

I. Dooman—elevator operator	$400.00	
S. Skinner—elevator operator	400.00	
R. Bingham—elevator operator	420.00	
J. Lind—receiving clerk	460.00	
P. Connor—porter	480.00	$2,160.00

Cleaning:

Rollins Supply 45.00

Exterminator:

Shur-Deth Exterminators 30.00

Window shades:

North Side Shade Co.—cleaning 105.00

Total janitor and house............................$2,340.00

HEAT, LIGHT AND POWER:

Wages:

R. Stone—engineer	$900.00	
J. Baker—assistant engineer	540.00	$1,440.00

Fuel:

Gas Company... 586.00

Electricity:

Electric Company 390.00

Water:

Dept. of Water... 78.00

Total heat, light, and power $2,494.00

REPAIRS AND MAINTENANCE:

Decorating:

Superior Decorators—public space	$ 75.00	
Superior Decorators—apartments	345.00	$ 420.00

Electrical:

Midway Electric—supplies 54.00

Elevator:

Otis Elevator Co.—monthly charge........................... 158.00

Carpentry:

Hagstrom Lumber Co. 45.00

Plumbing:

New Market Hardware....................................... 96.00

Sundry:

New Market Hardware....................................... 81.00

Total repairs and maintenance ....$ 854.00

ADMINISTRATIVE:

Manager—I. Rogers ....$ 600.00

Management... 627.00

Employee Benefits:

Payroll taxes	$202.00	
Group insurance	$120.00	$ 322.00

Advertising:

Evening American 162.00

Telephone:

Bell Telephone Company 53.00

Sundry:

Petty cash—stamps, etc.	44.00	
Tablet & Ticket—name cards	24.00	
Horder's—stationery	31.00	99.00

Total administrative...................................$1,863.00

TOTAL OPERATING COSTS $7,551.00

THE TRANSCRIPT

Name of Building   SHADYSIDE APARTMENTS
Street and No.   4000 Lakeshore Drive   City   Shadyside
Revenue for the Month of   November
And Accounts Receivable as of   November 30th

Apartment (or Other Unit) Number	Number of Rooms	NAME OF TENANT	Date Lease Expires *New Lease Has Been Obtained Effective on Expiration of Present Lease	CHARGES FOR CURRENT MONTH			Debit Balance *(Credit Balance) at Beginning of Month	Total Debits	Less Collections During the Month	Debit Balance *(Credit Balance) at End of Month
				Rent	Extra Services	Total Charges				
50	4	JONES	May 31	285	10	295	90	385	355	30
51	3	SMITH	*Nov. 30	240	9	249	0	249	249	0
52	4	MANAGER		0	0	0	0	0	0	0
53	5	VACANT		0	0	0	0	0	0	0
OTHERS	192	OCCUPIED		14,775	581	15,356	1,110	16,466	15,069	1,397
OTHERS	32	VACANT		0	0	0	0	0	0	0
	240	TOTALS		15,300	600	15,900	1,200	17,100	15,673	1,427

OCCUPANCY DATA

Occupied   199   84.3 per cent
Vacant   37   15.7 per cent
Total   236   100. per cent
Manager   4
240

"OTHER CHARGES" DETAILED

Electricity $345
Carpentry   235
Bulbs   20
Total $600

SAMPLE FORM 3

This type of record is shown in Sample Form 3; the cross footings of figures at the bottom must balance. In other words, the transcript proves that the sum of rental and other income earned, plus beginning balances owing, less collections made, produces a result equal to unpaid balances at the end of the month.

Subsidiary records which are the source of information from which the transcript is prepared may vary greatly, depending upon the type of property and methods of office procedure. Generally, the manager should maintain some type of accounts receivable ledger in which an account is carried for each tenant. Such ledger may be a stock loose-leaf sheet for a post binder, or it may be in the form of a card inserted in a *visible record* tray. The tenant ledger page, or card, contains name of tenant, space description, terms of lease, and columns for entries of charges, credits, and balances.

Offices having a large volume of rent collection work may use a machine bookkeeping system or an electronic data processing system. A bill or invoice to the tenant is prepared: one copy is kept as a *ledger,* or receivable record, until paid, and one copy is used as a receipt to be signed and given to the tenant when payment is received. More copies may be prepared for branch offices.

Lease records take a variety of forms. The description on the tenant ledger may be adequate in a small office, but in a large office some additional record or control of leases is necessary. One system (see Sample Form 4) involves the maintenance by the accounting department of a *visible record* tray of cards, one card for each rentable unit in a building. On each card is recorded the unit number, the tenant's name, the number of rooms, the expiration date of the existing lease, and a brief note about special clauses in the lease.

At regular intervals the accounting department examines these cards, and gives the proper executive a list of leases expiring in the near future. After the

RECORD OF LEASE

SHADYSIDE APARTMENTS

Lessee may cancel

in event of death

APT. NO.	NO. ROOMS	NAME	RENTAL	SPEC. CLAUSE	EXPIRATION	
• 50	• 4	• Jones	285	•	May	31

SAMPLE FORM 4

renting office has obtained the signature of the tenant, the new lease goes to the accounting department and a new card is prepared. Then, the old and new card and the new lease go to the proper executive. The lease is filed and the new card returned to the tray. Thereafter, the card remains in the tray for general reference and comparison with the transcript to determine that proper rent charges have been made.

Other forms and records essential to the handling of income are a lease application, the lease itself, or a modified short form of *rental agreement,* and the receipt. All of these may vary according to local custom and practice, and standard forms are usually developed by the local Board of Realtors.

For purposes of control, it is desirable that a receipt be issued for *every* item of cash received, and that a carbon copy of the receipt be retained. The copies may be used as a ledger posting source and as a basis for determining daily total receipts for bank deposits. The copy also may be audited subsequent to issuance, in order to verify that the collector properly recorded on the receipt the rental period covered by the payment.

Records for Expenses

In many small management offices having only a few employees, ordering of services, supplies, and repairs may be done orally with no record kept, so that complete reliance is placed on the memory of the individual. In the larger or more modern offices, written orders are issued for all purchases, so that no misunderstanding on the terms of the order will develop. Thus, invoices may not be approved for payment unless first compared with the order. In large properties which operate with a receiving room, an extra copy of the purchase order is sent to the receiving clerk so that he may anticipate arrival and verify the quantity and condition of supplies received.

There is room for individuality in the styling of checks used for payment of bills. Most managers use a plain check and note on its back the dates of invoices covered. Others send the bill along with the check, and ask that it be receipted. Still, others use voucher checks which provide for description of the items being paid in the *voucher portion* of the check.

If the owner lacks confidence in the manager to the extent that he requires bills to be receipted by the vendor, then he should not engage the manager. The practice of reporting bills paid that are not paid (permitting the manager to use the funds for personal gain temporarily), has been indulged in not infrequently in the past. The code of ethics of The Institute of Retail Management precludes intermingling of owner's funds with those of the manager, and if this policy is followed, there is no need to have bills receipted.

Methods of reporting expenditures to the owner were touched upon earlier in this chapter. Because of the wide divergence in the nature of properties operated, there has been no universally accepted style of classifying disbursements. Nevertheless there is ample need for logical but simple methods of classification and presentation of data on disbursements. Institutional owners frequently prescribe the classification style to be used in their properties. Office building managers have accomplished much in standardization of their account classification. The following are major groupings into which they classify operating expenses:

1. *Operating:* cleaning and janitor (supplies and labor), electrical (current, repairs and labor), heating (fuel, repairs, and labor), air conditioning (supplies, repairs and labor), plumbing (repairs), elevators (repairs and operator wages), and general (administrative, etc.)
2. *Maintenance:* tenant alterations, tenant decorating, and general repairs
3. *Fixed Charges:* insurance, property taxes, and depreciation

Federal housing bodies have designed extensive systems of account classification, which include the following typical groupings of expenses: renting expense, administrative, operating, maintenance, depreciation, taxes and insurance, and financial.

Many forms have been developed for listing expenses by type in alphabetical order (eliminating the possibility of logical comparisons) such as: ash removal, advertising, boiler repairs, and decorating.

For apartment buildings in general, a modified version of the uniform account classification used in hotels is very effective. This style is illustrated in Sample Form 2, and classifies expenses into four general groups with subsidiary classifications in each group. Any style of grouping which summarizes comprehensively and which is kept up consistently is useful in making management decisions.

Auxiliary Records

The foregoing discussion has been directed primarily to the problems and methods for *reporting to the owner.* The actual routines involved in management may embrace a large number of auxiliary forms and records, many of which are discussed in other chapters.

When arrangements for decorating a tenant's space are completed, a written order should be prepared with one copy to the decorator, one to the tenant, and one for accounting. Stock forms for this purpose may be purchased, or they may be individualized for a building. Their use limits the likelihood of misunderstanding.

Buildings maintaining their own decorating crew need a reporting system in order to control costs. A regular decorating order should be prepared in advance for every job, so that a permanent record of work done may be had. The head painter should prepare a written weekly report showing total man-hours of each worker, listed by jobs. He should also record quantities of materials used on each job. It then becomes possible for the accounting department to compute total labor and material costs for each job, and this affords a basis for analysis and comparison of alternative methods.

Many variations of payroll accounting systems are offered commercially, and where large numbers of employees are involved, these are desirable. A memorandum such as Sample Form 5 is submitted with the paid bills, if there are very few employees. A summary such as Sample Form 6 is desirable where there are five or more employees, because it gives proof of accuracy and facilitates understanding.

Normally, the property manager is charged with the duty of maintaining social security records and filing of reports. The payroll summary, therefore, serves as a source from which to post entries into the payroll ledger. That ledger in turn produces the information necessary for preparation of social security tax returns.

Whether the manager is engaged to handle all insurance phases or not, he should nevertheless keep fully advised on the status of all insurance coverages. The best record (see Sample Form 7) is a separate card for each policy. However, more policies may be recorded on the same card, if they provide identical coverage, run for the same period, and expire on the same date. The necessary information should be obtained by actual inspection of the policy, because questions of insurance coverage and losses often confront the manager.

If the person receiving a tenant's service request cannot personally supervise its disposition, he should prepare a written order directing someone else to perform the task. This order should specify name and address of tenant, date issued, name of person to whom addressed, date of completion, and nature of work performed. The person who performed the work should then return the order to the main office, so that the manager may note conclusion and determine whether further attention is needed (including a charge for the work if proper).

MEMO OF DEDUCTIONS

EMPLOYER___Shadyside Apartments___Employee ___I. Rogers___

Salary from___November 1___to___November 15___ $ 300

Value of room or apartment $ 142.50

Total Pay Earned $ 442.50

Deductions:

F.I.C.A.	$ 14.40
Federal Withholding	41.20
State Withholding	6.00
Group Insurance	15.00
Other	0
Total Deductions	$ 76.60

NET CHECK # 2115 .... $223.40

M—126

SAMPLE FORM 5

PAYROLL SUMMARY

BUILDING Shadyside Apartments   PAY PERIOD Nov. 1–Nov. 15   DATE PAID November 15

NAME	Ex-emp-tions	Occupation	Monthly Rate	Period From	Period To	Earnings Salary	Earnings Extra	Earnings Total	FICA	Deductions Fed. withholding	Deductions State withholding	Deductions Ins.	Deductions Other	Deductions Total	Net Pay	Check Number
I. Doorman	4	Elevator Operator	$400	11–1	11–15	$200		200	9.60	11.60	4.00	15.00		40.20	159.80	2108
S. Skinner	3	Elevator Operator	400	11–1	11–15	200		200	9.60	16.00	4.00	15.00		44.60	155.40	2109
R. Bingham	2	Elevator Operator	420	11–1	11–15	210		210	10.08	23.10	4.20	15.00		52.38	157.62	2110
J. Lind	4	Receiving Clerk	460	11–1	11–15	230		230	11.04	16.10	4.60	15.00		46.74	183.26	2111
P. Connor	2	Porter	480	11–1	11–15	240		240	11.52	28.80	4.80	15.00		60.12	179.88	2112
J. Baker	3	Ass't. Engineer	540	11–1	11–15	270		270	12.96	29.00	5.40	15.00		62.36	207.64	2113
R. Stone	5	Engineer	900	11–1	11–15	450		450	21.60	51.10	9.00	15.00		96.70	353.30	2114
I. Rogers	2	Manager	600	11–1	11–15	300		300	14.40	41.20	6.00	15.00		76.60	223.40	2115
TOTALS						2,100		2,100	100.80	216.90	42.00	120.00		479.70	1,620.30	

```
┌─────────────────────────────────────────────────────────────────────┐
                         INSURANCE CARD
 Jan   Feb   Mar   Apr   May   Jun   Jul   Aug   Sep   Oct   Nov   Dec
       EXPIRES              Name of Assured
 ─────────────────────────
   Month         Day
 Year                       Location
 ─────────────────────────────────────────────────────────────────────
 Policy No.                 Company
                                               Amount
 ─────────────────────────────────────────────────────────────────────
                            Property
                                               Premium
 ─────────────────────────────────────────────────────────────────────
                                               Rate
 ─────────────────────────────────────────────────────────────────────
                                               Term
 ─────────────────────────────────────────────────────────────────────
                                               Register
 ─────────────────────────────────────────────────────────────────────
                            Broker
                                               Form
 ─────────────────────────────────────────────────────────────────────
   Remington Rand, Inc.           Library Bureau Form Cat. No. 30–8005.1
└─────────────────────────────────────────────────────────────────────┘
```

SAMPLE FORM 7

ANALYSIS

The foregoing discussions deal with accounting control of money and property. Far too little attention has been devoted by managers to the equally important need for statistical and analytical data. Many opportunities occur, especially in large buildings, for trend analyses which cannot be made by merely reviewing the monthly list of receipts and disbursements.

For example, it had long been customary to compute occupancy of property only on the last day of the month. No clear indication of any trend may be obtained from this inaccurate data. There are, however, at least three possible methods of computation. First and foremost, a true computation may be made by counting the facilities which actually produce income for the period. (Note, a room rented for a half month counts only as half occupied for the whole month.) Accurate computations of rental per room may be obtained month by month simply by dividing total rentals earned by the number of rooms from which those rentals were earned.

A highly useful comparison, made available by these reports, is the rental earned per occupied square foot of rentable area. In office building management, the *square foot* of rentable floor area is universally accepted as the unit of measure. The same unit may be used for residential properties, though the more popular unit is the *room*.

There is a third unit of measure which has never gained much support, namely the *rent value* basis.

Apt. No.	Rooms	Square Feet	Rental Value	Rental Earned
A...........	4	560	$165.00	$165.00
B...........	4	510	120.00	120.00
C...........	4	540	130.00	130.00
D...........	4	550	165.00	....
Totals	16	2160	$580.00	$415.00

AVERAGE OCCUPANCY — *Percentage*

Computed on rooms basis .... 75.00 (= 12/16)
Computed on square feet .... 74.54 (= 560 + 510 + 540/2160)
Computed on rent value................. 71.55 (= 415/580)

THE THREE METHODS OF COMPUTING OCCUPANCY

Many other ratios may be analyzed from these classified reports, such as heating cost per square foot of radiation, average decorating cost per room, ratio of decorating cost to rental earned, and ratio of total operating expenses to gross income.

A unique system of observing the trend of operations is followed by one realtor who presents to his owner each month a statement showing income and expenses for the twelve months ended that date. The form is designed so that it can be compared *shingle style* to similar reports for prior months. Thus, it can readily be observed whether the net earnings in the twelve months ended, for example, November 30 are better or worse than the twelve months ended August 31. This idea can be modified by tabulating on one page the cumulative twelve-month figure (each month) for gross income and the cumulative twelve-month figure (each month) for net income from operations.

The annual summary of operations (being a simple addition of twelve monthly reports) is reasonably easy to prepare and is of inestimable value in self-examination. Comparison of the annual report with those of other years can yield startling observations. Comparison of ratios of various items of expense for the year with similar data in other buildings becomes almost an exciting game and often challenges the manager to a remedy that would not otherwise be obtained. Yet, too many managers permit this great opportunity for improvement of results, and incidentally for solidifying their owner relations, to slip away.

The Budget

A budget is an excellent—in fact, essential—aid to effective and intelligent management. It may be aptly described as a thoughtful prediction of what will take place in the period indicated. Its form should be the same as that of the annual summary of operations. Its preparation need not be complicated, if records of performance in prior periods are available; but, in the absence of such data, a real challenge confronts the manager. He then must draw on his experience, refer to analyses of comparable properties, and exercise care in estimates of income and expenses.

A budget should not deliberately be constructed as a background against which actual results look favorable, nor should it set goals beyond the reach of reality. Its purpose is to serve as a warning when comparisons of actual results month by month show major variations from the predictions in the budget. As a long term *planning device,* it also assists in planning major policy adjustments on rental rates, on major repair, and on improvement projects. When the manager studies results over a number of years and sets up a prediction for the current year, a broad perspective develops which it is not possible to attain in the routine of day-to-day work.

Corporate Accounting

Many properties in modern times are held in corporate ownership for the benefit of a number of investors, former bondholders, syndicate investors, etc. Competent accounting personnel in the manager's office may be required to render a full corporate or fiscal service, which naturally produces additional income to the manager. In effect, this service begins where the manager's report leaves off. It contemplates full general ledger records.

The manager's monthly report is limited in scope because it basically is concerned with cash. It therefore tends to ignore accruals of income and expense which have not been collected or paid or which have been collected or paid in advance. If one tenant pays six months' rent in advance, the monthly report records it as income, but on the corporate owner's books it will appear as income only when it is earned. If the exterior of the property is painted, the expense will be paid in one month, but corporate accounting permits the expense to be charged monthly over a period of years. Therefore, the statement of net income on an accrual basis becomes more accurately descriptive month by month.

Normally, officers of a corporation are persons having another occupation. Consequently, the bulk of the administrative work falls upon the property manager. This may include correspondence and interviews with the investors, preparation and submission of annual reports to investors, investigation and analysis of property tax assessments, and supervision and control of borrowing arrangements of the corporation. These functions vary somewhat from the normal management function, yet they are nevertheless closely allied.

Whereas, banks, trust companies, and public accountants may offer fiscal services, the corporation property owner rarely can find a more satisfactory method of administration than that available through the services of a competent property manager.

TAX SERVICE

As our society moves on to higher and higher standards of living, the complexities of life are increased; the results are greater and greater burdens of responsibility and expense placed upon the government. For generations we have been increasing public responsibility in the field of education, we have required a broader and more efficient type of police and fire protection, we have insisted upon an enlarged program of public health, and we have been constantly exploring new horizons of public welfare.

In a democracy it seems inevitable that the people, who wield the sovereign power, will constantly enact legislation designed to broaden the comforts of life. In the final analysis this means that an increasing proportion of the national income will be acquired by taxation in order to implement the mandates of the people. This taxation has become increasingly important as a part of the cost of doing business and as a part of the responsibility of those who administer business.

The increase in the importance of tax analysis service has already been reflected in a steady growth in the number of professionals engaged in the field. There are countless tax consultants, tax accountants, and tax lawyers who devote their entire professional careers to problems of reducing the tax burdens of clients whom they represent. Their growth is due to the fact that more and more personal and business decisions are made on the basis of the tax implications of a course of action. This is true, to a great or greater extent, in the field of real estate as in the field of business as a whole.

We have seen throughout this text that the scope of activity of the property manager has constantly increased throughout the history of real estate management. The complexities of the problem of property administration are responsible for the evolution of the manager's duties and the change in the form of real estate ownership. The owners of income real estate are more and more disposed to turn properties over to managers for *complete* administration. The manager is not only responsible for the physical operation of the property, he also assumes full responsibility for the collateral activities related to its ownership. This has brought property management face to face with the administration of the tax program of the real estate involved, and with the research program vital to the correct implementation of decisions in the entire field of property administration.

The manager of larger income properties today has a complex series of tax problems. These include local real estate property taxes, personal property taxes, state property taxes, social security taxes, corporation taxes, income taxes, excise taxes, and sales taxes. These tax problems require the development of skills by the manager or members of his organization. The first of these skills involves duties of an administrative nature in the tax program. Pertinent records bearing upon taxes must be faithfully kept, in order that tax reports may be prepared and filed on behalf of clients. Tax calendars must be prepared to ensure the prompt preparation and filing of such reports, as well as the prompt payment of the amounts involved. The entire process requires administrative interpretation founded upon a thorough knowledge of the tax regulations covering each individual situation.

The second area of skill envisions activities of an analytical nature. The manager or the tax department must know the application of the law if he is to find opportunities for a saving to the client. Property owners must be counseled on the advantages to be gained from various programs of operation as against alternate programs. Finally, it is the duty of the real estate manager, as a representative of perhaps scores of real estate owners, to exert influence on the public authorities either for more efficient public administration or for a favorable interpretation of existing regulations.

In larger operations where tax consultants, tax accountants, and tax lawyers are either engaged by or are under retainer to the property management firm or individual property owners, the real estate manager is frequently placed in the position of the owner's representative; thus it is often the case that he must counsel with professionals in these specialized fields. This consultation cannot be adequately handled unless the manager, or a member of his organization, is sufficiently conversant with the specialty to make decisions intelligently on the owner's behalf. Certainly it is wise for the manager to prepare himself for this type of administration, since by so doing he not only increases the value of his services to the property owner, but justifies the base of his potential fee for real estate administration.

The most important duties that must be undertaken by the manager in administering an adequate tax service to clients, are discussed below.

Local Real Estate Taxes

The valuation placed on an individual property by the local assessor is the basis of the real estate tax bill. This assessment must be analyzed critically. In most cases the local assessor follows a manual of standards. The critical analysis of the assessment should be an audit of the assessed valuation on the basis of the provisions of the manual. Such an audit involves a verification of measurement—such as land frontage, depth, square feet of floor area, cubic capacity, etc. The age of the property and the amount of depreciation allowed should likewise be verified as well as the assessor's classification of the property and its unit replacement cost. In addition to the check on the factual background of the assessment, the analysis should substantiate all of the computations by which the total tax was extended. This would include the application of the tax rate to the recorded assessed valuation.

If the original analysis of the assessor's valuation indicates reason for a protest on the basis of an excessive assessment, such a protest should be prepared and made to the assessor before the assessment is recorded as final. If insufficient relief is obtained by means of this protest, the manager should present an appeal to the next higher authority—usually a board of tax appeals.

In the process of preparing and presenting a local protest, it may become the duty of the property manager on behalf of the property owner to choose and engage tax experts. When such is the case, the manager should exercise care to define exactly the basis of employment and to procure in writing, if possible, the fees for the service.

In addition to protest on the individual valuation, objections to the overall tax rate are frequently filed on a cooperative basis by many owners of real estate or real estate management firms. In this case it may become the responsibility of the individual manager to participate in the engagement of tax attorneys for such work, and to share in the underwriting of their fee. Where the real estate manager has complete responsibility for the administration of a given piece of property, it is his duty to see that adequate funds are available to pay real estate taxes and to see that these tax payments are made on or before date due. Wherever possible and desirable, reserve funds should be established for the payment of taxes. If such a procedure is not possible, arrangements must be made for temporary financing, in order to avoid expensive penalties for delinquency.

Local Personal Property Taxes

Many types of real estate are subject to assessment on the value of personal property in addition to local real estate taxes. In such cases it is necessary to prepare and file with the assessor a proper schedule of personal property subject to tax. This type of local taxation varies with local custom and usage, and it is vital for the real estate manager to be entirely familiar with local laws in order to take advantage of accepted practices. Here again it is the manager's responsibility to arrange for the timely payment of the tax.

State Property Taxes

In most areas the valuations for state property taxes usually coincide with the local assessor's figures. However, these valuations should be checked for the accuracy of assessment procedures as well as mathematical computations. If protest machinery is available and the valuations appear to be excessive, the property owner's interests should be represented in such protests.

Social Security Taxes

As the nominal employer or employer's agent, the real estate management office is responsible for the collection and payment of social security taxes, and for representing the property owner's interests as they may be influenced by the operation of the law.

Contributions to federal old age insurance must be arranged by the manager through the collection of employer and employee contributions, and accurate records must be kept. A large portion of this activity is made up of accounting department details.

The payment of state unemployment compensation taxes is also a matter of accounting department routine, but this tax requires administrative supervision. Its operation is an additional motivation for careful personnel selection designed to reduce worker turnover and minimize the number of benefit claims as well as the tax rate which applies. In many cases, the property owner's interest must be represented through the challenge of and opposition to claims made by former employees where the circumstances of dismissal make claims questionable.

Federal excise taxes on wages must be compiled where such taxes are payable, and proper returns (annual) must be computed and filed along with the tax payment.

Federal Income Taxes

Although most individual property owners are required to handle their own income tax problems based upon the inclusion of property income in their broader personal returns, corporations represented by property management firms in many cases rely upon the manager's accounting department for the preparation and filing of federal income tax schedules.

The largest area of service to property owners is focused on advice to clients concerning decisions which may be vitally influenced by income tax regulations. Such advice is extremely helpful to owners who do not themselves have an opportunity to become familiar with the complex income tax laws. Careful study of federal income taxes (and state income taxes where they exist) is an important aspect of the alert manager's job performance. In larger management organizations, it is desirable to have one member of the firm accept the responsibility of being fully informed about the federal income tax law.

Excise Taxes

In the operation of hotels, office buildings, and other large properties, it may become the responsibility of the real estate manager to collect federal excise taxes. They may include taxes on dues and admission, the sale of electric light bulbs, the charges for telephone messages, and others. Whenever the management of an individual building includes the operation of separate merchandise or service departments (such as restaurants, bars, drugstores, or telephone switchboards), the manager at the outset of his assignment should make a careful investigation of his responsibility with respect to the levy and collection of excise taxes. Frequently, managers have been embarrassed to find, after operating a certain type of enterprise for a number of months, that they are obligated for taxes which they failed to collect as the result of ignorance of the law.

Sales Taxes

In states having a sales tax law, a return must be prepared and the tax paid when taxable sales are conducted. The property manager may find that it is his responsibility to collect sales tax on electricity resale, newspapers, hotel food and beverage operations, gasoline and oil sales—in fact on any and all taxable goods sold in subsidiary operations which may come under the direct administration of the manager. Here again the manager should check local sales tax regulations at the outset of his management assignment in any building where sales are conducted.

BREADTH OF TAX SERVICE

Throughout this text we have discussed specialized fields of operation in which the manager is called upon to offer service. At the beginning we stressed that it is impossible for a manager to become an expert in all of the fields of specialization in the overall field of real estate management. In the operation of a one-man property management office, the individual property manager is limited by the amount of time available for study and by the amount of detailed knowledge which can be acquired and retained by one individual. It should be the objective of the manager to assemble a sufficient amount of knowledge in each of the areas of specialty to be able to intelligently discuss problems with his client and to capably select specialists whose efforts will be devoted to the property manager's interests.

In large real estate management organizations, it is possible to have a number of specialists as part of the firm's operations. Such large organizations should be made up of a group of experts in various fields, each of whom has gained authority through specialized training, specialized study, and specialized experience.

In the field of tax service to clients, the individual manager should be concerned mainly with basic routines and with the engagement of special tax counsel whenever it is needed. In large organizations, such counsel may be handled directly by the management firm, that is, if it embraces one or more persons whose tax studies have been sufficient to equip them with the required breadth of knowledge.

Research in Management

The use of research by business enterprises is a comparatively new activity. One might define business research as "any activity designed to increase the area of knowledge."

In the final analysis, *management* is largely a matter of making decisions. The word *decision* in the dictionary is defined as a process of deciding. To decide means to "determine authoritatively; to bring to a conclusive result or to resolve." In the process of deciding, one must rely upon one's knowledge. It is impossible to conceive of a fallacious decision based upon complete knowledge. The failure of management decisions must, therefore, be due to imperfect or incomplete data. Thus, the objective of management is to equip and fortify itself with as much factual data as possible, in order that decisions be as nearly perfect as possible.

Research is a matter of broadening the factual data upon which decisions are based. It is the process of enlarging the scope of one's knowledge. Research can and should be carried on in every field in which decisions are required.

Throughout this text we have endeavored to give students a modicum of knowledge. More than that, however, we have emphasized the need for constant reevaluation of management data, and for periodic reexamination of economic, political, and social conditions.

The property manager, who seeks to do an outstanding job in the field of real estate administration must continually recognize the need for additional data in order to justify the authenticity of his decisions. He will devote a portion of his time, or a portion of the efforts of his staff, to the gathering of information and the creation of ideas which may not be possessed by competitors. This is research.

There is virtually no limit to the program of research that can be carried on by the property manager or the property management organization. It can extend from the examination of the rent market to the study of paint. It can embrace the fields of sociology, psychology, engineering, and political science. The *range* of research is, in fact, of less importance than its *quality.*

One of the most common errors of all business research is to let it become subjective in nature. Too many people undertake investigations to confirm their judgment. Too few businessmen undertake investigations from a purely objective point of view—simply to find out more about a subject or where a trend is leading.

Real estate management is a business which is vitally concerned with economic, political, and social trends. During its brief history, many of these trends have operated in a manner adverse to the interest of property owners and real estate managers. Regardless of this fact, those managers who have been in possession of data which clearly indicated the direction of these trends were in the best position to cope with ensuing impacts.

In chapter 2 we pointed out that every real estate manager should be an active researcher in the field of the real estate market. Even the manager who operates individually should build regularly a data bank covering the operation of cause and effect which are outlined in that chapter. In larger organizations, a library should be established and, if possible, served by a full-time librarian. Rather than simply a library of books, this should be a collection of data files with cross-references for easy access to the information they contain. All appraisals, studies of buildings, press clippings on buildings, city plans, etc., should be sent to this library for filing rather than to the general file. Such data should be protected against loss and should be removed from the library for study only after a record of the withdrawal has been made with the librarian.

The opportunities for research are not restricted to the analysis of market or economic trends. A number of real estate management organizations conduct broad research into the wearing qualities of carpets, linens, electric light bulbs, and materials used in the maintenance of buildings. Research can also embrace time studies of personnel operations to the end of improving efficiency and ultimately reducing cost.

In addition to the practical benefits of research as a means of implementing sounder decisions, the program can be extremely valuable from a public relations standpoint. Press releases based on research findings represent a most desirable form of publicity, since they associate the manager or management firm with a higher level of knowledge. Moreover, it is an extremely effective aid to the sale of management service to exhibit to a prospective client a reference library or research laboratory.

The management firm that establishes a well-operated research program will soon find itself in possession of information which has broad value in the community. In some cases, this information and its interpretation can be profitably sold to individuals, firms, or agencies having a need for factual data. Even where opportunities do not exist for the sale of information gained through research, the public relations value of becoming a recognized authority in the real estate field is far greater than the cost of supporting such a program.

REVIEW QUESTIONS

1. Name the customary classifications under which operating expenses are grouped when reporting expenditures to the owner.
2. What is a *payroll summary?* When is it used and how? Prepare a sample.
3. What should a manager's monthly report to the owner include?
4. What is a *record of lease?* How and when should it be used?
5. What is meant by the *transcript system* of recording, and what is its value to the property manager and to the property owner?
6. How would you compute property occupancy?

7. What form or system for cost control would you use if your building employed its own crew of decorators?
8. To what effective use can annual reports be put?
9. What effective use can you make of a budget?
10. What are the general purposes of records in property management?
11. What system would you use when placing an order for decorating a unit?
12. What is meant by local real estate taxes? Explain.
13. What is the duty of the real estate manager who holds the complete responsibility of property operation with regard to real estate taxes?
14. Name some of the taxes with which a property manager will come into contact.
15. What are the property manager's responsibilities regarding excise taxes?
16. What are personal property taxes? Why are they important to the property manager?
17. Why is knowledge of the source of social security tax payments essential to the property manager?
18. Define business research.
19. What is the importance of research in management?
20. Does research have any public relations value to the individual property manager or the property management firm?
21. What skills should a property manager possess in dealing with the problem of taxes?

SELECTED REFERENCES

"Are you Overpaying Real Estate Taxes on Your Income Property?" *Mortgage and Real Estate Executives Report,* Aug. 1, 1973, p. 1–2.

DeSalvo, Joseph S. "Effects of the Property Tax on Operating and Investment Decisions of Rental Property Owners." *National Tax Journal,* Mar. 1971, pp. 45–50.

Glassman, Sidney. *Tools for Creative Property Management.* Chicago, Ill., Institute of Real Estate Management, 1974, 52p.
    See "Operating Statements as They Relate to the Property Manager."

Hanford, Lloyd D., Sr. "Budgets: Test of Management Conference." *Journal of Property Management,* Sept.–Oct. 1971, pp. 239–241.

Hanford, Lloyd D., Sr. *The Property Management Process.* Chicago, Institute of Real Estate Management, 1972. 86p.

CHAPTER 27

Insurance

INTRODUCTION

The inclusion of a chapter on insurance in a text primarily concerned with the field of real estate management is a natural outgrowth of the trend toward complete stewardship of properties on the part of real estate managers. The owner of a building is entitled to expect that he will be relieved of the burden of every detail incident to his ownership of the property.

One of the foremost problems of ownership is the matter of fully underwriting the risks as much as possible. Since these risks vary in different localities and under different operating conditions, it is normal to expect that the real estate manager, or real estate management firm, will become expert not only in appraising the extent of the risks involved, but also in knowing with whom these risks may be safely and adequately insured.

In addition to his interest in the writing of insurance as a service to his owner-client, the real estate manager has been motivated to enter this field as a service to his tenants as well. Over the years it has appeared desirable for the real estate manager to enlarge the service nature of his office to embrace the needs of the community. Certainly the writing of insurance for tenants and members of the general public is a logical by-product of the manager's close contact with the public.

In the insurance industry almost every aspect revolves around service. Anyone anticipating doing any sizeable amounts of insurance business should be prepared to be of service many times (not only at the initial sale) throughout the benefit period of the policy written.

By far the largest percentage of property managers have assumed the role of broker, rather than agent in their handling of insurance. There is a fine distinction between these two roles. The *broker* is a person or firm who represents the buyer of insurance. In such a capacity he determines the risk involved from the buyer's point of view, scans the insurance market for the best and most economical protection, and then places an order for the proper insurance on behalf of this client. It is traditional for the insurance company or agency to pay the broker's commission in such instances, but the broker is nonetheless the representative of the insurance buyer rather than the insurance company or agency.

An insurance *agency* is an insurance office, serving as the representative of insurance companies. As such, the *agency* is presumed to represent the companies' point of view. Many property managers, who began representing their clients as brokers, have subsequently developed a sufficiently large volume of insurance to justify their operating as agents. In most such instances, the insurance phase of the real estate manager's business has been separated from the management business and has been set up under a separate identity as an insurance agency.

Thus, the proper role of the real estate manager in the field of insurance is that of broker. In instances where management firms are associated with insurance agencies, it should clearly be the responsibility of the management firm to represent the client in all insurance dealings. In any case, special emphasis should be given not only to the risk involved but to the company or companies with which the real estate manager is placing the business. The insurance companies chosen should be highly rated, have a good reputation (especially for paying claims), and have strong financial backing. Such information is easily obtained by contacting the department of insurance in the state in which the manager is a licensed broker.

RESPONSIBILITIES OF INSURANCE BROKERS

Just as we have noted throughout our study of the field of real estate management, each added activity brings with it an added responsibility. The insurance underwriting phase of management operations is no exception to this general rule—in fact, the duties of representing a client in the field of insurance are extremely important and must be meticulously carried out.

From the point of view of the real estate manager, it may be said that the responsibilities in connection with insurance underwriting fall in two general categories. The first of these imposes upon the real estate manager the necessity for an adequate knowledge of insurance underwriting. He must know which types of insurance are available and to what extent each of these types of insurance offers effective coverage. He must be in a position to appraise accurately the risks involved in the ownership of property, in the employment of labor, and in the field of public responsibility. He must have the facilities to keep abreast of new forms of underwriting and new conditions of each type of coverage.

The business of insurance is a highly complex and involved specialty. The real estate manager who seeks to discharge his responsibility in the insurance field adequately must prepare himself by careful study of the types of policies currently available. A number of excellent texts on insurance are available in almost all business libraries, and we recommend that the student of real estate management avail himself of such texts in order to obtain a fundamental knowledge of the general practices in the field of underwriting. This is because here we are merely offering the student suggestions about the methods of developing a volume of insurance business. This will succeed if the student has already obtained a sufficient knowledge of the business to render him a capable insurance representative.

Before proceeding to a discussion of the methods of obtaining insurance business in a real estate management office, we should mention the second (and more important) phase of the manager's responsibility in the operation of an insurance department. This has to do with the extremely important mechanics of operating in the insurance field. Records of policies must be painstakingly kept so that expirations will be handled in ample time and with adequate planning. These records of policy expirations should not only embrace those policies which have been underwritten by the real estate manager, but should include complete insurance records on all property under the management of the individual or firm, in order that the manager himself may be assured that his client is adequately covered. This is true even in those instances where the insurance policies are actually written through another agency or brokerage connection.

This mechanical responsibility does not end with the record-keeping phase designed to protect the client against lapses in his policy, but also embraces the continuous review of the risks involved in order to assure the client of perpetual, adequate coverage. For example, in the period between 1929 and 1947, it was necessary frequently to adjust fire insurance coverage in order to compensate for the very material increases in construction cost which characterized this period. Moreover, during the war years (when building restrictions forbade the construction of many types of building), it was particularly important that property owners be protected against rent losses during what might have been an extended period in which it was impossible to replace a building destroyed by fire.

This responsibility to provide regular review of risks is especially important in the office of the property manager, whose duties not only cover the writing of insurance, but also the stewardship of the physical property involved. The property manager must be sure that regular anniversaries are set up for inspecting the use of properties on the part of tenants from the point of view of determining whether or not changes have taken place (in such use), which might involve an alteration of the risk to be underwritten. This is true especially in the case of commercial and industrial tenants, where changes in types of merchandise carried or kinds of goods manufactured may materially alter the cost of providing adequate insurance—in fact, may jeopardize the effectiveness of insurance coverage.

HOW MUCH INSURANCE BUSINESS?

We shall assume that the real estate manager who has determined to add the writing of insurance to his services and responsibilities has provided himself with adequate knowledge and mechanical facilities to perform properly the duties contemplated. As noted above, many aids are available in the form of recorded knowledge. Insurance companies of all kinds are peculiarly well equipped to supervise the setting up of suitable mechanical systems within the office of the real estate manager. Many insurance agencies specialize in the development of brokerage contacts among property managers and real estate firms; and these agencies will place facilities at the disposal of the manager or firm, as their representative, in order to ensure competency and to facilitate sales.

The problem, then, becomes one of determining how the real estate manager is to obtain a volume of insurance business and how much business he should set as his goal. The answer to these questions depends upon the circumstances in which the real estate manager finds himself. Through the years, surveys have shown that the most beneficial way to obtain new business and increase the volume of sales each year is through personal referrals from present clients. Advertisements are sometimes productive but insufficient alone. Obviously, the best way to obtain personal referrals is simply to render good service and then ask clients if they know other tenants who might have pending insurance needs. Deciding how much business a property manager should set as his goal is an extremely difficult question to answer. First and foremost, the property manager must determine how much of his time is occupied in managing. This then will suggest how much insurance business he should seek to occupy his remaining time.

Generally speaking, operations in the field of real estate management (aside from institutional and governmental operation) can be divided into several categories. The first of these types of operation—and perhaps the most common—is what we generally call *the one-man office.* This is the office of a real estate man who operates a general business embracing real estate brokerage, property management, loan placement, and insurance. The second general category is the real estate firm which embraces these same activities but is large enough to be departmentalized and to employ specialists in each of the separate fields. The third but somewhat uncommon category is the very large operation, in which the same ownership operates a real estate firm (including brokerage, management, appraisal, etc.) and owns or controls an insurance agency with which it is associated.

Let us first analyze our problem from the point of view of the *one-man office.* In such an office, the amount of time that the proprietor will spend in real estate brokerage, real estate management, and insurance will depend upon his choices between short-term gains and long-term benefits. All business operates in cycles, but real estate is peculiar in that it prospers materially in "up" cycles and virtually disappears in "down" cycles. In times of good business, it certainly can be said that the most profitable pursuit for the proprietor of a one-man office lies in the sale of real estate. Here the commissions are larger and the sales resistance lower. Real estate management and insurance, on the other hand, are more difficult to exploit from the sales point of view. It takes a longer time to build an adequate business from these sources, and the rewards of effort are not as great in each individual sale. However, it can be accurately said that *it is impossible for a proprietor of a general real estate and insurance business to devote himself exclusively to real estate brokerage in good times and to have a satisfactory management and insurance business in bad times*. This is especially true with insurance where constant attention must be given to sales on a day-after-day basis to obtain a satisfactory volume of premiums.

From a purely practical and human point of view, there is almost no man anywhere who finds himself equally happy doing all of the things which must be done by the proprietor of a one-man office. Almost everyone prefers one form of activity over another. Some proprietors of small real estate firms will get their greatest enjoyment from the actual administration of real estate. Others will obtain the most pleasure from closing a real estate sale or will find the solicitation of management business a stimulating task. And others will prefer the negotiation of mortgages. Still others may get their greatest thrill out of the writing of insurance.

The successful proprietor of a one-man business must so plan his time that a proper proportion will be spent in developing each of the types of business which are sought by the office itself. This is extremely difficult to do. In any case, experience shows that most proprietors of one-man offices generally end up specializing in one or perhaps two phases of the overall field. The fact is that if a man's ambition, and outlook, are such as to propel his interest in all of the fields of the business, he will generally enlarge his organization by the employment of other persons who will specialize in the operation of various phases of the business, thus leaving the proprietor free to devote more and more of his time to selling efforts. In most cases, this type of business ultimately changes into the second category—a departmentalized (larger) office.

The departmentalized real estate business, which embraces real estate brokerage, mortgage lending, property management, appraisal, and insurance, is the most logical type of organization in which a volume of insurance business is attainable. In common practice, the proprietor of such a firm becomes a sort of one-man holding company in which the head of each separate department is in effect admitted to partnership in his phase of the business. This is especially true of insurance departments, for the head of the department is almost universally compensated on the basis of volume of premiums earned by the office. In such instances the old saying, "the sky is the limit," should be the goal of the insurance underwriting activities of the firm, since the proprietor of a large real estate firm must constantly keep in mind that the "bread-and-butter" departments of the firm are mortgage lending, property management, appraisal, and insurance. The real estate brokerage department (which may for long periods of time produce the greatest earnings) is a highly volatile avenue of revenue, which operates at a loss throughout periods of depression.

In brief, it is suggested that the idea of the one-man office be examined carefully. Since service is the main factor, it follows that the real estate manager should carefully consider not taking on too much of a load since he has only himself to carry it. Other things being equal, a larger departmentalized office is unquestionably indicated. If the real estate manager is fortunate enough to have such an office, and if he can employ a specialist in each of the various fields, there is no reason he cannot successfully promote all of them to their fullest capacities. Indeed, there are numerous large insurance agencies today that are not only associated with, but owned and operated by, real estate management and/or brokerage firms.

SOURCES OF BUSINESS AND HOW TO TAP THEM

Whereas the insurance business in the United States has almost no limit in underwriting the risks assumed by individuals in modern society, the real estate manager who enters the insurance field does so because he has, by the very nature of his business operations, a specialized interest in three groups of prospects.

The first of these is obviously the owners of real property—clients and prospective clients of the real estate management firm. The manager who operates an apartment building for a client can be assumed to have established a firm and close business relationship with that client. The very fact that the client has turned over the stewardship of a valuable piece of property to the real estate manager would seem to justify a belief that the client had determined to place considerable reliance on the manager's general acumen. It seems logical to assume further that proper solicitation on the part of the real estate manager might result in his also being named insurance representative of the building owner. In such an instance, the real estate manager would have an opportunity to write at least the insurance to cover the owner's risk anent the ownership of the property managed. If the manager's contact with the client was sufficiently close and well established, it might be expected that he might also write the client's personal insurance and that of his family. If the client (as is most often the case) is the proprietor of another business in a different field, he then becomes a prospect for industrial or commercial insurance in that field. This *chain* of business can be worked almost ad infinitum, since the client undoubtedly will have friends who may be solicited on the basis of the satisfactory service which was rendered to the initial client. This is the way insurance solicitation is conducted, when the soliciting agency has sufficient ambition and drive to ferret out additional business.

In addition to the buildings that it manages, the real estate management firm's insurance department should solicit insurance business from other building owners in conjunction with its property management business solicitation. Insurance in the field of property ownership is a properly specialized field. It is to be assumed that the property manager who is in the insurance business will have devoted himself (or his insurance specialist) to a most exhaustive study of the problems surrounding the underwriting of the risks of property ownership. As in the case of all modern business, advantages in knowledge ultimately produce advantages in business volume. Unless the property manager is willing to devote the time necessary to acquire this demonstrable superiority in the field of property insurance, his chances of ultimate success are negligible. Without question, expert insurance solicitation and administration are valuable tools for the property manager in building confidence in his firm and hence in obtaining real estate management business.

As a by-product of the property management business, the real estate manager is generally in close contact with a large number of purveyors from whom he buys services and materials used in the operation of buildings. These suppliers are to be found in a wide variety of businesses. They embrace coal and heating oil dealers, contractors of all kinds, service agencies, and material vendors. Inasmuch as the real estate manager is a substantial buyer of these services and materials, he has at least a basis for claiming reciprocal trade. Whereas this claim for reciprocal business can be carried beyond ethical limits, there is absolutely nothing unethical in intelligent, constant, and effective solicitation of such business. As a matter of fact, business in the United States is increasingly done on a reciprocal basis, and many businessmen have heretofore failed entirely to exploit the reciprocal possibilities of their own field. This failure is characteristic of small rather than large business. If you would seek enlightenment in the manner in which large corporations trade in reciprocal relations, an analysis of any one of the major corporations of the country will produce illuminating facts.

In the field of insurance, where there is a good deal of policy standardization as to rate and coverage, there is every reason for the real estate manager to feel entitled to reciprocal treatment from those with whom he does a volume of business. It is recommended that the real estate manager in the insurance field base at least a part of his solicitation upon a careful analysis of the reciprocal possibilities afforded in his routine operations.

The third logical center of contact upon which the real estate manager may expect to found his insurance business is that covered by his roll of tenants. This latter group does not fall within the scope of specialization noted in connection with property owners (because their requirements run the entire gamut of risks), and the real estate manager unquestionably enjoys the advantage of close contact with tenants which should at least give him an *edge* over the customary insurance solicitors.

The amount and extent of direct solicitation of tenants is a matter to be determined by the real estate manager operating the insurance department.

As has been pointed out elsewhere in this text, there is no substitute in any form of sales work for direct solicitation. The best way to get business is to ask for it, and the best way to ask for it is in person or through a representative's personal call.

Over and above direct solicitation, however, there are many methods which can be employed by the insurance department in the successful underwriting of tenants' insurance. First, it is extremely important for the tenant to realize that the real estate manager, or management firm, is in the business of selling insurance. This knowledge can be impressed upon the tenant in any one of several ways.

In a previous chapter we pointed out that so-called *stuffers* can be inserted in rent bills and rent receipts. These *stuffers* are merely small pieces of advertising literature in which the tenant's attention may be called to the fact that the management firm offers a full line of insurance, or in which the tenant is specifically told about a certain kind of policy which is being offered. The advertising departments of insurance companies are peculiarly prolific in inventing timely advertising pieces for the sale of particular policies. Thus, at the beginning of the golfing season the tenant may be reminded to take out a golfer's liability policy, or at the beginning of the winter season the tenant may be reminded that accident policies are a handy thing to have in case one slips on the ice. These advertising *stuffers* have the distinct virtue of being repetitive. They come along with the regularity of the rent bill and tend to build up in the tenant's mind a firm knowledge that the manager is at least alert in his insurance offerings.

Window displays or general office displays are particularly effective in convincing tenants that it is the sincere desire of the manager to be of service in the insurance field. Here again, insurance companies are alert to their opportunities and, frequently, arrangements can be made for interesting window and/or office displays to serve this end.

In previous chapters in discussing the renewal of leases and the operating of the collection system, we called attention to the value of training employees to report unusual occurrences in the lives of the tenants in their buildings. If this type of friendly espionage service is developed, it can be used by the insurance department as well. For example, if one of the tenants in an apartment building has a bad fall and breaks a leg, an alert and able solicitor can quite easily write one or more accident insurance policies among the neighbors of the unfortunate. Resistance to the purchase of accident policies is never so low as when a close friend has had a costly accident. Similarly, if a tenant buys a new and expensive radio or piano, it is certainly timely to ask him whether or not he wishes to increase his household furniture coverage.

Nothing is as convincing or as flattering to a tenant as the realization that the property manager is sufficiently interested in him to know when such special occasions arise. Everyone likes to do business with a man who knows his business. Making money is typically American, and the man who is alert to an opportunity to increase his revenue is secretly admired.

The fact is that 90 percent of all the insurance sold in the United States is sold by people who are *on their toes*. Insurance is a necessity for virtually every person in the country with any property. The whole technique of insurance selling revolves around convincing people that it is wise and economical for them to protect themselves. In general, most people are inadequately insured. It is safe to say that tenants often will not be adequately insured and hence will be the most likely prospects for a wide variety of insurance coverage when properly approached and educated on insurance needs. As we have suggested above, *the man unsold is the man untold*.

KINDS OF COVERAGE

The basic purpose of insurance is to reduce insofar as possible the chance of loss through unforeseen and hence uncontrollable calamity. This chance is often described as *risk*.

In the complex social and economic structure in which we live, the risks to life, limb, and property are many and varied. As a result, the common need for a wide variety of protection has brought into being an equally broad range of risk protection in the form of insurance policies. The most common categories of coverage are as follows: Standard Fire Insurance, Extended Coverage and Collateral Fire Lines, Consequential Loss, Use and Occupancy, General Liability and Workmen's Compensation, Inland Marine Insurance, Automobile Insurance, Casualty Lines, and Surety Bonds.

The reader cannot expect this chapter to adequately ground him for a career in insurance. However, for the beginning student, we offer the following brief description of the basic types of insurance named above.

Standard Fire Insurance

The evolution of the so-called *standard* fire insurance policy was intended to simplify the adjustment of losses, clarify dealings with agents whose operations were far from the home offices of their companies, and protect the insuring public. The adoption of such standard policies was motivated also by the advantage of compliance with court decisions based upon identical policy provisions.

Several standard fire policies are in use. For the purpose of describing one such standard we shall refer to the policy now in use in Colorado, Illinois, Kentucky, Michigan, New Mexico, Ohio, Oklahoma, South Dakota, Tennessee, and Wyoming. This policy (like all others) consists of two separate parts. First, the agreement and contract and, second, various stipulations and conditions. The agreement or contract is sufficiently complete so that it could stand alone as a contract of insurance. It includes space for description of the property, and for the attachment of various endorsements which may be used to alter the terms of the contract. This agreement or contract, sometimes called the insuring clause, briefly states that the company, the name of which is included, in consideration of the stipulations and of a stated amount of premium, does insure for a stated term the person whose name is given, against all direct loss or damage by fire, except as later provided, to an amount not exceeding a stated value, to the described property while located as described.

In the synopsis of the contract to which we have just referred, there are the following general stipulations and agreements with which the student should become thoroughly conversant:

1. Concealment, Fraud

This provision indicates that the policy shall be void if, whether before or after a loss, the insured has concealed or misrepresented any material fact or circumstance concerning the insurance.

2. Uninsurable and Excepted Property

This clause points out that the policy does not cover accounts, bills, currency, deeds, evidences of debt, money, or securities (nor, unless specifically named thereon in writing, bullion or manuscripts).

3. Perils Not Included

This clause points out that the company shall not be liable for loss by fire or other perils caused directly or indirectly by: (a) enemy attack by armed forces, including action taken by military, naval or air forces in resisting an actual or an immediately impending enemy attack; (b) invasion; (c) insurrection; (d) rebellion; (e) revolution; (f) civil war; (g) usurped power; (h) order of any civil authority except acts of destruction at the time of and for the purpose of preventing the spread of fire, provided that such fire did not originate from any of the perils excluded by this policy; (i) neglect of the insured to use all reasonable means to save and preserve the property at and after a loss, or when the property is endangered by fire in neighboring premises; (j) nor shall his company be liable for loss by theft.

4. Other Insurance

This clause points out that other insurance may be prohibited, or the amount of the insurance limited, by endorsement attached thereto.

5. Condition Suspending or Restricting Insurance

This clause suspends the insurance in case the hazard of fire is increased by any means within the control or knowledge of the insured, or while the building is vacant or unoccupied beyond a period of sixty consecutive days, or as a result of explosion, or riot, unless fire ensues, and in that event for loss by fire only.

6. Waiver Provisions

This clause points out that no provision in connection with the policy shall be held to be waived by any requirement or proceeding on the part of the insuring company relating to appraisal or to any examination provided for.

7. Cancellation of Policy

This points out that the policy shall be cancelled at any time at the request of the insured, in which case the company shall upon demand surrender the policy and refund the excess of paid premium above the customary short rates for the expired term. It also provides that the policy may be cancelled at any time by the company upon presentation of a five days' written notice of cancellation.

8. Mortgage Clause

This clause generally provides for the terms and conditions under which the mortgagee and the mortgagor's interests are to be handled in case of fire.

9. Pro-Rata Liability

This clause points out that the company shall not be liable for a greater proportion of any loss than the amount thereunder insured shall bear to the whole insurance covering the property against the peril involved, whether collectable or not.

10. Requirements in Case Loss Occurs

This clause provides that the insured shall give immediate written notice to the company of any loss; protect the property from further damage; separate the undamaged and damaged personal property and put it in the best possible order; furnish a complete inventory of the destroyed, damaged, and undamaged property; show in detail quantities, costs, actual cash value, and amount of loss claimed; and, within sixty days after the loss, unless such time is extended in writing by the company, the insured shall render to the company proof of loss.

11. Appraisal

This clause provides that, in case the insured and the company shall fail to agree as to the actual cash value or the amount of loss, then on the written demand of either, each shall select a competent and disinterested appraiser who shall determine the actual value.

12. Company's Options

In this clause the company reserves the option to take all, or any part, of the property at the agreed or appraised value and to repair, rebuild, or replace the property destroyed or damaged with other of like kind and quality within a reasonable time.

13. Abandonment

This clause provides that there can be no abandonment to the company of any property.

14. When Loss Payable

Here is recited the time under which the company shall make settlement for a loss.

The standard form of policy being discussed generally contains a special form designed for the type of property insured. For example, separate forms are used for apartment buildings, commercial buildings, fireproof apartment buildings, duplex apartments, and so forth.

Extended Coverage and Collateral Fire Lines

Since the standard fire contract contains many exclusions, it has become the practice of those desiring broader protection to provide for insurance of those hazards which are specifically excluded by the terms of the fire contract or do not fall within the scope of the coverage provided by the fire contract. Such hazards are frequently covered by what is known as the extended coverage endorsement. In simple terms this extended coverage merely includes in the risk assumed by the company the perils of windstorm, hail, explosion, riot, riot attending a strike, civil commotion, aircraft, vehicles, and smoke.

Consequential Loss, Use, and Occupancy

In the discussion of the two forms of fire policy above we have been principally concerned with damage to *the extent of the actual cash value* of the property destroyed or damaged. We have not been concerned with the loss resulting from the interruption of business as a consequence of the direct property loss. In many cases, this latter type of loss actually exceeds the amount of the direct property loss. In the case of the La Salle Hotel fire in Chicago, for example, the loss of revenue on the part of the hotel, as a going business, was considerably more serious than the loss of the damaged property.

The insurance against consequential loss is sometimes called business-interruption insurance. It embraces rent, rental value insurance, leasehold insurance, use and occupancy insurance, and profits and commissions insurance. A number of other risks may also be covered by this type of insurance, such as temperature damage insurance and rain insurance.

General Liability and Workmen's Compensation

Liability insurance, of which workmen's compensation is a special and highly important branch, deals with liability imposed by law on one party for damage to the persons or property of others.

Every person presumably owes a duty to exercise a certain degree of care with respect to his own acts and the condition and use of his own property so that others may not be injured. Failure to do so is called *negligence*. All forms of liability insurance stem from the law of negligence. This law of negligence recognizes two classes of wrongs, namely crimes and torts. Crimes are wrongs against the state, and they are punishable by fine and/or imprisonment. Torts are wrongs committed against persons and are subject to so-called civil action resulting in a judgment for damages payable to the party injured. One class of torts consists of the failure to use proper care with respect to one's acts or the maintenance and use of one's property. Such failure is a form of negligence.

Described briefly, general liability policies break down into the following groups: employer's liability, automobile liability, real property liability, product liability, and bailee's liability. These policies are frequently extremely complicated and do not have the degree of standardization which characterizes fire policies. They are an important part of the insurance business, however, and are vital to all classes of the property manager's insurance prospects.

Inland Marine Insurance

Most people might think of *inland marine* insurance as having to do with boats on inland waterways. This is not true. *Inland marine insurance* acquired its name because the early insurance of articles in transport was almost entirely confined to goods being shipped over oceans. In present day insurance jargon, *inland marine insurance* covers imports, exports, domestic shipments, personal property floaters, and a host of other types of property mobile in nature. From the point of view of individuals, inland marine insurance is the type which embraces insurance on cameras, collections, furs, golf equipment, guns, jewelry, outboard motors and boats, personal property, silverware, and wedding presents.

Automobile Insurance

Virtually everyone in America is so thoroughly familiar with automobile operation and ownership that there appears little need of discussing in any detail the types of automobile insurance. However, in addition to the fire, theft, and public liability insurance with which we are all familiar, there are numbers of other types of motor vehicle insurance. Among these are special dealer insurance contracts, insurance for fleet (several cars) owners, commercial automobiles, public automobiles, and trailers.

Casualty Lines

The insurance generally described as casualty insurance includes burglary, robbery and theft, plate glass, steam boiler and machinery, and various accident coverages. Accident and health insurance is generally included in the casualty group.

There are various forms of theft insurance including residence and outside theft insurance, messenger, interior robbery and safe burglary insurance, interior robbery policies, paymaster policies, mercantile safe burglary insurance, storekeeper burglary and robbery policies, office burglary and robbery, bank burglary and robbery, safe deposit burglary and robbery, and other forms.

Accident and health insurance is likewise varied in character. Accident insurance, for example, is generally classified as commercial accident, industrial, noncancelable, limited, workmen's collective, and group accident. Health policies are classified in the following groups: house-confinement, nonhouse-confinement, life idemnity, waiting period, noncancelable, partial disability, and limited.

There are various types of both plate glass and power plant insurance which also are in the casualty group.

Surety Bonds

A surety bond is an agreement under which a carrier agrees to answer for the debts, defaults, or miscarriages of another. Because these contracts are required by law to be executed in writing and sealed, they are generally called *surety bonds.* These bonds are by custom divided into two broad classifications, namely, fidelity bonds and other surety bonds. The principal under a fidelity bond has an implied obligation to serve his employer, the obligee, honestly and faithfully. The principal under other forms of surety bonds usually owes the obligee a duty expressly imposed upon him by contract. Thus, under a fidelity bond, the primary obligation is implied, and, under other surety bonds, it is usuall; expressed in the form of a written contract. A wide variety of surety bonds is in general use today in private and public affairs.

The above brief description of some of the general forms of insurance commonly being written in the United States today will give the student an idea of the broad opportunity for risk protection that is available to the property manager who accepts the challenge to provide the much-needed protection of insurance to those with whom he comes in contact.

(Acknowledgment is made of the generosity of The National Underwriter Company of Cincinnati, Ohio, in allowing the author to use certain material contained in The National Underwriter Company's copyrighted book entitled *Practical Fire and Casualty Insurance,* by J. Edward Hedges, Ph.D., University of Indiana.)

REVIEW QUESTIONS

1. What are the *bread and butter* departments of a large departmentalized real estate business? Explain the importance of each.
2. Define *inland marine* insurance.
3. Define an *insurance agency.* Discuss briefly the pros and cons of this activity from the viewpoint of the property manager.

4. If you were a property manager and wanted to supplement your real estate business with insurance brokerage, outline the steps you would take to do so.
5. Name and describe the types of insurance operation usually found in real estate offices.
6. Suppose you operate a "one-man-business," and real estate business is bad, and you "jump" into insurance. Then, times in real estate turn improve. You forget the insurance. What is the result? How should you conduct the insurance end of your business in both bad times and good times?
7. Suggest ways of letting your tenants know you are in the insurance business.
8. Can expert insurance administration for a client prove valuable to the manager in his real estate business? Explain.
9. Is it considered good practice to write insurance for tenants? Justify your answer.
10. How are most real estate managers led into the insurance field?
11. What is an *insurance broker?* What are his duties and responsibilities to the client?
12. Would it be considered ethical to solicit insurance business from plumbing concerns, material suppliers, and others with whom you as a real estate manager do business?
13. What is meant by insurance against consequential loss?
14. What is *liability insurance?* How important is liability insurance to a property manager's insurance prospects?
15. List the major points covered by the standard fire insurance policy.
16. Name the types of insurance. Describe each briefly.
17. How does one secure broader protection in fire insurance policies?

SELECTED REFERENCES

Friedman, Edith J. *Real Estate Encyclopedia.* Englewood Cliffs, N. J., Prentice-Hall, 1960. 1458p.
See pp. 1330–1364: "Insurance in the Real Estate Office."

"Guide for Managing an Insurance Program." *IREM Operating Techniques,* Sept. 1966.

"Insurance: Package Policy." *IREM Operating Techniques,* Dec. 1965.

Kulp, C. A. and Hall, John W. *Casualty Insurance.* 4th ed. New York, Ronald Press, 1968, 1072p.

Long, John D. and Gregg, Davis W. *Property and Liability Insurance Handbook.* Homewood, Ill., Richard D. Irwin, 1965. 1265p.

Wescott, Ray D. and Fessler, George R. *The Insurance Primer.* 10th rev. ed. Santa Monica, Calif., Medical & Technical Books, 1974. 172p.

CHAPTER 28

The Manager's Relation to Physical Problems

INTRODUCTION

In the previous edition of this book, one chapter was devoted to the maintenance aspects of property management, while in still earlier editions as many as five chapters had been presented on this basic topic. Here the subject is dealt with only tangentially, and no technical details of "how to do it" are presented at all. This is because we intend to deal only with a theoretical point of view that corresponds to the modern way of thinking about the matter.

The major maintenance problems which must be met by the property manager fall into four categories:

1. Those maintenance activities that have as their objective the protection of the physical integrity of the building structure.
2. The maintenance responsibilities involved in guaranteeing the functional operation of a given building from the standpoint of providing maximum utility for its occupants.
3. The standard problems of housekeeping and cleanliness.
4. The maintenance operations that are undertaken solely for merchandising purposes—in other words, those where expenditures are made with a view toward increasing the competitive appeal of individual buildings to the renting public.

But times have changed. Today it is usually enough for the property manager to have an awareness of the categories of problems just mentioned. At the same time he must know whom to retain with the expertise to deal with these problems directly. This is the idea developed in the remaining pages.

DISCUSSION

As professionalization increased in America, professional persons' concern with the physical processes of their particular vocations became more obscure. Fewer railroad executives had been members of train crews or had operated a telegraph key. Fewer steel company executives had worked on a blast furnace or in a rolling mill.

In the early history of real estate management, the so-called management man was usually a product of the building trades who, in a period of recession, sought employment "taking care of buildings" to tide him over a slack period of construction.

As the field has matured, the present-day property manager is concerned more with economics, financing, personnel, and the other subjects covered by this text than he is with decorating, plumbing, or machinery maintenance. Certainly those skills are required in the process of maintaining the physical integrity and mechanical functioning of the properties under management, but the largest and most sophisticated property management organizations in the country probably do not have a single carpenter, painter, electrician, plumber, or plasterer on their payrolls. These artisans are on the payrolls of the *buildings* which are managed by the management firms or are employees of a contracting firm employed by the manager.

All businesses have training programs under which future executives are exposed to various phases of the business which they are learning. Property management trainees go through a period of apprenticeship during which they become acquainted with the physical maintenance of structures for which their firms are responsible. While it is desirable that the professional property manager have a rudimentary knowledge of the labor, skill, and materials employed in all phases of building maintenance, it is certainly not necessary that he master the techniques of every tradesman for whose work he will ultimately be responsible.

From a practical standpoint, the property manager's prime responsibility is to train himself and his associates in the disciplines of cleanliness, order, neatness, and continuous operability of every part of his buildings and their equipment. His training should be such that he can and will spot even the most obscure imperfections in any of the maintenance programs that are required to ensure a property's maximum utility and desirability. He must likewise be sensitive to flaws in the conduct of the service organization and its provision of a smooth flow of its product as designed in the operating program. He should be especially aware of the scale of values of service and materials used in the maintenance process and should make sure that those values are being delivered in accordance with his responsibility to his client.

Just as a physician's effectiveness is established by the thoroughness of his examination of his patient, so too does the manager's effectiveness as a building administrator depend upon his alertness to detail in his inspection of the property or properties under his management. Such inspections should have certain characteristics. First, they must be *regular* so that it is impossible for a building to deteriorate in any respect without its being discovered in a relatively short period of time. Second, they should be *complete* in covering the structure and its equipment so that, when finished, the manager is certain that he has covered every significant bit of information which a thorough inspection will reveal. To assure himself of this fact, the manager should provide himself with a complete checklist not only of physical factors but of personnel performance as well. An example of such a checklist is shown.

Whereas we have said the modern property manager does not allow himself to become too deeply involved in the physical problems of managing buildings, he must not lose sight of the fact that he is *completely responsible* for every expenditure of funds made on behalf of the owner of the property. One of the most fruitful exercises a manager can carry on is a thorough review of each operating statement prior to its being sent to a client. In a large organization where certain managers handle certain accounts, it is a wise rule for each account executive to perform this function each month. By so doing, he can become aware of every expenditure made on behalf of the client and, if any expenditures require explanation, he can familiarize himself with the details and be prepared to discuss them with the familiarity that the client would expect. As office experience will demonstrate, nothing substitutes in an owner's mind for a manager's familiarity with every detail of his responsibility for the client's affairs. Moreover, nothing builds confidence as thoroughly as a demonstration of this familarity. As a matter of fact, it is recommended policy that after an operating statement has been reviewed by the manager, he should prepare a letter to accompany it in which every item that possibly might be questioned is covered in advance. By following such a process the questions that enter the owner's mind when he receives the statement do not have a chance to build up without the facts being made clear at the outset. While we still maintain that the manager need not have the capability of performing a physical maintenance chore, nothing so enrages the average owner/client *as to be charged for* a major expenditure for a physical improvement with which the manager is not conversationally familiar or in which he cannot document his direct participation.

In summary, the modern property manager is not the "Jack of all trades" that he had to be in the early days when the profession was in its infancy, and life—by today's standards—was less complex. In fact, as in all other professions now, specialization to one degree or another has become the rule. It logically follows that the property manager will add stature to himself and his firm, and he will tend to maximize his earnings to the extent that he specializes in those prestigious activities that also are highly revenue-generating. Maintenance of the physical condition of managed properties, of course, is an important function. It does not earn money, however, but only saves it (i.e., in the sense that an ounce of prevention is worth a pound of cure). Selling insurance, as discussed in the previous chapter, is both a dignified and profitable activity by comparison. It follows that the busy property manager should specialize on things like selling insurance, given the additional fact that the maintenance function can be handled on a contract basis by firms and agents who have special qualifications for that sort of routine work.

REVIEW QUESTIONS

1. You are the manager of a large office building constructed in the 1930s. Tenants in several of the busy offices complain about the inadequacy of the electrical power supply. How would you handle this problem?
2. You are the manager of a large office building constructed in the 1970s. Suggest ways for implementing a regular and comprehensive preventive maintenance program.

SELECTED REFERENCES

"Real Estate Management Operating Techniques and Products." Bulletin Series. Chicago, Institute of Real Estate Management, 1945 to date.

Sack, Thomas F. *A Complete Guide to Building and Plant Maintenance.* 2d ed. Englewood Cliffs, N. J., Prentice-Hall, 1971. 677p.

Appendix

CONTENTS

IREM
MANAGEMENT AGREEMENT
A SHORT EXPLANATION

The **IREM MANAGEMENT AGREEMENT** is another service of the Institute of Real Estate Management of the National Association of Realtors.® As with any form agreement, it should be carefully reviewed to be certain that all of the various blanks are completed and that this form agreement fully and completely sets forth the understanding between you, as the manager of the property, and the owner, your client. It may also be desirable to discuss this with competent legal counsel. The following explanation should be of some assistance to you in filling in the blanks as well as understanding the basic format of the agreement so, if necessary, proper modification may be made.

Introductory Clauses
This sets forth by and with whom the agreement is made, and the blanks should be so completed.

Section 1. In this section, you should set forth the specific address of the property which you are to manage, as well as the effective term of the agreement. You will note that you should insert additionally, the time for notification in the event that there is a termination. You should also be sure that you check paragraph 6 (c) to be sure that it comports with your understanding.

Section 2. This section sets forth your responsibilities as manager. Subparagraphs (a) through (c) should be reviewed carefully to be sure that they are in accordance with the understanding between you and your client. Note that subparagraph (b) obligates you to provide monthly statements of receipts, disbursements and charges against the property to the person whose name and adress you should insert in the blanks. Furthermore, you are obligated under this section to remit the net proceeds of any rent payment to the person whose name and address you should insert in the next series of blanks in the next paragraph. In the event of multiple ownership, the percentage of the net rent should also be set forth. In the case of disbursements for charges in excess of receipts, you should, of course, send a monthly bill. Note also that you must obtain a bond, at your own expense, for your employees who will be handling money.

Section 3. This section sets forth the obligations of the owner. Here, too, you should be certain that subparagraphs (a) through (e) properly reflect the agreement between you and your client. Subparagraph (a) obligates the owner, among other things, to sign leases for terms not in excess of the period of time that you should set forth in the blank in that section. This subparagraph allows you, as the manager, to collect late rent charges and other charges which may result from your activities as manager without having to account to the owner. Subparagraph (b) requires the owner to undertake the negotiation of contracts and nonrecurring items not to exceed a certain dollar amount which you should insert in the blank. You should inform the owner that he is required by subparagraph (d) to refund tenants' security deposits at the expiration of the lease and, if required to do so by law, to pay interest on such security deposits. Many states now require the payment of interest on such security deposits. You should consult with your legal counsel to determine what other obligations may be required by state or local laws.

(over)

Section 4. By this section, the owner further agrees to idemnify the agent and to provide adequate insurance for the property. The blank in sub-paragraph (a) should be completed to set forth the period of time within which the owner is to provide insurance. Subparagraphs (b) through (d) set forth other indemnification requirements. Review these carefully also.

Section 5. This section should be filled in to set forth your fees. Sub-paragraph (e) should be completed if there are other areas for which you are to be compensated.

Section 6. This section sets forth various matters relative to the property. Subparagraph (a) requires that you obtain permission before making any structural changes and then only in accordance with the specific power and direction given by the person whose name and address should be inserted in the blank in that subparagraph. Each of these subparagraphs should be reviewed to be sure they are in accordance with your understanding and that they comport with your state or local laws.

Section 7. This section provides for cancellation. You should insert the time period for written notice that is required for cancellation as well as the percentage amount that you will receive in the event of such termination.

NOTE

Care should be taken in using any form agreement so as to be sure that it does completely comport with your undertsanding with your client and that it is in compliance with state and local laws. If in doubt, competent legal counsel should be consulted.

This is short explanation for Standard Form No. 7-11, The Management Agreement prepared by the Institute of Real Estate Management, 155 East Superior, Chicago, Illinois 60611.
© Copyright 1974, Institute of Real Estate Management of the National Association of Realtors, Chicago, Illinois.

Between

OWNER_____

and

AGENT_____

for Property located at_____

Beginning_____19_____

Ending_____19_____

MANAGEMENT
AGREEMENT

In consideration of the covenants herein contained,_____

_____(hereinafter called

"OWNER"), and_____(hereinafter called "AGENT"),
agree as follows:

    1. The OWNER hereby employs the AGENT exclusively to rent and
manage the property (hereinafter called the "Premises") known as_____

_____

_____

upon the terms hereinafter set forth, for a period of_____years beginning

on the_____day of_____, 19_____, and ending on

the_____day of_____,19_____, and there-
after for yearly periods from time to time, unless on or before _____days
prior to the date last above mentioned or on or before _____days prior
to the expiration of any such renewal period, either party hereto shall notify
the other in writing that it elects to terminate this Agreement, in which case
this Agreement shall be thereby terminated on said last mentioned date.
(See also Paragraph 6(c) below.)

2. THE AGENT AGREES:

(a) To accept the management of the Premises, to the extent, for the period, and upon the terms herein provided and agrees to furnish the services of its organization for the rental operation and management of the Premises.

(b) To render a monthly statement of receipts, disbursements and charges to the following person at the address shown:

Name   Address

_____   _____

_____   _____

and to remit each month the net proceeds (provided Agent is not required to make any mortgage, escrow or tax payment on the first day of the following month). Agent will remit the net proceeds or the balance thereof after making allowance for such payments to the following persons, in the percentages specified and at the addresses shown:

Name   Percentage   Address

_____   _____   _____

_____   _____   _____

_____   _____   _____

In case the disbursements and charges shall be in excess of the receipts, the OWNER agrees to pay such excess promptly, but nothing herein contained shall obligate the AGENT to advance its own funds on behalf of the OWNER.

(c) To cause all employees of the AGENT who handle or are responsible for the safekeeping of any monies of the OWNER to be covered by a fidelity bond in an amount and with a company determined by the AGENT at no cost to the OWNER.

3. THE OWNER AGREES:

To give the AGENT the following authority and powers (all or any of which may be exercised in the name of the OWNER) and agrees to assume all expenses in connection therewith:

(a) To advertise the Premises or any part thereof, to display signs thereon and to rent the same; to cause references of prospective tenants to be investigated; to sign leases for terms not in excess of_____years and to renew and or cancel the existing leases and prepare and execute the new lease without additional charge to the OWNER; provided, however, that the AGENT may collect from tenants all or any of the following: a late rent administrative charge, a non-negotiable check charge, credit report fee, a subleasing administrative charge and/or broker's commission and need not account for such charges and/or commission to the OWNER; to terminate tenancies and to sign and serve such notices as are deemed needful by the AGENT; to institute and prosecute actions to oust tenants and to recover possession of the Premises; to sue for and recover rent: and, when expedient, to settle, compromise and release such actions or suits, or reinstate such tenancies.

IREM CONDOMINIUM MANAGEMENT AGREEMENT A SHORT EXPLANATION

The IREM **CONDOMINIUM MANAGEMENT AGREEMENT** is another service of the Institute of Real Estate Management of the National Association of Realtors®. As with any form agreement, it should be carefully reviewed to be certain that all of the various blanks are completed, and that this form agreement fully and completely sets forth the understanding between you as the manager and the owner. It may also be desirable to discuss this with competent legal counsel. The following explanation should be of some assistance to you in filling in the blanks as well as understanding the basic format of the agreement so, if necessary, proper modification may be made.

Introductory Clauses—The introductory clauses should be carefully reviewed in that this agreement is designed for the initial management of the condominium prior to the time that the unit owners association is organized ("Board"). If this agreement is to be entered into subsequent to the organization of the Board, then the first part of the agreement should be modified accordingly.

The appropriate state condominium property act and sections should be included in the blanks where called for. In addition, you should set forth the number of years for which the Developer is authorized to engage you as the managing agent. If the Board is already in existence, then this section should be modified.

Section 1. If this form is to be used for an interim period, to expire when the Board is formed, then this section should be appropriately amended and should reflect an interim fee agreement. If a longer term agreement is the understanding between the parties, it may be desirable to have some type of provision allowing for a shorter notice cancellation without penalty than would be provided under section 13.

Sections 2 and 3. These sections set forth the responsibilities of the agent. Each of the items set forth in Section 3, paragraphs (a) through (k) should be carefully reviewed to be sure that they are in accordance with the understanding between you and your client. Be sure that you fill in the dates for subparagraphs (b), (c) and (d). The blank in subparagraph (g) should include state legal requirements, if any. Also, if this agreement is used *after* the condominium development is completed and the Board established, special attention should be paid to subparagraph (k) and it should be modified accordingly. This is because the subparagraph relates to initial construction of the project, and could be inappropriate if the condominium is in existing operation.

Section 4. You should fill in the amount of expense that you will have the authority to incur without prior consent.

Section 5. This section allows you to undertake individual agreements with other unit owners without any conflict of interest. However, be sure that you have a clear understanding with each unit owner for whom services are to be performed that it will be his own obligation, not that of the Board.

(over)

Section 6. This section provides for bank accounts, advances of funds, etc. Note that paragraph (c) requires that you bond all employees who handle or are otherwise responsible for monies of the owners.

Section 7. This section provides for the fees you will charge and the method of calculation. This section might require modification so as to clearly reflect your understanding with the client. Also note that provision is made to include other similar matters.

Section 8. This section should be reviewed carefully to be certain that it properly reflects your understanding with your client concerning designation of an employee as the Building Manager. You may wish to include the provision of office or living space to the manager at the expense of the client, or for telephone and other expenses to be paid by the client.

Section 9. This section provides for a "contact" person for the agent.

Section 10. This section limits the authority of the agent as to structural changes but, does allow you to make emergency repairs.

Section 11. This section provides for indemnification to you. It is an important clause to review carefully so as to be sure that peculiarities in your state law will be properly met and that you, as an agent, will not be obligated beyond the terms and conditions of the management agreement.

Sections 12 and 13. These sections provide for cancellation of the agreement upon certain terms and conditions. Be sure that if there are to be other grounds for termination, that they are set forth in the agreement.

Section 14. This section establishes the notification procedure as may be required under the agreement.

Section 15. This section sets forth the binding effect of the agreement.

NOTE

Care should be taken in using any form agreement so as to be sure that it does completely comport with your understanding. If in doubt, competent legal counsel should be consulted.

This is short explanation for Standard Form No. 7-12, The Condominium Management Agreement prepared by the Institute of Real Estate Management, 155 East Superior, Chicago, Illinois 60611.
© Copyright 1974, Institute of Real Estate Management of the National Association of Realtors, Chicago, Illinois.

Between

OWNER_____

and

AGENT_____

For Property located at

_____

_____

Beginning_____19____

Ending_____19____

CONDOMINIUM MANAGEMENT AGREEMENT

THIS AGREEMENT, made and entered into this_____day of

_____, 19____, by and between_____

_____

(the "DEVELOPER"), not individually but on behalf of all of the owners

from time to time of units in_____(the
"Condominium") and on behalf of the owners' association to be organized
pursuant to Section_____

_____or the not-for-profit corpora-
tion to be organized pursuant to Section_____
of said Act (the "OWNERS"), and_____
(the "AGENT");

WITNESSETH:

WHEREAS, under the provisions of the purchase contract with the
purchaser of each condominium unit, the Declaration of Condominium
Ownership and the By laws required under the provisions of the_____

Condominium Property Act, the OWNERS delegate the authority to manage
the Condominium initially to the DEVELOPER and thereafter to an elected
Board of Managers, which may be the Board of Directors of a not-for-profit
corporation organized by the Owners (the "BOARD"); and

WHEREAS, under the provisions of the purchase contract with the purchaser of each condominium unit, the Declaration of Condominium Ownership and the By-laws required under the provisions of the_____

Condominium Property Act, the DEVELOPER is authorized to engage a
management agent on behalf of the OWNERS under a contract to expire not
later than_____years after the first unit is occupied; and

WHEREAS, the DEVELOPER, on behalf of the OWNERS, desires to
employ the AGENT to manage the Condominium, and the AGENT desires
to be employed to manage the Condominium;

NOW, THEREFORE, it is agreed as follows:

1. The DEVELOPER, on behalf of the OWNERS, hereby employs the
AGENT exclusively to manage the Condominium for a period of_____
years, beginning on the date the first unit in the Condominium is occupied,
and thereafter for yearly periods from time to time, unless on or before sixty
days prior to the expiration of the initial term or on or before thirty days prior
to the expiration of any such renewal period, either party hereto shall notify
the other in writing that it elects to terminate this agreement, in which case
this agreement shall be terminated at the end of said period.

2. The AGENT agrees to manage the Condominium to the extent, for the period, and upon the terms herein provided.

3. More particularly, the AGENT agrees to perform the following services in the name of and on behalf of the OWNERS, and the DEVELOPER, on behalf of the OWNERS, hereby gives the AGENT the authority and powers required to perform these services:

(a) The AGENT shall collect and, as necessary, receipt for all monthly assessments and other charges due to the OWNERS for operation of the Condominium and all rental or other payments from concessionaires, if any, provided that the AGENT shall have no responsibility for collection of delinquent assessments or other charges except sending notices of delinquency.

(b) The AGENT shall maintain records showing all its receipts and expenditures relating to the Condominium and shall promptly submit to the DEVELOPER or the BOARD a cash receipts and disbursements statement for the preceding month and a statement indicating the balance of deficit in the AGENT'S account for the Condominium on or before the _____ day of the following month.

(c) The AGENT shall prepare and submit to the DEVELOPER or the BOARD, on or before _____ of each year, a recommended budget for the next year showing anticipated receipts and expenditures for such year.

(d) Within _____ days after the end of each calendar year, the AGENT shall submit to the OWNERS a summary of all receipts and expenditures relating to the Condominium for the preceding year, provided that this service shall not be construed to require the AGENT to supply an audit. Any audit required by the OWNERS shall be prepared at their expense by accountants of their selection.

(e) Subject to the direction and at the expense of the OWNERS, the AGENT shall cause the common elements of the Condominium to be maintained according to appropriate standards of maintenance consistent with the character of the Condominium, including cleaning, painting, decorating and such other annual maintenance and repair work as may be necessary.

(f) On the basis of the budget, job standards and wage rates previously approved by the OWNERS, the AGENT shall hire, pay, negotiate collective bargaining agreements with, supervise and discharge engineers, janitors and other personnel required to maintain and operate the Condominium properly. All such personnel shall be employees of the OWNERS and not of the AGENT. All salaries, taxes and other expenses payable on account of such employees shall be operating expenses of the Condominium.

(g) The AGENT shall execute and file all returns and other instruments and do and perform all acts required of the OWNERS as an employer under the Federal Insurance Contributions Act, the Federal Unemployment Tax Act, Subtitle C of the Internal Revenue Code of 1954 and the_____

Income Tax Act with respect to wages paid by the AGENT on behalf of the OWNERS and under any similar Federal, State or Municipal law now or hereafter in force (and in connection therewith the OWNERS agree upon request to execute and deliver promptly to the AGENT all necessary powers of attorney, notices of appointment and the like).

(h) Subject to the direction of the OWNERS, the AGENT shall negotiate and execute on behalf of the OWNERS contracts for water, electricity, gas, telephone and such other services for the common elements of the Condominium as may be necessary or advisable. The AGENT shall also purchase on behalf of the OWNERS such equipment, tools, appliances, materials and supplies as are necessary for the proper operation and maintenance of the Condominium. All such purchases and contracts shall be in the name and at the expense of the OWNERS.

(i) The AGENT shall pay from the funds of the OWNERS all taxes, building and elevator inspection fees, water rates and other governmental charges, and all other charges or obligations incurred by the OWNERS with respect to the maintenance or operation of the Condominium or incurred by the AGENT on behalf of the OWNERS pursuant to the terms of this agreement or pursuant to other authority granted by the OWNERS.

MANAGEMENT PRICING

Property _____

No. of Units____ Residents____ Offices____ Stores____ Boat Slips _____

Age and present condition of property & improvements

_____

_____

Miles from Office_____ Number of Employees_____

Gross Common Area Charge _____

Management/Leasing_____ Leasing _____

	No. Per Month	Hours Each	Total Hours	Cost
I. *PROPERTY MANAGER'S SERVICES*				
A. Inspections	___	___	___	___
B. Site Visits	___	___	___	___
C. Capital Improvement Supervision	___	___	___	___
D. Owner/Investor/Association Meetings	___	___	___	___
E. Travel time: $___per hr. X___hrs.	___	___	___	___
F. Office Hours Per Month	___			
G. Travel Expense___mi X___¢ per mi.				___
TOTAL COST				___
II. *EXECUTIVE SERVICES*				
A. Owner/Investor/Association Meetings	___	___	___	___
B. Site Visits	___	___	___	___
C. Surveys/Consultations	___	___	___	___
D. Inspections	___	___	___	___
E. Statement Review	___	___	___	___
F. Budget Preparation	___			
G. Travel time: $___per hr. X___hrs.			___	___
H. Travel Expense___mi X___¢ per mi.				___
TOTAL COST				___
III. *ACCOUNTING AND CLERICAL SERVICES*				
A. Receipts accounted for—days per mo.	___	___	___	
B. Disbursements: invoices, payments	___	___	___	
C. Monthly billing	___	___	___	
D. Payroll: checks issued	___	___	___	
E. Owner/Assoc. Statement preparation	___	___	___	
F. Resident Statement and preparation	___	___	___	
G. Statement duplication	___	___	___	
H. Owner consultation	___	___	___	
TOTAL COST				___
IV. *SUBTOTAL BEFORE OVERHEAD AND PROFIT*				___
V. *OVERHEAD AND PROFIT*	*Percent of Total*			
A. General Overhead	___			___
B. Marketing	___			___
C. Profit and Contingencies	___			___
VI. *TOTAL MONTHLY FEE*				
$_____Fee − Units = $_____each				___
$_____Fee − Gross = _____%				

Compiled by_____ Approved _____

(Page 1 of a four-page form)

THE INSTITUTE OF REAL ESTATE MANAGEMENT   Form '40A
of the
NATIONAL ASSOCIATION OF REAL ESTATE BOARDS   _____ 19___

APARTMENT BUILDING INSPECTION REPORT

Name of Property _____ Address _____

Type of Property _____

No. of Stories _____

Report Submitted by _____

No. of Apts.: 1's _____ 1½'s _____
2's _____ 2½'s _____ 3's _____ 3½'s _____
4's _____ 4½'s _____ 5's _____ 5½'s _____
6's _____ 7's _____ 8's _____ Total _____

EXTERIOR

Items	Character and Condition	Needs	Estimated Expense Involved
Grounds			
1. Soil			
2. Grass			
3. Shrubs			
4. Flowers			
5. Trees			
6. Fences			
7. Urns			
8. Walks			
9. Cement flashings			
10. Parking curbs			
Brick and Stone			
11. Front walls			
A. Base			
B. Top			
C. Coping			
D. Tuck pointing			
E. Cleanliness			
12. Court walls			
A. Base			
B. Top			
C. Coping			
D. Tuck pointing			
E. Cleanliness			
13. Side walls			
A. Base			
B. Top			
C. Coping			
D. Tuck pointing			
E. Cleanliness			
14. Rear walls			
A. Base			
B. Top			
C. Coping			
D. Tuck pointing			
E. Cleanliness			
15. Chimneys			

(Page 2)

GENERAL INTERIOR

Items	Character and Condition	Needs	Estimated Expense Involved
Vestibules			
1. Steps			
2. Risers			
3. Floors			
4. Marble slabs			
5. Walls			
6. Ceilings			
7. Door mats			
Vestibule Doors			
8. Glass			
9. Transoms			
10. Hinges			
11. Knobs			
12. Door checks			
13. Door finish			
14. Kick plates			
15. Handrails			
Mail Boxes			
16. Glass			
17. Doors			
18. Locks			
19. Name plates			
20. Speaking tubes			
21. Signal buttons and connections			
Stair Halls			
22. Steps			
23. Landings			
24. Handrails			
25. Woodwork			
26. Carpets			
27. Walls			
28. Ceilings			
29. Skylights			
30. Windows			
31. Shades			
Rear Halls			
32. Steps			
33. Landings			
34. Walls			
35. Ceilings			
36. Handrails			
37. Garbage cans			
38. Waste-paper receptacles			
39. Windows			
40. Shades			

Items	Character and Condition	Needs	Estimated Expense Involved
Elevators			
41. Signal buttons			
42. Doors			
43. Cab floors			
44. Cab walls			
45. Cab ceilings			
46. Control mechanism			
47. Cables			
48. Pulleys			
49. Motor			
50. Shaft walls			
51. Shaft ceiling			
52. Shaft floor			
53. Floor numbers on doors			
Public Light Fixtures			
54. Entrance			
A. Brackets			
B. Fixtures			
C. Bulbs			
D. Switch			
55. Vestibule			
A. Brackets			
B. Fixtures			
C. Bulbs			
D. Switch			
56. Halls			
A. Brackets			
B. Fixtures			
C. Bulbs			
D. Switch			

BASEMENT

Items	Character and Condition	Needs	Estimated Expense Involved
Laundries			
1. Floors			
2. Walls			
3. Ceilings			
4. Stoves			
5. Driers			
6. Tubs			
7. Faucets			
8. Toilet bowls			
9. Lavatories			
10. Drains			
11. Windows			
12. Doors			
13. Shades			
Boiler Room			
14. Floor			
15. Pipes			
16. Fuel bin			
17. Fire hazards			

(Page 4)

Items	Character and Condition	Needs	Estimated Expense Involved
Boiler Room (cont'd)			
18. Ceiling			
19. Walls			
20. Windows			
21. Doors			
22. Cleanliness			
23. Shades			
24. Ash cans			
Boiler			
25. Flues			
26. Tubes			
27. Valves			
28. Diaphragms			
29. Flange unions			
30. Grates			
31. Ash pits			
32. Pointing on brickwork			
33. Motors			
34. Draft controls			
35. Chimney			
36. Thermostats			
37. Hydrostats			
38. Stoker			
39. Insulation			
40. Combustion chambers			
41. Water level			
Hot-Water Heater			
42. Tank			
43. Insulation			
44. Ash pit			
45. Incinerator			
46. Submerged system			
47. Hydrolator			
Pumps			
48. Motors			
49. Sump			
50. Pressure			
51. Circulating			
Lockers			
52. Floors			
53. Walls			
54. Ceilings			
55. Doors			
56. Fire hazards			
57. Aisles			
Refrigeration Units			
58. Motors			
59. Cleanliness			
60. Accessibility			
General			
61. Plaster			
62. Trash and junk			
63. Screens			

(Page 1 of a four-page form)

THE INSTITUTE OF REAL ESTATE MANAGEMENT

of the

NATIONAL ASSOCIATION OF REAL ESTATE BOARDS

Form '40B

_____ 19_____

APARTMENT INTERIOR INSPECTION REPORT

Name of Property_____ _____ Address _____

Apt. No._____   No. of Rooms_____

Report Submitted by_____

Items	Character and Condition	Needs	Estimated Expense Involved
Vestibule			
1. Door			
2. Hinges			
3. Lock			
4. Safety chain			
5. Doorplate			
6. Transom			
7. Floor			
8. Walls			
9. Ceiling			
10. Light fixtures			
11. Light switches			
Coat Closet			
12. Door			
13. Floor			
14. Interior walls			
15. Ceiling			
16. Shelves, rods, hooks			
Living Room			
17. Floor			
18. Baseboards			
19. Walls			
20. Ceiling			
21. Windows			
22. Doors			
23. Light fixtures			
24. Electric outlets			
25. Electric switches			
Dining Room			
26. Floor			
27. Baseboards			
28. Walls			
29. Ceiling			
30 Windows			

Items	Character and Condition	Needs	Estimated Expense Involved
Dining Room (cont'd)			
31. Doors			
32. Light fixtures			
33. Electric outlets			
34. Electric switches			
35. Buffets			
36. Plate rails			
Kitchen			
37. Doors			
38. Transoms			
39. Locks			
40. Floor			
41. Baseboards			
42. Walls			
43. Ceiling			
44. Light fixtures			
45. Electric outlets			
46. Electric switches			
47. Stove			
48. Sink			
49. Cupboards			
50. Refrigerator			
51. Pantry			
52. Doorbell			
53. Ventilating fan			
54. Dumb waiter			
First Bedroom			
55. Doors			
56. Floor			
57. Baseboards			
58. Walls			
59. Ceiling			
60. Windows			
61. Light fixtures			
62. Electric outlets			
63. Electric switches			
64. Closets			
Second Bedroom			
65. Doors			
66. Floor			
67. Baseboards			
68. Walls			
69. Ceiling			
70. Windows			
71. Light fixtures			
72. Electric outlets			
73. Electric switches			
74. Closets			
Third Bedroom			
75. Doors			
76. Floor			

Items	Character and Condition	Needs	Estimated Expense Involved
Third Bedroom (cont'd)			
77. Baseboards			
78. Walls			
79. Ceiling			
80. Windows			
81. Light fixtures			
82. Electric outlets			
83. Electric switches			
84. Closets			
Maid's Room			
85. Doors			
86. Floor			
87. Baseboards			
88. Walls			
89. Ceiling			
90. Windows			
91. Light fixtures			
92. Electric outlets			
93. Electric switches			
94. Closets			
First Bathroom			
95. Doors			
96. Floor			
97. Walls			
98. Ceiling			
99. Window			
100. Tub			
101. Shower			
102. Shower curtain			
103. Lavatory			
104. Toilet bowl			
105. Flush tank			
106. Faucets			
107. Light fixtures			
108. Electric outlets			
109. Electric switches			
110. Towel racks, etc.			
111. Cabinets			
Second Bathroom			
112. Doors			
113. Floor			
114. Walls			
115. Ceiling			
116. Window			
117. Tub			
118. Shower			
119. Shower curtain			
120. Lavatory			
121. Toilet bowl			
122. Flush tank			
123. Faucets			

460

Items	Character and Condition	Needs	Estimated Expense Involved
Second Bathroom (cont'd)			
124. Light fixtures			
125. Electric outlets			
126. Electric switches			
127. Towel racks, etc.			
128. Cabinets			
Windows and Shades			
129. Frames			
130. Sashes			
131. Sills			
132. Stops			
133. Weights			
134. Locks			
135. Glass			
136. Weatherstripping			
137. Shades			
138. Blinds			
139. Curtain fixtures			
Linen Closet			
140. Door			
141. Floor			
142. Ceiling			
143. Walls			
144. Shelves			
145. Drawers			
146. Electric lights			

NOTES

(Page 1 of a four-page form)

THE INSTITUTE OF REAL ESTATE MANAGEMENT
of the
NATIONAL ASSOCIATION OF REAL ESTATE BOARDS

Form 50A

_____ 19____

OFFICE BUILDING INSPECTION REPORT

Name of Property...Address...

Type of Property...Office Area Rental Rate..

No. of Store..Store Area Rental Rate..

Report Submitted By...Basement Area Rental Rate....................................

Owner..

EXTERIOR

Items	Character & Condition	Needs	Est. Expenses
Roofs			
1. Type			
2. Flashing			
3. Valleys			
4. Drains			
Walls - North			
5. Type			
6. Base			
7. Top			
8. Tuck pointing			
9. Stone sills			
10. Coping			
11. Parapet walls			
12. Terra cotta			
13. Metal trim			
Walls - East			
14. Type			
15. Base			
16. Top			
17. Tuck pointing			
18. Stone sills			
19. Coping			
20. Parapet walls			
21. Terra cotta			
22. Metal trim			
Walls - West			
23. Type			
24. Base			
25. Top			
26. Tuck pointing			
27. Stone sills			
28. Coping			
29. Parapet walls			
30. Terra cotta			
31. Metal trim			
Walls - South			
32. Type			
33. Base			
34. Top			
35. Tuck pointing			
36. Stone sills			
37. Coping			

GENERAL EXTERIOR

Items	Character & Condition	Needs	Est. Expenses
Walls - South (Cont'd)			
38. Parapet walls			
39. Terra cotta			
40. Metal trim			
Walls - Court			
41. Type			
42. Base			
43. Top			
44. Tuck pointing			
45. Stone sills			
46. Coping			
47. Parapet walls			
48. Terra cotta			
49. Metal trim			
Chimney			
50. Type			
51. Comment			
Sidewalk Elevators			
52. Permits - expiration date			
53. Make			
54. Type			
55. Capacity			
56. Parts, oil, grease contr.			
57. Sidewalk doors			
58. Shaft			
59. Platform size			
60. Shaft gates			
61. Motors			
62. Pumps			
63. Tanks			
64. Generator			
65. Signal			
66. Safety locks			
67. Controls			
68. Pits			
69. Signs			
70. Comments			
Bldg. Entrance			
71. Doors			
72. Hinges			
73. Locks			
74. Checks			
75. Side lights			
76. Transoms			
77. Canopy			
78. Signal button			
79. Lighting			
80. Building name			
81. Street numbers			
82. Entry steps			
Exterior Fire Escapes			
83. Signs			
84. Access windows			
85. Access ladders			
86. Maintenance			
87. Ladder treads			
88. Hand rails			
Sidewalks			
89. Comments			

GENERAL EXTERIOR

Items	Character & Condition	Needs	Ext. Expenses
Light Wells			
90. Skylights			
91. Roof			
92. Comments			
Fire Hazards			
93. Defective wiring			
94. Trash and rubbish			
95. Oil, gasoline or paint storage			
96. Gas leaks			
97. Self-closing doors			
98. Breeching and flues			
99. Dumbwaiter enclosures			
100. Hot ash disposal			
101. Defective fire hose			
102. Fire extinguishers			
Windows - Office			
103. Type			
104. Frames			
105. Stops			
106. Sash			
107. Sills			
108. Lintels			
109. Anchor bolts			
110. Glass			
111. Glazing			
112. Caulking			
113. Weather strip			
114. Screens			
115. Locks			
Windows - Store			
116. Frames			
117. Transoms			
118. Sash			
119. Glass			
120. Caulking			
121. Glazing			
122. Screens			
123. Hinges			
124. Sash			
125. Locks			
Penthouse - Elevator			
126. Roof			
127. Walls			
128. Steps			
129. Doors			
130. Windows			
131. Flooring			
132. Fire protection devices			
Other Roof Structures			
Miscellaneous Extras			

(Page 1 of an eight-page form)

THE INSTITUTE OF REAL ESTATE MANAGEMENT
of the
NATIONAL ASSOCIATION OF REAL ESTATE BOARDS

Form 50B

_____ 19____

OFFICE BUILDING INSPECTION REPORT

Name of Property..Address...

Type of Property..Office Area Rental Rate..

No. of Stores..Store Area Rental Rate...

Report Submitted By..Basement Area Rental Rate...

Owner...

INTERIOR

Items	Character & Condition	Needs	Est. Expenses
Lobby			
1. Ceiling			
2. Walls			
3. Floors			
4. Lighting fixtures			
5. Glass			
6. Directory			
7. Signs			
8. Mail box			
Interior Doors			
9. Type			
10. Glass			
11. Rails			
12. Stiles			
13. Hand rails			
14. Hinges			
15. Locks			
16. Pulls			
17. Push plates			
18. Kick plates			
19. Mail slot			
Stairway			
20. Treads			
21. Risers			
22. Gates			
23. Bannisters			
24. Handrails			
25. Walls			
26. Ceilings			
27. Windows			
28. Skylights			
29. Electric lights			
Corridors			
30. Ceilings			
31. Walls			
32. Wood trim			
33. Floors			
34. Hardware			
35. Doors			
36. Glass			
37. Lighting fixtures			
38. Lighting switches			

(Page 2)   **GENERAL INTERIOR**

Items	Character & Condition	Needs	Est. Expenses
Corridors (Cont'd)			
39. Convenience outlets			
40. Waste paper receptacle			
41. Sand jars			
42. Fire hose			
43. Fire extinguishers			
44. Required signs			
45. Safety code violations			
46. Hopper rooms			
47. Maintenance			
Office Interiors			
48. Ceilings			
49. Walls			
50. Floors			
51. Lighting			
52. Fixtures			
53. Switches			
54. Elec. outlets			
55. Radiators			
56. Air conditioning			
57. Doors			
58. Transoms			
59. Hardware			
60. Baseboards			
Windows			
61. Type			
62. Frames			
63. Sash			
64. Sills			
65. Stops			
66. Weights			
67. Glass			
68. Glazing			
69. Caulking			
70. Weatherstripping			
71. Locks			
72. Screens			
Elevators-Passenger			
73. Permit expiration date			
74. Serviced by			
75. Contract			
76. Full maintenance			
77. Parts, oil, grease contr.			
78. Make			
79. Type			
80. Capacity (weight)			
81. Capacity (passengers)			
82. Lobby door fronts			
83. Corridor door fronts			
84. Operatorless			
85. Pit			
86. Full automatic			
87. Self leveling			
88. Door operator			
89. Electric			
90. Air			
91. Manual			
92. Cab size			
93. Cab trim			

Items	Character & Condition	Needs	Est. Expenses
Elevators-Passenger (Cont'd)			
94. Cab walls			
95. Cab doors			
96. Cab lighting			
97. Cab ceiling			
98. Cab floor			
99. Cab ventilation			
100. Position indicators			
101. Floor indicator			
102. Signal lanterns			
103. Signal buttons			
104. Emergency switches			
105. Telephone			
106. Elevator shafts			
107. Pits			
108. Walls			
109. Guide rails			
110. Hoisting cables			
111. Compensating cables			
112. Governor cables			
113. Sheaves			
114. Motors			
115. Generators			
116. Governors			
117. Signs in shaft			
118. Floor numbers on shaft walls			
119. Floor numbers on door			
120. Miscellaneous			
121. Control panels			
122. Threshold lights			
Elevators - Freight			
123. Permit expiration date Contract			
124. Serviced by			
125. Full maintenance			
126. Parts, oil, grease contr.			
127. Make			
128. Type			
129. Capacity, pounds			
130. Platform size			
131. Platform lighting			
132. Shaft doors			
133. Cab gates			
134. Hoisting cables			
135. Compensating cables			
136. Governor cables			
137. Pit			
138. Motors			
139. Generators			
140. Signal buttons			
141. Signal buzzers			
142. Shaft numbers			
143. Shaft safety signs			
144. Guide rails			
145. Comments			
Public Rest Rooms-Men			
146. Floors			
147. Floor drain			

(Page 4)

Items	Character & Condition	Needs	Est. Expenses
Public Rest Rooms-Men			
(Cont'd)			
148. Walls			
149. Wainscote			
150. Ceiling			
151. Watercloset enclosure			
152. Watercloset type			
153. Tank			
154. Flushing valve			
155. Vacuum breaker			
156. Seat			
157. Bowl			
158. Lavatory			
159. Trim			
160. Soap dispensers			
161. Urinal			
162. Type - wall - floor			
163. Flushing valve			
164. Stall panel			
165. Hardware on door			
166. Locks			
167. Deodorants			
168. Ventilation			
169. Light fixtures			
170. Switches			
171. Window			
172. Waste receptacle			
173. Towel Cabinets			
174. Mirrors			
175. Signs			
Public Rest Rooms-Women			
176. Floors			
177. Floor drain			
178. Walls			
179. Wainscote			
180. Ceiling			
181. Watercloset enclosure			
182. Stall doors			
183. Stall doors hardware			
184. Watercloset type			
185. Tank			
186. Flushing valve			
187. Vacuum breaker			
188. Seat			
189. Bowl			
190. Toilet tissue holder			
191. Lavatory			
192. Trim			
193. Soap dispenser			
194. Mirrors			
195. Vanity shelf			
196. Deodorants			
197. Ventilation			
198. Light fixtures			
199. Switches			
200. Windows			
201. Waste receptacle			
202. Sanitary napkin vendors			
203. Signs			

Items	Character & Condition	Needs	Est. Expenses
Basement Stairway			
204. Entrance door			
205. Treads			
206. Risers			
207. Hand rails			
208. Walls			
209. Landings			
210. Ceilings			
211. Light			
Basement Area			
212. Floors			
213. Sump pumps			
214. Walls			
215. Ceilings			
216. Fire doors			
217. No. of exits			
218. Sprinkler system			
219. Lighting			
220. Convenience outlets			
221. Ventilation			
222. Elevator service			
223. Storage space			
224. Heating			
225. Utility space			
226. Carpenter shop			
227. Plumber			
228. Paint shop			
229. Superintendent office			
Men Employees Rest Room			
230. Showers			
231. Watercloset			
232. Type			
233. Lavatory			
234. Urinal			
235. Lavatory trim			
236. Floor			
237. Walls			
238. Ceilings			
239. Lighting			
240. Heating			
241. Ventilating			
Men's Locker Rooms			
242. Floors			
243. Walls			
244. Ceiling			
245. Lighting			
246. Switches			
247. Heating			
248. Ventilation			
249. Doors			
250. Fire hazards			
Women Employees Rest Room			
251. Showers			
252. Watercloset			
253. Type			
254. Lavatory			
255. Trim			
256. Floor			
257. Walls			

(Page 6)

Items	Character & Condition	Needs	Est. Expenses
258. Ceiling			
259. Doors			
260. Heating			
261. Ventilation			
262. Lighting			
263. Switches			
Women's Locker Rooms			
264. Floors			
265. Walls			
266. Ceiling			
267. Lighting			
268. Heating			
269. Ventilation			
270. Doors			
271. Fire hazards			
Boiler Room			
272. Floor			
273. Walls			
274. Ceiling			
275. Fire doors			
276. Fire hazards			
277. Ventilation			
278. Lighting			
279. Switches			
Boilers			
280. Type			
281. Pressure, high			
282. Pressure, low			
283. Flues			
284. Tubes			
285. Draft control			
286. Valves			
287. Blow-off pit			
288. Vents			
289. Grates			
290. Fire box			
291. Pointing fire brick			
292. Steam line insulation			
293. Fuel, kind			
294. Storage tanks			
295. Coal chutes			
296. Coal bins			
297. Stokers			
298. Oil burners			
299. Gas burners			
300. Injectors			
301. Low water cutout			
302. Pop-off valves			
303. Gauges, pressure			
304. Gauges, water level			
305. Automatic controls			
306. Diaphragms			
307. Flanges			
308. Gaskets			
309. Packing glands			
310. Draft regulators			
311. Smoke detectors			
312. Steam condensate return			

Items	Character & Condition	Needs	Est. Expenses
Vacuum Pump Make			
313. Storage tank			
314. Control (elec.) make			
315. Control (elec.) voltage			
316. Water level float switch voltage			
317. Combination negative & pressure gauge			
318. Strainer			
319. Motor			
320. Type			
321. Horse power load			
Hot Water Heaters			
322. Inside lining			
323. Steam coils			
324. Insulation			
325. Gaskets			
326. Thermostat			
327. Steam trap			
328. Safety valve			
329. Fire box			
330. Fuel			
331. Burner			
Pumps			
332. Sump			
333. Pressure			
334. Feed water			
335. Circulating			
336. Vacuum			
Water Softeners			
337. Type			
338. Sand filters			
339. Valves			
340. Differential gauges			
341. Tank, filter			
342. Softener			
Salt Tank			
343. Coating			
344. Float valve			
345. Overflow			
346. Tank			
Compressors			
347. Filters			
348. Automatic switch			
349. Safety valve			
350. Drive			
351. Motor H.P.			
352. Tank capacity			
353. Purpose of comp. air			
Vacuum Pump-Cleaning System			
354. Automatic switch controls			
Air Conditioning			
Window Units			
355. Miscellaneous			
a.			
b.			
c.			

(Page 8)

Items	Character & Condition	Needs	Est. Expenses
d. **Window Units (Cont'd)**			
e.			
Central System			
356. Type			
a.			
b.			
c.			
Original Installation			
357. Age			
358. Refrigeration			
359. Unit			
360. Refrigerant			
361. Compressor			
362. Capacity			
363. H.P. connec. load			
364. Performance			
365. Cooling tower			
366. Air distribution			
367. Ducts			
368. Insulation			
369. Grills			
370. Thermostats			
371. Zones			
372. Fans			
373. Performance			
Electric Panel Room			
Electric Energy Service			
374. Transformer capacity			
375. Voltage			
376. Cycle			
377. Power			
378. Lighting			
379. Phase single			
380. Phase three			
Panel Board			
381. Maker			
382. Amperage capacity			
383. Power circuits			
384. Lighting circuits			
385. Emergency circuits			
386. Stand by circuits			
387. Spare circuits			
388. Fuses			
389. Circuit breakers			
390. Meters			
391. Lighting meter			
392. Power meter			
393. Tenants meter			

INDEX

Index